STORY
S-T-R-E-T-C-H-E-R-S
FOR THE
PRIMARY GRADES

Activities to Expand
Children's Favorite Books

Shirley C. Raines and Robert J. Canady

gryphon house

Mt. Rainier, Maryland

ACKNOWLEDGMENTS

CHAPTER 1

Jacket illustration from **CROW BOY** by Taro Yashima. Copyright © 1955 by Mitsu and Taro Yashima. Reprinted by permission of The Viking Press, a division of Penguin USA.

Jacket illustration by Ted Lewin from **THE DAY OF AHMED'S SECRET** by Florence Parry Heide and Judith Heide Gilliland. Illustrations copyright © 1990 by Ted Lewin. Reprinted by permission of Lothrop, Lee and Shepard Books, a division of William Morrow and Company, Inc.

Jacket illustration from **JOSEPHINA THE GREAT COLLECTOR** by Diana Engel. Copyright © 1988 by Diana Engel. Reprinted by permission of Morrow Junior Books, a division of William Morrow and Company, Inc.

Cover illustration from **MATTHEW'S DREAM** by Leo Lionni. Copyright © 1991 by Leo Lionni. Reprinted by permission of Alfred A. Knopf, Inc.

Jacket Illustration from **MY SHADOW** by Robert Louis Stevenson, illustrated by Ted Rand. Copyright © 1990 by Ted Rand. Reprinted by permission of G.P. Putnam's Sons, a division of The Putnam and Grosset Book Group.

CHAPTER 2

Jacket illustration from **ALL KINDS OF FAMILIES** by Norma Simon, illustrated by Joe Lasker. Text copyright © 1976 by Norma Simon. Illustrations copyright © 1976 by Joe Lasker. Reprinted by permission of Albert Whitman and Company.

Library of Congress Catalog Number: 92-53142

Design: Graves, Fowler & Associates
Cover Photo: Burwell & Burwell

Raines, Shirley C.
  Story stretchers for the primary grades : activities to expand children's favorite books / Shirley C. Raines and Robert J. Canady.
    p. cm.
  Includes bibliographical references and index.
  ISBN 0-87659-157-8
  1. Early childhood education--Activity programs--Handbooks, manuals, etc. 2. Children's literature--Bibliography. 3. Teaching--Aids and devices--Handbooks, manuals, etc. 4. Children--Books and reading--Handbooks, manuals, etc. I. Canady, Robert J. II. Title.

LB1139.35.A37R3 1992   372.6'4'044
                             QB192-570

Jacket illustration by Lynn Sweat from **AMELIA BEDELIA'S FAMILY ALBUM** by Margaret Parish. Illustrations copyright © 1988 by Lynn Sweat. Reprinted by permission of Greenwillow Books, a division of William Morrow and Company, Inc.

Jacket illustration from **JULIUS, THE BABY OF THE WORLD** by Kevin Henkes. Copyright © 1990 by Kevin Henkes. Reprinted by permission of Greenwillow Books, a division of William Morrow and Company, Inc.

Jacket illustration by James Ransome from **HOW MANY STARS IN THE SKY** by Lenny Hort. Illustrations copyright © 1991 by James Ransome. Reprinted by permission of Tambourine Books, a division of William Morrow and Company, Inc.

Jacket illustration from **THE RELATIVES CAME** by Cynthia Rylant, illustrated by Stephen Gammell. Text copyright © 1985 by Cynthia Rylant. Illustrations copyright © 1985 by Stephen Gammell. Reprinted by permission of Bradbury Press, a division of Macmillan.

CHAPTER 3

Jacket illustration from **ARTHUR'S BIRTHDAY** by Marc Brown. Copyright © 1989 by Marc Brown. Reprinted by permission of Little, Brown and Company.

Jacket illustration from **CHESTER'S WAY** by Kevin Henkes. Copyright © 1988 by Kevin Henkes. Reprinted by permission of Greenwillow Books, a division of William Morrow and Company, Inc.

Jacket illustration from **FROG AND TOAD TOGETHER** by Arnold Lobel. Copyright © 1971, 1972 by Arnold Lobel. Reprinted by permission of HarperCollins Publishers.

Jacket illustration from **IRA SAYS GOODBYE** by Bernard Waber. Copyright © 1988 by Bernard Waber. Reprinted by permission of Houghton Mifflin Company.

Jacket illustration from **WILFRID GORDON MCDONALD PARTRIDGE** by Mem Fox, illustrated by Julie Vivas. Text copyright © 1984 by Mem Fox. Illustrations copyright © 1984 by Julie Vivas. Reprinted by permission of Kane\Miller Book Publishers.

CHAPTER 4

Jacket illustration from **ALEXANDER AND THE TERRIBLE HORRIBLE, NO GOOD, VERY BAD DAY** by Judith Viorst, illustrated by Ray Cruz. Text copyright © 1972 by Judith Viorst. Illustrations copyright © 1972 by Ray Cruz. Reprinted by permission of Aladdin Books, a division of Macmillan Publishing Company.

Jacket illustration from **KOALA LOU** by Mem Fox, illustrated by Pamela Lofts. Text copyright © 1988 by Mem Fox. Illustrations copyright © 1988 by Pamela Lofts. Reprinted by permission of Harcourt Brace Jovanovich, Inc.

Jacket illustration from **THREE BRAVE WOMEN** by C.L.G. Martin, illustrated by Peter Elwell. Text copyright © 1991 by C.L.G. Martin. Illustrations copyright © 1991 by Peter Elwell. Reprinted by permission of Macmillan Publishing Company.

Jacket illustration from **THUNDER CAKE** by Patricia Polacco. Copyright © 1990 by Patricia Polacco. Reprinted by permission of Philomel Books, a division of The Putnam and Grosset Group.

Reprinted by permission of Running Press, 125 S. 22nd Street, Philadelphia, PA. from **THE VELVETEEN RABBIT** by Margery Williams, Copyright © 1981 by Running Press.

*To all teachers who read to their
students every day*

—Raines and Canady

CONTENTS

PREFACE

THE IDEA OF A LITERATURE -BASED CURRICULUM is one which we have been proposing in our teacher education courses for years. We, like many of you, used children's literature as an integral part of the curriculum when we taught children, but we always felt there were many more possibilities for connecting the books to other areas. When we were classroom teachers, we used many of the ideas in this book. However, as wonderful new books came on the market and as heightened interest grew in providing a "whole language" environment and in "developmentally appropriate practices" in the primary grades, it seemed the right time to collect our ideas, organize them and place them in the hands of teachers, librarians, reading specialists and parents.

STORY S-T-R-E-T-C-H-E-R-S FOR THE PRIMARY GRADES: ACTIVITIES TO EXPAND CHILDREN'S FAVORITE BOOKS is the third in a series of books for a literature-inspired curriculum organized around thematic units. We wrote the book in response to requests we received from first, second and third grade teachers; reading specialists; librarians; and children's bookstore owners. The first two STORY S-T-R-E-T-C-H-E-R books were written primarily for the preschool and kindergarten classrooms, but bookstore owners and librarians told us teachers were adapting them for their first and second graders. We were tremendously pleased. They are totally appropriate because "active learning" should be the foundation for the curriculum from preschool through primary grades.

We wrote this series of story s-t-r-e-t-c-h-e-r books as a vehicle to support teachers who develop classrooms where children grow to love books, poems, jokes, riddles, songs and the stories of our many rich cultures. As professors and researchers, we study and teach about children's language, literacy and interests in literature. We know that the books and the story s-t-r-e-t-c-h-e-r-s support teachers in their quest for well-developed literacy environments where listening, speaking, reading and writing permeate the curriculum.

We are indebted to the students and teachers in our courses at George Mason University and Marymount University who read the books to children and who field-tested many of the story s-t-r-e-t-c-h-e-r-s. We also appreciate the teachers from other colleges and universities where we have taught who encouraged us to write our ideas into a book. Thank you, classroom teachers from Northeastern State University in Oklahoma, North Carolina Wesleyan and the University of Alabama, for being our colleagues. You will find teachers' names mentioned throughout the book when we adapted ideas from their classrooms.

We have been fortunate to find colleagues among publishers as well. We are indebted to the many fine professionals at Gryphon House. We could not have written this book without Leah Curry-Rood, who has a keen eye for stories which intrigue and delight and a vast knowledge of children's literature. She and Mary Rein also helped to select the additional references for each unit. We are also indebted to Leah and the staff at Gryphon House for securing permission from authors, illustrators and publishers to include their books. Sarabeth Goodwin produced and formatted the three story s-t-r-e-t-c-h-e-r books, making them attractive and user-friendly. Kathy Charner skillfully edited the manuscript and shared our goal of keeping "active learning" center stage. We are also grateful to Larry Rood, the President of Gryphon House, who directs the many facets of a publishing firm which makes a difference in writers' reputations and in how their works are received by the vast audience of educators.

Over the years, when we spoke about a literature-based curriculum, print-rich environments and literacy learning, teachers often asked if we had a book about these ideas.

Now, we can say, "Yes, three books—STORY S-T-R-E-T-C-H-E-R-S: ACTIVITIES TO EXPAND CHILDREN'S BOOKS; MORE STORY S-T-R-E-T-C-H-E-R-S; and our latest book, STORY S-T-R-E-T-C-H-E-R-S FOR THE PRIMARY GRADES: ACTIVITIES TO EXPAND CHILDREN'S FAVORITE BOOKS."

Shirley C. Raines, Ed.D., Associate Professor, George Mason University, Fairfax, Virginia

Robert J. Canady, Ed.D., Professor, Marymount University, Arlington, Virginia

INTRODUCTION

"READ IT AGAIN!" "I WANT TO READ THAT BOOK!" "I LIKE BOOKS BY THIS AUTHOR." "I LIKE THE STORY AND THE PICTURES." Every teacher is delighted to hear these comments. A good teacher knows by the giggles, the sighs, the absolute stillness and by the way the listeners inch closer that a book is a "read-it-again" story. The love of a good story—the classic ones, the outrageously funny ones, the sad tales, the tall tales, the rhythms and rhymes of language that get stuck in our minds, the bold graphics, the weepy watercolors, the muted charcoals, the funny cartoons—the reasons children shout, "Read it again!" and "I want to read that book!" are as varied and rich as the authors' and illustrators' imaginations.

As former classroom teachers and now as teacher educators, we know the importance of reading to children every day. From our research on literacy and from our experiences in the classroom, we know that children who have an environment at home and at school where they are read to and where they interact with adults about books usually become good readers. We encourage you to use story s-t-r-e-t-c-h-e-r-s not only for their importance in motivating children to read by connecting the child, the story and the curriculum, but also because the activities are inherently interesting and appealing.

About The Format Of The Book

Knowing first, second and third graders love good stories, we devised "story s-t-r-e-t-c-h-e-r-s" as a means to extend that enthusiasm and better connect children's books and teaching ideas with other areas of the curriculum. Story s-t-r-e-t-c-h-e-r-s are teaching ideas for active learning based on the stories in children's favorite books. STORY S-T-R-E-T-C-H-E-R-S FOR THE PRIMARY GRADES is a literature-inspired approach to planning eighteen units

or themes often found in the primary grades curriculum.

The themes of the units are topics which teachers, librarians, reading specialists and principals told us were regularly a part of the curriculum in first, second and third grades. There are 18 units with five focus books per unit, and each book has read-aloud suggestions for the book and five story s-t-r-e-t-c-h-e-r-s per book. We review the storyline and illustrations under the photograph of the cover of the book. STORY S-T-R-E-T-C-H-E-R-S FOR THE PRIMARY GRADES contains 90 read-aloud suggestions and 450 story s-t-r-e-t-c-h-e-r-s for 90 different children's books.

In each chapter, the books selected for the theme are stretched into different centers, activities and areas of the curriculum. We have story s-t-r-e-t-c-h-e-r-s for art, creative dramatics, games, classroom library, mathematics, music and movement, science and nature, special projects, special events and the writing center. Each book is stretched into the five activities which best fit that book.

We selected 90 children's books, some old favorites, classics which have stood the test of time, and we included some new favorites which teachers, librarians, bookstore owners and children called to our attention. From the hundreds of new books on the market, we selected ones we thought would appeal to children, then we asked teachers to read them to their classes and tell us the children's responses. We also verified that the books we feature are currently in print and readily available.

You may wonder why some of your children's favorites were not selected. There are many excellent children's books which cannot be stretched easily or extended into activities for other areas of the curriculum. To extend the book somehow takes away from the "essence" of the story. Some of these books have a particularly powerful theme, like THE TENTH GOOD THING ABOUT BARNEY (Viorst, 1971) or KNOTS ON A COUNTING ROPE (Martin & Archambault, 1987). While these books, with their sensitive themes or keenly-edged plots, are wonderful selections for reading aloud and for discussion, somehow it trivializes them to stretch the book to other areas of the curriculum. However, these books become even more potent when paired with other books which can be stretched, and their main ideas are studied within a unit on "Pets" or "Families" or "Self-Concepts."

Integrated Thematic Units

While an integrated unit by its nature includes activities across the curriculum, the theme is often either a science or a social studies one. The science and social studies concepts are developed through the "shared experience" of the story or the informational book and the story s-t-r-e-t-c-h-e-r-s which follow. Collectively, each unit contains five read-aloud suggestions and twenty-five story s-t-r-e-t-c-h-e-r-s inspired by the five children's literature books we selected as focus books. As with all story s-t-r-e-t-c-h-e-r activities, indeed all good instruction, the teacher will make the associations and connections which best fit the developmental needs of the age group and the individual interests of each child, while building the concepts which meet the curricular needs.

The units most often associated with social studies include "I am Me, I am Special, Look What I Can Do," "Friends," "Families," "Feelings," "Another Time and Place" and "Celebrations." Social studies is a part of every unit through the concepts presented in the read-aloud sessions, the discussions in the classroom library and the extended writing suggested for the writing center. While the primary focus of the unit on "Pets, Dogs and Cats," is the social studies theme of being a responsible pet owner, the unit also emphasizes science.

Other thematic units defy categorization, such as "Machines and Things," a combination of a little physics, people's responses to machines (social studies),

and a lot of imagination. "Life in the Sea, Real and Imagined" includes some books based in reality and others that explore the sea through imagination, while clearly delineating fact from fantasy. Another example of a unit which transcends categorization is "I Care about my World, the Environment." While much scientific information is given in the five focus books, our responsibility to care for the earth is both a scientific and social studies concern. Likewise the theme of weather seems scientific, yet studies how people react to various types of weather, and so could logically fit in either social studies or science. Other science units include "Animal Life" and "Life in the Sea, Real and Imagined." Both include substantive science activities, but call upon the imagination to blend in language arts, music, drama and art.

At the request of teachers and reading specialists, all the units contain strong reading, writing, listening and speaking activities. However, we have developed some units in which the primary focus is language and the story, such as "Mysteries, Secrets and Adventures," "Poems, Chants, Rhythms and Rhymes," " Native American Legends and Folktales from Around the World" and "Tall and Funny, Funny Tales." "Fun with Words" is a language arts unit where children play with knock-knocks, jokes, riddles, homonyms, idioms and funny sayings that are a part of children's rich language heritage. "Bears in Tall Tales, Funny Tales, Stories and Poems " is a unit we included because bear books tend to be favorites among young readers.

Read-ALoud And The Reading Process

It has been said that to become a great musician one must know the music and then make the music come to life by bringing one's self to the playing. The teacher as a reader of children's books is like the great musician. The teacher knows the literature and makes it come to life by bringing herself or himself to the reading. In the following pages, there are 90 children's books which can come to life through the teacher's reading. Just as the music on a great score has notations as to how the music should be played, we have taken the liberty of making notations that suggest how to present the story, but it is the reader who brings the story to life.

In the section titled, "Read-Aloud Suggestions," we present our notations, which emphasize reading as an interactive thought/language process. The suggestions are based on relating the children's prior knowledge and experiences to the main idea of the story, asking children to offer predictions and confirming information drawn from their own experiences, language patterns and reading. They integrate the concepts and new information by using them in the story s-t-r-e-t-c-h-e-r-s which follow the read-aloud time. The students build more connections to the concepts, main ideas and imaginative extensions through the activities which each book stimulates. The reading strategies modeled by the teacher in the read-aloud time involve the children as active and imaginative thinkers.

After the read-aloud suggestions, we offer at least five ways to orchestrate the curriculum to take advantage of the story's underlying concept, or illustrations, or an association easy for the child to make. These activities which connect the child and the curriculum are "story s-t-r-e-t-c-h-e-r-s."

Often the story s-t-r-e-t-c-h-e-r-s ask children to "revisit" the text and the illustrations. In the story s-t-r-e-t-c-h-e-r-s for the classroom library, we suggest many individual and guided reading activities. The story s-t-r-e-t-c-h-e-r-s also include many rich listening, speaking and drama possibilities to help children develop a strong "sense of story."

In addition to the read-aloud suggestions and other language arts activities, we assume that teachers who use children's literature as an organizing foundation for the curriculum will also provide large blocks of time in the schedule for children to read books of their own choosing. In addition to the focus books for each unit, the classroom library should include an array of other books on the theme which the children can choose to read. A diverse collection of books from different genres is needed in the classroom library to allow children to follow their own reading interests. Of course, some of the children's favorite books should be a part of the permanent classroom collection.

The Writing Process

As you scan the story s-t-r-e-t-c-h-e-r-s, you will notice that for most books there are suggestions for the writing center. Integral to the concept of a classroom in which children are active language users, is the belief that children's writing is as natural a response to a story as is listening, dramatizing, discussing and reading. The suggestions we offer for the writing center are based on a developmental view or children's writing. Children's thinking about a story or about a concept naturally leads to their writing about what they know, what they observe, what they wonder or can imagine.

Writing is a "constructivist" process. Children construct their writing from the printed symbols they know, whether it is the invented spelling of the first grader, or the uncertain sentences of the third grader writing his or her first book. The premise of "whole language" classrooms, where teachers use "developmentally appropriate practices," is that the child be encouraged to use whatever she or he knows. Approximations of standard spelling are accepted because they represent what the child knows now. The teacher understands that by constructing the language in print and speech, children grow in their ability to write and to spell.

Throughout the book, you will see the suggestion that children read their writing to an editing or listening group. This step helps children view writing as a process. The first step is pre-writing or thinking about what one would like to write and how it might be developed. For many children in the primary grades, pre-writing may mean drawing a picture or talking with a writing partner. The second step is writing a draft. If one gets "stuck" and needs more ideas or response from the audience, the writer or teacher calls for a writing conference. The author reads his or her draft and listeners make suggestions and ask questions centered around the author's main question of the audience: "What else would you like to know?"

Having heard their suggestions, the author decides whether or not to answer their questions change or rewrite the draft. First graders who are just learning to edit for content will usually add sentences to the end of their story, rather than rearrange it. Second and third graders can rewrite drafts by rearranging and inserting new content. After one or many drafts, the teacher and child can decide whether to edit the piece for publication. Writing is meant to be read; therefore, we provide many opportunities for children to share their compositions. Whether a regular time is set aside each day for "author's chair," for a child to sit in a special chair and read his or her writing to the audience, or dramatize it with puppets, or present a particularly potent part of the piece with musical accompaniment, the ways of sharing one's writing are as rich and diverse as the children's imaginations. From pre-writing to publication, the amount of editing and rewriting depends upon the children's abilities and desires. Children should not be expected to edit everything they write for publication. As they refine their understanding of what makes a good story or informational piece, they can select those pieces of writing with the most potential and edit them to publication stage. (See the directions in the Appendix for one way to bind a book.)

Teachers often ask when they should give instruction in writing. Certainly, the teacher is a role model, and many story s-t-r-e-t-c-h-e-r-s the suggest that teachers brainstorm with children about possible content, compose group stories and model the editing process with the teacher's own writing or a group story. By connecting good works of literature with the writing process, the teacher helps focus the students' attention on specific aspects of story structure. From good children's literature, the teacher can provide examples which can help children develop attention-getters for the beginnings of their stories, use more descriptive words, write dialogue, connect episodes and find just the right point at which to end the story for an effective climax.

By assisting children throughout the writing process, the teacher can ascertain what specific help each needs. We suggest keeping a portfolio, letting the students select pieces they enjoyed writing or think reflect their best writing. The writing portfolios can be shared with parents and used to help the children see their own progress throughout the year. (For a more thorough discussion of the reading and writing process, see our book THE WHOLE LANGUAGE KINDERGARTEN from Teachers College Press.)

Choice Is A Powerful Motivator

Choice is integral to the operation of a classroom which uses children's literature as an organizing structure. In addition to the obvious choices of which books they read from a well-stocked classroom library, there are other choices children can make throughout the day, throughout the curriculum. Children who exercise choice become more creative, expressive and motivated. In the DEVELOPMENTALLY APPROPRIATE PRACTICES (1987) document from NAEYC, and in the central premise of what makes a whole language classroom, is "children making choices" throughout the day. There is a balance of child-choice and teacher-directed activities. Children have large blocks of time when they can choose which story s-t-r-e-t-c-h-e-r-s they will complete, which topics they will write about, how they will share their writing, which science and nature problem they will investigate and how they will display their findings in mathematical terms.

Representational Competence

Just as children are active learners who choose from an array of possible activities, there is also the expectation in the classroom that children will develop their "representational competence," that is, their abilities to **re**present what they have learned. Whether they use a calendar to keep track of the weather for a month, a balance to compare weights, a graph to chart preferences for certain authors, the children are being asked to solve problems by collecting data, summarizing or demonstrating their findings, and selecting ways to represent their solutions. While rather simple by adult standards, this systematic observation, conscious record keeping and discovery of ways to share findings with others, and the problems and explanations generated by children employ sound scientific and mathematical understandings. In addition to becoming more competent in reading and writing, children who do science and mathematics story s-t-r-e-t-c-h-e-r-s learn a vocabulary which they come to know by **re**presenting what they have learned. (See the article by Raines,

1990, for more information about representational competence.)

The Literature Is The Experience

We would be remiss, however, to omit the very essence of a curriculum where good children's literature is central to expanding their ever widening view of the world. In addition to the literally thousands of ways the curriculum is made more interesting by hearing and reading the stories and information books written by some of the best authors of our century, we know that "the literature itself is the experience." The young child who confidently says, "I can read that book," and plunges into A HOUSE IS A HOUSE FOR ME does so because the author tells a predictable but interesting story. While savoring the content of the story, the child is also relishing the style of the writing. The girl who pours over Ruth Heller's illustrations in ANIMALS BORN ALIVE AND WELL, then rushes over to proclaim she knows what a mammal is, has learned a valuable concept, but the fact that the literature is written factually, yet rhythmically, made the child return to read it again. The beautiful illustrations also drew her back to connect the words, the concepts and the beauty of the text. Over the course of three weeks, the child discovered other Ruth Heller books and announced, "I like books by this author." When a child's begins to identify favorites, the literature has become the experience.

We would also be remiss as teachers, curriculum planners, and lovers of good picture books if we failed to appreciate the art of children's books. Someone said that children's books are the last source of inexpensive, yet great art for families. Many picture books are collections of great works of art. Illustrations give children the opportunity to observe closely and hold in their own hands truly great drawings, paintings, pastels and watercolors. The impressionistic watercolors by Itoko Maeno in MINOU, Lynne Cherry's bold celebration of rainforest colors in THE GREAT KAPOK TREE, the lavishly decorated borders and exquisite ornamentation in Jan Brett's BERLIOZ THE BEAR, and Jan Spivey Gilchrist's black and white pencil drawings with depths of shading in NATHANIEL TALKING are just a few of the picture books that offer a wonderful experience both because of the literature and because of the magnificent art.

We have included the full names of authors and illustrators, rather than just their initials, so that you can become familiar with them and request their other books.

How To Use The Book

We suggest you use STORY S-T-R-E-T-C-H-E-R-S FOR THE PRIMARY GRADES: ACTIVITIES TO EXPAND CHILDREN'S FAVORITE BOOKS as a resource and adapt and devise activities for your students which best meet their needs. Some teachers select a different focus book for each day of the week and include all the story s-t-r-e-t-c-h-e-r-s as a base for their curriculum plan for the unit. Other teachers read all the five focus books during read-aloud sessions and complete only one story s-t-r-e-t-c-h-e-r for each day of the week. Most importantly, they are adopting, adapting, revising and devising the story s-t-r-e-t-c-h-e-r-s to meet their children's needs.

Whether you are a student teacher, beginning teacher or seasoned veteran, the goal is to connect the child, the story and the curriculum through good books. Librarians, reading specialists, principals and curriculum directors have found many inventive ways to incorporate story s-t-r-e-t-c-h-e-r-s into their work in support of classroom teachers. We appreciate the reception educators have given STORY S-T-R-E-T-C-H-E-R-S: ACTIVITIES TO EXPAND CHILDREN'S FAVORITE BOOKS and MORE STORY S-T-R-E-T-C-H-E-R-S: MORE ACTIVITIES TO EXPAND CHILDREN'S FAVORITE BOOKS. At conferences and conventions, teachers often tell us their "success stories" and sometimes even bring us samples of the children's work in response to a story s-t-r-e-t-c-h-e-r we have recommended. We eagerly await the response to STORY S-T-R-E-T-C-H-E-R-S FOR THE PRIMARY GRADES and the many success stories you will tell us about your students.

References From The Introduction

Bredekamp, Sue. Ed. (1987). **DEVELOPMEN-TALLY APPROPRIATE PRACTICE IN EARLY CHILDHOOD EDUCATION PROGRAMS SERVING CHILDREN FROM BIRTH TO AGE 8.** Washington, DC: National Association for the Education of Young Children.

Martin, Bill, Jr., & Archambault, John. (1987). **KNOTS ON A COUNTING ROPE.** New York: Henry Holt.

Raines, Shirley C. (1990). Representational competence: (Re)presenting experiences through words, action, and images. **CHILDHOOD EDUCATION.** 66(3), 139-144.

Raines, Shirley C. & Canady, Robert J. (1989). **STORY S-T-R-E-T-C-H-E-R-S: ACTIVITIES TO EXPAND CHILDREN'S FAVORITE BOOKS.** Mt. Rainier, MD: Gryphon House.

Raines, Shirley C. & Canady, Robert J. (1991). **MORE STORY S-T-R-E-T-C-H-E-R-S: ACTIVITIES TO EXPAND CHILDREN'S FAVORITE BOOKS.** Mt. Rainier, MD: Gryphon House.

Raines, S. C. & Canady, Robert J. (1990). **THE WHOLE LANGUAGE KINDERGARTEN.** New York: Teachers College Press.

Viorst, Judith. (1971). Illustrated by Eric Blegvad. **THE TENTH GOOD THING ABOUT BARNEY.** New York: Atheneum.

I AM ME,
I AM SPECIAL,
LOOK WHAT I CAN DO!

Josephina, the Great Collector
Matthew's Dream
The Day of Ahmed's Secret
Crow Boy
My Shadow

I AM ME, I AM SPECIAL, LOOK WHAT I CAN DO!

JOSEPHINA, THE GREAT COLLECTOR

By Diana Engel

Josephina is a collector of treasures. Everywhere she goes she finds something to bring home with her to put in her room. The only problem is that Josephina shares her room with her sister Rose, who likes everything neat and tidy. The two sisters try to solve the problem by taking part of the collection to Uncle Mario's house. But while Rose and Uncle Mario are enjoying some of his hot biscuits, Josephina is collecting some items from his curio cabinet that she wants to take home. Finally, in disgust, Rose moves out. Even Josephina's beautiful seashell collection cannot take her mind off how much she misses her sister. Josephina solves the problem by taking all her collections outside to their playhouse, which she decorates beautifully. The illustrations in Diana Engel's Josephina stories are chock-full of details, yet the action remains the center of attention.

Read-Aloud Suggestions

The collectors in your classroom are easy to identify. They are often the ones with desks stuffed with papers, and the ones who bring boxes of objects for "show and tell." Begin the discussion of the book by asking the class collectors to tell how they got started collecting. Ask where they display and keep their collections. Show the children the cover of JOSEPHINA, THE GREAT COLLECTOR. Tell them Josephina has a problem with her collections. Read the book and discuss how your class collectors solved their collection problems. Let the children who are collectors and who would like to display their treasures sign up for a display day. Announce the other JOSEPHINA, THE GREAT COLLECTOR story s-t-r-e-t-c-h-e-r activities.

STORY STRETCHER

For Art: Josephina's Displays

What the children will learn
To create displays with focal points

Materials you will need
Tablecloth, lengths of fabric, blocks, construction paper, tape, index cards, markers, sea shells or a child's collection of objects, optional—lamp, baskets and gift boxes

What to do
1. If possible, observe a librarian or an art teacher creating a display.

2. Ask the person to use the term "focal point" as she or he discusses what they are doing and why.

3. Discuss a variety of ways to create a focal point, by placing a block under the cloth to make a special object higher than others, by placing an item in a spotlight or by positioning it in the center of the display.

4. Collect the supplies for a display of sea shells or a special collection from one of the children.

5. Work with a small group of collectors to create the special display.

Something to think about
Try a variety of ways of creating focal points. Encourage the children to look at store windows and notice focal points. Ask children who cannot bring their collections to class to make pictures of how they have their treasures displayed at home.

STORY STRETCHER

For Classroom Library: Circle Story

What the children will learn
To identify the main events in a story

Materials you will need
Chart tablet or posterboard, markers or colored pencils

What to do
1. With small groups of children, look through the illustrations in JOSEPHINA, THE GREAT COLLECTOR.

2. Find the illustrations of main events in the story.

3. Write JOSEPHINA, THE GREAT COLLECTOR at the top of a sheet of chart tablet paper or a piece of posterboard.

4. Draw a large circle and divide it into six pie pieces.

5. Ask one child to draw something in the first pie section, that illustrates the beginning of the book, when the two sisters are playing together happily.

6. In the second pie piece, have another child show Josephina becoming a collector.

7. In the third section, ask someone to draw the problem—that Josephina's collections are taking over the two sisters' room.

8. In the fourth section, show Uncle Mario's house.

9. In the fifth section, show Rose moving out of their room.

10. In the last part of the circle, ask a child to draw a picture of Josephina decorating the playhouse.

11. Talk with the children about the fact that this is a circle story: the opening scene of the children playing together and the ending scene are the same.

Something to think about
Select other stories which are appropriate for circle stories. Ask the children to look through their own writings and select a story to illustrate by making a circle story. Also use circle stories as a means to brainstorm main events, or as a pre-writing activity for planning a story.

For Cooking: Uncle Mario's Biscuits

What the children will learn
To make drop biscuits or muffins

Materials you will need
Drop biscuit or muffin mix, mixing bowls, wooden spoons, measuring cups and spoons, milk or water, shortening, cookie sheet or muffin pan, toaster oven, chart tablet, marker, knives, butter or margarine, jelly

What to do
1. Invite a father, grandfather or uncle to lead the baking activity.

2. Print the recipe on the chart tablet for the children to follow.

3. Divide the class into small groups so that each child can par-

ticipate in the measuring and mixing.

4. Bake the drop biscuits or muffins in a toaster oven or in the cafeteria oven.

5. Serve them with butter or margarine and jelly.

Something to think about
If you do not have a father or male relative who will volunteer, ask a cafeteria worker to help. This allows the children to get to know one of the school helpers.

For Mathematics: Josephina's Patterns

What the children will learn
To recognize and organize patterns

Materials you will need
Collection of sea shells, boxes or bags, construction paper, butcher paper

What to do
1. With small groups of children, look at the endpapers of Diana Engel's JOSEPHINA, THE GREAT COLLECTOR.

2. Have the children describe the pattern of the seashells that decorate the pages.

3. Distribute boxes or bags of sea shells to each person in the group.

4. Ask each child to make a pattern on the construction paper.

5. Let the children read each other's patterns.

6. Vary the activity by asking them to create vertical and diagonal patterns.

7. Let partners work together and combine designs on large sheets of butcher paper.

Something to think about
Other collectibles that are good for this activity are matchbox cars, animal cards, baseball cards, rocks

and household items like buttons or different patterns of silverware.

For Science And Nature: Cooperative Learning— Researching Our Collection

What the children will learn
To use reference materials

Materials you will need
Collection of sea shells; boxes, baskets or bags; index cards; pens or pencils; reference books

What to do
1. Working in small groups, give the children an assortment of sea shells.

2. Let them sort them into boxes, baskets or bags by types.

3. Ask each group to make a display of their shell collection and to identify their shells by working together. Tell them they are resources for each other.

4. Have them label each type of shell by printing the names on an index card.

5. At this point, they will need to refer to the reference books. Demonstrate how to match the shells to the pictures.

6. Let the children compare the shells in each of their displays and decide of which types they have more and the kinds of shells that are most unique in each of their collections.

Something to think about
To encourage group interactions, place one unique type of shell in each group's collection. Also try to identify at least one child per group who has "sea shell expertise" so that the children learn to rely on each other for information.

I AM ME,
I AM SPECIAL,
LOOK WHAT
I CAN DO!

MATTHEW'S DREAM

By Leo Lionni

Matthew, the mouse, and his family live in a dusty attic surrounded by old newspapers, discarded toys and broken furniture. Matthew's parents want him to grow up to be a doctor so he can provide for the family. But Matthew doesn't know what he wants to be until the day he goes with his classmates to an art museum. There he becomes enchanted with the paintings and with a mouse named Nicoletta who loves art. Matthew thinks about painting all the time, even dreams about beautiful paintings and about Nicoletta. When he grows up, he marries Nicoletta and spends his life as a famous painter. When asked the name of his largest painting, he replies, "Matthew's Dream." In classic Lionni style, the story and the art complement each other, simply, boldly and beautifully.

Read-Aloud Suggestions

Ask the children what they want to be when they grow up. Discuss what you wanted to be when you were growing up. Talk about how parents sometimes "dream aloud" for their children. Show the children the cover of MATTHEW'S DREAM and see if the cover reminds them of other books. Perhaps they remember Leo Lionni's style and some of his other books. Ask the children to predict what the title may mean. Read MATTHEW'S DREAM. After hearing the story once, the children will want to look at the illustrations again. Point out the different types of artistic expression, such as impressionism, pointillism, cubism and modern art. Discuss the plans for a trip to an art museum and the other story s-t-r-e-t-c-h-e-r activities planned for children to discover which types of art they enjoy the most. Emphasize that a positive self-concept means that you enjoy your opinions and that your tastes in art do not have to be the same as your friends.

STORY STRETCHER

For Art: Prints Of Famous Paintings

What the children will learn
To recognize some famous pieces of art

Materials you will need
Prints of famous works of art

What to do
1. With the help of the librarian or an art specialist, select several paintings that will appeal to children of the age you teach.
2. Each day of the week show a print to the children and talk about the artist and the painting.

3. Let the children think of titles for the work. Then tell them the titles the artists used, and see if they think the titles are appropriate.
4. During the next weeks, share very different periods and styles of art.
5. Encourage diversity of tastes and opinions.

Something to think about
If you have an artist from your state who is famous or even a locally famous artist, display her or his prints in the classroom.

ANOTHER STORY STRETCHER

For Art: Matthew's Dream Collages

What the children will learn
To make collages

Materials you will need
White construction paper, different colors of tissue paper, scraps of construction paper, scissors, glue sticks

What to do
1. Let the children tear or cut tissue paper or scraps of construction paper into irregular shapes.
2. Have them glue the pieces onto white construction paper to create a pleasing design.
3. Display the torn paper collages and title them with the children's names, such as "Michelle's Dream," "Damien's Dream," or "Tina's Dream."

Something to think about
Leave the same art materials out for several days. Children need time to experiment with the possibilities of a medium before their products will become more creative.

For Music And Movement: Color Dance

What the children will learn
To see colors and patterns as they move in response to the music

Materials you will need
Long colored scarves or crepe paper streamers, slow waltz music, tape or record player

What to do
1.   Read the section of MATTHEW'S DREAM where Nicoletta and Matthew see changing patches of color that move in response to the distant music.

2.   With the children seated in a circle, begin to play the waltz music.

3.   Have the children move their upper bodies in response to the music.

4.   Select a few children and begin moving around the circle. Tap a few at a time to get up and move in response to the music.

5.   While the children are moving, distribute the colored scarves or crepe paper streamers and continue the movement until the music stops.

Something to think about
If you have children who feel too self-conscious to join in the movement, let them be the audience, and at the end of the session, ask them to tell some of the colors they saw as the children's scarves or streamers overlapped.

For Special Event: Trip To An Art Museum Or A Gallery

What the children will learn
To express their opinions about works of art that appeal to them

Materials you will need
Paper and pencils

What to do
1.   Make transportation arrangements and secure parental permissions.

2.   Train the volunteers who will accompany the group by talking with them about your objectives for the trip, distributing brochures about the museum and pointing out any paintings or sculptures you want the children to notice in more detail.

3.   Assign no more than four children per volunteer.

4.   Encourage the children to express their opinions.

5.   Have them write down the names of some of the paintings and artists whose works they particularly enjoyed.

Something to think about
Many museums have educational programs planned for children. Visit the museum ahead of time and follow the children's tour. With the educational program director, plan a tour that will best fit your children's interests and attention span. It is far better to plan a shorter tour than a long one.

For Writing Center: When I Grow Up . . . .

What the children will learn
To use the theme from the story to write another episode

Materials you will need
Assorted of sizes of writing paper, pencils, colored pens

What to do
1.   With the children who come to the writing center during choice time, talk about Matthew's parents' dream for him and Matthew's dream. Discuss

Matthew's decision to follow his own talents and dreams.

2.   Converse with the children about their special talents and what they think they would like to do as a career when they grow up.

3.   Encourage the children to draw themselves in three or four possible careers and then imagine what their lives might be like.

4.   Ask the children to write about themselves and why they think this would be a good career possibility for them.

Something to think about
Teaching with an integrated unit approach allows the children to have many choices. If some children are already writing other pieces, allow them to continue. In creative expression, allow as much freedom in choosing a topic as is possible.

1
I AM ME,
I AM SPECIAL,
LOOK WHAT
I CAN DO!

THE DAY OF
AHMED'S SECRET

By Florence Parry Heide and

Judith Heide Gilliland

Illustrated by Ted Lewin

Ahmed is a young boy who works in the city of Cairo selling bottled gas and making deliveries with his donkey drawn cart. All day long Ahmed has a secret. As he travels through the day, selling, meeting and greeting people, eating, resting and thinking of his family, he has his secret with him to give him a special feeling. We travel with Ahmed and find out how children in Cairo work to help their families. We also see the city through Ahmed's eyes and those of his father, as Ahmed recalls the way his father describes the city. At the end of the day, Ahmed gathers his entire family to tell his secret—he can write his name. The story ends with Ahmed's beautiful thought that perhaps his name will live like the old buildings in the city, live for a thousand years. Lewin's watercolors are more than illustrations, they are exquisitely rich paintings filled with the colors, sights, bustle and character of the ancient city.

Read-Aloud Suggestions

Discuss with the children what their special roles are in their families, their jobs, their responsibilities. Talk about what would happen if they forgot to do their jobs. Continue by talking about how in many parts of the world children must help their families by working to earn money. Show the cover of THE DAY OF AHMED'S SECRET. Look at a map or a globe and point out Cairo, the city where the story takes place. Read the book and at the end look closely at the way Ahmed writes his name. Give each child a sheet of paper and ask them to write their names in large bold print or cursive handwriting. Re-examine the illustrations and read again some of the descriptions of the sights, sounds, smells and the constant sand of the desert city.

S T O R Y   S T R E T C H E R
For Art: Sand Painting

What the children will learn
To add texture to their paintings with sand

Materials you will need
Construction paper or manilla paper, scraps of paper, tempera paints, brushes, sugar shakers, sand

What to do
1. Whenever Ahmed thought of his city, Cairo, he always thought of the sand in the streets and the sand in the desert outside the city. Discuss the traditional technique of using sand to add texture.

2. Using scraps of paper, brush on some paint, then sprinkle it with sand.

3. Let it dry briefly, then lift the paper, stand it on its end and let all the loose sand shake off. Show the children the texture that remains.

4. Discuss Ahmed's mentioning the sand throughout the story. If pictures were painted of the streets of Ahmed's city, the sand technique could emphasize the feeling and give texture to the painting.

5. Let the children brainstorm about other pictures they could paint using the sand technique, such as a day at the beach, playing in the sand box at the playground or mixing concrete for a cement patio.

6. Ask the children to paint any picture they choose, either one that reminds them of Ahmed's day, or some special day they enjoyed where sand was a part of the activity.

Something to think about
Older children can mix colored sand and layer it into baby food jars to create sand murals.

S T O R Y   S T R E T C H E R
For Classroom Library: Recording Ahmed's Story

What the children will learn
To read dialogue and record a story

Materials you will need
Cassette tape recorder, tape, fork, glass, listening station, headphones

What to do
1. With a small group of children, plan how to record THE DAY OF AHMED'S SECRET. Either you read the story as told by Ahmed or ack a child who is a proficient reader to make the recording. Assign children to do the speaking parts of Hassan, the old woman and Ahmed's father.

2. Ask one child to tap a glass gently with a fork to make a page-turning signal.

3. Rehearse the reading and record the book.

4. Place the cassette tape in the listening station.

Something to think about
Invite an Egyptian friend or someone who has traveled in the Middle East to share with the class some examples of art and photographs or slides of Cairo or another middle eastern city. Leave the materials on display in the class library.

For Special Event: A Bazaar, A Market Day

What the children will learn
To price, barter and sell some items

Materials you will need
Posterboard, markers, crepe paper, scissors, tape, stickers for price tags

What to do
1. Look again at the scenes in THE DAY OF AHMED'S SECRET that show the bazaar, the busy streets of the marketplace.
2. Talk about our American equivalent, the sidewalk sale or the flea market with small stalls.
3. Discuss ways family members sell items, such as a garage sale, yard sale, a community or church bazaar or rummage sale.
4. Let the children tell about some of their experiences at these types of sales, either as sellers or customers.
5. Plan a class bazaar or market day by asking the children to bring in items they would like to sell. Decide how to keep track of the items contributed. Discuss pricing and bartering, counting money and keeping track of the amount sold and inventory.
6. Place tables around the room and let the children make posters and signs advertising their bargains.
7. Schedule an afternoon of shopping and invite several other classrooms to come to shop.
8. After the bazaar, have the children evaluate their pricing, bartering, effectiveness as sales people, proficiency at counting money and what they will do with any leftover merchandise.

Something to think about
Try to make the experience as authentic as possible. For younger children, plan a less elaborate event and assist with the money exchanges. For older children, consider some ongoing enterprise, such as a yearlong class project.

For Writing Center: Writing Our Names In Different Languages

What the children will learn
To recognize their names in different languages

Materials you will need
Collection of nice papers, inks and pens that the different language writers prefer

What to do
1. Ask Arabic writers to come to class and demonstrate to the children how to write their name. Be sure to include Ahmed's name.
2. Ask writers of several different languages to come to class on different days.
3. Let the children practice writing their names in more than one language.
4. Display their names around the room.

Something to think about
If you live in a community where several different languages are seen on signs and logos, copy them or bring advertisements to the classroom and let the children decide what is being communicated based on the context of the sign.

For Writing Center: Ways I Help My Family

What the children will learn
To compare chores and wyas to help without being told

Materials you will need
Writing paper, pencils, colored pens, markers, crayons or paints, paper, brushes, easels

What to do
1. Discuss THE DAY OF AHMED'S SECRET with the children who come to the writing center. Ask the children to talk about some of the ways they help their families.
2. Suggest that the children write about a typical weekend at their home and some of the ways they are helpful, both with routinely assigned chores and without being asked.
3. Have the children illustrate their writing with materials of their choosing.
4. Display their pictures and stories around the room as a part of the emphasis on the "I Am Me, I Am Special, Look What I Can Do" unit.

Something to think about
Taking responsibility is an important part of building one's self-concept. Help the children appreciate each other's contributions to family life as well as the ways they work together in the classroom.

I AM ME, I AM SPECIAL, LOOK WHAT I CAN DO!

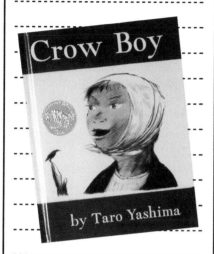

CROW BOY

By Taro Yashima

The story takes place in Japan, where Chibi, a bashful little boy from the country, goes to school. His classmates call him stupid and slowpoke. No one plays with him and he does not participate in the class activities. When the class gets a new teacher, Mr. Isobe, they gain a new appreciation of how much Chibi knows about the garden, the woods, plants and insects. Mr. Isobe spends a lot of time talking with Chibi and displays his art work and writing on the wall. When the class has a talent show, Chibi imitates the voices of crows. The children are so taken by their new understanding of all that Chibi knows about nature and birds that they begin calling him Crow Boy, a name he really likes. Years later when Chibi brings charcoal to sell in the village, everyone still calls him by his favorite name, Crow Boy. This Caldecott Honor book is illustrated with charcoals and highlighted with colored paints.

Read-Aloud Suggestions

Even though CROW BOY was written in 1955, unfortunately, the problem of children calling each other names and not understanding a different child is still with us. Talk about nicknames and how much fun they are. Then go on to discuss how children sometimes call each other names that are not fun. Discuss how our feelings are affected by what other people say to us. Read CROW BOY. Let the children tell how they felt at the beginning of the story when Chibi's classmates called him stupid and slowpoke. Contrast their feelings at the beginning of the story and at the end. Discuss what made CROW BOY unique and why he liked his nickname.

S T O R Y   S T R E T C H E R

For Art: Chibi's Charcoal Drawings

What the children will learn
To experiment with charcoals for drawing

Materials you will need
Charcoals, scraps of paper, tissues, manilla paper, hair spray

What to do
1.   Look again at the illustration in CROW BOY where the teacher placed Chibi's black and white drawings on the bulletin board.

2.   Talk about how the teacher made Chibi feel so special by recognizing that his art work was very unique. Discuss how much you like the children's art in your classroom because everyone is special.

3.   Show the children the charcoals and let them try making lines of different widths with the points and sides of the charcoals.

4.   Demonstrate how to shade by smudging the charcoal with a tissue or the end of a finger.

5.   Let the children experiment with drawing and writing with the charcoals.

6.   Ask them to make a black and white drawing. When the children finish their drawings, spray them with hair spray so the charcoal will not smudge.

Something to think about
Display the children's art work by matting them with construction paper or the reverse side of used poster board. Let the children choose the color of mat. Make a black and white display and another display of prints matted in bright reds, yellows and blues.

S T O R Y   S T R E T C H E R

For Cooking: Crow Boy's Rice Balls

What the children will learn
To taste rice served in a different manner

Materials you will need
Rice, water, butter, saucepan, honey, mixing bowls, wooden spoons, wax paper or aluminum foil, optional—hot plate

What to do
1.   Work with a small group of children and repeat the cooking experience several times so that all can participate.

2.   Prepare the rice by following the directions on the package. If you cannot cook in your classroom, cook the rice ahead of time at home.

3.   Allow the rice to cool.

4.   Divide the rice into portions by placing it in smaller mixing bowls.

5.   Let the helpers take a handful of rice.

6. Drizzle a small amount of honey over the handful of rice and let the children shape it into a ball.

7. Place on wax paper or aluminum foil and write children's names alongside their rice balls.

8. Serve for a snack.

Something to think about
If you have a student who is of Asian heritage, ask his or her parents to make a variety of rice dishes for the children to try.

STORY STRETCHER

For Science And Nature: Chibi's Listening Walk

What the children will learn
To listen and observe the sounds of the natural world

Materials you will need
Chart tablet or posterboard, marker

What to do
1. With the whole class, read again the section of CROW BOY where he listened so intently to the sounds of nature.

2. Have the children close their eyes and take an imaginary walk out of your school building into a woods or a park. Help them visualize the walk by taking them step by step from the school to the area.

3. After the children appear to be thinking about the woods or the park, ask them to slowly open their eyes and tell you the sounds they imagined hearing.

4. Write the sounds on a sheet of chart tablet paper or posterboard.

5. Take a listening walk to a park, woods or other natural setting near your school.

6. When you return from the walk, ask the children to tell you the sounds they heard. Whenever someone mentions a sound they had previously imagined, write the

sound and place a check mark beside it.

Something to think about
On other days take listening walks to hear the sounds of people working or the sounds of transportation.

STORY STRETCHER

For Special Event: Talent And Hobby Show

What the children will learn
To appreciate each person's unique talents

Materials you will need
Posterboard, marker, easel

What to do
1. With the class as a whole, plan a talent and hobby show. Mention several children whose talents and hobbies are well-known by the class and others the class may not know about.

2. Discuss talent and hobby shows that class members may have attended.

3. Plan tables to display children's hobbies and a time for entertainment when the children will perform.

4. Meet in smaller groups and let the children discuss what they might do. Be sure to include budding hobbies, such as cooking, puppetry, rock collecting, crafts.

Something to think about
Combining a hobby and talent show allows more children to be comfortable participating. It also allows children to appreciate each other's uniqueness.

STORY STRETCHER

For Writing Center: Nicknames I Would Like

What the children will learn
To compose a short characterization

Materials you will need
Writing paper, pencils, colored pens

What to do
1. Talk with the children about Chibi and his new nickname, CROW BOY, and what it meant.

2. Ask the children to tell the nicknames they are called by family members and friends..

3. Go on to discuss what nicknames they would like to have and why the names would fit. For instance, a child might be called "Slugger" because he or she is good at hitting baseballs. Tell the children that when they write the reasons why the nicknames are appropriate, they are writing characterizations.

4. Let the children write their nicknames in colored pens with decorative writing.

5. During a time when the whole class is together, let the children take turns sitting in the "author's chair" and sharing the nicknames and the characterizations they wrote.

Something to think about
Younger children who are less proficient writers may draw pictures illustrating why they deserve their nicknames. Older children might try writing a whole collection of nicknames that fit an imaginary group of friends.

MY SHADOW

By Robert Louis Stevenson

Illustrated by Ted Rand

This classic Robert Louis Stevenson poem has been turned into cheerful illustrations of children from around the world playing. Each phrase of the poem is illustrated with a child or children and the ever-present shadows. A delightful celebration of individuals, of friends and of the discovery of shadows. Ted Rand's pictures and the charm of the well-known poem are sure to make it a teacher and a child favorite.

Read-Aloud Suggestions

Tell the children that you know something that stays with you all the time when you are in the light. No one else has one just like yours. Let them guess what it might be. When someone guesses a shadow, have the children notice their faint shadows inside the classroom. Then ask some students to stand near the windows and look at their shadows. Read Robert Louis Stevenson's MY SHADOW. After reading it through once without stopping, read the poem again and have the children notice the shadows on each page. Go outside and let the children play with their shadows and observe moving shadows and the still shadows of buildings, playground equipment and trees. While outside, announce all the shadow story s-t-r-e-t-c-h-e-r-s.

S T O R Y   S T R E T C H E R

For Art: Shadow Silhouettes

What the children will learn
To use shadows to make silhouettes

Materials you will need
Overhead projector, chair, tape, black construction paper, pen, scissors, glue, white typing paper or construction paper

What to do
1. Tape black paper onto the wall.

2. Have a child sit in a chair with his or her profile to you.

3. Turn on the overhead projector and shine it on the child, creating a shadow on the wall.

4. Draw around the shadow on the black paper.

5. Cut out the shadow—the silhouette.

6. Let the children glue their silhouettes onto white typing paper or construction paper.

Something to think about
Let the children choose their favorite color for the silhouettes and glue them onto contrasting colored paper. As a writing extension, have the children compose diamond poems about themselves (see the story s-t-r-e-t-c-h-e-r for the writing center) and attach them to the backs of the silhouettes.

S T O R Y   S T R E T C H E R

For Classroom Library: Choral Reading

What the children will learn
To read expressively and in unison

Materials you will need
Chart tablet, red and blue markers

What to do
1. After reading the book, MY SHADOW, several times, print the words on chart tablet paper. Alternate colors of marker for each page.

2. Form the children into two groups, and let one group read the blue lines and the other group read the red lines. Use a variety of methods to form groups: boys and girls; counting off 1, 2, 1, 2; saying red, blue, red, blue; dividing by last names, A-K and L-Z.

3. Demonstrate how to do choral reading and let the children practice several times. Have them pay attention to the punctuation and read with expression.

4. Practice choral reading with longer poems, and let each group read a stanza, rather than alternating lines.

Something to think about
Make a class *Big Book of Favorite Poems*. Include a favorite poem from each child and poems for each of the units you routinely teach.

STORY STRETCHER

For Creative Dramatics: Favorite Character And Favorite Story Shadow Puppets

What the children will learn
To follow directions and to dramatize characters

Materials you will need
Overhead projector, sheet or screen, construction paper, scissors, stapler, long straws or tongue depressors

What to do
1. Make a construction paper shadow puppet of a favorite class storybook character, such as Curious George, Frog or Toad, Amelia Bedelia.

2. Staple the puppet onto a holder, such as a long straw or tongue depressor.

3. Turn the overhead projector on and light up a sheet or screen. Move the puppet across the screen of the projector.

4. An alternative is to light up the sheet and place the puppets behind the sheet and move them. Then the audience sees the shadows of the puppets.

5. Let the children make puppets of their favorite characters. Encourage groups of children to make puppets for entire stories and dramatize them for the class.

Something to think about
Younger children will enjoy guessing who each child's puppet character is. Let the child improvise dialogue or answer the questions

the children pose to the puppeteer. Older children often make scenery and write plays that are extensions of favorite stories.

STORY STRETCHER

For Games: Bouncing Balls

What the children will learn
To improvise games

Materials you will need
Rubber balls, chalkboard, chalk, different sizes of balls and equipment from found objects and materials, paper and pencils

What to do
1. Look at the children in MY SHADOW who are playing with "an india-rubber ball." Discuss why it is called india-rubber: because the trees from which the rubber was made came from India. Notice the little girl bouncing the ball under her leg.

2. Have the children sit in a semi-circle, and roll a ball to different students. When a child catches the ball, ask him or her to describe a game that is played with a ball.

3. Make a list on the chalkboard of the games played with balls—soccer, basketball, baseball, tennis, football, dodge ball. After the children have thought of the obvious ones, encourage them to think of others. If they get stalled, tell them of a game you may have played as a child, such as stick ball or throwing the ball over the roof of the house.

4. Encourage the children to tell about games with balls that they have improvised to entertain themselves when no one is around to play. For instance, bouncing a ball against a wall, rolling a golf ball into a cup, throwing a ball at a target.

5. Bring out all the balls you have and roll them around in the

semi-circle. Ask each child to think of a game he or she could play with a ball.

6. Then randomly divide the children in pairs and ask them to improvise a game and play it together.

7. As the children design the games, they will begin making up rules for how to play.

8. Ask the children to teach their game to another pair of children. At this point, have them write down the rules and draw diagrams so that others can play the game.

9. Let the children take turns teaching their games to the class.

Something to think about
Plan with the physical education teacher and teach the children a variety of games with balls which children from around the world would play.

STORY STRETCHER

For Writing Center: I Am A Diamond, I Am Me Poems

What the children will learn
To use descriptive words

Materials you will need
Chalkboard, chalk, large index cards, pens and pencils, glue

What to do
1. Draw a large diamond on the chalkboard.

2. Draw a line inside the diamond at the top. Write a story book character's name on the line, such as "Curious George."

3. Below the character's name, draw two lines and write two words that tell who Curious George is, such as "monkey" and "character."

4. Draw three lines in the center of the diamond and write three adjectives that describe Curious George, such as "funny," "curious," "helpful."

5. Below the center of the diamond, draw two lines and continue to describe Curious George with adjectives such as "friend," "escaper."

6. End by drawing one line in the bottom tip of the diamond and write "Curious George" again.

7. Have the children write descriptions of themselves. If they like, on the three lines in the middle of the diamond, they can write games they enjoy.

8. Let the children print their "I Am Me" diamond poems on large index cards and glue them onto the backs of their shadow silhouettes.

Something to think about
Older children can add more lines and have four lines in the middle of the diamond. They can also do contrasting diamonds telling about themselves at home versus school, or at school versus the summertime.

References

Engel, Diana. (1988). **JOSEPHINA, THE GREAT COLLECTOR**. New York: Morrow Junior Books.

Heide, Florence Parry, & Gilliland, Judith Heide. (1990). Illustrated by Ted Lewin. **THE DAY OF AHMED'S SECRET**. New York: Lothrop, Lee & Shepard Books.

Lionni, Leo. (1991). **MATTHEW'S DREAM**. New York: Alfred A. Knopf.

Stevenson, Robert Louis. (1990). Illustrated by Ted Rand. **MY SHADOW**. New York: G. P. Putnam's Sons.

Yashima, Taro. (1955). **CROW BOY**. New York: The Viking Press.

Additional References for I Am Me, I Am Special, Look What I Can Do

Bunting, Eve. (1989). Illustrated by Donald Carrick. **THE WEDNESDAY SURPRISE**. New York: Clarion Books. *Anna surprises everyone by teaching her grandmother to read. The family thought Grandmother was just babysitting!*

Engel, Diana. (1989). **JOSEPHINA HATES HER NAME**. New York: William Morrow and Company. *After Grandma explains that Josephina was named after Grandma's talented and daring older sister, Josephina begins to appreciate her unusual name.*

Guthrie, Donna. (1988). Illustrated by Dennis Hockerman. **A ROSE FOR ABBY**. Nashville: Abingdon Press. *Young Abby's compassion and courage inspire her neighbors and family to start a soup kitchen in the church. The rose is an unexpected "thank you."*

Little, Lessie Jones, & Greenfield, Eloise. (1978). Illustrated by Carole Byard. **I CAN DO IT BY MYSELF**. New York: Thomas Y. Crowell. *Donny is determined to buy his mother's birthday present all by himself, and even though he gets scared, he succeeds.*

Williams, Vera B. (1986). **CHERRIES AND CHERRY PITS**. New York: William Morrow and Company. *The author's neighbor, Bedemmi, draws pictures and tells stories as she draws. We experience the power of this young girl's imagination.*

FAMILIES

All Kinds of Families
Julius, The Baby of the World
How Many Stars in the Sky?
The Relatives Came
Amelia Bedelia's Family Album

ALL KINDS OF FAMILIES

By Norma Simon

Illustrated by Joe Lasker

Simon's book is an excellent beginning for a unit on families because it warmly and affectionately portrays many different types of families and family life. The text and illustrations help children think of themselves as family members and to see what changes in families and what remains the same. The book celebrates of family special events, holidays, stories and feelings at both sad and happy times. Lasker alternates pages of black line drawings with soft, warmly colored illustrations.

Read-Aloud Suggestions

Tell about your family—the family you were a part of growing up and the family you are a part of now. Select several children who have different kinds of families and ask them to tell who their family members are. Continue by asking children to tell how their families have changed. Elicit comments about extended families, grandparents, uncles, aunts, cousins. Have someone tell about a time when the greatest number of people from their family came together for a special event. Read ALL KINDS OF FAMILIES. After the reading, relate the earlier discussion of families to the illustrations in the book. Ask some children to tell about family gatherings they were reminded of by the pictures in the book. End the session by announcing the books you will read aloud for the unit. Encourage children to find library books about families as well as to read the ones you have collected for the classroom.

STORY STRETCHER

For Art: My Family Portrait

What the children will learn
To illustrate their immediate family

Materials you will need
Construction paper or manilla paper, crayons, markers, colored pens, glue

What to do
1. Talk with the children about the bulletin board you would like to make for the unit, one that shows all their families.

2. Have the children draw their family portraits. Then let the children choose a contrasting color of construction paper and make a mat or a border for their family portraits.

3. Ask the children to title their portraits using their names— "Marty's Family," "Christy's Family."

4. Arrange the bulletin board.

Something to think about
After the drawings have been up for a few days, have the children bring in family photographs to add to the bulletin board. Place them near the children's drawings and let the children add captions.

STORY STRETCHER

For Classroom Library: My Name Comes From

What the children will learn
To associate their names with family members or meanings of names

Materials you will need
Name books, such as baby name books or reference books on name meanings; chart tablet or posterboard; markers

What to do
1. Display the reference books on names.

2. Ask a child who has the most unusual name in class if he or she was named after someone in the family.

3. Look up the meaning of the child's name in a reference book and write it on the chart tablet.

4. Let the class add to the name charts until everyone is included.

Something to think about
Be sure to include reference materials for a variety of cultures. If these materials are not available to you, ask the children to provide information or invite parents or older students from different cultures to come to class and talk about their names. Younger children can talk about family members' nicknames. Older children can trace name changes over time

and family moves to this country, or changed spellings of names over time. In some Native American cultures, special names are sacred and are used in ceremonies. Do not ask these children their Indian names, but use the names they use at school.

STORY STRETCHER

For Cooking: Our Family Recipes

What the children will learn
To read recipes and to associate them with family times

Materials you will need
Materials for parent newsletter, sample recipe

What to do
1. In a parent newsletter, ask for copies of favorite family recipes for a class recipe book.

2. Include a sample recipe from your family and ask parents to write their recipes in the same format. For example, list the ingredients and steps for preparing the recipe "Granny Irene's Pineapple Upside-Down Cake,"

3. Encourage the families to include simple recipes for snacks as well.

4. Collect the recipes and review them.

5. Select recipes that would make good snacks.

6. Invite family members to come to class and lead small groups of children in preparing the snack recipes or have them send enough of the snack for the entire class to sample.

Something to think about
Duplicate copies of the recipes and bind them into a book for the students to give to their families. Younger children can write a sentence about why they like this food or remember a family event where the recipe was served. Older children can interview the relative to whom the recipe belongs and write a brief history of the recipe to include in the book.

STORY STRETCHER

For Music And Movement: Music My Family Enjoys

What the children will learn
To recognize a variety of family music preferences

Materials you will need
Cassette player and tapes, record player, chart tablet or posterboard, markers

What to do
1. Find out what types of music different families enjoy.

2. Ask several of the children whose families have strong musical interests to bring cassette tapes or records of music their families always play at family gatherings.

3. Listen to different selections on different days of the week.

4. Make a list of the main instruments that are used in the recordings.

5. Emphasize how music is a part of family life and family celebrations.

Something to think about
If any of the families of your children include professional musicians, ask them to play for the class. Invite amateur musicians who are members of family groups to play for the class.

STORY STRETCHER

For Writing Center: Writing To Someone In My Family

What the children will learn
To express their feelings in letter form

Materials you will need
Different kinds of stationery or papers, scratch paper, envelopes, pencils and pens

What to do
1. With the small group of children who come to the writing center, read a few family letters you have received.

2. Let the children talk about letters and greeting cards they have received in the mail.

3. Discuss relatives to whom they would like to write. Ask the children what special message they would like to communicate.

4. Let the children write a practice letter, help them edit it, then ask them to transpose the letter onto the stationery they want to use.

Something to think about
Children who do not know their extended families can write a letter to a member of their immediate family.

2
FAMILIES

JULIUS, THE BABY OF THE WORLD

By Kevin Henkes

Lilly thinks her new baby brother is disgusting. She has to share her room with him and keep her voice down while he sleeps. She cannot understand why her parents think he is the most beautiful baby in the world. When Lilly tries some of the things Julius does, like screaming and crying, she is sent to the uncooperative chair. Lilly runs away from home seven times in one morning. All her parents' attempts to help Lilly like Julius fail until the day when Cousin Garland says she thinks Julius is disgusting. Lilly didn't like her cousin talking about Julius like that; after all, Julius is her brother. Henkes' drawings are black ink and full color art with lots of lavender backgrounds, but splashed with brighter pastels as well as reds and pinks. The pictures are rich in pattern and detail. The humor in the story and illustrations are sure to make this selection a favorite one.

Read-Aloud Suggestions

Ask children who have baby brothers or sisters to tell what they do to help take care of the baby. Show the cover of JULIUS, THE BABY OF THE WORLD. If you have already read other Kevin Henkes books, the children may recognize Lilly. She is introduced in CHESTER'S WAY, a book covered in the "Friends" unit. Ask the children what Lilly is doing on the cover—trying to scare Julius with one of her disguises. Read the book and at the end discuss how Lilly felt at the beginning of the book, some of her funnier antics and how she felt at the end of the story.

STORY STRETCHER

For Art: Lavender And Pastel Family Pictures

What the children will learn
To use pastels and chalks for drawing

Materials you will need
Pastel chalks, scraps of construction paper, manilla paper, lavender construction paper, hair spray

What to do
1. With the children who choose to come to the art center during choice time, look at Henkes' use of lavender throughout the book, on the end papers and as background for important scenes.

2. Have the children find the lavender in every picture.

3. Let the children experiment with the pastels on scraps of construction paper.

4. Allow them to choose whether they want to make pastel pictures on the lavender construction paper.or use the manilla paper and include some lavender chalk.

5. After the children have finished their drawings, spray them lightly with hair spray to make the pastel adhere to the paper without smudging.

Something to think about
Keep the pastel chalks available throughout the week. It takes time for children to explore the possibilities of a medium and gain some sense of control over the material.

STORY STRETCHER

For Classroom Library: Story Retelling Tapes

What the children will learn
To retell stories using pictures

Materials you will need
Cassette recorder and player, tapes, stapler

What to do
1. Make a cassette recording of JULIUS, THE BABY OF THE WORLD. Be sure to provide a page-turning signal, such as clicking a stapler near the microphone of the tape recorder.

2. Turn over the tape. Ask children who have babies in their families to retell the story of JULIUS, THE BABY OF THE WORLD by looking at the pictures. Again, be sure to record a page-turning signal.

3. Mark one side of the tape with a drawing of a book and the other with a drawing of a child's face.

4. Place the cassette tape at the listening station in the classroom library.

Something to think about
Older children can form story retelling groups and take turns telling the story in a round robin fashion. Younger children can alternate, with the teacher telling the story on one page and the child, the next page.

For Creative Dramatics: A Parade Of Lilly Disguises

What the children will learn
To improvise costumes

Materials you will need
An assortment of old clothes, construction paper crowns, boots, hats, old costume jewelry, optional—dolls, baby clothes

What to do
1. With the children who are interested, look at the illustrations of Lilly in her many disguises, including her yellow crown and red boots.

2. Let the children talk about how they like to play dress-up at home with their brothers or sisters.

3. Have the children dress up in a variety of Lilly disguises.

4. Later on in the day, have a Lilly parade of disguises and read JULIUS, THE BABY OF THE WORLD again.

Something to think about
On another day, show the picture at the end of the book of Lilly and Julius playing together in their disguises. Add dolls and baby clothes and let the children dress up the dolls as if they were Julius in his disguises.

For Music And Movement: Lullabies From Our Families

What the children will learn
To sing a variety of lullabies

Materials you will need
Copies of lullabies, chart tablet, marker, cassette tapes, recorders

What to do
1. Copy the words from several famous lullabies onto sheets of chart tablet paper. Selections could include, "Hush Little Baby," "Lullaby and Good Night," "Rockabye Baby."

2. Teach the songs to the children.

3. Have the children sing the lullabies that were sung to them when they were babies.

4. Include lullabies from a variety of cultures and ones that parents improvised.

Something to think about
Invite the music teacher to sing and play lullabies. Older children can write lullabies with a modern twist. One third grader wrote a lullaby for the baby sitter to sing to her baby sister.

For Writing Center: Signs For My Room

What the children will learn
To write poster messages to their families

Materials you will need
Scraps of posterboard or construction paper, markers, crayons

What to do
1. Look through the illustrations of JULIUS, THE BABY OF THE WORLD. Find all the signs and posters Lilly wrote to tell her feelings about Julius and about the property in her room.

2. Ask the children what messages they would like to write to communicate with their brothers and sisters.

3. Provide the materials and let the children make the signs as well as write the messages.

4. Have the group brainstorm some messages that might make their class function better, such as signs telling where to place homework, labels for the art center shelves or reminders about keeping the game and puzzle pieces organized.

Something to think about
Use as much humor as possible to get across rules for class operation. Let the children think of funny ways to communicate the messages on the posters.

HOW MANY STARS IN THE SKY?

By Lenny Hort

Illustrated by James E. Ransome

A young boy cannot sleep because Mama's away. He gazes out his bedroom window and begins to count the stars. It is a lovely summer evening, so he goes out in the backyard to count more stars, then up in the tree house to see even better. His father cannot sleep either since Mama is away, so he joins his son in counting the stars. They still cannot sleep, so they drive into the city and go to Mama's tall office building to count stars, but the lights of the city make it impossible to see the stars. The father has an idea; they drive out into the country, and look up at a sky so clear that they can see the Milky Way. Finally, exhausted, they lie down in the bed of the pickup and sleep under the stars. This story of family feelings, of missing Mama yet sharing a special time with Father, is much more than a story about counting stars. Ransome's realistic oil paintings are rich and deep with interesting visual perspectives.

Read-Aloud Suggestions

Begin the discussion of HOW MANY STARS IN THE SKY? by asking what children do when their mothers or fathers are away. What takes their parents away? Do the children have trouble sleeping? Show the children the cover of the book, but place your hand over the title and tell them that you want them to listen to the story and then think of a good title for it. Read HOW MANY STARS IN THE SKY? in a soft, dreamy, reassuring voice. After the story is read, ask the children what surprised them about the book. Several will be interested in the father's response when he found his son outside at night counting the stars. Many children will say their parents would be very angry if they went outside at night. Other children will comment that it must be a weekend because the father would not have taken the son on such a long drive at night. Some children will mention they were surprised that the father and son slept in the back of the truck. Ask the children to suggest some titles for the book. After several have been suggested, read all the titles again and notice the ones the students seem to like best. Then read the title on the cover and see whether the children prefer one of their titles or the author's.

STORY STRETCHER

For Art: Starry, Starry Night

What the children will learn
To mix oil paints for night scenes and practice different brush strokes

Materials you will need
Large quantities of blue, black, purple, gray, dark green and white oil paints; smaller quantities of other oil paints; popsicle sticks or coffee stirrers; meat trays for palettes; canvas or particle board; heavy cardboard; paintbrushes of different sizes

What to do
1. With small groups of children, look again at the dark and beautiful illustrations from HOW MANY STARS IN THE SKY?

2. Have the children discuss how the painter used different shades of purple and green and darker shades to show the night.

3. Let the children experiment with mixing the oil paints.

4. Demonstrate several brush strokes, long and continuous ones for the sky, short choppy ones for the leaves of the trees, dots from the end of a small brush for the stars.

5. Allow the children to experiment with the oil paints, then ask them to paint a night sky and fill it with stars.

Something to think about
Invite the art teacher, a parent who is an artist or an older child to come to the classroom and demonstrate the strokes. If you have someone come in to assist with the class, be sure to participate in the activity with the children as a learner, not as the teacher. In addition, having the art supplies set up in a center means you do not need so many individual materials; the children can take turns using the same supplies.

STORY STRETCHER

For Classroom Library: Recording The Story

What the children will learn
To read dialogue

Materials you will need
Copies of the dialogue scenes, cassette recorder, cassette tape, stapler

What to do

1. With three children who volunteer for the recording, read the story again.

2. Select the scenes that have dialogue and rehearse with the children playing the father, the son and the narrator.

3. Record the story once.

4. Listen to the tape, and let the children identify the places they want to change or improve.

5. Record the story again with the changes. Be sure to record a page-turning signal, such as the click of a stapler.

6. Place the children's tape in the listening center along with the copy of the book.

Something to think about
Use hand signals as prompts for younger children to know when to read. If the reading is too difficult, let them simply retell the scenes based on the illustrations. Let older children write dialogue to replace what the narrator says.

STORY STRETCHER

For Music And Movement: Star And Nighttime Songs

What the children will learn
To sing the songs

Materials you will need
Music and chart tablet, markers

What to do

1. On large sheets of chart tablet paper, copy the words to some favorite children's songs with the theme of nighttime. Some possible titles are "When You Wish Upon a Star," "Star Light, Star Bright," "Twinkle, Twinkle, Little Star."

2. Teach the children the words to the songs by echo singing. Sing the entire song through, then break it into phrases and have the chil-

dren echo your singing until they have the tune.

3. Retain the large charts as pages for your *Big Book of Music.*

Something to think about
If you are not musically inclined, instead of singing the songs, read them as poems or chants. Assign different groups the phrases, and use the songs as choral readings. Another possibility is to invite older children who play musical instruments to come to the classroom and accompany your students as they sing these simple songs.

STORY STRETCHER

For Science And Nature: Simple Astronomy

What the children will learn
To find out more information about the stars and Jupiter and to share some new facts with their families

Materials you will need
Simple astronomy books, index cards, pencils

What to do

1. Have the children tell you all the stars mentioned in the story. If needed, read the story again.

2. Show the children how to use the reference books.

3. Find out information about the Big Dipper, the planet Jupiter, the Milky Way and the Sun.

4. After reading about the stars and Jupiter, let each child write one piece of new information on individual index cards.

5. Leave the reference books in the science area throughout the week and let children browse through them, write more index cards and practice identifying well-known constellations.

6. At the end of the week, let the children sort through the cards and group them in categories—the Big Dipper, Jupiter, Milky Way, Sun.

Something to think about
Since this is a unit on families, one of the most important things that parents want to know about their children is what they are learning at school. Ask the children to think of some ways they can share with their families what they have learned about the stars and Jupiter.

STORY STRETCHER

For Writing Center: When Mother Gets Home

What the children will learn
To compose what happened next in the story

Materials you will need
Writing paper, pencils, materials for illustrations

What to do

1. Ask the children to write what will happen when the mother in the story returns home the next day.

2. Let children think silently for a few minutes and jot down some possibilities before they begin to write.

3. Ask those students who already know what they want to write to begin writing.

4. With the remaining students, brainstorm some possibilities.

5. Display the stories near the "Starry, Starry Night" oil paintings.

Something to think about
Younger children can extend the story by first drawing a picture of what they think will happen when the mother returns home the next day. For older writers, this story is an excellent one for modeling how to write dialogue into a story. Often what the children decide to write is the son telling the mother what happened the night before.

2
FAMILIES

THE RELATIVES CAME

By Cynthia Rylant

Illustrated by Stephen Gammell

This warm, delightful story is told with jaunty, funny pictures of the relatives' trip from the mountains of Virginia to the home of the child telling the story. Each scene shows how the family's daily life is changed because the relatives are there. Rylant tells of bountiful tables filled with food, cramped sleeping, extra breathing in the house and music and games. The sadness, yet relief, when the visitors go home is a feeling many children understand. The passing of time is represented by the grapes, just turning purple when the relatives leave Virginia, deep purple when they return home. Gammell's colored pencil illustrations are rich in detail without being cluttered, featuring expressive faces and humorously exaggerated actions. THE RELATIVES CAME is a Caldecott Honor Book.

Read-Aloud Suggestions

Discuss a long family trip you have taken. Talk about all the preparations that were needed. Mention some of the food you took and games and activities you did to keep yourselves entertained across the miles. Solicit some comments from the children. Read THE RELATIVES CAME. Stop occasionally to enjoy the funny expressions and to point out the actions in the pictures. After the reading, let the children tell about some of the visits they have had from relatives and how they felt when the relatives left. Announce the story s-t-r-e-t-c-h-e-r activities associated with the book.

STORY STRETCHER
For Art: Colored Pencil Sketches Of Family Visits

What the children will learn
To use different techniques to create shading and emphasis in a picture

Materials you will need
Colored pencils, sharpeners, optional—paper of various textures

What to do
1. Look again at Stephen Gammell's illustrations in THE RELATIVES CAME. Discuss the fact that the book is a Caldecott Honor book, which means that the artist was given an award for his effective illustrations.

2. Examine how Gammell created the shading and shadows and how he used bright colors to outline some shapes to create emphasis.

3. Ask the children to draw pictures of relatives' visits or their own family's visits. Instead of using black lead pencils, suggest they use the colored pencils. En-

courage them to try some of Gammell's shading, shadowing and emphasis techniques.

4. Let the children experiment with the effects of different textures of paper on the colored pencil shading.

5. Display their family drawings in the class library with the book jacket of THE RELATIVES CAME.

Something to think about
Older children can illustrate their own versions of family visits to accompany the stories they write in the writing center. Younger children may enjoy doing a colored pencil mural of the book and dividing the scenes.

ANOTHER STORY STRETCHER
For Art: Sculpting Funny Station Wagons And Cars

What the children will learn
To sculpt using simple tools

Materials you will need
Playdough or modeling clay, coffee stirrers or straws, scissors, popsicle sticks, pencils, spatula, meat trays

What to do
1. Look at the funny illustrations of the multi-colored station wagon.

2. Ask a volunteer to sculpt the station wagon.

3. Encourage the other children who are interested to make other funny cars.

4. Demonstrate how to use a variety of simple tools—the straw, popsicle stick, pencil, point of scissors blade—to create lines.

5. After the sculptures are finished, gently lift them from the table by sliding a spatula around the edges. Place the sculptures on

meat trays so they can be easily moved.

6. Display the station wagon in the class library. Display the other funny cars around the room.

Something to think about
Do not emphasize the end product too soon. Let the children experiment over the course of the week. Like all art media, playdough, modeling clay and potters' clay require several sessions before the artists can gain enough control to use the material creatively.

STORY STRETCHER

For Classroom Library: Verbal Renditions Of Our Pictures

What the children will learn
To tell in words what they have expressed in drawings

Materials you will need
Cassette recorder, tapes, tape player, stapler, construction paper

What to do
1. In small groups, ask the children to come to the classroom library and tell about their colored pencil drawings from the art story s-t-r-e-t-c-h-e-r.

2. Have the children tell what happened before the scene they drew, what happened in the scene they drew and what happened next.

3. Tape record the children's verbal renditions.

4. Place the cassette recordings in the library area and staple the children's pictures together in the order that the children's stories are heard on the tape.

5. Make a construction paper cover for the children's drawings.

Something to think about
Not all of the sessions of children telling stories need to be placed on tape. Some should be savored just for the moment. However, tape recording often motivates the children to work on their oral language and to plan their stories.

STORY STRETCHER

For Creative Dramatics: Dramatizing The Two Families' Preparations

What the children will learn
To improvise scenes, feelings, dialogue

Materials you will need
None needed

What to do
1. Read THE RELATIVES CAME again.

2. Talk about how much preparation is needed for the one family to get ready for the trip.

3. Brainstorm a list of things that would have to be done, such as deciding which clothes to pack, selecting toys and games to take, preparing the food for the trip, servicing the car, packing the car, closing up the house.

4. Invite children to play the part of the organizer of the trip.

5. Assign other volunteers to the remaining roles and improvise the scenes.

6. Then with another group of actors, improvise the preparations necessary for the family who receives the relatives in their home for the long visit.

Something to think about
It is best to work in small groups for improvisations. If you have a reluctant group of actors, take on the role of mother or father, and the children will usually join you.

STORY STRETCHER

For Writing Center: Family Trips And Visits

What the children will learn
To write, edit and publish family stories

Materials you will need
Paper, pencils, markers, contact paper, tape, stapler

What to do
1. Tell the children you would like to publish some family stories for the class library to go along with the focus books for the unit.

2. Discuss the steps in the writing process: pre-writing—getting ideas and planning their stories; writing and rewriting; editing; and finally, publishing the books.

3. Model the steps by writing family stories with small groups.

4. Encourage the children to add their own individual stories and assist in the editing until they are ready for published book form.

Something to think about
Some schools have volunteers who can type the children's stories on the computer or assist older children in typing, and volunteers who work in publishing centers where children can go to select covers and format their books. While these volunteers are a wonderful support for a class or a school where children write often, it is still important for the teacher to model the steps and go through the entire process several times before turning these final steps over to the volunteers.

AMELIA BEDELIA'S FAMILY ALBUM

By Peggy Parish

Illustrated by Lynn Sweat

The Rogers family is so happy with Amelia Bedelia's work that they want to give her a party and invite her family. To plan the party, Mrs. Rogers asks Amelia who should be invited. Amelia Bedelia takes down the family picture album and tells Mrs. Rogers about all her relatives. In usual Amelia Bedelia fashion, there are differing funny interpretations of what each family member does. For example, when Amelia Bedelia describes her mother as a loafer, Mrs. Rogers thinks that means that she is lazy, but oh, no, Amelia Bedelia says that means she bakes loaves of bread. The story ends with another Amelia Bedelia surprise when Mrs. Rogers tells her to invite everybody. So Amelia goes into the street and invites everybody to come to her party. Lynn Sweat's drawings of Amelia Bedelia have become as familiar as Peggy Parish's clever characterization of the mixed-up maid.

Read-Aloud Suggestions

If Amelia Bedelia books are already known by the children, simply telling them you will be reading an Amelia Bedelia story will bring cheers and claps. Ask the children why they like these stories. Read AMELIA BEDELIA'S FAMILY ALBUM. Pause after reading about Amelia Bedelia's mother being a loafer, and let the children predict what Amelia Bedelia will say in response to Mrs. Rogers' questions about each family member who follows. Show some pictures of your family members and make up Amelia Bedelia descriptions of them. Let the children think of others they might write. For example, show a picture of a man who is a tax collector. Then let the children draw a picture of him going along picking up thumbtacks.

STORY STRETCHER

For Classroom Library: Our Amelia Bedelia Family Album

What the children will learn
To predict Amelia Bedelia meanings of words

Materials you will need
Children's writings from the writing center

What to do
1. Place the children's illustrated writings of their AMELIA BEDELIA family members in the classroom library.

2. Encourage the children to go in pairs to the classroom library and share the guessing. The two children look at the pictures on the outside of the cards, then guess what Amelia Bedelia would say. Then one child reads the Amelia Bedelia definition.

Something to think about
To make the Amelia Bedelia pictures into a more permanent book for the library, place the pictures on large index cards and slip them into the plastic sleeves in a photo album. The children can then read one side of the picture and turn the page to read the funny definition.

STORY STRETCHER

For Creative Dramatics: Which Amelia Bedelia Family Member Am I?

What the children will learn
To pantomime actions

Materials you will need
Scraps of paper, pen or pencil, box

What to do
1. Read AMELIA BEDELIA'S FAMILY ALBUM again.

2. Write the names of Amelia Bedelia's family members on scraps of paper and place them in a box.

3. At random, let each child draw the name of a family member from the box.

4. Let the children take turns pantomiming the different relatives while the audience guesses their identities.

Something to think about
Young children can use props and dress-up clothes to dramatize their actions. Older children can pantomime the Amelia Bedelia family members from the book and the descriptions the class wrote in the writing center.

For Creative Dramatics: Amelia Bedelia's Family At Our School

What the children will learn
To interpret meanings literally

Materials you will need
None needed

What to do
1.   Invite members of the school staff, such as the secretary, principal, librarian, reading specialist, cafeteria workers or others to come to your classroom on different days of the week and announce themselves as members of AMELIA BEDELIA'S family.

2.   You pretend to be Mrs. Rogers and ask the family member what he or she does. Then let the actors give their Amelia Bedelia description of themselves.

3.   Ask all the Amelia Bedelia family actors to join the class for the party (see the special event story s-t-r-e-t-c-h-e-r).

Something to think about
Take photographs of the school staff who come as Amelia Bedelia's family and add them to the family album in the class library.

For Special Event: An Amelia Bedelia Mixed-Up Family Portrait

What the children will learn
To plan a party

Materials you will need
Chart tablet, markers, paper, pencils, decorations, food, party games

What to do
1.   Talk about the kind of party Amelia Bedelia might have since she seems to get everything mixed up.

2.   Brainstorm some ideas for party games. Write all the ideas on chart tablet. For example, instead of "Pin the Tail on the Donkey," it might be "Pin the Head on the Donkey."

3.   Think about some mixed-up party food, such as pineapple upside-down cake or party mix with pretzels and nuts. Everything served at the party should be mixed-up.

4.   Plan the party decorations with giant drawings from AMELIA BEDELIA'S FAMILY ALBUM.

5.   Write party invitations and address them to the family members.

6.   Let children choose the invitations for Amelia Bedelia family members at random, and come to the party dressed like that family member.

Something to think about
Write a parent newsletter explaining the special party and the use of Peggy Parish's Amelia Bedelia stories to help children learn literal and inferential interpretations of words.

For Writing Center: Funny Families

What the children will learn
To write funny meanings for words instead of usual meanings

Materials you will need
Old magazines or catalogs, scissors, glue, construction paper or manilla paper, colored pencils, crayons or markers

What to do
1.   Let the children cut out pictures from magazines or catalogs and pretend the people pictured are members of their families.

2.   Fold the sheets of construction paper or manilla paper into halves vertically, like greeting cards.

3.   Glue the picture of the person on the outside.

4.   Write the name of the person and what he or she does on the outside.

5.   On the inside draw a picture illustrating what the person does and write the Amelia Bedelia interpretation of the person's job.

6.   Place the individual Amelia Bedelia family pictures in the classroom library.

Something to think about
Younger children may have difficulty coming up with Amelia Bedelia definitions. They can draw one of their own family members and then work with you to come up with a funny description.

References

Henkes, Kevin. (1990). **JULIUS, THE BABY OF THE WORLD**. New York: Greenwillow.

Hort, Lenny. (1991). Illustrated by James E. Ransome. **HOW MANY STARS IN THE SKY?** New York: Tambourine Books.

Parish, Peggy. (1988). Illustrated by Lynn Sweat. **AMELIA BEDELIA'S FAMILY ALBUM**. New York: Greenwillow.

Rylant, Cynthia. (1985). Illustrated by Stephen Gammell. **THE RELATIVES CAME.** New York: Bradbury Press.

Simon, Norma. (1976). Illustrated by Joe Lasker. **ALL KINDS OF FAMILIES**. Niles, IL: Albert Whitman.

Additional References for Families

de Paola, Tomie. (1980). **NOW ONE FOOT, NOW THE OTHER**. New York: G. P. Putnam's Sons. *When his grandfather suffers a stroke, Bobby lovingly teaches him to walk again, just as Grandfather once taught him.*

Greenfield, Eloise. (1974). Illustrated by John Steptoe. **SHE COME BRINGING ME THAT LITTLE BABY GIRL**. New York: J. B. Lippincott. *A child's disappointment and jealousy over a new baby sister are dispelled as he becomes aware of his new role as the big brother.*

Lyons, George Ella. (1990). Illustrated by Mary Szilagyi. **BASKET**. New York: Orchard Books. *A powerful, simple story of family love, symbolized by Grandma's white oak basket and the song that goes with it.*

Polacco, Patricia. (1988). **THE KEEPING QUILT**. New York: Simon and Schuster. *A handmade quilt binds together four generations of a Russian-Jewish immigrant family, symbolizing family continuity amid changing customs.*

Schertle, Alice. (1989). Illustrated by Lydia Dabcovich. **WILLIAM AND GRANDPA**. New York: Lothrop, Lee and Shepard Books. *A visit with Grandpa is William's chance to discover that some things about a little boy never change, even when he grows up to be a "big old grandpa."*

3

FRIENDS

Chester's Way
Frog and Toad Together
Arthur's Birthday
Ira Says Goodbye
Wilfrid Gordon McDonald Partridge

CHESTER'S WAY

By Kevin Henkes

Chester and Wilson, Wilson and Chester, are always together and always doing things just alike. They cut their sandwiches in diagonals just alike, double-knot their shoes just alike, even play croquet and baseball just alike. Then when Lilly arrives in the neighborhood, they notice she has her own way of doing things. Chester and Wilson avoid her. They would not even talk with her on the telephone until that fateful day when Lilly came to their rescue and scared away some bigger guys with her scary cat disguise and her squirt gun. After that, Lilly taught Chester and Wilson how to live a more adventuresome life by cutting their sandwiches with cookie cutters, dressing up in disguises and popping wheelies. The three are inseparable—until Victor moves into the neighborhood. Henkes' delightful illustrations are black line drawings washed with cheerful watercolors.

Read-Aloud Suggestions

Select some well-known best friends from the classroom. Describe some of the ways in which they are just alike and some of the things that they like to do together. If you have new children in the classroom, ask them what things they liked to do with a best friend from the old school or neighborhood. After a brief discussion, read CHESTER'S WAY. Pause after the scene where Lilly is first introduced and ask the children to predict what will happen next. Keep the predictions brief; stop after only two or three. Ask for predictions after the scene where Chester and Wilson are hiding behind the tree, watching Lilly in her funny disguises, and after Lilly rescues Chester and Wilson. Finally, at the end of the book, ask each child to think to himself or herself what might happen to the friends now that Victor has moved into the neighborhood. Then give each a sheet of paper to draw the next scene or write a new story about Chester, Wilson, Lilly and Victor.

STORY STRETCHER

For Art: Lilly's Disguises

What the children will learn
To make paper bag disguises or costumes

Materials you will need
Brown paper bags, markers, scissors, tape or glue or staples, optional—yarn, funny masks, Groucho Marx moustache and glasses

What to do
1. With the children who choose to come to the art area during free choice time, look again at Kevin Henkes' illustrations of Lilly and her disguises.

2. Let them try on some of the disguises you have collected.

3. Point out the illustration of Lilly in her paper bag mask.

4. Brainstorm with the children some disguises they could make.

5. Assist with cutting out eyes and making slits in the sides of the bag so that it will fall down over the children's shoulders.

6. Let the children wear their disguises and sit with their friends while you read the story again.

Something to think about
Ask parents or children to contribute funny old masks. Some children may prefer to draw the continuing story of the friends, rather than make the disguises. Whenever possible, give the children choices to promote their independent thinking.

STORY STRETCHER

For Cooking: Lilly's Decorated Sandwiches

What the children will learn
To make their own sandwiches

Materials you will need
Milk, knives, plates, napkins, bread, peanut butter, jelly, cookie cutters, optional—apples, oranges, strawberries, raisins

What to do
1. Prepare a special area of the classroom for snacks. If possible, schedule snack time for a longer period, or let children go in small groups to the snack table so they can enjoy the preparation and the conversation, while making their sandwiches.

2. Leave the cookie cutters there for those children who want to cut their sandwiches in different shapes the way Lilly did.

3. Let the children use raisins and cut orange slices, apple slices

and strawberries to decorate their sandwiches like faces, if they want to make a sandwich like Lilly's.

Something to think about
Enjoy the snack as an unhurried period of the day when children can enjoy each other's company. Casual conversation among friends is one of the keys to oral language development.

STORY STRETCHER

For Music And Movement: Bicycle Hand Signals

What the children will learn
To recognize signals and practice bike safety

Materials you will need
Chart tablet, posterboard, marker

What to do
1. If you have children whose brothers or sisters are members of the school safety patrol, invite them to the classroom to show the hand signals they use to direct pedestrians.

2. Ask the safety patrol to discuss special problems with bicyclers and pedestrians.

3. Ask them to demonstrate hand signals they give to bicyclers.

4. Demonstrate hand signals bicyclers can use to inform walkers, drivers and other bike riders before they turn.

5. Practice the signals patrollers use and ask pairs of friends to use bicycle hand signals throughout the day.

Something to think about
This story s-t-r-e-t-c-h-e-r emphasizes both a movement activity and a social studies activity: learning to obey signals and rules. Younger children will enjoy dressing up like the safety patrollers, who are often fifth graders. Third graders who are excellent bike rid-

ers can plan a bike safety demonstration for first and second graders.

STORY STRETCHER

For Games: Chester And Wilson's Game—Croquet

What the children will learn
To play croquet with friends

Materials you will need
Croquet set with mallet, balls, wickets, scraps of paper, pencil, hat or fishbowl

What to do
1. Briefly explain the object of the game: to move one's ball through the series of wickets.

2. Demonstrate how to hit the ball.

3. Let a few children begin playing. Soon they will be confronted with the problem of how to get their ball through the wicket when another player's ball is in the way.

4. After they seem to have the knack of playing, assign the different colored balls to characters in the story. For example, the red striped ball is Chester's, the green Wilson's, the blue Lilly's and the yellow can be Victor's.

5. Draw names from a hat or a fishbowl to determine who gets to be Chester, Wilson, Lilly and Victor for the day.

6. Play croquet for at least a week for the children to develop some skill.

Something to think about
Consult with the physical education teacher in your school and plan instruction in the finer points of croquet to accompany this story s-t-r-e-t-c-h-e-r for outside play.

STORY STRETCHER

For Writing Center: Writing With A Friend, The Next Episodes

What the children will learn
To confer with a friend and extend the story through a new episode

Materials you will need
Writing paper, pencils

What to do
1. Pair the children into writing partners, friends who will write the next episodes of the Chester, Wilson, Lilly and Victor story together.

2. Some children will begin writing immediately from ideas prompted by your reading the book aloud.

3. Assist those children who are having difficulty getting started by letting them look at Henkes' last illustration of Chester, Wilson and Lilly wearing their Groucho Marx plastic moustaches and glasses and peering over a rock at Victor.

4. Suggest that they draw what might happen next.

5. Brainstorm with others by asking what would happen if a new neighbor, just their age, moved in next door.

6. Let the writers who are interested continue their writing and rewriting until they are ready to read their "next episode" stories to the class.

7. Place special chairs in the read-aloud area and let the authors sit in the "authors' chairs" while they read their stories.

Something to think about
Give children a choice of writing a story about Chester, Wilson, Lilly and Victor, continuing on a project they are presently working on or starting a new one that interests them more.

FROG AND TOAD TOGETHER

By Arnold Lobel

Lobel's collection of five stories of friendship between Frog and Toad has become a favorite. In the first short story, when Toad writes a list of what he will do for the day, the list gains control. In the second tale, Toad admires Frog's garden and takes all his gardening advice quite literally. The third story is about how the two friends control their willpower when faced with a cookie jar filled with freshly baked cookies. In the fourth story, Toad and Frog are inspired by a book they have read about dragons and giants and decide to test their bravery. In the last story, Toad dreams he is introduced on stage as, "the greatest Toad in all the world," and goes on to act, walk a high wire, play a piano and dance while his friend Frog grows smaller and smaller in the audience. Lobel's green and brown illustrations, the simple dialogue, and the clever plots make the book a children's choice as well as a Newberry Honor book.

Read-Aloud Suggestions

While any of the five stories has excellent possibilities for story s-t-r-e-t-c-h-e-r-s, the first story, "The List," is the basis for the activities which follow. Read as many of the five stories as time permits, but end the session with "The List." End the read-aloud session by having the children select from the many different story s-t-r-e-t-c-h-e-r-s or "list" activities. Ask each person to go to the writing center at some point during the morning to make a list which includes "Surprise." (The surprise is the "Willpower Cookies.")

STORY STRETCHER

For Art: Frog's Favorite Green, Toad's Favorite Brown

What the children will learn
To mix colors

Materials you will need
Blue, yellow, red tempera paints, coffee stirrers, plastic margarine tubs, brushes, paper

What to do
1. With the group of children who choose to come to the art area during free choice, look again at Arnold Lobel's illustrations of Toad and Frog. Notice the lovely shades of green and brown, even the brown ink used to print the titles of each story.

2. Let the children experiment, mixing blue and yellow to make green. Have some children start with more blue and some with more yellow and decide which they need less of to make green.

3. Encourage the children to paint various shades of green on their papers until they get the shade they prefer and the shade they think Frog would prefer.

4. Let the children experiment, mixing colors to get brown.

5. Ask them to paint various shades of brown on their papers until they get the shade they prefer and the shade they think Toad would prefer.

Something to think about
This art story s-t-r-e-t-c-h-e-r could be used to teach color mixing and shading for art, to write mathematical equations for the color mixing or to experiment for science and observe the color changes as the paints dry.

STORY STRETCHER

For Classroom Library: Friends Retelling Their Favorite Frog and Toad Stories

What the children will learn
To recall main events in a story and to improvise dialogue

Materials you will need
Paper and pencils, optional—cassette recorder and tapes

What to do
1. Post a list of times for children to sign up for story retelling sessions. Have each child who is interested sign up for a time and list the title of the story.

2. Emphasize the basic story structure, not word-for-word retelling of the story.

3. Encourage children to write a list of points they want to remember or make small drawings of scenes that will help them recall the story.

4. Conduct the sessions in small groups with others in that time slot acting as the audience for the story retellers.

5. Tape-record the session if the child chooses.

Something to think about

Once the children know the Frog and Toad characters well, let them improvise other adventures for the friends.

For Cooking: Lists For Baking Willpower Cookies

What the children will learn

To follow the directions for baking cookies

Materials you will need

Chart tablet or posterboard, marker, cookie recipe, ingredients and utensils or refrigerator cookie dough, cookie sheet, knife, spatula, toaster oven if a larger oven is not available

What to do

1.   With a small group of children, plan the cookie baking activity. Look at a cookbook or read the package directions.

2.   Have the children make a list of items needed to bake the cookies.

3.   Talk about the fact that a recipe is a list of steps to follow to prepare food.

4.   Let the children make a rebus chart, listing all the steps in baking cookies. (See the appendix for a sample rebus recipe). Use symbols from recipe books, such as a drawing of a bowl for mixing, cups and spoons for measuring.

5.   Mix and bake cookies following the recipe.

6.   Serve for a snack while you read more Frog and Toad stories. (See the additional references list at the end of the unit.)

Something to think about

Small groups of older children can follow the recipe with little supervision.

For Mathematics: Graphing Friends' Favorite Stories

What the children will learn

To show data in more than one form

Materials you will need

List from classroom library activity, posterboard or chart tablet, marker, five crayons of different color, construction paper in five different colors, scissors, glue

What to do

1.   Take the list of story retellers from the classroom library and bring it to the mathematics area.

2.   Ask the children to look at the list and decide which Frog and Toad story is the class favorite, based on the story retellings.

3.   Have them brainstorm ways to show that data. For example, they could count the number of different stories for each session, then add them together to get a total. They could make a chart with the titles of each story at the top and then make a hash mark for each time the story was retold. Make the chart by writing the titles of the five stories in different colored crayons or markers, then make a hash mark in that same color under the title. Another way would be to cut construction paper strips or cubes of the same color and paste them on to form a vertical graph.

4.   Let the children choose which method they want to use.

5.   After the favorite stories have been tallied, poll the remaining children in the class and let them add their choices to the data.

Something to think about

For younger children, make up the chart and guide them in recording their choices using the crayons or the construction paper cubes. For older children, simply give them the problem: to find out which Frog and Toad story of the five read in class, is the class favorite. They can also do comparisons of the Frog and Toad stories in this read-aloud selection with those in the other Arnold Lobel book, FROG AND TOAD ARE FRIENDS (1970).

For Writing Center: A List Of Daily Activities

What the children will learn

To use a list as a plan for the day

Materials you will need

Chart tablet, posterboard, marker, paper, pencils

What to do

1.   Bring the class list of activities written in the read-aloud session to the writing center.

2.   If the children need your assistance to begin, discuss the list Toad wrote, planning his entire day.

3.   Children can work on their own and make a list for their day, from the beginning to the end. Remind them to write the word, "Surprise," on their list.

4.   Ask the students to keep their list with them throughout the day and mark off the activities as they occur.

5.   End the day by having the children write down any special assignments they have for tomorrow or special plans for after school.

Something to think about

Write lists throughout the week to model how adults use writing to help them do what is expected of them.

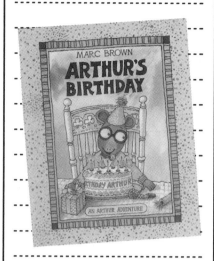

ARTHUR'S BIRTHDAY

By Marc Brown

Arthur delivers his birthday party invitations to his friends only to find that his party and Muffy's party are scheduled on the same day. For a week, their friends are upset, not knowing which party to attend. Finally, the boys decide to stick together and go to Arthur's party, while the girls plan to go to Muffy's. Then Arthur comes up with an ingenious plan that makes it possible for them to attend both. Marc Brown's humor, cartoon-like drawings and plot are as ingenious as Arthur's plan.

Read-Aloud Suggestions

Ask the children what their favorite day of the year is. Invariably, someone will answer, "My birthday." Show the cover of ARTHUR'S BIRTHDAY and let the children predict who will come to Arthur's party. If you have read other Arthur stories, they will recall the names of his best friends, Buster, the Brain, Binky Barnes and Francine. Let the children who have birthdays this month tell their favorite flavors of birthday cake, their favorite party games, and how their families celebrate birthdays. Tell them that Arthur planned his birthday party, but it looks like some of his friends may not come. Read ARTHUR'S BIRTHDAY. Pause after the scene in which Arthur delivers his party invitation to Muffy and she finds out Saturday afternoon is his birthday party as well as hers. Let the children try to decide what Arthur and Muffy can do so that all their friends can attend their parties. Continue reading, and stop before the scene where Francine and Arthur hide in the tree house writing notes to their friends. Have the children guess what Arthur and Francine are plotting. Finish the story and announce all the "friends" story s-t-r-e-t-c-h-e-r-s that are based on ARTHUR'S BIRTHDAY.

STORY STRETCHER

For Art: Friends Decorate For Arthur's Party

What the children will learn
To recycle throwaways, "trashables," to make party decorations

Materials you will need
Plastic bottles, egg cartons, paper towel tubes, milk cartons, plastic hosiery containers shaped like eggs, construction paper, tape, scissors

What to do
1. Make a collection of throwaways.

2. Gather construction supplies.

3. Begin the art project by asking pairs of children to work together, making party decorations.

4. In small groups, have them brainstorm some possible uses.

5. Set a date for the projects to be finished.

6. Plan a display of the projects and invite other classes to detour through your classroom on the way to lunch or the playground so they can see the students' inventive uses of recyclable materials.

7. Store the decorations for future parties.

Something to think about
While Arthur's story merits making birthday party decorations, this activity can be scheduled at any time of the year. The children can make recycled decorations for a harvest celebration in the fall or Valentine's Day in the winter or St. Patrick's Day in the spring.

STORY STRETCHER

For Cooking: Decorating Arthur's And Muffy's Cakes

What the children will learn
To decorate a cake

Materials you will need
Unfrosted cakes, contrasting colors of cake frosting, knives or spatulas, margarine tubs with warm water, optional—sprinkles, raisins or small candies, powdered sugar, doilies

What to do
1. Either bake two cakes in class or ask a parent or class volunteer to bake the cakes ahead of time.

2. Demonstrate how to spread the frosting by dipping the knife or spatula in warm water, then into the frosting mix before spreading on the cake.

3. Working in small groups, let the children decorate the cakes, starting with the sides first.

4. Decorate the cakes with different colors of frosting, and sprinkles, raisins or small candies.

5. Decorate one of the cakes without frosting the top. Place a doily on the top and sprinkle powdered sugar over it, then remove the doily to reveal a pretty pattern.

Something to think about
Encourage parents to bring their child's birthday cake or cupcakes to the class unfrosted, and let the children decorate them. It makes the celebration more festive and gives the children another way to practice their fine motor coordination.

For Games: Birthday Party Games

What the children will learn
To play party games and practice their good manners

Materials you will need
Several party games—pin the tail on the donkey, a piñata, spin the bottle, hide-and-go-seek, other party games the children recommend

What to do
1. Mention the gift Francine gave Arthur, a bottle marked "Francine's Spin the Bottle Game." Explain that this is not the "kissing" game of spin the bottle, but a "Take a Walk with a Friend" game. The spinners have to walk around the room together.

2. List some other games the children like to play at their parties.

3. Collect all the game materials.

4. On the following day, play the games throughout the day inside or outside or at the end of the day.

Something to think about
For a cross-cultural perspective, have children from different cultures plan the party activities.

For Mathematics: Marking Friends' Birthday Calendars

What the children will learn
To use calendars as devices to record important events

Materials you will need
Calendars collected from home or photocopied, markers and chart tablet or chalkboard and chalk

What to do
1. Distribute the calendars, or have the children bring theirs from home.

2. Let them mark their classmates' birthdays for each month.

3. Make a chart listing all the months of the year beginning with the present month.

4. With the children, count the number of children who have birthdays in each month.

5. Write the names of the months and the number of children who have birthdays each month. Add the number of birthdays for each month to get a total for the entire twelve months.

6. Ask the children to tell you how they know if the answer is correct. They should say that the total number of birthdays equals the total number of children in the class.

Something to think about
Young children have difficulty with understanding time. For first graders, mark the birthdays for this month only. Let them place a mark on birthdays and on today's date and count the number of days

in between. Older children can graph their findings to tell which month has the most birthdays.

For Writing Center: Party Invitations

What the children will learn
To write formal invitations including all the important information

Materials you will need
Party invitations you have received, stationery or paper, construction paper, glue, crayons, markers, old envelopes of various sizes

What to do
1. Discuss with the children the important information one must include to write a good invitation. Let the children generate the list of important points.

2. If possible, show the children a party invitation you have received. Read it to them and see if all the points they mentioned were covered.

3. As a group, list the important information for a party for Arthur that the class will host in the classroom.

4. Divide the children into four groups.

5. Let each group use the information to compose their own invitations to the office, cafeteria, janitorial and library staff to come to Arthur's party.

Something to think about
Try to keep writing experiences as authentic as possible. Writing real invitations and receiving replies helps the children appreciate the importance of writing in their daily lives.

FRIENDS

IRA SAYS GOODBYE

By Bernard Waber

Ira's sister breaks the news that his best friend Reggie is moving to Greendale. The following days are filled with sadness and excitement. Ira is sad and feels betrayed that Reggie is excited about the move. Reggie brags about his new house, new people he will meet and new fun things he can do when he moves to Greendale. Ira thinks about all the things he and Reggie like to do together, trading baseball cards, playing hide and seek, performing magic tricks, taking care of their pets. Even their two pet turtles will have to be separated. How the children express their feelings as well as how they plan to keep in touch are meaningful to primary age children whose friends move often. Waber's illustrations of Ira and Reggie as well as their families are the ones readers got to know in IRA SLEEPS OVER.

Read-Aloud Suggestions

If possible, bring a picture of one of your friends who has moved away. Show the photo to the children and talk about how much you miss your friend. Tell about where your friend moved, and how happy your friend is living in the new place. If there is a child who will be moving soon, emphasize that while he or she is excited about moving and will enjoy the new place, the child will be missed at school. Show the cover of IRA SAYS GOODBYE and ask the children to recall another popular book of Bernard Waber's, IRA SLEEPS OVER. Talk about the fact that Ira and Reggie are very good friends, good enough friends to admit that each sleeps with a teddy bear. Read IRA SAYS GOODBYE. Do not pause during the reading, as the dialogue in the story can be too easily interrupted. Read Ira's dialogue very sadly and Reggie's quite excitedly. At the end of the story, tell what you and your friend who moved away do to stay in touch. Let children with friends who have moved away tell about how they keep in touch.

STORY STRETCHER

For Creative Dramatics: Friends' Magic Show

What the children will learn
To perform simple tricks with a partner

Materials you will need
Top hat, cane, magician's cape, card table, simple reference books on magic

What to do
1.   Survey the children and find several who know how to do magic tricks.

2.   With the magicians, plan their stage names and introductions, and let them chose assistants.

3.   Chose an M.C., (Master or Mistress of Ceremonies.)

4.   Advertise the magic show for several days in advance.

5.   Schedule several practice sessions behind a curtain or in another room in the school.

Something to think about
Older children can organize a magic show for the kindergarten.

STORY STRETCHER

For Mathematics: Sorting Baseball Cards

What the children will learn
To sort by more than one attribute

Materials you will need
A collection of baseball cards, chart tablet and marker or chalkboard and chalk, two long strings of yarn or long shoelaces

What to do
1.   With the group of children who chose the mathematics area, brainstorm as many different ways as possible to sort the baseball cards.

2.   Write the categories for sorting on the board or chart tablet: for example by league, by team, by position, by home state, by home runs, by runs batted in, by years of playing, by rookie, by veteran.

3.   Divide the cards among the children.

4.   Form two loops with the yarn or shoelaces.

5.   Sort the cards from the two most popular teams into the two loops. Set the rest of the cards aside.

6.   Then sort again by positions, infield and outfield, etc.

Something to think about

First graders will probably sort by team. If they play baseball, they also may sort by position. The third graders can sort the cards by the more advanced categories and use a Vinn diagram of overlapping circles to sort cards that fit in two categories.

S T O R Y   S T R E T C H E R

For Music And Movement: Friends Looking For Friends

What the children will learn

To interpret and identify distance by signals

Materials you will need

None needed

What to do

1. Arrange ahead of time for two friends to hide together somewhere in the classroom.

2. With all the children seated, tell them that two students from class pretending to be Ira and Reggie are in a secret hiding place.

3. Whisper in one child's ear the place where the two friends are hiding. Designate that child as the "signaller."

4. Select another child to be the "seeker." As he or she looks for the two friends who are hiding, the signaller must say, "getting warmer," when the seeker is near their hiding place, or say, "getting colder," when the seeker is going away from the hiding place.

5. Continue playing the game, designating a new Ira and Reggie to hide while everyone closes their eyes. The seeker gets to be the next signaller.

Something to think about

Begin the game of hide and seek with the children in the classroom who do not get as much attention or who may not be as popular as other children.

S T O R Y   S T R E T C H E R

For Special Project: Our Town

What the children will learn

To discover interesting activities in their community

Materials you will need

Bulletin board, community tourist brochures, construction paper, glue, scissors, stapler

What to do

1. Read again the part of the story where Reggie brags about all the things that are so special about Greendale, the new town where he will be living. There is the aquarium, the fun park with a roller coaster, the duck pond with swans and, most of all, the Greendale Tigers, the football team his uncle Steve plays on.

2. Discuss with the children all the interesting activities that new people moving in would like to know about your town or community.

3. If possible, collect an assortment of tourist brochures and use them as reminders of special places and events.

4. Ask the children what they do on the weekend that would be helpful for newcomers to know.

5. Let them make a kids' bulletin board of what children should know about their new town.

Something to think about

Contact each classroom in the school and invite children who are new to the school and the community to come and see the displays.

As an alternative, let younger children draw their favorite weekend activities for the bulletin board. Older children might write an information guide for the new arrivals.

S T O R Y   S T R E T C H E R

For Writing Center: Letter To A Classmate Who Has Moved

What the children will learn

To write a letter to a friend

Materials you will need

Stationery, envelopes, stamps

What to do

1. With the small group who chose the writing area during choice time, compose letters to a friend who has moved.

2. Talk about missing a child who has moved. If no one from the class has moved yet, then find the name of a child who moved last year.

3. Discuss some of the changes that have taken place since the child moved away. Samantha lost her two front teeth. Jaime has both his front teeth now. Michael can ride a bike. Mrs. Andres, the teacher from last year, has a baby girl.

4. Have the children try to think of some activities that the child who moved away liked.

5. Compose a group letter telling about the activities and the news.

6. Let all the children sign the letter.

Something to think about

Younger children may want to draw pictures to include in the letter. Have older children write individual letters, and divide the writing assignment so that each is writing about a different activity the child who moved away enjoyed.

3
FRIENDS

Wilfrid Gordon McDonald Partridge
Written by Mem Fox   Illustrated by Julie Vivas

WILFRID GORDON MCDONALD PARTRIDGE

By Mem Fox

Illustrated by Julie Vivas

Wilfrid lived next door to an old people's home. Many of the people who lived there were his friends. He liked Mrs. Jordon because she played the organ. He liked Mr. Hosking because he told scary stories. He liked Mr. Tippett because he played cricket. He liked to run errands for Miss Mitchell who didn't walk too well. He liked Mr. Drysdale's booming giant voice, but his special friend was Miss Nancy Alison Delacourt Cooper because she had four names like he did, and he could tell her all his secrets. One day, Wilfrid overheard his parents saying that Miss Nancy had lost her memory. The remainder of the story is about how Wilfrid helped her find her memory. Mem Fox's story of this special friendship is made even more captivating by Julie Vivas' colorful, warm watercolors which are almost caricatures of Wilfrid and his older friends.

Read-Aloud Suggestions

If you have ever had a friendship with a person who is much older than you, talk about the person with the children. Ask if any of the children have special older friends or neighbors. If they do not, have them discuss their special feelings for their grandparents and what makes the grandparents unique, a special talent or a special interest. Read WILFRID GORDON MCDONALD PARTRIDGE. After reading the book, talk with the children about memories and the importance of older people talking about their lives. Look again at the illustrations and let the children describe things they own that remind them of Wilfrid's gift to Miss Nancy. Ask them what they would put in their special basket of memories. Let them think of things that remind them of special places, things that make them laugh, things that remind them of people they love, things that are as precious as gold to them, and things that give them warm feelings. End the session by announcing all the "friends" story s-t-r-e-t-c-h-e-r-s based on WILFRID GORDON MCDONALD PARTRIDGE, especially "Baskets Of Memories."

STORY STRETCHER

For Art: Caricatures

What the children will learn
To exaggerate features in their self-portraits

Materials you will need
If possible, pictures that are drawn as caricatures, drawing paper, colored pencils

What to do
1. Show the caricatures, and look at how the artist has highlighted some special feature by making it very large, often the nose, eyeglasses, hands or feet.

2. Look at the pictures of Wilfrid and the people from the old people's home. Let the children decide what features the artist is highlighting or exaggerating.

3. Discuss how you think an artist would draw as exaggeration of you: perhaps your large eyeglasses would be even larger, your bushy hair even bushier or your big hands bigger.

4. Ask the children which of their features an artist would exaggerate.

5. Ask the children who are interested to draw themselves or a member of their family in caricature form.

Something to think about
Some first graders may have difficulty with self-portraits that are too distorted. If so, let them draw favorite scenes from the story. Emphasize with all ages that if we had a caricature artist visit the class, he or she would make us look funny, so ask everyone to make a funny, exaggerated picture.

STORY STRETCHER

For Classroom Library: Cassette Recording Of Wilfrid Gordon McDonald Partridge

What the children will learn
To dramatize voices and to record themselves

Materials you will need
Cassette recorder, tapes, listening station, headphones, stapler

What to do
1. Tape-record yourself reading WILFRID GORDON MCDONALD PARTRIDGE. Use different voices for the voices of the older people.

2. At the end of the reading, talk with the children about the fact that as we get older, sometimes our voices change and become quivery. However, some voices remain stable.

3. Ask a small group of children to retell the story in their own words on the other side of the tape.

4. Do a dry run of the taping by letting the children take turns telling about the pictures.

5. Listen to the recording, and let the children decide anything they would like to change in their retelling.

6. Place the tape of your reading and of the children's story retelling in the class library with a copy of the book.

Something to think about
Consider asking an older friend who has an interesting voice to make the initial recording of the book.

STORY STRETCHER

For Mathematics: Sorting Shells

What the children will learn
To sort shells by their type and size

Materials you will need
Large collection of shells, small baskets or shoe boxes, glass jars

What to do
1. Collect a wide assortment of seashells.

2. Show the children the illustration of Wilfrid's lovely seashells from last summer.

3. Then spread your collection of shells out on the table and ask them if there are any that are alike.

4. Provide small baskets or shoe boxes, and let the children enjoy sorting the shells.

5. Display the shells in glass or clear plastic containers.

Something to think about
The focus of this mathematics activity is sorting; however, it could also become a science story s-t-r-e-t-c-h-e-r by identifying the shells by their proper names and the animals that once lived in them. Many mathematical problems could be made by comparing the quantities, weights and types. Younger children will simply enjoy having some interesting objects with which to practice counting.

STORY STRETCHER

For Special Event: Invitation To Older Friends

What the children will learn
To relate to older people

Materials you will need
Writing paper, pencils, envelopes, stamps

What to do
1. Discuss Wilfrid Gordon McDonald Partridge's friendships with several older people whom he admired. Recall the people from the story and what Wilfrid liked about them.

2. Mention some older friends of yours and what you like about them.

3. Tell the children that to be friends does not mean you must be the same age.

4. Invite older, retired people to come to class and share their special talents. Arrange for an older person who enjoys music to come to class and play an instrument, like Mrs. Jordan who played the organ.

5. Continue the invitations throughout the friends unit. Have an older adult who is a good story-teller come to class. Remind the children that the guest is like Wilfrid's friend, Mr. Hosking, who told scary stories. Invite an active older person to tell about his or her sport, like Mr. Tippett who liked cricket. Invite someone with a lovely deep voice to read to the class, and remind them that the voice is like that of Wilfrid's friend, Mr. Drysdale.

Something to think about
If it is not possible to have retired, older adults visit the classroom, then the class can go to a nearby retirement home. Let the children sing and also bring drawings of the children's school and families.

STORY STRETCHER

For Special Project: Baskets Of Memories

What the children will learn
To symbolize events and feelings that are good memories

Materials you will need
An array of baskets, special tin boxes or lovely gift boxes; tissue paper or gift wrap paper

What to do
1. In a parent newsletter, request that the children bring baskets, tins and special boxes to school. If some parents have extras, collect more for the children who may not have any.

2. In small groups, read again the story of Wilfrid and his friendship with Miss Nancy.

3. After the reading, let each child list the special items that are reminders of a special event, place or an activity they enjoy.

4. Have each child remember something that is very old, something that makes them cry, something that makes them laugh, something that is precious and

something that makes them feel warm.

5. Ask the children to bring these items to school.

6. On the following day, when the children arrive with their memory items, let them fill their baskets and make "memory baskets."

7. Arrange a beautiful display of the baskets for the children to enjoy for several days.

Something to think about
Encourage older children to write about their memory basket, and display their writing with the baskets. If possible, arrange for some special display spots throughout the school, such as in the office reception area and in the school library. Include a copy of the book in the display. Let the children compose a note explaining the symbolism of the memory baskets and how the baskets relate to the story of WILFRID GORDON MCDONALD PARTRIDGE.

References

Brown, Marc. (1989). **ARTHUR'S BIRTHDAY**. Boston: Little, Brown and Company.

Fox, Mem. (1985). Illustrated by Julie Vivas. **WILFRID GORDON MCDONALD PARTRIDGE**. Brooklyn, NY: Kane/Miller Book Publishers.

Henkes, Kevin. (1988). **CHESTER'S WAY**. New York: Greenwillow.

Lobel, Arnold. (1971). **FROG AND TOAD TOGETHER**. New York: HarperCollins.

Waber, Bernard. (1988). **IRA SAYS GOODBYE**. Boston: Houghton Mifflin.

Additional References for Friends

Henkes, Kevin. (1986). **A WEEKEND WITH WENDELL**. New York: Greenwillow Books. *Sophie does not enjoy energetic, bossy Wendell's weekend visit until Sunday, when she starts making some of the rules too, thereby moving them towards real friendship.*

Jones, Rebecca C. (1991). Illustrated by Beth Peck. **MATTHEW AND TILLY**. New York: Dutton Children's Books. *A city neighborhood is the backdrop for this story of two friends who discover the city is a lonely place if they don't have each other to play with.*

Kellogg, Steven. (1986). **BEST FRIENDS**. New York: Dial Books for Young Readers. *Kathy feels lonely, angry and betrayed when her best friend goes away for the summer. In the fall, a shared puppy helps to heal the wounds. This is a realistic look at the complexity of children's friendships.*

Lobel, Arnold. (1979). **DAYS WITH FROG AND TOAD**. New York: Harper and Row. *Frog and Toad spend their days together, but find that sometimes it's nice to be alone.*

Winthrop, Elizabeth. (1989). Illustrated by Martha Weston. **THE BEST FRIENDS CLUB**. New York: Lothrop, Lee, and Shepard Books. *Lizzie learns that she can share her best friend and can enjoy it, too.*

4

FEELINGS

Koala Lou

Three Brave Women

Thunder Cake

The Velveteen Rabbit

Alexander and the Terrible, Horrible, No Good, Very Bad Day

KOALA LOU

By Mem Fox

Illustrated by Pamela Lofts

Koala Lou is her mother's delight and tells her often by saying, "Koala Lou, I DO love you." But when Koala Lou's mother has other babies, she is too busy to notice every little thing that Koala Lou does. Koala Lou decides the one best way to get her mother's attention is to win one of the games in the Bush Olympics. Despite her long training and her many practice runs up the gum tree, Koala Lou loses the gum tree climbing contest to Koala Klaws. She is so upset that she runs away and hides. That evening she returns home and is greeted by the words she most wanted to hear, "Koala Lou, I DO love you." Pamela Lofts' colorful illustrations are endearing and so animated that the story can be told by just looking at the illustrations. She has included a number of other bush animals in addition to the ones mentioned in story.

Read-Aloud Suggestions

Since this unit is about feelings, talk with the children about some of the special things their parents say to them or do for them to express their affection. Perhaps it is a nickname or the way they tuck them in at night or the special time they spend together on the weekend. Read KOALA LOU and discuss how Koala Lou thought she had to do something extraordinary for her mother to tell her she loved her. Let the children talk about their feelings and their concern about their parents' feelings when they are playing games and sports. This is a book that the children will ask you to read again because they like the feelings and they like identifying the unusual bush animals.

STORY STRETCHER

For Art: Olympic Decorations

What the children will learn
To plan and decorate the classroom using available materials

Materials you will need
Usual classroom supplies, construction paper, posterboard, markers, crepe paper, tape, paper and pen

What to do
1. Have the children look at the decorations for the Bush Olympics in KOALA LOU.

2. Then ask them to look around the room for some possible materials they could use to decorate for "Our Bush Olympics." For example, a jump rope could be the finish line, clipped edges of construction paper could decorate booths for games, and crepe paper streamers could divide areas.

3. Make note of the possibilities and divide the class into decorating teams, each with a captain who is responsible for checking with other teams so that one set of decorations doesn't overlap onto another team's work.

4. Let the class decorate the classroom over a period of days.

Something to think about
Often children in today's society are accustomed to buying party decorations. Encourage children to recycle materials and use items in unusual ways. Another related art story s-t-r-e-t-c-h-e-r would be to let the children devise their own spectator hats like the elaborate ones worn in KOALA LOU.

STORY STRETCHER

For Classroom Library: Koala Lou, I DO Love You

What the children will learn
To read the recurring phrases on cue

Materials you will need
Cassette recorder and tapes, glass, fork, listening station, headphones

What to do
1. With a small group of children in the class library or a quiet area in the classroom, make a recording of KOALA LOU. Have the children recall the phrase which is repeated throughout the book, "Koala Lou, I DO love you!"

2. Either you or a child who is a proficient reader reads the story.

3. Assign one child to make the page-turning signal, gently tapping a glass with a fork.

4. Decide on a hand signal or cue so that the children will know when to say their line.

5. After recording the story, place it at the listening station with the book.

Something to think about
Young children profit from repeated readings of books. Encourage children who are less proficient readers to select a favorite story to hear again and again, and then let them read it to you.

For Games: Our Version Of Bush Olympics

What the children will learn
To improvise some cooperative games

Materials you will need
Ropes, balls, chairs, boxes, hoops

What to do
1. Read KOALA LOU again, and pause for the children to think of variations on the games played in the Bush Olympics. Also invent team games that require cooperation: for example, scavenger hunts, obstacle courses and team relays.

2. Let the children divide into teams. Each team is responsible for assembling the materials needed for the game, diagraming how to set up the game and leading the rest of the class in playing the game.

3. Emphasize the inventiveness of each game.

4. Continue to play the games, and notice the children improve with practice.

5. Let them modify their games, after they have played them for a while, and add new twists, such as running relay games backwards, or collecting all the scavenger hunt materials and deciding good places to hide them.

Something to think about
Play games that depend on cooperation for the players to succeed, rather than emphasizing competition for its own sake. The children can also try some Koala Lou exercises, such as jogging, lifting light weights and doing push-ups. (This story s-t-r-e-t-c-h-e-r was adapted from an idea by Kathryn Castle.)

For Science And Nature: Koala And Other Bush Animals

What the children will learn
To identify the koala, emu, platypus, kookaburra and other bush animals

Materials you will need
Reference books containing pictures of Australian animals, large index cards, pencils

What to do
1. Place the reference books in the science and nature area along with a copy of KOALA LOU.

2. Let the children compare the illustrator's animated versions of the animals with photographs of the real animals.

3. Plan to spend time talking about the animals featured in the book, but decide on some others that might have come to the Bush Olympics.

4. Let each child write facts they would like to remember about the animals. Ask for at least one card from each student.

Something to think about
Create a display about Australian animals from pictures drawn by the children. Tack up a large map of Australia as the backdrop for the display. If a child has a toy koala, add the stuffed animal to the display.

For Writing Center: Journal Writing, Feelings About Winning And Losing

What the children will learn
To use their journals as a means of writing about their feelings

Materials you will need
Notebooks or journals for each child, pencils, pens

What to do
1. Talk with the children about journals and diaries. Perhaps share with them about a time in your childhood when you kept a journal or a diary.

2. Journals can be shared, or they can be private and only read by the writer. Discuss with the children how it often helps to have someone read about our feelings. They can empathize with us because they have had similar experiences.

3. Ask the children to write about a time when they won and a time when they lost a game, and how that made them feel.

4. Let each child decide whether or not she or he wants you to read the journal entry on winning and losing.

5. If the child wants you to read about her or his feelings, then write a few lines expressing how you felt when you read the child's writing.

Something to think about
Other writing experiences that can be prompted by KOALA LOU include writing about sibling rivalry, changing the story so that Koala Lou wins, making the setting another country and describing the animals that might be there. Some children may like to write about other bush animals and make them the main characters in a set of stories.

THREE BRAVE WOMEN

By C.L.G. Martin

Illustrated by Peter Elwell

While sitting on the front porch swing with Mama and Grammy, Caitlin screeches that she hates Billy Huxley because she thinks he will tell everyone she is afraid of spiders and that she wears duck underpants. When a big spider crawled up Caitlin's leg, she slipped off her long pants and left them on the sidewalk. Billy saw her. Grammy and Mama tell Caitlin about times when they were scared and angry. Both their tales of being scared of spiders make Caitlin feel better. Then the three of them hatch a plan to show Billy Huxley that Caitlin isn't afraid. In the process, all three women decide they are brave. Elwell's line drawings with watercolors are perfect renditions of the three generations of brave women. Grammy's facial expressions are terrific.

Read-Aloud Suggestions

Ask the children if they are afraid of insects and spiders. Have them describe how they feel and the lengths they go to avoid the creatures. Show the cover of THREE BRAVE WOMEN and introduce the characters, Grammy, Caitlin and Mama. Read THREE BRAVE WOMEN and be prepared for some extra giggles over the duck underpants. Pause only once in the reading of the story to let the children predict the plan the three women will come up with to prove to Billy Huxley that Caitlin is not afraid. After the reading, ask the children what surprised them about the story. Continue by discussing the ways that the author built suspense.

STORY STRETCHER
For Art: Giant Chalk Bugs

What the children will learn
To draw sidewalk chalk drawings

Materials you will need
Colored chalk, paper

What to do
1. Read the scene where Caitlin goes to Billy Huxley's house and finds him drawing giant chalk bugs on the sidewalk.

2. Have the children imagine what the giant chalk bugs might look like. Let them make a sketch on paper.

3. Allow the children to go outside and draw giant chalk bugs on the sidewalk.

Something to think about
Sidewalk chalk artists can be found in many European and South and Central American cities. Ask the librarian to find some reference materials about these artists.

STORY STRETCHER
For Music And Movement: Composing Spider And Insect Songs

What the children will learn
To take a familiar tune and rewrite the lyrics to fit the book or an experience they have had

Materials you will need
Posterboard or chart tablet, marker

What to do
1. On chart tablet paper or posterboard, print the lyrics to some favorite childhood fingerplays and songs about insects, such as "Eencey, Wincey Spider," "I'm Bringing Home a Baby Bumblebee" and "Little Miss Muffet."

2. Sing the songs with the children.

3. Let the children think of lyrics that would fit the story of THREE BRAVE WOMEN. For example,

The eencey, wincey spider went up Caitlin's pant leg.
Off came the pants and Caitlin did run.
Out came Billy Huxley and laughed and laughed and laughed.
And the eencey, wincey spider went up the pants again.

4. Have groups of children sing their new versions of the songs.

Something to think about
Teach younger children the songs and use them as a Big Book shared reading experience. As the children sing, run your hand or a pointer under the words in a fluid motion. Children can practice reading with the *Big Book of Songs*.

For Science And Nature: KWL—Investigating Reporting

What the children will learn
To complete a KWL chart

Materials you will need
Chart tablet, posterboard, four markers or chalks of different colors and chalkboard that can remain for several days without being erased, nonfiction books on spiders

What to do
1. Make a large chart with three columns, and print "Spiders" at the top. Then write a "K" at the head of the first column, a "W" at the top of the second column and place an "L" at the head of the third column.

2. Introduce the KWL chart as a means of keeping track of data. The "K" represents what we already know about the topic of spiders. The "W" stands for what we want to find out or want to know, and the "L" represents what we have learned.

3. In the "K" column, write what the children say they already know about spiders from hearing the story of THREE BRAVE WOMEN.

4. Ask the children what they already knew about spiders from their own experiences. Write key words from their comments in the "K" column with a different marker.

5. Then, ask the children what they would like to know about spiders—some of the questions they have. For example, Are all spiders poisonous? Do all spiders eat flies? How do spiders spin webs?

6. Using the non-fiction reference materials, let the children find out as much as they can about spiders.

7. After several days of observation and investigation, answer the questions from the "W" column with the "L" column, what we learned. Also, add other information that the children found interesting and facts they want to be sure and remember.

8. Retain the chart in the science area for a few days.

Something to think about
First graders sometimes have difficulty thinking of questions for the "W" column. Either help them think of questions by providing a few, or make a "K" & "L" chart. Use the "K" column, complete the science and nature story s-t-r-e-t-c-h-e-r, and then write the "L" column of the chart.

For Writing Center: Front Porch Swing Stories

What the children will learn
To recall family stories

Materials you will need
Paper, pencils, drawing paper, colored pencils, markers, crayons

What to do
1. Talk about Caitlin, Grammy and Mama sitting in the front porch swing and remembering family stories, such as the times when Grammy was afraid of worms, mice and spiders, and the story of Mama overturning the boat when she saw a spider.

2. Have the children share some funny family stories.

3. Ask the students to tell their parents or grandparents the story of THREE BRAVE WOMEN, then ask their relatives if they have any funny insect or spider stories.

4. Request that the children either tape-record the family story, or, after the relative has told the story, draw a picture that will help them remember what happened.

5. At school the next day, have the children begin writing their front porch swing or family stories.

Something to think about
Younger children can tell about their pictures and write key scenes from the story. Older children can write, edit and publish their stories to add to the library collection along with THREE BRAVE WOMEN.

For Writing Center: "When I Was Afraid" And "When I Was Brave" Stories

What the children will learn
To express their feelings in writing

Materials you will need
Writing paper, pencils, art supplies of the children's choice to illustrate their stories

What to do
1. Contrast Caitlin's feeling scared and angry at the beginning of the story with her feeling brave at the end of the story.

2. Ask the children to recall times when they felt afraid or times when they felt brave.

3. After a few children have shared their recollections, encourage some to write their stories.

Something to think about
The children can choose whether to write the "front porch swing funny family stories" or to write "when I was afraid" or "when I was brave" stories.

THUNDER CAKE

by Patricia Polacco

The narrator remembers when she was a little girl and visited her grandma's farm in Michigan. She called her grandmother, "Babushka," and it was her Babushka who helped her overcome her fear of thunderstorms by baking a "Thunder Cake." Ingeniously, the grandma has the little girl count each time she sees the lightning, then stop counting when she hears the thunder. The number means the storm is that many miles away. While the storm is coming, they bake a Thunder Cake. The gathering of the ingredients, including some unusual ones like tomatoes, and the baking of the cake occupy the little girl's mind. By the time the storm arrives, they are eating cake and having tea. The charming illustrations are colorful, most expressive and animated. The facial expressions of Babushka and the granddaughter strengthen any child's resolve not to be afraid of thunderstorms, especially when there is Thunder Cake to be baked.

Read-Aloud Suggestions

Preferably on a stormy day, read THUNDER CAKE. Have the children tell about their fear of storms. One child recalled that his dog was so scared of storms that she scratched and shredded the screen door, trying to get in the house from the backyard. Look at the front cover of the book, and let the children decide the time and place of this story. See if they can predict what is about to happen, based on the cover illustration. Read THUNDER CAKE through from cover to cover without pausing. End the session by announcing the story s-t-r-e-t-c-h-e-r-s based on the book, including baking THUNDER CAKE.

STORY STRETCHER

For Art: Fabric Swatches In My Drawings

What the children will learn
To illustrate using a fabric swatch as part of the picture

Materials you will need
Scraps of patterned cloth, scissors, construction paper, tracing paper, glue, crayons, colored pencils, markers

What to do
1. Have the children who choose art activities during choice time look again at Patricia Polacco's illustration in THUNDER CAKE and notice the many different patterns in Babushka's skirt, blouse and bonnet and in the little girl's dress and bonnet as well as on the bed covers, tablecloths and rugs.

2. Let the children cut at least one swatch of fabric they would like to use in their drawings to illustrate the story of THUNDER CAKE or a story they would like to write.

3. The children can either draw the illustration then cut the fabric to fit by tracing a pattern of part of the drawing, or they can start with a swatch of fabric, glue it on and draw the illustration around it.

Something to think about
If you have children whose grandparents came from Russia and have some of the beautiful patterned pieces of clothing or quilts, ask them to bring them to the class and let the children enjoy them.

STORY STRETCHER

For Classroom Library: Recording THUNDER CAKE With Sound Effects

What the children will learn
To use sound effects to create drama

Materials you will need
Pots and pans or drums, collection of objects from around the room

What to do
1. Tell the children you would like to have a special recording of THUNDER CAKE to place at the listening station in the classroom library. You would like to have it with sound effects.

2. Let the children think of ways they could make the sound of thunder, wind and rain.

3. Have them experiment with a variety of objects, such as beating on a big bread pan to sound like the roll of thunder, hitting a large pot to make a clap of thunder, beating a drum or tapping fingers on metal for the sound of rain.

4. When they have found the sound effects they like, record them and hear how they sound on tape.

5. Practice reading the story and prompting the sound effects.

6. Record the story, and let the "sound effects" mixers be the first children to hear the entire story at the listening station.

Something to think about
Older children might be interested in adding sound effects to some of their own stories and recording them for the listening station.

For Cooking: Baking Thunder Cake

What the children will learn
To follow the directions in a recipe

Materials you will need
Ingredients listed in the book for making Thunder Cake, mixing bowl, measuring cups and spoons, wooden spoon, baking pans, oven, plates, forks, milk, chart tablet or posterboard, marker

What to do
1. Onto chart tablet paper or a sheet of posterboard, copy the recipe for "My Grandma's Thunder Cake" from the end of the book.

2. Divide the children who are interested in helping bake the cake into groups of collectors, mixers, frosters, servers.

3. Let the collectors read the recipe, collect all the ingredients and set them up in the cooking area in the order that they will be needed.

4. Have the mixers measure and mix all the ingredients as well as pour the cake mixture into the baking pans.

5. Ask the frosters to take the cake from the oven when it is baked, let it cool and frost the cake.

6. The servers can cut the cake and serve it on plates with cartons or glasses of milk.

Something to think about
Try to plan at least one cooking story s-t-r-e-t-c-h-e-r for each unit. Sign up two sets of parents to provide the ingredients for each unit.

For Music And Movement: Hiding From The Storm

What the children will learn
To move in response to the music while seeking the one who is hiding

Materials you will need
Fast, energetic classical music with a frantic beat, cassette or record player

What to do
1. Let one child hide while the other students close their eyes. The one who is hiding is the grandchild in THUNDER CAKE.

2. Tell the children that when the music starts, the searchers are to feel the energy of the music and move in the way it makes them feel. While they are moving, they are to be searching for the little girl who has hidden from the storm.

3. Begin the music, and let the children get a sense of the urgency in the tempo.

4. Select four children, and let them dart around the room, searching for the Thunder Cake granddaughter.

5. The other children remain seated. They clap the beat or wave their arms or pat their knees, whatever response they feel keeps time to the music and still lets them remain seated.

6. The searcher who finds the hidden child gets to be the next one to hide. Four new searchers are tapped to continue the game of music and movement.

Something to think about
With the help of a music teacher, locate a piece of classical music that has a storm as the theme. Let the children listen for different parts of the storm and talk about how they feel throughout the score.

For Writing Center: Stormy Stories

What the children will learn
To recall a time when a storm caused some unusual happenings

Materials you will need
Writing paper, pencils, chart tablet, marker

What to do
1. Let the children tell some of the things they liked about the story of THUNDER CAKE.

2. Then ask them to recall a time when they were frightened by a storm, or when the storm caused something to happen which was unexpected. Write some of the examples on the chart tablet. The list might include stopping by the side of the road in a blinding rainstorm, branches falling on rooftops, lightning flashing and lighting up a room in a ghostly way, a blackout at school when there was a power failure.

3. Have the children take one of their real experiences or an imagined one and write a story about a storm .

Something to think about
Some children may be more interested in focusing their writing on special times with their grandmothers, rather than fears in storms. Both writing ideas are appropriate because they both emphasize feelings.

THE VELVETEEN RABBIT

By Margery Williams

Illustrated by Michael Green

This famous story has been printed by many different publishers and any unabridged version of the story is appropriate to read aloud. However, Michael Green's pen and ink illustrations are particularly appealing for primary age children, helping them to grasp the little bunny's longing to become real. The other nursery animals looked down on the velveteen rabbit, all except the skin horse who gave him sage advice. It was only when the little boy loved the little bunny for a long time that he became real. A genuinely touching classic story that no young child should miss and no teacher should miss sharing. It is a tale to be savored and loved again and again.

Read-Aloud Suggestions

Hold a toy bunny rabbit on your lap. Show the children the cover of the book and have them compare the two bunnies, the stuffed velveteen rabbit and a real bunny. Some children may have already heard the book, but they will want to hear it read again. Ask them not to tell the ending or what happens that is sad or happy. Divide the book into at least three sections—the arrival of the toy bunny and the discussion with the skin horse about what it means to be real; the section where the little boy starts sleeping with the bunny and plays with him out in the garden all summer; and the final section in which the boy becomes ill and the little bunny is thrown away only to find some special magic. After reading the first section, have the children remember the story to that point. The next day read the second section, and at the end of the reading, have them recall the story. Another day or late on the same day, read the final part of the story and let the children tell you the parts that made them happy, sad and surprised.

STORY STRETCHER

For Art: Tri-Fold Pictures—Beginning, Middle, End Pictures

What the children will learn
To identify main events at key points in the story

Materials you will need
Large sheets of manilla paper or butcher paper, colored pencils

What to do
1.   Have the children fold their papers so there are three sections, each with the same width.

2.   On the outside fold, ask them to draw something that reminds them of the beginning of the story.

3.   Open the paper up to the second fold and illustrate a part of the story that happened in the middle of the story.

4.   Open both folds and expose the center of the paper. Draw a scene from the end of the story.

Something to think about
Ask the children to take some of their favorite pieces of writing and make tri-fold illustrations of their own stories.

ANOTHER STORY STRETCHER

For Art: Decorating The Nursery Fairy

What the children will learn
To use collage materials for decorations

Materials you will need
Scraps of satin, velveteen, aluminum foil, gift wrap paper, ribbon, sequins or glitter, glue, construction paper or posterboard, scissors, colored pencils

What to do
1.   Read the description of the nursery fairy who makes the toys become real.

2.   Ask the children to imagine what she might look like.

3.   Show the artists the collage materials and ask them to draw and decorate the magic fairy.

4.   Display the collages in the class library area with a copy of the book.

Something to think about
Some children might enjoy sewing a nursery fairy costume for their dolls. Invite a doll dressmaker to come to class and help the children sew doll clothes or to add decorations to dresses the dolls already have. Some children may want to make posterboard fairies that stand

up like paper dolls and dress them in the sparkling collage dresses.

For Classroom Library: Puppet Show

What the children will learn
To follow the sequence of the story and know when to enter the scene

Materials you will need
Stuffed animals and toys to represent the characters, table

What to do
1. Ask children to bring in stuffed animals and toys to represent all the characters in the story of THE VELVETEEN RABBIT.

2. Identify the human characters. You, the teacher, can be the nurse. Let a child be the little boy and another be the doctor.

3. Select two very verbal children to pretend to be the Velveteen Rabbit and the Skin Horse.

4. Make a puppet stage from an overturned table. Turn a table over on its side and seat the puppeteers behind the overturned table in the order that they appear in the story.

5. Read the story and let each animal appear as his or her name is mentioned. Have the children move the animals from side to side as if speaking.

6. Let the human characters appear in front of the puppet stage and pantomime the actions implied by the story.

7. On other days, let different children become different characters.

Something to think about
Older children may write dialogue and act out the story. For more elaborate productions, designate a stage manager and scenery decorators and turn the play into a puppet drama.

For Music And Movement: Nursery Toys Dance

What the children will learn
To move like toys

Materials you will need
Recording of music from "The Nutcracker," cassette tape or record player

What to do
1. Tell the children about the musical, "The Nutcracker," and "The Dance of the Toys," where the toys come to life.

2. Ask the children to imagine how the toys in the nursery of THE VELVETEEN RABBIT might move. Let them improvise movements for the toy train, the wind-up mouse, the model boat, the jointed wooden lion, the skin horse and the soft velveteen rabbit.

3. Let the children choose which toy they want to be.

4. Play the recording of "The Dance of the Toys" and let them pretend they are becoming real.

5. You can be the lovely fairy, and as you tap them with your "magic wand," they begin to dance.

Something to think about
Do the activity on several different days so the children get to pretend to be different toys.

For Writing Center: What Would Happen If One Of My Toys Became Real?

What the children will learn
To imagine a similar plot but with different characters

Materials you will need
Drawing paper, colored pencils, writing paper, pencils

What to do
1. Hold the bunny from read-aloud time. As a pre-writing activity, improvise some dialogue and begin telling a story about what might happen if he became real.

2. Collect some toy stuffed animals from around the room, and let the children think of other stories about them.

3. Have the children identify their favorite toys and ask them to imagine what might happen if they became real.

4. Let the children begin sketching main scenes from the stories they are imagining.

5. After they have a sense of the story they want to tell, ask them to write.

Something to think about
Children can write individual stories but still work as writing partners. At intervals in the writing process, they can stop and read to their partners what they have written so far. The partner can listen and ask questions about any part he or she does not understand.

4
FEELINGS

ALEXANDER AND THE TERRIBLE, HORRIBLE, NO GOOD, VERY BAD DAY

By Judith Viorst

Illustrated by Ray Cruz

Alexander's terrible day begins with him waking up with chewing gum in his hair and continues with so many irritating happenings that he thinks the only way to survive is to move to Australia. All his friends and family seem to be having a good day, except for Alexander. The common childhood mishaps, the bickering, the misunderstandings and the out-of-sorts feelings are ones with which adults and children can identify. Finally, Alexander realizes that everyone has bad days, "even in Australia." Ray Cruz' illustrations are detailed black line drawings with textures, patterns and shading that set just the right tone for the story.

Read-Aloud Suggestions

Write on the chalkboard, "I'm having an Australia day," but do not tell the children what it means. Tell about one of your mornings when everything seemed to go wrong. Let the children join in the discussion and describe some mornings when they know it is going to be a difficult day. Read ALEXANDER AND THE TERRIBLE, HORRIBLE, NO GOOD, VERY BAD DAY. Do not interrupt the reading for discussion since each scene builds to the added frustration Alexander is feeling. Then, ask the children if they have ever had "an Alexander day or an Australia day." Reverse the mood and ask what Alexander's story might be like if he were having a "wonderful, marvelous, terrific, very good day." Use the scenes of the original story as the structure for the reversed mood story. Let the children imagine how Alexander might feel throughout the day, and end with how he remembers his "wonderful, marvelous, terrific, very good day" in his home town. (Some of the suggestions for the read-aloud session and the story s-t-r-e-t-c-h-e-r-s were first published by Raines in IDEAS AND INSIGHTS: ACTIVITIES FOR ELEMENTARY LANGUAGE ARTS.)

STORY STRETCHER

For Art: Adding Details To Drawings

What the children will learn
To use dots, crosshatching strokes, patterns and shading to make details in drawings

Materials you will need
Smooth typing paper or manilla paper, pencils, pencil sharpeners

What to do
1. Have the children look closely at the illustrator's drawings in ALEXANDER AND THE TERRIBLE, HORRIBLE, NO GOOD, VERY BAD DAY. Help them notice the many different ways Ray Cruz added details to the pictures—points or dots, patterns and stripes in clothing, cross-hatching to show grains in the wood and many, many tiny lines to add texture to hair and faces.

2. Let them experiment with a variety of lines using the pencils. Sharpen them often to add the fine detail.

3. Ask the children to draw about one of their "Alexander days" and choose at least one of the techniques Cruz used to add detail to their drawings.

4. Display some of the drawings in the class library area with the copy of the book and also in the writing center.

Something to think about
Some teachers are concerned that teaching children drawing techniques will somehow interfere with their creativity. We have found the opposite to be true. If children are taught techniques and encouraged to observe the ways other artists use lines or colors, the students will begin to incorporate these techniques into their work in some inventive ways.

STORY STRETCHER

For Cooking: Alexander's Cupcakes

What the children will learn
To decorate cupcakes

Materials you will need
Cupcakes, milk, canned frosting, raisins, sprinkles, little candies, mixing bowl, spatula, knives, margarine tubs, warm water

What to do

1. One of the scenes that gets a lot of laughs in ALEXANDER AND THE TERRIBLE, HORRIBLE, NO GOOD, VERY BAD DAY occurs at lunch time when Alexander discovers that his mother forgot to put dessert in his lunch bag. Remind the children of that scene and tell them that for a snack today they can decorate cupcakes for Alexander—and for themselves, of course.

2. Bake the cupcakes ahead of time.

3. Set up all the decorating materials on a separate table.

4. Demonstrate how to spread the frosting with a knife or spatula dipped in warm water.

5. Serve the cupcakes with cartons of cold milk.

Something to think about
Let the children plan a variety of nutritious lunch menus. Make copies to take home to their parents. Title the menus, "If My Lunch Box Could Talk."

STORY STRETCHER

For Creative Dramatics: Scenes From An Alexander Day

What the children will learn
To use movement as a means to communicate scenes from the story

Materials you will need
Note pad, pencil, chalkboard, chalk

What to do

1. On a note pad, list all the scenes from the book and the number of children required to pantomime each scene.

2. Go to individuals and groups of two and three children and, in secret, sign them up for a scene from the book that they would like to act out.

3. Have them describe to you what they will do, and give any hints that might make their miming more effective.

4. On the chalkboard, list the names of the children in the order that they will pantomime the scenes.

5. The children pantomime, and the audience guesses what scene the students are acting.

Something to think about
For younger children, provide a few simple props and allow the audience to ask questions such as "Did it happen at the beginning of the book or the end of the book?"

STORY STRETCHER

For Mathematics: Shoes, Shoes And More Shoes

What the children will learn
To represent quantities with numerals, symbols and graphs

Materials you will need
The children's shoes, paper, pencils, shoe boxes, posterboard, marker, construction paper, scissors, tape, optional—play money, cash register

What to do

1. Assign tasks for the shoe store, such as inventory takers, clerks, customers, cashier, owner.

2. The inventory takers collect all the shoes in the class and list them by writing down descriptions of the shoes: for example, sneakers with red stripes and velcro, white leather high-tops, canvas with leather strings.

3. After all the descriptions are written, have the children categorize the shoes, high-top sneakers, low-top sneakers, leather lace-ups, canvas slip-ons.

4. Make a graph showing all the different categories of shoes. On a sheet of posterboard, write the categories of shoes at the top, then count and write down the number of shoes in that category.

5. Cut out little shoes from construction paper to represent the categories. Let each child put a symbol on the chart to represent her or his shoes.

6. Have the clerks decide on prices for the shoes and mark the boxes or tag the shoes for a display table.

7. Let the customers come in and decide to buy their own shoes.

8. The inventory takers remove a shoe symbol from the chart each time a pair of shoes is sold.

9. The cashier takes their "money" and makes "change."

Something to think about
This activity can be as structured as we describe above, or you can simply assemble the materials, let the children play shoe store, and observe what happens. Add another dimension to the operation by suggesting that the children write advertisements for a shoe sale.

STORY STRETCHER

For Writing Center: Our Terrible, Horrible, No Good, Very Bad Days And Our Wonderful, Marvelous, Terrific, Very Good Days

What the children will learn
To create moods in their writing

Materials you will need
Paper, pencils

What to do

1. Recall the brainstorming during the read-aloud session when the children described some terrible days they had experienced and what happens when they are hav-

ing wonderful, marvelous, terrific, very good days.

2. Ask the children who are interested to write one or both types of stories and illustrate them.

3. Help the children edit their writing by working with writing partners, listening groups or editing groups (see a more detailed description of these writing activities in the Introduction to the book).

4. Publish the children's stories in book form (see the Appendix for directions).

5. Place the books on display in the class library. Add library cards and let the children check them out to read.

Something to think about
The degree of editing one does of children's writing is a matter of teacher and school preference. However, it is imperative that the child be involved in each stage of the writing and editing process. There are many pieces of writing in which we leave the children's invented spellings, but in books that will circulate throughout the year, and during times when children's spelling will change and mature significantly, we help the child edit and spell the words correctly for the final, published book form. We talk with them about how professional book editors work the same way. They are supposed to help writers spell all the words correctly so that the books can be read easily by a large number of people.

References

Fox, Mem. (1989). Illustrated by Pamela Lofts. **KOALA LOU**. San Diego: Harcourt Brace Jovanovich.

Martin. C. L. G. (1991). Illustrated by Peter Elwell. **THREE BRAVE WOMEN**. New York: Macmillan.

Polacco, Patricia. (1990). **THUNDER CAKE**. New York: Philomel Books.

Viorst, Judith. (1972). Illustrated by Ray Cruz. **ALEXANDER AND THE TERRIBLE, HORRIBLE, NO GOOD, VERY BAD DAY**. New York: Macmillan.

Williams, Margery. (1981). Illustrated by Michael Green. **THE VELVETEEN RABBIT OR HOW TOYS BECOME REAL**. Philadelphia, PA: The Running Press.

Additional References for Feelings

Chardiet, Bernice & Maccarone, Grace . (1990). Illustrated by G. Brian Karas. **THE BEST TEACHER IN THE WORLD**. New York: Scholastic, Inc. *Bunny is too embarrassed to admit that she didn't know how to carry out her teacher's errand. The "best teacher in the world" shows her it is better to ask questions than to pretend.*

Cohen, Miriam. (1989). Illustrated by Lillian Hoban. **SEE YOU IN SECOND GRADE!** New York: Greenwillow Books. *The children take a nostalgic look back at their first grade year from the vantage point of the end-of-the-year picnic. Will second grade be as much fun?*

Hines, Anna Grossnickle. (1988). **GRANDMA GETS GRUMPY**. New York: Clarion Books. *Five cousins spend the night at Grandma's, and they learn that Grandma's patience wears thin when they romp out of control.*

Henkes, Kevin. (1987). **SHEILA RAE, THE BRAVE**. New York: Greenwillow Books. *Sheila Rae was brave, indeed, but when she did finally get scared, she was very glad to see her little sister.*

Scheffrin-Falk, Gladys. (1991). Illustrated by Barbara Garrison. **ANOTHER CELEBRATED DANCING BEAR**. New York: Charles Scribner's Sons. *Boris is jealous of his friend Max's fame as a dancer. Max's understanding, plus patient teaching and hard work, produce **another** celebrated dancing bear!*

Teacher Reference

Raines, S. C. (1987). "Australia Days," In Watson, D. S. (Ed.) **IDEAS AND INSIGHTS: ACTIVITIES FOR THE ELEMENTARY LANGUAGE ARTS**. Urbana, IL: National Council of Teachers of English.

CELEBRATIONS

Something Special for Me
Barn Dance!
Mirandy and Brother Wind
One Zillion Valentines
I'm In Charge of Celebrations

SOMETHING SPECIAL
FOR ME

By Vera B. Williams

Rosa's mother saves the tip money she earns at the Blue Tile Diner to buy Rosa a special birthday present. Grandma, Aunt Ida and Uncle Sandy also drop their change in the special jar where the birthday money is kept. When Rosa's birthday arrives, she goes shopping with Mama to select her special present. The story goes on to tell all the things she thinks of buying and ends with a surprise when she selects an old accordion. Beautifully illustrated in bright watercolors with patterns painted on the borders, Williams' illustrations are as rich as the family and community life they portray.

Read-Aloud Suggestions

Ask a child who has a birthday coming up soon what she or he wants as a special present. After the child's replys, say that would be "something special for you." Show the children the cover of the book and let the child who has a birthday soon read the title to the class. Read SOMETHING SPECIAL FOR ME, stopping at the scenes where Rosa and Mama are shopping. Have the children predict whether or not Rosa will buy each item for her birthday present. Children often request that you read this book again. Read it again or spend time looking through the pictures and commenting on the effective way the author/illustrator used bright colors and patterns around the borders of the pages.

S T O R Y S T R E T C H E R

For Art: Special Border Pictures

What the children will learn
To decorate using patterns

Materials you will need
Watercolors, brushes, margarine tubs with water, watercolor paper or any thick paper, scissors, glue

What to do
1. Trim about a half-inch from each edge of a sheet of paper.

2. Let the children paint their watercolor paintings on the smaller sheet and put these aside to dry.

3. Show them the illustrations in SOMETHING SPECIAL FOR ME and note the many different types of borders with different patterns.

4. Let the artists paint borders on a full sheet of paper.

5. Position their watercolors on the border papers and glue them into place.

Something to think about
Using magic markers, let the children make their own patterned book jackets. Cover the paper with contact paper and use it on one of their books.

S T O R Y S T R E T C H E R

For Classroom Library: "Little Pictures" Mean A Lot

What the children will learn
To make pictures which represent scenes

Materials you will need
Cassette tape, tape player, glass, fork, chalkboard, chalk, flannel board, construction paper, markers or crayons, scissors, glue, old emery boards

What to do
1. Alone or with a group of children, record yourself reading SOMETHING SPECIAL FOR ME. Be sure to record a page-turning signal, such as gently tapping a glass with a fork.

2. Look through the pictures and notice how the illustrator represented some scenes with small, simple pictures, such as the birthday cake, the stack of bills, the skates, the hat, the accordion.

3. Read each scene and let the children decide upon a small picture they could draw to remind them of what was happening. List their ideas on the chalkboard.

4. Assign children to make the "little pictures" that represent the scenes.

5. Glue a short strip of old emery board onto the back of the children's "little pictures."

6. Play the recording of you reading the book and let the listeners arrange their "little pictures" on the flannel board to represent each scene.

7. Store the flannel board pieces with the tape, and place both in the class library area along with the book.

Something to think about
Children who are often reluctant to come to the library area because they like more active and social learning enjoy story s-t-r-e-t-c-h-e-r-s which are "hands-on" manipulations of the story.

STORY STRETCHER
For Creative Dramatics: The Blue Tile Diner

What the children will learn
To dramatize the activities at a busy diner

Materials you will need
Tables, silverware, plates, cups, saucers, glasses, note pads, pencils, posterboard, optional—cash register and play money

What to do
1. With the children's assistance, collect the supplies for a creative dramatics center.

2. Let the children plan and arrange their diner.

3. Have the class decide on a name for the diner that fits your classroom.

4. Plan a menu with prices for the diner.

5. Leave the children to their own devices to improvise their play at the diner. Arrange to have six or seven people play at a time so that they have to negotiate roles. Make only one rule—you have to play a different role each day.

Something to think about
When children are selecting activities during choice time, be sure to ask children who have not played in the diner whether they want to go there or not.

STORY STRETCHER
For Mathematics: How Much "Something Special" Costs

What the children will learn
To read prices

Materials you will need
Catalogs, advertisements, want ads, index cards, pencils, thumbtacks, bulletin board, Post-it notes

What to do
1. Survey the class and decide some of the things they would like to have as "something special" for their birthdays.

2. Decide on the best places to find out how much the items might cost. Place the catalogs, advertisements and want ads on a table.

3. Have the children write their names and what they would like for their birthdays on an index card. Ask them to be specific. Instead of just writing bike, they should say dirt bike with knobby tires.

4. Tack their cards to a bulletin board.

5. Let the children browse through the catalogs, advertisements and want ads searching for new and used items that meet their descriptions. Whenever a shopper finds something that meets another birthday shopper's description, he or she can write a Post-it note and tell the person where to look.

Something to think about
Younger children could cut out pictures of what they would like, then practice counting out enough play money to purchase the item. Older students might do some comparison shopping between stores or between new and used items.

STORY STRETCHER
For Writing Center: My Birthday Celebration

What the children will learn
To write descriptively and expressively

Materials you will need
Writing paper, pencils

What to do
1. Have the children retell a favorite part of SOMETHING SPECIAL FOR ME.

2. Let them share the story of a special shopping day or a special birthday they enjoyed.

3. Encourage them to write about the event using descriptive language which helps the reader know exactly where they were and what they were doing.

4. Discuss how the reader or listener of SOMETHING SPECIAL FOR ME feels.

5. Encourage the children to express how their special day of celebration made them feel.

6. After the children have finished their compositions, let those who want to read their writing sit in the "author's chair" and read their pieces to the entire class.

Something to think about
Help the children edit their work by letting them read their pieces to you. Then select two or three lines where descriptive or expressive language could be added. Let the child think aloud how she or he might rewrite the sentences.

BARN DANCE!

By Bill Martin, Jr. and

John Archambault

Illustrated by Ted Rand

From his bedroom window, a little boy hears the faint sound of music coming from the barn. He sneaks down to the barn to find the scarecrow playing his fiddle and all the farm animals dancing. Finally, he can resist the music no longer and joins in the fun. Just as the owl calls that it is almost morning, he finds his way back through the barnyard, through the house and into bed. A story told in verse, BARN DANCE! is truly a celebration of sights, sounds and a young boy's vivid imagination. Ted Rand's illustrations are line drawings with watercolors. The night scenes with the full moon lend just the right magic to the mood.

Read-Aloud Suggestions

Discuss harvest festivals and how the farmers used to celebrate their harvest. After all the corn was pulled, the hay was stacked, the apples and the pumpkins picked and stored in the barn, the farmers celebrated their bountiful harvests by having a barn dance. A fiddler and sometimes other musicians played for the dance, and a "caller" gave the directions for the square dancers. Show the children the cover of the book and have them notice the fiddling scarecrow with a crow on top of his head and the little boy crawling through the fence. Read BARN DANCE! at least twice and keep the rhythm of the poem as you read. During the second or third reading, pause for the children to finish phrases that rhyme.

STORY STRETCHER

For Art: Crayon Resist Night Paintings

What the children will learn
To paint using a technique which shows nighttime

Materials you will need
Construction paper or manilla paper, crayons, margarine tubs, thin black and purple tempera paints, water, brushes

What to do
1. Look at Ted Rand's illustrations of the BARN DANCE! and call attention to the night skies in each scene.

2. Demonstrate the crayon resist technique on a small scrap of paper. Draw a picture with a crayon, bearing down hard to leave a lot of wax on the paper.

3. Paint over the crayon drawings, alternating the diluted black and purple tempera paints.

4. Encourage the children to illustrate night scenes near their homes or scenes they imagine they would see visiting the farm for a barn dance.

Something to think about
Watercolors can be used for the paint washes over the crayon drawings; however, it takes a lot of watercolor paint to achieve the darkness of the tempera paints.

STORY STRETCHER

For Classroom Library: Reading Partners Create Night Magic

What the children will learn
To use their voices to create a mood

Materials you will need
Cassette tape, recorder, extra copies of the book, stapler, listening station, headphones

What to do
1. Read the book again and create a special mood with the way you raise and lower your voice. Exaggerate the voice a bit so the children notice the emphasis.

2. Let pairs of children select the page they want to read into the tape recorder. If many children want to be involved, have small groups record each page as a choral reading. Have them practice their lines to create the night magic mood.

3. Click a stapler near the microphone as the page-turning signal.

4. Record the book and place the tape at the listening station in the classroom library.

Something to think about
Let third graders record several children's books for the first graders to have as read-along tapes. Have small groups of first graders

visit the third grade class and tell which of the tapes they like best.

For Cooking: Harvest Apple Snacks

What the children will learn
To name and enjoy eating a variety of apple products

Materials you will need
Tablecloth, napkins, knives, cutting board, baskets, as many different varieties of apples as you can find in your locality, dried apples, apple juice, apple cider, optional—apple fritters, fried apple pies, apple pies, apple dumplings

What to do
1. With some helpers, arrange the apples in baskets.

2. Talk with the children about all the apples and apple products.

3. Have a tasting party and sample different apple products throughout the week.

4. Show the children how to cut their apples through the middle so that there is a "star" inside, formed by the seeds.

5. Discuss the apple harvest and how the apples were stored in the barn in the fall to keep for eating throughout the winter.

6. Open the BARN DANCE! book to the last page and prop it open on the table so the children can see the little boy propped up in bed, munching on his apple from the barn dance, while the sky is turning a rosy pink as the sun rises.

Something to think about
Write to the tourism board of one of the states that grows a lot of apples, and they will send you information about growing and harvesting apples as well as recipes for many different dishes.

For Music And Movement: Our Own Barn Dance

What the children will learn
To dance basic square dance steps

Materials you will need
Tape or record of square dance music with calls, tape or record player

What to do
1. Invite some square dancers to come to class and demonstrate some basic square dance steps.

2. Play the music and let the children get the rhythm by clapping their hands, slapping their knees and stomping their feet.

3. Practice some of the calls and steps with partners.

Something to think about
Talk with the children about how barn dances and square dances were the way that country folks celebrated the harvest. Read some other books which show apple bobbing, corn husking and horse shoe tosses. Play some of these games and celebrate the lively music and fun of being with friends.

For Writing Center: Sequels to BARN DANCE!

What the children will learn
To use the underlying story structure to create a sequel

Materials you will need
Chalkboard, chalk, writing paper, pencils, drawing paper, crayons, markers, colored pencils

What to do
1. Read BARN DANCE! again.

2. Ask the children what might happen if the little boy sneaked outside, and he lived near a zoo instead of a farm.

3. Let the children brainstorm different possibilities by referring back to BARN DANCE! Write their ideas on the chalkboard. Since this is brainstorming, accept every idea the children suggest.

4. Have the students think of other possible settings, like living near a pet store where the animals start to dance , or living near a music store where the instruments start to dance.

5. Encourage the children to write a story using the types of scenes from BARN DANCE! to change them by varying the settings.

Something to think about
With first and second graders, try group dictation of one idea, and then let the children write about their own if they are interested. Third graders might write sequels for stories.

5
CELEBRATIONS

MIRANDY AND BROTHER WIND

By Patricia C. McKissack

Illustrated by Jerry Pinkney

Mirandy is planning how she will strut in her finest clothes so she can win the beautifully decorated cake at the cakewalk. The couple who wins must impress the judges by making the best moves, with complicated kicks, pivots, swirls and twirls, when they must prance and dance to the music. Mirandy wants to win the cakewalk so badly that she goes to different members of the family and the community to ask advice about how to catch the wind to make him her partner. She doesn't want slow Ezel and refuses his invitations to do the cakewalk. However, in the end, Ezel has a surprise. The dialogue with older members of the community contains some black dialect. The story is beautifully written and placed in an historical context. Pinkney's full-page, full-color watercolor illustrations are worthy of the Caldecott Honor medal the cover of the book bears.

Read-Aloud Suggestions

Ask the children to look at the cover of MIRANDY AND BROTHER WIND and decide if this story happened in the present or in the past. The little girl's old-fashioned clothes are a clue. Point out that the picture in the wind is Mirandy's imagination but that many of the events in the story could have happened. Discuss "cakewalks" as parties, a time when a community came together to celebrate and dance. Let the children describe some beautifully decorated cakes they have seen which they would like to win as a prize. Have children who know fancy dance steps show a few, or let a child show the others what it means to strut—to walk with one's shoulders thrown back and a jaunty step. If none of the children volunteer, then you demonstrate how to strut. Read MIRANDY AND BROTHER WIND without interruption. After the book is read, let some children show how they think Mirandy and Ezel might have danced to win the cake.

S T O R Y   S T R E T C H E R
For Art: Painting Scarves

What the children will learn
To use fabric as a canvas

Materials you will need
Liquid embroidery paints, large pieces of cotton broadcloth in bright colors, tape measure, scissors

What to do
1. Look at Jerry Pinkney's illustrations of Mirandy and Ezel dancing with the scarves at the cakewalk.

2. Help the children cut lengths of fabric at least twelve inches long by at least six inches wide.

3. Demonstrate how to use the liquid embroidery paints.

4. After the painted scarves have dried, let the children strut with them at the cakewalk.

Something to think about
Older children can unravel the edges of the broadcloth and make a fringe before painting their scarves. Invite someone who is good at stitchery to demonstrate embroidery with needle and thread and embroidery hoops.

S T O R Y   S T R E T C H E R
For Classroom Library: Story Retelling

What the children will learn
To use the illustrations as visual clues to the story

Materials you will need
None needed

What to do
1. With a small group of children, look again at Pinkney's illustrations of MIRANDY AND BROTHER WIND.

2. Let the students browse through the book, tell what they like about the watercolor pictures and pick out favorite scenes.

3. Give the book to one child to turn the pages, and let the other children retell the story in their own words.

Something to think about
If you have a reluctant reader in your classroom, letting the child retell the story in his or her own words helps you assess whether or not the child is developing a sense of story. Encourage reluctant readers by asking them to select books that would make good audio-tapes for the listening station.

For Cooking: Decorating A Cakewalk Cake

What the children will learn
To use cake decorating tools

Materials you will need
Simple cake decorating tube and tips, bowl, spatula, knives, forks, cake frosting, food coloring, waxed paper, tape, margarine tubs, warm water, sheet cake or layer cake

What to do
1. Invite a cake decorator to come to class and show the children how she or he uses the various tips to create rosettes, borders, designs and writing on cakes.

2. Let the children help mix the colors of frosting and fill the decorating tubes and sleeves with frosting to assist the decorator.

3. Tear sheets of waxed paper for each child. Tape them in place on the table top. Place a small amount of frosting on the waxed paper for a pretend top of a cake.

4. Have the children experiment with their own designs using the decorating tools or making swirls and patterns with simple tools, such as the edge of the spatula, a knife or fork.

5. With the children who are interested, decorate the sheet cake or the layer cake for the cakewalk prize.

6. Serve the cake after the cakewalk dancing.

Something to think about
Place cake decorating books in the classroom library. Even though the text may be too difficult for young readers, they will enjoy the pictures.

For Music And Movement: Cakewalk

What the children will learn
To improvise prancing and dancing moves

Materials you will need
Recording of a song with a good beat, tape recorder or record player, chalk or masking tape, cake from cooking story s-t-r-e-t-c-h-e-r

What to do
1. With chalk or masking tape, make a large square in the center of the classroom.

2. Select one child as your partner and whisper to the child that you want him or her to prance and dance with you in response to the music.

3. Start the music and have the children stand outside the square and clap their hands. Sway until you and your partner are moving in harmony.

4. Begin strutting and prancing, like Mirandy and Ezel, swaying back and forth, swirling and twirling and moving all around the perimeter of the inside of the square.

5. At the end, tell the children you were doing the cakewalk.

6. Form several other partners and let them do the cakewalk.

Something to think about
It isn't necessary for everyone to do the cakewalk; there needs to be an audience, but encourage wide participation. Some third grade students are hesitant to have girl and boy partners. Don't force the hand holding. Simply have them move and be aware of what their partners are doing.

For Writing Center: Stories My Parents And Grandparents Tell

What the children will learn
To recall family stories

Materials you will need
Writing paper, pencils, art supplies for illustrations

What to do
1. Read the "Author's Note" by Patricia C. McKissack from the front of the book.

2. Have the children recall any family stories they have heard about their relatives.

3. Let the children talk with their parents or grandparents and ask what kind of celebrations they had when they were young. Sometimes looking at family photo albums will prompt some good family stories.

4. Ask the children to write a story about something that happened to their parents or grandparents.

Something to think about
First graders may want to begin by drawing a picture of a family story or something that happened to them personally rather than to their parents or grandparents. Sharing an old picture from the family photograph album in a "show and tell" time can be a good pre-writing activity for family stories.

ONE ZILLION VALENTINES

By Frank Modell

Marvin loves celebrating Valentine's Day and shows his friend Milton how to make valentines. When they make about a zillion, they have a problem and have to decide how to deliver all the valentines. Even when they have given valentines to everyone they know, they still have many left over. They improvise a plan for getting rid of them. This delightful story is filled with marvelous surprises, natural dialogue and the warmth of a genuine friendship. Modell's illustrations are cartoon black line drawings colored with pinks, reds and roses to celebrate Valentine's Day.

Read-Aloud Suggestions

Wear a red shirt or blouse when you read ONE ZILLION VALENTINES and show the children a handmade valentine given to you by a friend or a child from a former class. Read the message inside and tell a bit about the sender. Show the front cover of the book and ask the children to guess how Marvin and Milton got so many valentines. After a few guesses, read the story. Pause at the end of their valentine making session and ask the children to predict what Marvin and Milton will do with all the valentines. At the end of read-aloud time, announce all the valentine celebration story s-t-r-e-t-c-h-e-r-s.

STORY STRETCHER

For Art: Valentines For Marvin And Milton

What the children will learn
To make a variety of valentine designs

Materials you will need
Construction paper, gift wrap ribbon, crayons, markers, colored pencils, pastel chalks, watercolors, brushes, scissors, glue

What to do
1. Look at the pages illustrating all the different designs on Marvin's and Milton's valentines.

2. Let the children select their art supplies and make as many different designs as they like. Encourage experimentation.

3. Have the valentine makers select two of their designs and place them on a valentine bulletin board, one for Marvin and one for Milton.

Something to think about
Provide a list of names of all the students in your classroom and send it to parents with a letter asking that children bring a valentine for each child in the classroom. Or, even better, ask parents to send extra art supplies to school, and let the children make a valentine for each of their classmates.

ANOTHER STORY STRETCHER

For Art: Valentine Placemats

What the children will learn
To design a holiday decoration

Materials you will need
Large heart-shaped box; red, rose and pink construction paper; markers; crayons; chalks; paints; brushes; scissors; contact paper

What to do
1. Let the children design valentine placemats for their families or for themselves. Begin by demonstrating how to hold the heart-shaped box in place and draw around the edge to make a pattern on the construction paper.

2. Cut out the hearts.

3. Decorate them with designs on one side and a valentine message on the other.

4. Cut two strips of contact paper.

5. Place the first strip of contact paper down on the table with the sticky side up.

6. Lay the valentine shape on top of the contact paper.

7. Place the second strip of contact paper over the top of the valentine, sticky side down.

8. Trim the excess contact paper from around the heart, leaving a thin margin all around so the contact paper will stay together.

9. Use the valentine placemats all during the week of Valentine's Day.

Something to think about
Avoid making patterns and designs for the children. Craft projects like this one can still be labeled art if the child is the originator of the designs. Laminating paper can be substituted for the contact paper.

For Games: Musical Hide And Seek

What the children will learn
To listen for clues

Materials you will need
Empty box from valentine candy, cassette tape or record, player

What to do
1. Select energetic music or a recording with a Valentine's Day message.
2. Sit the children in a circle on the floor.
3. Ask one child to be Marvin and hide the valentine candy box.
4. Let another child be Milton who closes his or her eyes while the box is being hidden.
5. When the music starts, the child who is Milton begins looking for the box. The children in the circle take turns giving Milton clues to the location by saying, "Milton, you are getting warmer," when the child is near the box. When the searcher moves away from the box, the children say, "Milton, you are getting colder."
6. When the box is found, the child who was Milton gets to hide the box while the teacher selects another child to be Milton.

Something to think about
With younger children, you can hide the box while they have their eyes closed. Then, when you start the music, everyone becomes Milton and searches until someone finds the box or until the music stops.

For Mathematics: More Than Enough Valentines

What the children will learn
To determine how many is enough by using one-to-one correspondence

Materials you will need
Posterboard or chart tablet, marker

What to do
1. Read the part of the story where Marvin and Milton make too many valentines.
2. Talk with the children about making valentines. Ask them how many they want to make and why. How many are too many? Let them decide that first they must establish who is to get a valentine. They may decide to make enough valentines only for the people in their classroom, or add some for family members, or add valentines for the office and cafeteria workers in the school.
3. Have each child write his or her name on the posterboard or chart tablet.
4. Let each person make a hash mark or a tally mark to represent the number of valentines he or she wants to make. Each mark must represent someone they want to receive a valentine.

Something to think about
Depending on the grade level of the students, many different types of mathematical problems could be solved by the valentine tally. First graders could practice counting and simple addition. Second graders could count by fives and total the entire chart. Third graders could determine ratios.

For Writing Center: Valentine Poems

What the children will learn
To write funny and sentimental valentine poems

Materials you will need
Valentines, markers or colored pens

What to do
1. Read a few funny and a few sentimental valentine messages.
2. Ask the children to compose valentine poems.
3. Write them on the valentines they made for the art story s-t-r-e-t-c-h-e-r.

Something to think about
Read valentine messages you have received and let the children guess whether it was sent by a student or one of your friends or a family member. Choose both funny and "mushy, mushy," sentimental types.

I'M IN CHARGE OF CELEBRATIONS

By Byrd Baylor

Illustrated by Peter Parnall

The author tells the reader about her celebrations in the Southwest desert. Last year, she celebrated 108 days, each in remembrance of a special event, such as the day she saw seven "dirt devils;" the night she saw falling stars; the day she saw a green parrot-shaped cloud; the time she looked into a coyote's eyes. Parnall's spare line drawings are highlighted with Southwest colors: golds, tans and browns with a few light turquoise and green touches.

Read-Aloud Suggestions

Announce to the children that today is a wonderful day, a celebration day. Tell them about something that happened today which was unexpected. Perhaps you saw a beautiful little bird or two scampering squirrels or someone did something special for you which was totally unexpected. Write a key word or phrase on the classroom calendar to remember the unexpected event. Show the children the cover of I'M IN CHARGE OF CELEBRATIONS and tell them that you will be reading about the Southwestern desert. If any children have visited the desert, ask them to talk about their experiences. Point out the Southwestern states on a map. Read the jacket information about the author and show the children Texas, Byrd Baylor's birthplace, and Arizona, where she lives now. Read I'M IN CHARGE OF CELEBRATIONS. Have the children tell about special days they remember.

S T O R Y   S T R E T C H E R

For Art: Unexpected Celebration Day

What the children will learn
To paint using an enlarged focal point

Materials you will need
Easels, tempera paints, brushes, butcher paper or manilla paper

What to do
1. With a group of children who choose to participate in the art activities, look again at the illustrations from I'M IN CHARGE OF CELEBRATIONS. Notice particularly the cover with an enlarged sun, and the inside illustrations of an exaggerated green parrot and very large triple rainbow. Discuss

these events as unexpected happenings.

2. Have the children tell about one of their special days when an unexpected event happened, a day they want to celebrate. Decide what drawing might represent what happened on their special days.

3. Let the children paint with the Southwestern colors the illustrator used or with any which fit their pictures.

4. Encourage the children to write titles or captions for their paintings.

5. Display the pictures in or near the classroom library.

Something to think about
Older children will enjoy painting pictures from the animal's perspective. For inspiration, have them look at Parnall's illustration of the coyote finding the feast the storyteller left behind.

S T O R Y   S T R E T C H E R

For Mathematics: Calendar Of Holidays And Unexpected Events

What the children will learn
To use a calendar to note number of days until an event and number of days since an event

Materials you will need
Large classroom calendar, marker, small calendars for each child, pencils

What to do
1. Ask parents to send in any excess calendars and date books they have at home.

2. Collect and display all the different types of calendars: school calendars, eighteen-month calendars, daily planners, weekly planners, month-at-a-glance, electronic calendars.

3. Select a large calendar to use as the classroom calendar and copy smaller versions for each student. For first and second graders, copy only this month.

4. Mark school holidays, children's birthdays and any recent events that the class wants to be sure to remember, as well as any that are planned, such as the hike in the science and nature story s-t-r-e-t-c-h-e-r.

5. Let the children use their calendars to count days and answer questions about time. For example, How many days until the next school holiday? How many days until Melinda's birthday? How many days until David's birthday? How many days until our next field trip?

6. Then use the calendars to count days and answer the reverse of those questions. How many days since the last school holiday, since Melinda's birthday, since David's birthday, since our last field trip?

7. On the calendar, mark celebration days of the unexpected type, like those in I'M IN CHARGE OF CELEBRATIONS. Record them for a month.

Something to think about
Begin with the children marking their calendars with celebrations they are in charge of. Also, younger students can add and subtract using the calendar as a number line. Older students can use days of the week and months to solve problems. For example, if there are nine months of school, how many days of those nine months are spent in school? How many days of the nine months are holidays? How many days of the nine months are "I'm in charge of celebration" days?

For Music And Movement: A Celebration Of Movement

What the children will learn
To listen for movement words, then move like the words imply

Materials you will need
None needed

What to do
1. Have the children sit in a circle on the floor.

2. Tell them that you are impressed with the way Byrd Baylor writes, particularly the way she tells about movement.

3. Read the scene of the seven "dust devils" or whirlwinds.

4. Ask seven children to demonstrate what those movements might look like.

5. Continue the reading and select different children for each scene of I'M IN CHARGE OF CELEBRATIONS.

Something to think about
With younger children, let them improvise each scene, but you lead the whole class in the movements. With older students, consider adding rhythm band instruments, like drums and tambourines, to express the movements.

For Science And Nature: Field Notes From Our Hike

What the children will learn
To observe closely and to write key observation points

Materials you will need
Small note pads or index cards, pencils

What to do
1. Talk with the children about how scientists take field notes, which are their observations.

2. Write a sample field note, including the date, time, location and an observation of an insect, a plant, an animal or the weather.

3. Plan a hike to a natural area on the school grounds or in the neighborhood. Pair children as hiking partners. Have parent volunteers or older elementary students involved in the hike. Explain to them about the field notes exercise.

4. Enjoy the hike until you are surrounded by trees and plants or, if you live in an arid area, until you are out of sight of the school and in a more natural setting.

5. Have the children stop and select one specimen—insect, animal, plant—that they want to observe. Ask them to observe for several minutes without talking. The length of the observation time will vary depending on the age of the students.

6. Let the children tell their partners what they saw.

7. Have the students write key words and any sketches they need to help them remember their specimen.

8. Back in the classroom, divide the observers into teams, according to the specimen they chose for field notes. Have an insect team, a plant team and an animal team. Let them compare notes on what they saw.

Something to think about
Because of their curiosity about nature, the primary school age is a wonderful time to help children become keen observers. Practice field notes for several science and nature story s-t-r-e-t-c-h-e-r-s.

For Writing Center: Journal Entry—A Day To Remember For The Rest Of My Life

What the children will learn
To write about special events they want to remember

Materials you will need
Notebooks or journals for each child, pencils

What to do
1. Read the page from I'M IN CHARGE OF CELEBRATIONS where the author says that she keeps a notebook and writes down the date and notes about the celebration.

2. Write your own journal entry about a special day you want to remember the rest of your life because of some unexpected event. Describe what happened, how you felt, and how you celebrated.

3. Read the journal entry to the children and elaborate on what happened.

4. If your special celebration reminds the children of something that happened to them, let the students share their recollections.

5. Read your journal entry a second time and have the children listen for the main ideas—what happened, how you felt and how you celebrated.

6. Ask the children to write about one of their days that they want to remember for the rest of their lives. They can use your outline or they may write in story form.

Something to think about
Encouraging children to write to remember helps them understand the way writing is used by adults. It is also important for the children to view their teacher as a writer of the same types of writing they are expected to do.

References

Baylor, Byrd. (1986). Illustrated by Peter Parnall. **I'M IN CHARGE OF CELEBRATIONS**. New York: Charles Scribner's Sons.

Martin, Bill, Jr., & Archambault, John. (1986). Illustrated by Ted Rand. **BARN DANCE! New York: Henry Holt and Company.**

McKissack, Patricia C. (1988). Illustrated by Jerry Pinkney. **MIRANDY AND BROTHER WIND**. New York: Alfred A. Knopf.

Modell, Frank. (1981). **ONE ZILLION VALENTINES**. New York: Greenwillow Books.

Williams, Vera B. (1983). **SOMETHING SPECIAL FOR ME**. New York: Greenwillow Books.

Additional References for Celebrations

Bunting, Eve. (1988). Illustrated by Beth Peck. **HOW MANY DAYS TO AMERICA? A THANKSGIVING STORY**. New York: Clarion Books. *This book stresses the meaning of our great national celebration. We follow an immigrant family as they arrive in this country and give thanks for their safety and their freedom.*

Cohen, Miriam. (1987). Illustrations by Lillian Hoban. **DON'T EAT TOO MUCH TURKEY!** New York: Greenwillow Books. *The first grade Thanksgiving celebration can begin once everyone in the class is included.*

Dr. Seuss. (1959). **HAPPY BIRTHDAY TO YOU!** New York: Random House. *The incomparable Dr. Seuss, imagining for the reader a Seuss-like happy birthday of glorious nonsense.*

Polacco, Patricia. (1989). **UNCLE VOVA'S TREE**. New York: Philomel Books. *A story of the author's own childhood, when the whole family would gather on Uncle Vova's farm to celebrate Christmas in the Russian tradition.*

Schotter, Roni. (1990). Illustrated by Marylin Hafner. **HANUKKAH!** Boston: Little, Brown and Company. *Five young children and their family celebrate Hanukkah with all its special traditions and historical meaning.*

I CARE ABOUT MY WORLD, THE ENVIRONMENT

The Empty Lot
When the Woods Hum
The Great Kapok Tree
Farewell to Shady Glade
Brother Eagle, Sister Sky

I CARE ABOUT MY WORLD, THE ENVIRONMENT

THE EMPTY LOT

By Dale H. Fife

Illustrated by Jim Arnosky

While strolling through his vacant lot, Harry Hale asks himself, "What good is an empty lot?" He soon discovers it is far from empty. The woodpecker is the first creature to make his presence known, then a squirrel, a chickadee, a bluejay, three baby sparrows, a frog, dragonflies, beetles, a salamander, and even a mosquito. Harry closes his eyes and tries to relax so he can think about to whom he should sell his empty lot. Then he hears the twittering birds, the droning bees and the buzzing insects. When he opens his eyes, a mother quail and her four chicks parade by, then a cricket chirps, and a spider does acrobatics hanging from the limb of an oak. From a tree house, Harry sees children playing. In the end, Harry changes the "empty lot for sale" sign to an "occupied" sign. Arnosky's illustrations are watercolors with a humorous, moustache-adorned Harry as the central character.

Read-Aloud Suggestions

If there is an empty lot near your school, ask the children who they think lives there. Show them the cover of the book and have a child read the title, THE EMPTY LOT. Read the story without pausing for discussion until the very end, then let the children predict what Harry will write on his sign. After reading, let the children recall the animals and insects who made their homes on the lot. Ask if any other living things found homes there. Read the phrases about the trees, bushes and wild grasses. Begin planning the class visit to a nearby empty lot.

STORY STRETCHER

For Art: Peeking In On Nature

What the children will learn
To emphasize a part of an illustration

Materials you will need
Construction paper, crayons, markers, colored pencils, small blocks, scissors, stapler

What to do
1. Show the children the illustration of Harry peeking through the leaves at the three baby sparrows.

2. Have the children draw a favorite natural setting they enjoy.

3. Let each artist select a special area of their drawing that would be pretty to look at without seeing the whole picture.

4. Show the children how to do the following steps on their own. Place a sheet of construction paper over their drawings and mark a pencil dot on the paper that corresponds to the special area.

5. Select a round, square or triangle block and place it over the dot. Draw around the block to make a "peek" hole.

6. Cut out the peek hole.

7. Staple the construction paper cover with the peek hole over the drawing.

Something to think about
Arnosky's illustrations are watercolors painted on squares and rectangles with parts of the pictures extending beyond the borders, like a trail of ivy growing off the picture, the beak of a quail pointing off the edge, and tree limbs extending beyond the top of the square. Point out this technique to the children and encourage them to try it by first drawing a smaller rectangle on their drawing paper and using the border to extend their pictures.

STORY STRETCHER

For Classroom Library: Harry And Friends

What the children will learn
To retell the story from another perspective

Materials you will need
Chart tablet and marker or chalkboard and chalk, cassette tape and recorder, stapler

What to do
1. Read the story again and have the children pretend they are the insects, animals and plants that live in the empty lot. Have them imagine what they might say when they see Harry arrive.

2. Scan the story and make a list of where the creatures' thoughts could be inserted into the story.

3. Have the children volunteer to improvise what the creatures might be saying and write their names on the list beside the creatures.

4. Do a practice recording of the book and improvisations.

5. Ask one child to be responsible for recording the page-turning signal: click a stapler near the microphone.

6. Record a brief introduction to the book and make a sample page-turning signal so the listeners understand how to operate the tape.

7. Read the book and pause for the children to tell their improvised story, inserting the creatures' comments.

8. Record the original version of the story on the other side of the tape.

9. Place the tape and the book at the listening station in the library corner.

Something to think about
Older children might add what each of the potential buyers of the lot might say to Harry to try to persuade him to sell it.

STORY STRETCHER

For Mathematics: How Many Classifications?

What the children will learn
To determine categories for classification

Materials you will need
Posterboard or chart tablet, marker, paper, pencil

What to do
1. Read the story aloud and ask the listeners to write down the names of all the living things they hear.

2. Make a large poster of all the living things from the empty lot. Title the poster, "Occupants—Living Things on Harry's Lot."

3. Draw lines to form three columns. Let the children decide what the names of the three categories of living things could be, such as animals, insects, plants.

4. Categorize, list and count the living things mentioned in THE EMPTY LOT.

5. If the children choose smaller classifications, such as the plant category could be divided into grasses, bushes, trees, then make additional columns or more posters.

Something to think about
Categorizing is a mathematical and scientific exercise. Help the children understand that the classification system of "living things" can be broken down into categories and subcategories or sets and subsets.

STORY STRETCHER

For Science And Nature: What Lives On Our Empty Lot?

What the children will learn
To observe living things in a natural setting

Materials you will need
None needed

What to do
1. Find an empty lot with a natural setting and secure permission to visit it.

2. Ask for parent volunteers to accompany the class and discuss with the volunteers what your objectives for the experience are.

3. Discuss with the children ahead of time what they will be doing and let them help decide the rules, such as staying with the parent volunteer to whom they are assigned.

4. Take a walk to the empty lot and break up into small groups of no more than four children per adult.

5. Walk over the property and spend some time with eyes closed listening to the sounds, just as Harry did when he visited his empty lot.

6. Return to the classroom and discuss the sights, sounds and feelings experienced.

7. Follow up the discussion with a mathematics story s-t-r-e-t-c-h-e-r similar to the one listed above.

Something to think about
Empty lots are often environmental problems because of the trash and debris left there. Perhaps the children could help clean up an empty lot in the neighborhood.

STORY STRETCHER

For Writing Center: Write to Harry

What the children will learn
To write a persuasive letter

Materials you will need
Overhead projector, transparency, markers

What to do
1. With small groups of children, compose a group letter inviting Harry to visit his empty lot and giving reasons why he should not sell it.

2. Read the letter to the group and let them suggest changes or more persuasive ways of expressing their thoughts.

3. Let the children see how to edit draft to improve it. Cross out, insert, add carets, draw lines to move sentences around.

4. Reprint the finished letters and share the drafts and the finished letters with each group.

Something to think about
With first graders, try a group dictated letter with each child contributing at least one sentence. Print each child's sentence in a different color of ink and then let the child decide how to rewrite his or her sentence more persuasively.

I CARE ABOUT MY WORLD, THE ENVIRONMENT

WHEN THE WOODS HUM

By Joanne Ryder

Illustrated by Catherine Stock

In this intergenerational story, Papa shows Jenny a cicada he has kept for seventeen years. In the spring, Jenny and Papa visit the woods and hear the "hummers," the cicadas, make the woods sing. The story parallels the seventeen years between the cicadas' appearances and Jenny's growing up. At the end of the story, seventeen years later, Jenny tells her son, Ray, about the cicadas as Papa, now a grandfather, walks with them through the woods. A warm, affectionate life cycle story told through lovely watercolor and ink drawings showing the lush greens of the beautiful woods.

Read-Aloud Suggestions

Ask the children if they have heard crickets make noises. Then have them imagine what hundreds of crickets chirping would sound like. They would all blend together into a long chirping sound, where individual crickets could not be heard. Show the children the illustration of a cicada. Explain that when thousands of cicadas make noise, they create a loud humming sound that fills the woods. Read the title of the book, WHEN THE WOODS HUM, and tell the children that the number 17 is important in the story. Read the book and answer the children's questions about cicadas. Have them recall the importance of the number 17: that there are 17 years between the appearances of the cicadas. If the cicadas came this year, how old would the children be when the cicadas came again?

STORY STRETCHER

For Art: Bark Rubbings

What the children will learn
To make textures in their illustrations

Materials you will need
Bark, crayons, butcher paper or typing paper, tape, newspaper, choice of art materials

What to do
1. When walking in an empty lot or near a wooded area, pick up pieces of tree bark.

2. Bring the bark back to class and examine it more closely.

3. Demonstrate how to make rubbings by taping bark onto a folded newspaper, then placing pieces of butcher paper or typing paper over the bark and rubbing a crayon over the top of the paper. The texture of the bark shows through.

4. Have the children incorporate their bark rubbing into a drawing. Let them choose any art medium they wish to finish their pictures—tempera paints, watercolors, crayons, markers, charcoals, colored pencils, chalks.

5. Display the bark rubbing pictures in the science area and the classroom library.

Something to think about
Younger children can actually break the bark into smaller pieces and glue it onto their pictures in a collage effect. Older artists might try experimenting with a variety of bark and leaf rubbings to add texture to their nature illustrations.

STORY STRETCHER

For Music And Movement: Papa's Bath

What the children will learn
To visualize sights and imagine sounds

Materials you will need
None needed

What to do
1. Read the scenes where Jenny and Papa follow Papa's path, and where Ray, Jenny and Papa walk together.

2. Have the children close their eyes and imagine a wooded area where they have walked.

3. Talk them through an imaginary walk.

4. Have them open their eyes and describe what they saw and felt.

5. Ask the children to take an imaginary walk and pretend they are little Jenny. Using the same type of language, add movement words. For example, tell the children the leaves are just budding and Jenny reaches up with her left hand to touch some leaves on a low limb. The children then pre-

tend they are touching one of the tiny new leaves.

6. Continue the imaginary walk. Use descriptive language and have the children walk around the room moving as if walking along a path in the woods.

Something to think about
Visual and kinesthetic imagery is a good relaxation technique. Use the technique at different times throughout the week to help youngsters relax when events at school have been stressful.

For Science And Nature: Listening Walk

What the children will learn
To discriminate between sounds of nature and people-made sounds

Materials you will need
None needed

What to do
1. Take a walk to a wooded area or back to the empty lot from THE EMPTY LOT story s-t-r-e-t-c-h-e-r for science and nature.

2. Have the children sit quietly and listen for sounds of insects. Try to pick out the sounds of insects from those of birds, of the wind blowing the leaves and grasses and from the people-made sounds of voices, machines and traffic.

3. Concentrate on the listening aspects of the walk in the woods.

Something to think about
Try different kinds of walks in addition to the listening walk. For example, have one walk where the emphasis is on touching and feeling many different textures, or on noticing the many different shades of greens and browns that occur in nature.

For Science And Nature: Cicadas And Other Insects

What the children will learn
To recognize insects in different stages of development

Materials you will need
Simple reference books

What to do
1. Look at the last page of WHEN THE WOODS HUM, which contains drawings of the different stages of the cidada life cycle.

2. Refer back to the story and notice when Jenny and Papa saw each stage of the insect's life.

3. Examine other simple reference books on insects and compare the stages of life, the egg, nymph and adult.

4. Invite an entomologist or a science teacher from a high school who has students interested in insects to bring specimens to the classroom for the children to examine through hand-held magnifying glasses.

Something to think about
If possible, ask that some specimens be left in the classroom in the science and nature display for children to examine and compare to the reference books.

For Writing Center: Science And Nature Learning Logs

What the children will learn
To record a new learning

Materials you will need
Science journals or paper, pencils, colored pencils

What to do
1. From reading WHEN THE WOODS HUM and looking at reference materials and examining specimens, the children will learn many new facts about insects. Ask them to record in their science and nature logs at least three new pieces of information they have learned.

2. They can add illustrations to help them recall the information.

Something to think about
Writing in their learning journals or learning logs should become a natural extension for all the science and nature story s-t-r-e-t-c-h-e-r-s. Try to keep science and nature logs as the places for factual information, rather than story writing or personal narratives.

I CARE ABOUT MY WORLD, THE ENVIRONMENT

THE GREAT KAPOK TREE
By Lynne Cherry

Children will enjoy the adventure and the suspense of this Gulliver-like story, an environmental message wrapped in a magical tale. A wood chopper falls asleep, and in his dream, the creatures of the rain forest whisper to him not to chop down their tree. The boa constrictor, the bee, a troupe of monkeys, a toucan, a tree frog, a jaguar, a tree porcupine, an anteater, a three-toed sloth whisper to the woodsman. In the end, a child from the Yanomamo tribe implores the man to spare their tree. Cherry's full-page illustrations make the rain forest plants and animals come to life. They provide such a rich visual experience that the children will want to look at the pictures again and again. The end papers are a map of the tropical rain forests of the world, bordered with small drawings of the insects and animals that inhabit them.

Read-Aloud Suggestions

Read the "author's note" at the beginning of the book which describes the Amazon rain forest. Then open the book to the end papers and show the children where the tropical rain forests are on the world map. They are highlighted in green. Read the story without pausing. Hand the book to a child who has not shown as much interest in reading as others have. Ask him or her to take the book to the classroom library and invite a friend to go along to look at the pictures more closely and see some of the animals which are camouflaged in the pictures.

STORY STRETCHER

For Art: Green-On-Green Collages

What the children will learn
To create collages

Materials you will need
Different shades of green construction paper, pencils, colored pencils, markers, crayons, chalks, glue sticks, scissors

What to do
1. Have the children look at Lynne Cherry's beautiful illustrations in THE GREAT KAPOK TREE. Call attention to the many shades of green and the way she showed the veins in leaves by darkening the ridges and the way she drew white around the edges. Have the children notice how the insects and animals sit on top of a mass of greenery.

2. Show the children the different shades of green construction paper.

3. Let them draw many different types of leaf patterns on the construction paper and draw some darker veins or highlight the edges with white.

4. Cut out enough leaves to completely cover a sheet of paper.

5. Glue the leaves in place and add any combination of flowers, insects, animals to the pictures, but use the greenery as background.

Something to think about
Avoid providing patterns for the leaves. Have the children notice how the leaves are turned, twisted and shaped so that there is no exact pattern.

STORY STRETCHER

For Classroom Library: Whispers To Senhor

What the children will learn
To use their voices expressively

Materials you will need
Chalkboard, chalk, cassette recorder, player, stapler, listening station, headphones

What to do
1. Make a list of all the insects and animals that whispered in the wood chopper's ear.

2. Let children volunteer to read the different parts. Write the volunteers' names beside the rain-forest creatures' names on the chalkboard.

3. Practice reading the whispers.

4. Assign another child to be responsible for recording the page-turning signal on cue: click a stapler near the microphone.

5. Record the book with you reading the narrative and the children reading what the insects, animals and child whispered in the ear of Senhor, the wood chopper.

6. Place the recording and the book in the classroom library at the listening station.

Something to think about
Be sure to include children in this small group experience who are reluctant readers. Practice their dia-

logue with them in private so that they are confident readers for the recording session.

STORY STRETCHER

For Science And Nature: What Is A Kapok Tree?

What the children will learn
To state facts about the kapok tree

Materials you will need
Chalkboard, chalk, reference books on plants

What to do
1. Read the "author's note" at the beginning of THE GREAT KA-POK TREE. Have the children re-state any facts which were stated or implied about the tree.

2. Read THE GREAT KAPOK TREE and add other facts to the list.

3. Look up the kapok tree in reference books and read the information aloud to the children.

4. Let the students tell you other information to add to the list.

5. At the end of the information-gathering session, let the children restate in their own words what they want to be sure to remember about the tree.

Something to think about
Find out if there is a botanical garden near you which has a kapok tree growing there. A plant special-ist may be willing to provide additional information. Better still, plan a visit to the garden.

ANOTHER STORY STRETCHER

For Science And Nature: Animals Of The Rain Forest

What the children will learn
To identify rain forest animals

Materials you will need
Chart tablet or posterboard, marker, learning log notebooks or index cards, pencils, optional—reference books

What to do
1. Read THE GREAT KAPOK TREE again.

2. Have a child list on a chart the different animals mentioned in the story.

3. Compare the large illustrations of those animals to the smaller ones on the borders of the tropical rainforest map of the world.

4. Look closely at the smaller animal illustrations and list other animals not mentioned in the story, such as the coati, the mous-tached tamarin and the kinkajou.

5. Look at reference books and find out more about these animals. Leave the reference materials on display for several days for the children to browse through.

6. Have each child write a few sentences about an animal they learned more about. These can be entries in their science and nature learning logs or index cards that they leave at the display for other children to read.

Something to think about
On other days, concentrate on in-sects of the rain forest and plants of the rain forest.

STORY STRETCHER

For Writing Center: Writing To Environmental Groups

What the children will learn
To compose a letter requesting information

Materials you will need
Sample letters, writing paper, pen-cils, chart tablet and marker or overhead projector and transparen-cies, envelopes, stamps

What to do
1. Work with children in small groups.

2. Read the acknowledgements section on the back of the title page of THE GREAT KAPOK TREE. The author expresses her appreciation to the World Wildlife Fund in Washington, DC.

3. Tell the children that the World Wildlife Fund provides ma-terials to students about their pro-jects, but to receive them, they must write a letter requesting infor-mation.

4. Read the children part of a friendly letter you have received and part of a business letter. Help them to hear the difference in lan-guage and expression.

5. Let each small group compose a letter. Be sure to state in the letter that the class has read THE GREAT KAPOK TREE by Lynne Cherry.

6. Either print the letters on chart tablet paper or write them on a transparency on the overhead pro-jector.

7. Reread the letters and let the children edit them with you.

8. Have volunteers print or write the finished letters from each small group. Mail the letters to World Wildlife Fund, 1250 24th Street, NW, Washington, DC 20037.

Something to think about
Consult with the librarian for the names and addresses of other envi-ronmental groups who will pro-vide information to primary age children.

I CARE ABOUT MY WORLD, THE ENVIRONMENT

FAREWELL TO SHADY GLADE

By Bill Peet

A favorite children's author, Bill Peet was ahead of his time when in 1966 he wrote the story of animals being misplaced by the encroaching city land developments. Shady Glade was a cluster of some trees along a creek and home to sixteen inhabitants, some rabbits, a pair of possums, a skunk, some frogs and a raccoon. When raccoon hears the rumble of machines stripping the land, he contrives a plan to move the small band of inhabitants to a safe place. Their moving adventure and discovery of a safe haven is the tale. The dialogue, intrigue and colored pencil illustrations take the listener through environmental concerns while moving the story to a happy ending.

Read-Aloud Suggestions

No doubt, Bill Peet books are well-known to your students. Help them recall other Bill Peet books. (See the list on the book jacket for reminders.) Ask the children why they like Bill Peet stories. Of course, they will mention how funny they are. Look at the cover of FAREWELL TO SHADY GLADE and let a child sitting near you count the number of animals. Ask who the leader is. Raccoon has his paw pointed in the air and all the animals are looking at him, so he is obviously the leader. Read the story and pause at three suspenseful points in the story for a child to make a prediction about what the animals may do to solve their problem. After reading the story, ask how this Bill Peet story is different from the other, funny ones.

STORY STRETCHER

For Art: Pollution Solutions

What the children will learn
To draw contrasts of environmental hazards and cleaned-up sites

Materials you will need
Drawing paper, colored pencils, crayons, markers, chalks, charcoals

What to do
1. Show the children the illustrations from FAREWELL TO SHADY GLADE. Tell them Bill Peet used colored pencils for his drawings. Look at the peaceful pictures of Shady Glade at the beginning of the book, and the polluted sites the animals saw from the top of the train and the open countryside.

2. Fold drawing paper in half like a greeting card.

3. Ask the children to draw a polluted scene on the front of their card and a pollution solution on the inside.

Something to think about
Young children may concentrate on the beauty of nature and draw a place where the animals would like to live. Older children can draw a series of pollution solution pictures which highlight environmental issues in their town.

STORY STRETCHER

For Classroom Library: Story Retelling

What the children will learn
To retell a story in their own words

Materials you will need
Optional—cassette tape and recorder

What to do
1. With a small group of children, look through the illustrations in FAREWELL TO SHADY GLADE.

2. Ask the children which pictures they like the most and why.

3. After they have discussed the story and the illustrations, let them retell the story in their own words. They can take turns with reading partners or tell the story in round robin fashion.

4. Do not emphasize exact dialogue but rather the children's own renditions of the story.

Something to think about
With first graders, it is often helpful for the teacher to take a turn after each child to keep the flow of the story. After they become more skilled at retelling, let the children work on their own and decide how they want to retell their stories. While it is not necessary to tape-record all the story retelling sessions, children often are more ex-

pressive and enthusiastic when they can hear themselves on tape.

For Creative Dramatics: The Animals' Journey

What the children will learn
To improvise actions to illustrate scenes

Materials you will need
Chalkboard, chalk

What to do
1. List the sixteen inhabitants of Shady Glade on the chalkboard.

2. Let volunteers decide which animal movements they would like to dramatize. List the children's names beside their choices.

3. Have the children sit together according to the animal roles they have selected.

4. Read the book again and let the children improvise movements which dramatize the animals' journey.

Something to think about
If you teach young children, lead the children in the movements, rather than just reading. If some students are reluctant to participate, let them be the audience.

For Science And Nature: Visiting A Shady Glade

What the children will learn
To think about the environmental needs of the animals, insects and plants that inhabit a shady glade

Materials you will need
None needed

What to do
1. Select a shady glade to visit. If you live in a city, you may find a park with a creek running through it.

2. Secure permission for the class to visit the shady glade. Get parental permission forms signed, arrange for volunteer helpers and involve the children in planning the excursion.

3. With small groups of children per volunteer, enjoy the natural surroundings.

4. Spend time observing what lives and grows in the shady glade. Try to identify some of the trees. If there are sycamore, willow or cottonwood trees there, point out that these trees were in Bill Peet's FAREWELL TO SHADY GLADE.

Something to think about
After returning to the classroom, discuss the area, what they saw and enjoyed. Talk about the surrounding area. Is it in the center of the city, or in the country? Is it in jeopardy of being destroyed? Do any birds and animals live there?

For Writing Center: What We Like About Our New Home

What the children will learn
To write from the animals' perspective

Materials you will need
Writing paper, pencils, art supplies for illustrations

What to do
1. Read again the section of FAREWELL TO SHADY GLADE where the animals leave the train when it stops for the rock slide.

2. Talk about what they liked about their new home.

3. Ask the children to select one animal from the group and write as if they were that animal, telling what they like about their new home.

4. Have the writers add illustrations to their writings.

5. Display their extensions of the story in the class library with a copy of FAREWELL TO SHADY GLADE.

Something to think about
Let older children form writing groups and write a group story with each child taking a different animal's part.

I CARE ABOUT MY WORLD, THE ENVIRONMENT

BROTHER EAGLE, SISTER SKY

By Chief Seattle

Illustrated by Susan Jeffers

Chief Seattle's inspirational words spoken in the 1850s provide the text for BROTHER EAGLE, SISTER SKY. The introduction tells about the occasion of Chief Seattle's profound words. The Indian's immortal words begin with, "How can you buy the sky?" Quoting his mother and his father, the Chief calls all things our brothers and sisters and ends by imploring us to preserve our world— our environment—for our children and our children's children. Jeffers' illustrations are magnificently alive, yet of a mythical quality. The full-color art is produced with fine-line pen and dyes.

Read-Aloud Suggestions

Practice reading Chief Seattle's words several times before reading the book aloud to the children. Prepare them for the reading by telling about the occasion for Chief Seattle's words. Read BROTHER EAGLE, SISTER SKY. At the end, let any child talk freely about the message in the Chief's words or about the illustrations. After a bit of discussion, share the information from the last page of the book, which explains that Susan Jeffers saw a PBS Bill Moyers television special in which Joseph Campbell read Chief Seattle's words on television.

STORY STRETCHER

For Art: Foreground Decoration

What the children will learn
To notice and use different foreground treatments to add perspective

Materials you will need
Drawing paper, crayons, markers, colored pencils

What to do
1. Have the children notice the many different ways Susan Jeffers illustrates the foreground of her paintings: letting the viewer look through a meadow of flowers, a spider's web, branches of trees, and reflections in the water.

2. Ask the children to tell about a scene from nature they would like to draw, then think of something they could draw in the foreground.

3. Provide the art materials and let the children work at their own pace, drawing any scene from nature they wish.

Something to think about
Young children may need to decorate with flowers or things cut out from construction paper and pasted onto their drawings, rather than draw over them to make a foreground focal point.

STORY STRETCHER

For Classroom Library: Chief Seattle's Words

What the children will learn
To repeat their favorite lines from Chief Seattle's message

Materials you will need
Cassette tape, recorder, listening station, headphones, writing paper, pencils

What to do
1. Invite a male friend or parent with an impressive voice to record Chief Seattle's words. Introduce the recording and, at the end, introduce who the reader was.

2. Have the children listen to the recording at the listening station with headphones.

3. Ask them what their favorite parts of Chief Seattle's speech were.

4. Reread the lines after each child makes a selection.

5. If some children want to remember parts of Chief Seattle's speech, let them copy the lines and read them into the tape recorder.

Something to think about
Consider making a talking mural. Let the children illustrate their version of BROTHER EAGLE, SISTER SKY on a long sheet of butcher paper. Place the tape recording of Chief Seattle's speech and their favorite parts under the mural. Then, while they are looking at their finished mural, they can play the words of the Chief.

For Science And Nature: Plant A Tree

What the children will learn
To plant a tree

Materials you will need
A sapling or larger tree for the entire class and enough seedlings for each child to have a tree, shovels, compost, watering can

What to do

1. Read BROTHER EAGLE, SISTER SKY again and talk about the differences between pictures of the Indians on their horses emerging from the forest and the barren forest land they see.

2. Invite a nursery owner or a forester to show the children how to plant a tree.

3. Let the children help by digging the hole, preparing the soil, helping to set the tree in place, filling around it and watering it.

4. Plan a tree planting ceremony with the class and let a child read Chief Seattle's words. Invite parents and school personnel.

5. Collect enough seedlings from one of the forestry organizations or a community group to give each child a tree.

6. Write a parent newsletter about the tree planting and ask the families to make the seedling planting a family ceremony.

Something to think about
There are many different science and nature possibilities for story s-t-r-e-t-c-h-e-r-s based on BROTHER EAGLE, SISTER SKY. The children could investigate endangered species of birds, animals and plants. They could walk through protected wetlands or animal and bird sanctuaries, visit a river that has been cleaned up or explore an unspoiled meadow. Help young children to appreciate nature and assist in projects where they can make a difference.

For Science And Nature: I Can Make A Difference

What the children will learn
To contribute to preserving rather than destroying the environment

Materials you will need
Reference books on ways children can save the earth

What to do

1. Read several of the "save the environment" books written for children and let the students make their own list of things they can do at home, such as turning the water off when brushing teeth, taking showers instead of baths, using cloth instead of paper napkins, recycling glass, paper and plastics.

2. After the children have finished their list of ways to make a difference at home, make a list of what can be done in the classroom. For example, use recyclables in art and craft projects, use scraps of construction paper, use milk cartons for planters, turn off lights when bright sunlight is all that is needed, collect materials for recycling centers.

3. Design environmental awareness posters and write brochures to teach younger children what they can do to make a difference.

4. Establish environmental monitors each week, like class helpers, to think of at least five ways the class is helping the environment.

Something to think about
It is important to design environmental projects for young children that are "do-able" and "sustainable." The one time campaign of "picking up litter" from around the school grounds is a good beginning, but children need to learn that taking care of the environment is a daily concern.

For Writing Center: Reading Response Journal

What the children will learn
To express their feelings in writing

Materials you will need
Writing paper or notebooks, pencils

What to do

1. Begin a series of writing story s-t-r-e-t-c-h-e-r-s which include children writing their responses to literature. BROTHER EAGLE, SISTER SKY is a wonderful one to begin with because it is so inspirational.

2. Ask the children to read the book on their own, then write a brief response to the book telling how it made them feel, what they thought about after they finished the book and their favorite scenes.

3. When several writers have finished their reading responses logs, let small groups share their written responses to BROTHER EAGLE, SISTER SKY.

4. End the reading session with each child finishing this phrase, "I wonder. . . . . ." For example, "I wonder what Chief Seattle would think about our town if he were alive today."

Something to think about
Reading response logs should be both routine and special. Children should routinely list the date and

what they read that day, including the selection's title and page as well as some response to the book or story: whether they liked it or not, what surprised them— whatever their responses. When a particularly inspiring story has been read aloud as a featured book in the classroom, this is the time for a special response.

References

Seattle, Chief. (1991). Illustrated by Susan Jeffers. **BROTHER EAGLE, SISTER SKY**. New York: Dial Books.

Cherry, Lynne. (1990). **THE GREAT KAPOK TREE**. San Diego: Harcourt Brace Jovanovich.

Fife, Dale H. (1991). Illustrated by Jim Arnosky. **THE EMPTY LOT**. Boston: Little, Brown and Company and Sierra Club Books.

Peet, Bill. (1966). **FAREWELL TO SHADY GLADE**. Boston: Houghton Mifflin.

Ryder, Joanne. (1991). Illustrated by Catherine Stock. **WHEN THE WOODS HUM**. New York: Morrow Junior Books.

Additional References for I Care About My World, The Environment

Arnosky, Jim. (1990). **CRINKLEROOT'S GUIDE TO WALKING IN WILD PLACES**. New York: Bradbury Press. *The mixture of information, amusing illustrations of Crinkleroot on his walk and careful drawings of plants and insects, make this a valuable resource for preparing to walk in the woods.*

Burningham, John. (1989). **HEY! GET OFF OUR TRAIN**. New York: Crown Publishers, Inc. *At bedtime, a young boy takes a trip on his toy train, which becomes something of a Noah's Ark for endangered animals.*

Dorros, Arthur. (1990). **RAINFOREST SECRETS**. New York: Scholastic, Inc. *The rainforest ecosystem is described in words that make us see, smell, hear and understand the delicate balance of plant and animal life living togther.*

Greene, Carol. (1991). Illustrated by Loretta Krupinski. **THE OLD LADIES WHO LIKED CATS**. New York: HarperCollins. *When the old ladies are no longer allowed to let their cats out at night, the delicate balance of their island ecology is upset. A timely message.*

Peet, Bill. (1970). **THE WUMP WORLD**. Boston: Houghton Mifflin Company. *This 1970 story of the lovable Wumps, whose world is being invaded by Pollutians, has a message which is just as urgent today.*

WEATHER

The Sun, the Wind and the Rain
Hurricane
The Winter Hedgehog
Ollie's Ski Trip
Time of Wonder

THE SUN, THE WIND AND THE RAIN

By Lisa Westberg Peters

Illustrated by Ted Rand

A first lesson in geology, the author compares Elizabeth's sand mountain she made on the beach to the one she can see on the horizon. Scientifically correct, the text is a story of what happens when the wind and the rain reshape Elizabeth's sand mountain in one afternoon and reshape the real mountain over eons of time. The full-page, full-color illustrations are bright and clear with the texture and perspective of beautiful landscape paintings.

Read-Aloud Suggestions

Show the children the cover of the book and point out the different land formations, of beach, meadow and mountain. Introduce the little girl in the yellow sun hat as Elizabeth and tell them that her sand mountain is like the snow-capped mountain in the background. Read THE SUN, THE WIND AND THE RAIN and show the illustrations while you read. Announce the story s-t-r-e-t-c-h-e-r-s associated with the book and emphasize the science activities and displays.

S T O R Y   S T R E T C H E R

For Art: Sand Painting

What the children will learn
To add texture to paintings

Materials you will need
Tempera paints or watercolors, brushes, paper, table, sand, salt shakers

What to do
1. Let the children mix colors to achieve the color they want for the beach.

2. Place the paper flat on the table.

3. Demonstrate how to use the sand in the paintings by making a long brush stroke with a "beach" color and, before it dries, shaking sand from the salt shaker onto the painting.

4. Ask the children to make their own beach paintings and use the sand to add texture.

Something to think about
The illustrations in THE SUN, THE WIND AND THE RAIN use perspective affectively to show the foreground, the horizon and the background. Spend time with the children looking at the pictures and noticing how the artist com-

posed them to help us see what Elizabeth is seeing.

S T O R Y   S T R E T C H E R

For Classroom Library: Yellow Sun Hat and Tape

What the children will learn
To read the story and listen for cues

Materials you will need
Cassette tape and recorder, bucket of sand, plastic shovel

What to do
1. With a small group of children, make a recording of THE SUN, THE WIND AND THE RAIN.

2. Ask one volunteer to make the page-turning signal by placing the microphone near the bucket of sand and, each time the page is turned, push the shovel into the sand to create a rasping, scratchy sound.

3. Plan an introduction to the tape with the "page signaller," telling the listener that the sound of the shoveling sand means to turn the page.

4. Record another version of the tape with the children taking turns whispering into the microphone, "Something is going to happen." Then at the end of the story, have them say together, "THE SUN, THE WIND AND THE RAIN."

Something to think about
First graders might take turns reading along with the teacher, while older children could each take turns reading the pages.

S T O R Y   S T R E T C H E R

For Mathematics: How Much Sand Equals How Many Pebbles?

What the children will learn
To measure and determine equivalencies

Materials you will need

Sand, pebbles, plastic sand pails, shovels, balance, newspapers, dry measuring cups, markers, large index cards

What to do

1. If the children have not used a balance before, place it in the mathematics area for a day or two and let them experiment with balancing objects from around the room.

2. Place the sand, pebbles, pails, shovels and balance together on a table covered with newspapers for easy clean-up.

3. Encourage the children to balance the scales by placing sand in one pail and pebbles in the other.

4. After they have balanced the scales, let the children measure the sand and count the pebbles.

5. Have them write their equations on a large index card, along with their names. For example, 1/4 cup of sand = 112 pebbles.

6. Discuss why the equations are different. Because the size of the pebbles and the amount of each shovelful of sand differ, there are many different equivalencies that can be measured by balancing the sides.

Something to think about

Outside in the sand area of the playground, let the children determine how many buckets of sand are needed to make a mountain as tall as they are.

STORY STRETCHER

For Science And Nature: The Effects Of The Elements

What the children will learn

To replicate Elizabeth's experiences with a science experiment

Materials you will need

Chart tablet, markers, sand table or large plastic child's swimming pool, sand, sticks, pebbles, buckets, shovels, watering cans, water, optional—fan

What to do

1. Read the story of THE SUN, THE WIND AND THE RAIN again.

2. Ask the children what they would need to make a mountain like Elizabeth's on the beach. Print their list on chart tablet paper.

3. Have the children volunteer to bring in some of the supplies or borrow equipment, such as a sand table from another teacher in the school.

4. Engage the children in helping to set up the equipment and materials.

5. Have volunteers build mountains of sand, complete with sticks to represent the trees and pebbles to symbolize the animals, just as Elizabeth did.

6. When the builders have finished, ask the "rain people" to pour water slowly from their water cans. Let the observers tell what is happening.

7. Stop the rain and let the children compare what they see to the illustrations in the book.

8. Begin again and turn the slow rain into a rainstorm; have the rain people dump all their water on top of the sand mountain. Again, pause and compare the results to the pictures in the book.

9. Continue building and raining on the mountain until all the children have had an opportunity to participate as either "builders" or "rain people."

10. With older children, set up an experiment with an electric fan blowing the sand and look at the effects of wind and erosion.

Something to think about

It is important that the science experiments be "hands-on" experiences for the children.

STORY STRETCHER

For Writing Center: Words From Observations

What the children will learn

To record their observations

Materials you will need

Chalkboard and chalk, notebooks, pencils, colored pens

What to do

1. Discuss with the children how scientists talk about their observations, just like they did when they conducted "The Effects Of The Elements" experiment.

2. Have the children recall what happened.

3. On the chalkboard, print what they say occurred.

4. After they have finished describing what they saw, go back over the list and let them decide what happened first, second, third, and so on.

5. Ask the children to write in their science journals anything they want to remember from the experiment, anything that surprised them, or a different experiment they would like to try. Some children may choose to draw their observations or plans.

Something to think about

Connect the science experiment with writing and emphasize that scientists write field notes and observations as well as writing about their discoveries or surprises.

HURRICANE

By David Wiesner

HURRICANE could be used for a unit on weather or trees. Two brothers and their cat prepare for and ride out a hurricane. When they awake the next morning, a large tree has been toppled in their neighbor's yard. The boys play in the tree and imagine it to be a jungle, a pirate ship and even a space ship. When the tree trimmers come to cut up the tree, the boys grieve for the loss of their great tree. Wiesner's illustrations are large, realistic paintings with wonderful perspectives looking through the branches of the tree.

Read-Aloud Suggestions

Tell about a favorite tree in your yard or one you remember from childhood. Talk about what made it special. Have a few children describe their favorite trees. Look at the title of the book, HURRICANE, and have the children predict what a hurricane might have to do with trees. Read the book and pause briefly before the tree trimmers arrive for the children to predict what will happen next. On another day, discuss weather safety at school and at home. Use as an example the most prevalent hazardous weather for your area—tornado, flood, hurricane. Look at the pictures of how the family prepared for the storm and discuss what precautions are taken at school and at home to insure safety.

STORY STRETCHER

For Art: Blowing Across The Picture

What the children will learn
To use techniques to create the effect of rain

Materials you will need
Manilla paper or construction paper, colored pencils, markers, white- colored pencil, chalk, plastic knives

What to do
1. Look at the illustrations of rain blowing across the windows on the cover of HURRICANE.

2. Have the children think of ways they could create the same effects, such as slashing the colored surface with knife strokes going in the same direction, or using white-colored pencil or a chalk edge to make slash marks.

3. Let the children experiment with techniques they choose to add rain to their pictures.

4. Ask the students to make weather pictures and add rain to their drawings or paintings.

Something to think about
Experimentation is a necessary first step to creativity. Encourage divergent thinking and alternate ways to reach the desired end.

STORY STRETCHER

For Classroom Library: Reporting The Weather

What the children will learn
To write, read and speak based on information collected from sources

Materials you will need
Newspapers, videotapes, optional—camera, videotape player

What to do
1. Ask parent volunteers to videotape some weather reports for a week. If they have a cable channel with a weather station, have them tape reports on different types of weather.

2. Listen to the weather reports for descriptive vocabulary.

3. Read the weather reports and forecasts from a local newspaper.

4. Select at least two weather reporters for the day and let one write the weather report, by reporting what children should wear to school, and what the weather will be like when they get out of school.

5. Let the second reporter write a weather forecast based on what was read in the local newspaper. Again, have the forecaster write about the weather according to children's interests: what they need to wear to school the next day; whether they will be able to play outside; and what the weather will be like after school.

6. Use the public address system of the school to let the weather re-

porter and the weather forecaster read their reports to the school.

Something to think about
If you have access to a videotape camera and recorder, tape the weather report. Place a videotape player near the cafeteria door and, as children are waiting in line, play the weather videotapes. Classes can take turns doing the weather reports.

For Mathematics: Charting Our Weather

What the children will learn
To make simple graphs

Materials you will need
Chart tablet or posterboard, marker, calendar, construction paper, scissors, glue

What to do
1. Select one weather recorder per week and three helpers.

2. At the opening of the school day, ask the weather recorder to tell what the weather is like outside and record it on the calendar by writing the words or drawing symbols for sunshine, clouds, rain, etc.

3. At the end of the week, begin a weather graph by writing the different types of weather along the baseline or bottom of a sheet of chart tablet paper or posterboard. Draw columns to separate the categories.

4. Let the three weather helpers work under the direction of the weather recorder. Cut seven construction paper squares, one for each day of the week.

5. Glue the paper squares on the appropriate column of the graph by looking at the calendar and counting how many days for each type of weather.

6. Ask the weather recorder and helpers to show their graph to the rest of the class and explain how they constructed it.

7. Select another weather recorder and helpers for the next week. Continue the process for at least a month.

Something to think about
For third graders, read weather reports from the newspaper and decide the different types of mathematics used in a weather reports, such as numbers in temperatures, decimals in amount of rainfall, percentages in chance of rain.

For Science And Nature: Trees And Weather

What the children will learn
To observe the effects of weather on trees

Materials you will need
Note pads, pencils

What to do
1. Plan to look at trees throughout the month. As the weather changes, have children look out the windows or go outside and observe changes in the trees.

2. Designate two tree watchers to alert the class to changes in weather that may effect changes in the trees.

3. Begin by observing the trees when the wind is still.

4. Ask the children to either write or draw in their science logs or field notes, what they see happening to trees as the weather changes.

5. Continue the observations and field notes during different weather conditions. Note leaf changes, bark changes, movement and leaf or needle loss.

Something to think about
Use an "adopt a tree" approach and have small groups of children observe different kinds of trees. Compare notes and drawings. With younger children, take instant print pictures of the trees.

For Writing Center: My Big Tree

What the children will learn
To use the imaginary scenes in the book to prompt their own writing

Materials you will need
Writing paper, writing folders, pencils, markers or colored pens

What to do
1. Read the end of the book jacket where the author tells the source of his inspiration for the story—some scary weather and the big tree he enjoyed as a child.

2. If you have trees in the school yard or nearby, take small groups of children outside and look up through the branches of the trees.

3. Talk about tree climbing, tree houses and feelings about trees.

4. Back in the classroom, with small groups of children, recall big trees they have enjoyed.

5. Ask the children to write about real trees and their feelings and memories of them, or write an imaginary tale of what it would be like to be George and David pretending in the limbs of the fallen tree.

Something to think about
Let third graders write the story from Hannibal the cat's point of view.

THE WINTER HEDGEHOG

By Ann and Reg Cartwright

The smallest hedgehog is determine to stay awake and find out for himself what happens during the winter when all the other hedgehogs are hibernating. Despite his mother's warnings, he sets out to find winter. He observes changes in animal and bird behavior and continues his search. Then one morning he finds the beauty and peril of winter after a snowstorm. Hedgehog's adventure continues when he is accidentally rolled into a snowball by some children. In the end, while his family is awakening from their long winter's nap, the smallest hedgehog drops off into a deep sleep. The illustrations are bright and colorful with amber, browns and sharp contrasts in the winter scenes.

Read-Aloud Suggestions

Read a brief description of hedgehogs from an encyclopedia or an informational book about animals. Be certain to read about their hibernation, and let the children discuss what hibernation means. Show the cover of the book, THE WINTER HEDGEHOG. Based on the earlier information and discussion of hedgehogs as animals that hibernate, let the children decide if the title is a contradiction. Read THE WINTER HEDGEHOG through from beginning to end without pausing for predictions.

STORY STRETCHER

For Art: Thumbprint Animals

What the children will learn
To use a focal point and build a picture around it

Materials you will need
Inked stamp pad; paper towels; choice of markers, crayons, colored pencils or charcoals; manilla paper or white construction paper

What to do
1.   Press a thumb onto the inked stamp pad, then roll the thumb print onto a piece of paper.

2.   Let the children make their own thumbprints.

3.   Look at the thumbprints and notice the lines. Let the children think of animals the thumbprints remind them of: mouse or hamster fur, porcupine quills or coarse hedgehog fur.

4.   Ask the children to make a thumbprint hedgehog and draw a scene around their character.

5.   Display the thumbprint hedgehogs in the classroom library.

Something to think about
Cut 5 x 8 inch index cards into two inch widths, and let the children make hedgehog thumbprints and a small sketch on these strips. Laminate the card strips, punch a hole in the bottom and tie a piece of brightly colored yarn through the hole. These make great bookmarks!

ANOTHER STORY STRETCHER

For Art: Contrasting Views, Beauty And Danger

What the children will learn
To contrast with paints and color

Materials you will need
Tempera paints, brushes, white and gray construction paper, salt shaker, optional—easel

What to do
1.   Look through the illustrations from THE WINTER HEDGEHOG and point out the contrasting views of the "beautiful winter" and the "danger of winter."

2.   Notice the colors of the sky when Hedgehog is enjoying winter's beauty and when he is scared and understands his mother's description of winter as a dangerous time.

3.   Let the children paint their contrasting winter scenes to depict Hedgehog's "beautiful winter" and "dangerous winter."

4.   Remove the paintings from the easel to a flat table top.

5.   Demonstrate how to shake salt onto the wet paintings. When it drys it looks like it is snowing.

6.   Let the children make their salt snowstorms and then leave them to dry overnight.

Something to think about
Give children a choice of making contrasting Hedgehog pictures or their own interpretations of winter from their experiences.

For Classroom Library: Reading Dialogue

What the children will learn
To read dialogue and pause for narrator's speech

Materials you will need
Cassette tapes, recorder, listening station, headphones

What to do
1. With seven children, one for each character, plan how to read the book so that each child speaks the lines of the animal characters. You read the other words, much like a narrator.

2. Let the children practice their lines.

3. Rehearse the story reading several times.

4. Have one child introduce the tape by telling the listener to turn to the title page where the three yellow flowers are growing out of the snow. Also ask the child to say the word "turn" into the microphone whenever you give the cue. This becomes the page-turning signal for the listeners.

5. Record the book with the children reading dialogue on one side, and on the other side, record yourself reading the entire text.

Something to think about
When young readers listen to a tape and read along in the book, they have the added experience of linking auditory and visual modalities.

For Science And Nature: Hedgehog Visits The Animals

What the children will learn
To learn the names of animals' homes and classify the animals which hibernate

Materials you will need
Chart tablet or posterboard, marker, animal resource books, children's encyclopedia, large index cards, tape, pencils, colored pencils

What to do
1. On a sheet of chart tablet paper or posterboard, print the question, "Where could Hedgehog go in the storm?"

2. Look at the picture of Hedgehog snug and warm in Rabbit's burrow. Discuss the effects of weather on animal life.

3. Have the children list other animals that hibernate and tell where Hedgehog could go to sleep through the winter storm, such as the bear's cave, the squirrel's nest, the fox's den, the beaver's dam.

4. After you have begun the chart, let the children come to the science and nature center at their leisure and research other animal homes where Hedgehog could go.

5. On the index cards, ask children to write or draw additional places for Hedgehog to sleep through the winter storm and to tape these onto the chart tablet.

6. After a few days of information gathering, classify the animals by the ones that hibernate through the winter and those that do not.

Something to think about
Read more about hedgehogs and determine what they eat, how they reproduce, the dangers in their environment, and what their lives are like during the remaining seasons of the year, during different weather conditions.

For Writing Center: What Is Winter?

What the children will learn
To write contrasting descriptions

Materials you will need
Chalkboard, chalk, writing paper, pencils, choice of crayons, markers or colored pencils

What to do
1. Show the children the illustrations of cold, shivering Hedgehog trudging through the snowstorm and warm, snug Hedgehog safe in Rabbit's burrow.

2. Ask for descriptions of the illustration of Hedgehog in the snowstorm. Tell how he is feeling physically and emotionally as well as what he is seeing and thinking at the time.

3. Draw a line down the middle of the chalkboard, and on the left side, list the key words which the children use to describe Hedgehog in the winter storm.

4. Repeat the process and have the children describe Hedgehog when he is safe in Rabbit's burrow.

5. Write key words from the children's descriptions on the right side of the chalkboard.

6. Read over the lists and compare the descriptions.

7. Ask the children to fold their writing papers in half and write about contrasting events or feelings from the story or from their own experiences.

Something to think about
Suggest that some children might like to write a new Hedgehog adventure contrasting his family's winter and his winter.

OLLIE'S SKI TRIP

By Elsa Beskow

For his sixth birthday, Ollie receives his first real pair of skis. OLLIE'S SKI TRIP is the story of his waiting for the first snow and an imaginary skiing adventure to meet King Winter, accompanied by Jack Frost. Along the way, Mrs. Thaw threatens their beautiful winter scene. Ollie and his brother plead with Mrs. Thaw to stay away so they can ski and skate longer. Eventually, spring arrives, and they delight in the change of season while recalling their winter fun. Elsa Beskow's magical tale is charmingly illustrated with pictures large enough for the whole class to view.

Read-Aloud Suggestions

Show the children the cover of OL-LIE'S SKI TRIP and ask them to predict if this story is reality or fantasy. If you live in an area where there is skiing, invite the children to talk about their skiing experiences. Recall a present you received as a child and how hard it was to wait to use it. For example, you may have received a bicycle and could not ride it until the weather was nice out. Tell the children this is the story of Ollie and it begins with a present. Read OL-LIE'S SKI TRIP without pausing for the children to talk about the story. At the end, discuss the different types of weather and how they affected Ollie and his little brother. If interest continues, let volunteers retell the story by looking at the pictures.

STORY STRETCHER

For Art: Icicle Drip Prints

What the children will learn
To create a pattern of irregular shapes

Materials you will need
Long strips of colored poster-board, margarine tubs with water, ink pen, construction paper, scissors, glue, optional—eyedropper, colored pens, markers

What to do
1. Place colored posterboard flat on a table.

2. Dip a fingertip into water and let a drop of water drip down onto the posterboard, like a dripping icicle. Or if it is wintertime, use a real icicle. Hold it, and the warmth of the child's hand will melt the icicle into water drops.

3. Make a pattern of drops by moving either finger or hand.

4. Let the water drops dry overnight without moving them. The water will bleach out irregular shapes.

5. Draw around the water drop shapes with an ink pen.

6. Mat with contrasting or complementary shades of construction paper.

Something to think about
Invite a chef or caterer to carve an ice centerpiece for the children to enjoy.

STORY STRETCHER

For Creative Dramatics: Ollie's Friends

What the children will learn
To match visual and verbal cues

Materials you will need
Winter clothes, long coats, mittens, hats, real or pretend skis, skates, sleds, long cotton dress, apron, broom, paper bags

What to do
1. With the children who are interested in drama, look through the illustrations of OLLIE'S SKI TRIP and decide how many different characters they can portray.

2. Let the creative dramatics enthusiasts collect from home the clothing and props they will need to portray the characters.

3. Have the children separate the clothing and props for each character into paper bags.

4. At a whole class gathering, have the drama students dress up like their characters and parade around in a circle, pantomiming their characters' actions in the story.

5. Have the class guess the characters' identities.

6. If the class is having difficulty, let the characters tell some-

thing about themselves from the story.

Something to think about
Dressing up in costume helps many shy children because they have a disguise. Including children from the beginning in planning the event, gathering the props and dramatizing their characters also builds their confidence. On another day, let the characters act out the story by improvising as you read the book aloud.

For Music And Movement: Skater's Waltz

What the children will learn
To move in response to the rhythm of a waltz

Materials you will need
Recording of waltz music, cassette or record player

What to do
1. With the children sitting in a circle on the floor, listen to the recording of waltz music. Talk with them about how people often skate to music.

2. Let the children feel the music and begin to sway back and forth to the rhythm.

3. Skate around the room, picking up one foot and then the other, pretending to glide across the ice.

4. Invite a few children at a time to join you until all are up and skating.

Something to think about
If you have an ice skating rink near you, consider taking the children there and asking an instructor and some of his or her students to demonstrate some of the beginning skating moves. Ask skaters who are near the age of your students to be the ones to show your children how to skate.

For Science And Nature: Freezing And Thawing

What the children will learn
To observe changes in water forms

Materials you will need
Plastic pitcher, paper cups, trays, posterboard, marker, timer, refrigerator

What to do
1. Let each child pour water into a paper cup.

2. Place the cups in the freezer section of the refrigerator.

3. Make a chart on posterboard: on the left side, starting at the bottom, write down nearest half-hour, for example, 8:30. Then add the subsequent hour intervals for the next six hours, for example, 9:30, 10:30, etc.

4. Set a timer or alarm clock to ring every hour at the times you have printed on the posterboard.

5. When the timer rings, have the children touch the water in their cups and describe what it is like.

6. Write the descriptions on the posterboard across from the time. For example: 8:30—water lukewarm; 9:30—very cold, some ice crystals around the edge; 10:30—sheet of ice floating on the top; etc.

7. The next day reverse the process. Take the cups of frozen water from the refrigerator and observe them every hour until they are completely thawed out. Write the observations on the posterboard.

Something to think about
Make frozen drink popsicles for a cooking activity and serve as a snack treat.

For Writing Center: A Fairy Tale

What the children will learn
To write a fantasy story

Materials you will need
Writing paper, pencils, choice of materials for illustration

What to do
1. With small groups of writers, read the "about the author section" of OLLIE'S SKI TRIP. Talk with the children about Elsa Beskow's favorite type of story, the fairy tale.

2. Discuss OLLIE'S SKI TRIP and the characteristics of the story that make it a fairy tale. There are imaginary characters, a king—a magic fairy princess who brought spring, little people working in the King Winter's workshop making winter toys, and so on.

3. Brainstorm with the children about characters they would like in a fantasy story.

4. Ask the children to draw a picture with some characters they would like for a fantasy story.

5. Have partners talk with each other about their pictures. When they begin to think of things these characters might do, suggest they begin writing.

6. Continue the writing and editing process for those children who want to bind their stories into books. (See the Introduction for more information on the writing process and the Appendix for directions for binding a book.)

Something to think about
Primary age children often compose best when working from their drawings to their writing.

WEATHER

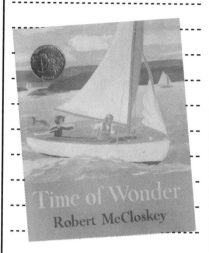

TIME OF WONDER

By Robert McCloskey

This Caldecott Medal book is the story of a summer in Maine, and the weather and change of seasons that controlled the family's activities, such as rowing, sailing, swimming and playing on the beach. The lull of long, lazy summer days is captured beautifully in the lyrical text and illustrations. The surprise of the hurricane and the family's departure adds drama to the ending. The book is excellent to read aloud.

Read-Aloud Suggestions

Before the read-aloud time, give the book to two children and ask them to look at the pictures without reading the words. At story time, have the two children take turns telling their story based on the illustrations. After the storytellers have finished, let the listeners decide what a good title for the story would be. Tape a piece of paper over the title of the book. Read McCloskey's story and, at the end, let the children again decide what a good title might be. After they have selected a title, uncover the title, TIME OF WONDER, and ask which title they prefer and why.

STORY STRETCHER

For Art: A Watercolor Weather Picture

What the children will learn
To paint with wet and dry brush techniques

Materials you will need
Watercolors, brushes, margarine tubs filled with water, scraps of paper, construction paper or watercolor paper, paper towels

What to do
1. Explain that the Caldecott Medal as an award given for excellence in illustrating. Look at the pictures in TIME OF WONDER and have the children discuss which scenes they like.

2. Examine the ocean scenes more closely and look at how McCloskey illustrated the waves and highlighted white caps.

3. Demonstrate how to paint with wet brushes and wet paints as well as dry brush strokes. Also, show the children how to roll the ends of their brushes in the paint to create a point, how to fan the brush out and how to spatter paint with the brushes.

4. Let the children experiment with the strokes on scraps of paper.

5. Let interested children paint watercolor scenes of weather or the ocean for display in the classroom library.

Something to think about
Watercolors are not an easy medium, yet children enjoy them because of the unpredictability of how the colors will flow. Emphasize the experience, rather than their finished product.

STORY STRETCHER

For Classroom Library: Partner Stories From Pictures

What the children will learn
To compose stories prompted by illustrations

Materials you will need
Variety of books about weather, cassette tapes, recorder, stapler

What to do
1. Remind a small group of children in the library corner of the two storytellers at read-aloud time who told a story based on the pictures in TIME OF WONDER.

2. Look through the weather books collected in the classroom library and let partners decide on a book they would like to tell a story about.

3. Allow the partners some time to look through their books and decide what they want to say.

4. Record the storytellers on one side of each tape. Be sure to include a page-turning signal, like the clicking of a stapler.

5. On the other side of each tape, ask a few parents or adults in the school to record the printed version of the weather books. Older

children also enjoy making tapes for younger ones.

Something to think about
Randomly assign partners by drawing names, or use children who are often partners. Do not always let children choose partners because it harms the self-esteem of children who are consistently not chosen or the last to be chosen.

ANOTHER STORY STRETCHER

For Classroom Library: Vacation In Maine, Word Study

What the children will learn
To determine the meaning of vocabulary words from the context of the story

Materials you will need
Chart tablet, markers

What to do
1. Read a few pages of TIME OF WONDER and ask the children if they heard any words that are new to them. Print the words on the chart tablet. Examples from the first few pages are bay, bayberry, cove, cormorants.

2. Read the paragraphs where these words occur and ask the children to guess what the words might mean.

3. Continue throughout the book, pausing every few pages to add to the list and letting the children predict the word meanings.

4. At the end, read back over the list and let children volunteer to tell each word's meaning or when the word appears in the story—when the children were playing on the beach, sailing, during the storm, etc.

Something to think about
It is important for beginning readers and listeners to know that they can figure out the meaning of words from the context. We want children to expect to get the meanings. Encourage the readers to skip a word if they do not know it and continue reading. When they finish the story, they can go back and look at the word and decide what it might mean. We want children to understand that there are many new words that they may not know because they do not live in Maine or in a fishing and boating community.

STORY STRETCHER

For Construction Project: Sailboats On Penobscot Bay

What the children will learn
To follow directions to construct a sailboat

Materials you will need
Flats of wood approximately 5 x 8 inches, triangles of fabric approximately 5 x 8 inches, scissors, wooden dowels or tongue depressors or large plastic straws, popsicle sticks, carpenter's glue, tacks, hammers, pencil, posterboard, tape, water table or child's plastic swimming pool

What to do
1. Ask a parent volunteer to cut the flats of wood, or if you have a woodworking bench in your school, let the children saw their own wood with adult supervision. As an alternative, cut pieces from styrofoam meat trays.

2. Attach the mast to the sailboat by tacking the dowel or tongue depressor in place. Add a drop of carpenter's glue to hold the mast firmly. Allow to dry overnight.

As an alternative, staple a large plastic straw onto the meat tray by bending the straw and stapling the end. Insert a pencil in the straw to make it stand upright.

3. Make a posterboard pattern of the sail.

4. Place the pattern on a piece of fabric and draw around the posterboard. Cut out the sail.

5. Attach the fabric sail to the mast by stapling the top end of the fabric to the top of the mast and the bottom of the fabric to the bottom of the mast, leaving the fabric loose to billow in the middle. If desired, roll a popsicle stick in the bottom of the sail and staple fabric over it to hold it taut. An alternative is to make the sail from construction paper, punch a hole in the top and bottom of the sail and slip it over the plastic straw mast. Place tape at the top of the sail to keep it from slipping off.

6. Float the boats on Penobscot Bay—the water table or a child's swimming pool.

Something to think about
Name your project for a body of water near your school. If possible, take a field trip there, and ask someone who has a sailboat anchored there or in dry dock to give the children a tour of their vessel.

STORY STRETCHER

For Writing Center: Remembering The Fog

What the children will learn
To create a mood by describing the fog

Materials you will need
Chalkboard, chalk, writing paper, pencils, optional—art supplies

What to do

1. Look again at the illustrations of the children walking through the woods in the fog.

2. Have children recall when they have been in fog and how it made them feel.

3. Ask the children to remember their fog experiences and write about them or about another weather condition that surprised them.

4. Let the children who are interested in editing their pieces for publication continue with the writing process. (See the Introduction about the steps in the writing process.)

5. Publish the children's stories in individual books or in a collection of stories about different weather conditions. (See the Appendix for an illustration of how to bind a book.)

Something to think about

Just as not all art work is something children want to take home to be framed, not all stories are worthy of rewriting, editing and publishing. Help children judge which of their pieces of writing they want to take to the next level and refine.

References

Beskow, Elsa. (1989). **OLLIE'S SKI TRIP**. Edinburgh: Floris Books.

Cartwright, Ann & Reg. (1989). **THE WINTER HEDGEHOG**. New York: Macmillan.

McCloskey, Robert. (1957). **TIME OF WONDER**. New York: Viking Penguin.

Peters, Lisa Westberg. (1988). Illustrated by Ted Rand. **THE SUN, THE WIND AND THE RAIN**. New York: Henry Holt and Company.

Wiesner, David. (1990). **HURRICANE**. New York: Clarion Books.

Additional References for Weather

Carrick, Carol. (1974). **LOST IN THE STORM**. Illustrated by Donald Carrick. New York: Clarion Books. *Christopher has spent the day on an island, visiting his friend Gray. It begins to rain, and the storm is raging before Christopher realizes that his dog has not come back with them from the beach. What will happen to the dog in the storm?*

Good, Elaine W. (1990). **FALL IS HERE! I LOVE IT!** Illustrated by Susie Shenk Wenger. Intercourse, PA: Good Books. *A book to help children recognize the weather changes which mean that fall is here.*

Good, Elaine W. (1989). **IT'S SUMMERTIME!** Illustrated by Susie Shenk Wenger. Intercourse, PA: Good Books. *Summer weather means hot sunny days and sudden thunderstorms and ripening crops.*

Lyons, George Ella. (1990). **COME A TIDE**. Illustrated by Stephen Gammell. New York: Orchard Books. *It rains and rains one spring in the Kentucky mountains, causing a flood, and when it's over, everyone helps clean up.*

Stevenson, James. (1988). **WE HATE RAIN!** *Grandpa tells Mary Ann and Louie all his tall tales about the big rains when he was young, and by the time he is finished, the rain has stopped!*

MACHINES AND THINGS

The Magic School Bus at the Waterworks

The Mouse and the Motorcycle

The Neighborhood Trucker

The Caboose Who Got Loose

Stay Away From the Junkyard!

MACHINES AND THINGS

THE MAGIC SCHOOL BUS AT THE WATERWORKS

By Joanna Cole

Illustrated by Bruce Degen

Mrs. Frizzle and her strange clothes and shoes are an embarrassment to her students. She has the children conduct strange science experiments and read five science books a week. But the magic of her teaching is what happens when they take the magic school bus on a trip to the waterworks. To prepare for the trip, the children investigate exactly how their city gets their water. Degen's illustrations are uproariously funny including inserts of children's hand-written notes on what they are learning.

Read-Aloud Suggestions

Without showing the cover of the book, turn to the title pages and have the children look at Ms. Frizzle and the students' expressions. Read the book from beginning to end. After reading, turn to the back of the book and read the "Notes from the Author: For Serious Science Students Only." Discuss how the author used fact and fantasy to communicate the main points about the need for water conservation.

STORY STRETCHER

For Art: Mural Of The Water Cycle

What the children will learn
To recall the steps in the water cycle

Materials you will need
Chalkboard, chalk, tables, butcher paper, tape, markers or tempera paints, brushes

What to do
1. With the children, recall all the steps in the water cycle. Let children check the book as a reference.

2. Print the steps on the chalkboard.

3. Have children volunteer to illustrate each step in the water cycle. Write their names beside the steps.

4. Place tables end to end, stretching across the classroom. Lay butcher paper across the tables and tape it so that it does not move.

5. Have the illustrators talk about what they will draw, starting with the cloud. Go down the line with each child explaining the point he or she will illustrate.

6. Let the children take turns working on the mural so they can share the art supplies.

7. When the mural is finished, display it in the classroom for a few days for the children to admire their art work and scientific knowledge.

8. Take the mural down and let the children add captions to their work, explaining the water cycle.

9. Display the mural with captions outside the classroom in the hallway for other children to enjoy.

Something to think about
An alternative for the mural is to have the children make self-portraits of themselves inside raindrops.

STORY STRETCHER

For Classroom Library: Informational Books About Water

What the children will learn
To collect interesting facts about water

Materials you will need
Chart tablet, marker, resource books and pamphlets on water conversation and the environment, large index cards or Post-it notes, tape

What to do
1. Look at the illustration of the children in the library collecting information about water. Read the cartoon bubbles of the children's comments.

2. Have the children dictate for you to write down at least ten water facts they learned from the book.

3. Ask the children to confirm the facts they learned in THE MAGIC SCHOOL BUS AT THE WATERWORKS by finding them in at least one other resource book.

4. Let the children decide how they will keep track of where they found the "confirming facts." They can record the source on an

index card or a Post-it note and tape it to the chart tablet list.

5. When the ten facts which interest them most have been confirmed, start another chart for information they learned while reading to confirm the water facts.

Something to think about
For younger children who do not yet read well enough to scan reference materials, plan to read from several resource books and ask them to recall whether or not this information was found in THE MAGIC SCHOOL BUS AT THE WATERWORKS.

STORY STRETCHER

For Mathematics: Measuring Water Consumption

What the children will learn
To equate water usage to quantities of water

Materials you will need
Chart tablet or posterboard, marker, measuring cups, gallon pitchers, two dishpans

What to do
1. Close the drain on the wash basin in the classroom.

2. Place the plastic dishpan in the basin. Have a child wash his or her hands, leaving the water running.

3. Then pour the water from the dishpan into the measuring pitchers.

4. Measure and record how much water was used.

5. Repeat the process, but this time have the child wash his or her hands by turning the water on to get hands wet, off while soaping and scrubbing, back on to rinse and off again while drying hands.

6. Measure and record the amount of water in the dishpan.

7. Compare the difference in amounts.

Something to think about
Continue the discussion and record household water usage per child for flushing toilets, showers, baths and hand washing. (Household usage idea adapted from Amy Cwalina, student teacher, George Mason University.)

STORY STRETCHER

For Science And Nature: We Are Plumbers

What the children will learn
To fit plastic plumbing pipes

Materials you will need
Plastic pipes, pipe wrenches, nuts

What to do
1. Invite a parent who is a plumber, or someone who enjoys working with his or her hands, to come to class and demonstrate how plumbers fit pipes together and test for water pressure.

2. Leave the plastic pipes and fittings on the science display table for the children to practice assembling.

3. Inspect the plumbing around the school, looking for different pipe materials and checking for leaks.

4. Have the plumber bring samples of water saving devices that can be installed at home and at school, such as aerators for faucets, dams for toilets and water-saving shower heads.

Something to think about
If a professional plumber comes to the class as one of the community helpers, let the children look inside the plumber's truck or van to see all the equipment needed to do the work.

ANOTHER STORY STRETCHER

For Science And Nature: Trip To The Waterworks

What the children will learn
To name the various parts of the water purification and pumping system

Materials you will need
Instant print camera

What to do
1. Visit the waterworks yourself and find out if it would be a good field trip for your class.

2. Follow the field trip requirements for your school for scheduling, securing parental permissions and making transportation arrangements.

3. Meet with parent volunteers who will accompany the class on the field trip, and have them read THE MAGIC SCHOOL BUS AT THE WATERWORKS.

4. Let the children tell the parents what they learned about water, water conservation and the waterworks from the story s-t-r-e-t-c-h-e-r activities.

5. Have three children tell about the water cycle mural.

6. Let the parents take some of the water resource books home with them to read so they can answer children's questions and can point out parts of the water purification and pumping system for the water supply.

Something to think about
For younger children, let the plumber help them set up a pumping system and large purification bowls to show them how the system works. Also invite a tropical fish store owner to set up an aquarium and demonstrate water pumping and purification on a smaller scale.

8
MACHINES AND THINGS

THE MOUSE AND THE MOTORCYCLE

By Beverly Cleary

Illustrated by Louis Darling

On vacation, Keith's toy motorcycle becomes a real motorcycle for Ralph, the mouse. Their attempt to keep the secret from the people and the mice in the story leads to intrigue. Ralph, usually a timid mouse, feels very brave riding the motorcycle. He has his bravery tested when he risks his life to deliver an aspirin to Keith's room and saves the boy from the ravages of a high fever. The book is written in thirteen chapters, which can be read over the course of a week. Besides the color illustration on the cover, there are two or three pen and ink sketches per chapter.

Read-Aloud Suggestions

THE MOUSE AND THE MOTORCYCLE is a good first chapter book for reading aloud to primary age children. Cleary describes the characters, settings and actions so vividly that the children's attention is sustained over the days needed to finish the book. Discuss chapter books and how you will read them. You will read the story throughout the week, and each day the children can predict what will happen next, but they will have to wait until the next day to find out. On the first day, read the first three chapters and let several students predict what will happen next. Each day before reading, let one or two children describe what happened the previous day to remind the class and to inform any child who was absent.

STORY STRETCHER
For Art: Playdough Machines

What the children will learn
To model motorcycles or other machines

Materials you will need
Playdough, plastic knives, styrofoam meat trays, optional—modeling clay

What to do
1. Read again the section of chapter two that tells about how the motorcycle looked to Ralph, the mouse.

2. Ask the children to sculpt motorcycles they would like to ride. Be sure to emphasize that they can be modeled on real or imaginary machines.

3. Each day for the read-aloud session, place some of the motorcycle models on a low table or on the floor near you while you read more of THE MOUSE AND THE MOTORCYCLE.

Something to think about
Do not assign children to do the art work, but instead encourage those who are interested to design their machines.

ANOTHER STORY STRETCHER
For Art: Scroll A Story

What the children will learn
To illustrate the main events

Materials you will need
Butcher paper, scissors, paper towel rolls, markers, masking tape

What to do
1. Talk with the children about how this book is different from other books you have read to them. They will not hear the whole story in one day, but instead it will unfold in a sequence of events over the course of a week.

2. Discuss how the book is different in another way. There are not very many pictures in the book.

3. Assign three children each day as illustrators.

4. After the read-aloud session, have them meet together and name at least three main events that happened in the day's chapters.

5. Ask each child to illustrate a different main event. They can draw their pictures on butcher paper. (The pictures are all on one continuous piece of butcher paper.)

6. Mark the space for each illustration by placing masking tape at the beginning and end of their scenes.

7. After the entire book has been read and all the main event scenes have been illustrated, tape the end of the butcher paper to a paper towel roll and roll the entire story scroll onto it.

8. Tape the edge of the beginning scene onto another paper towel roll.

9. Let the artists be the first children to retell the story by rolling the scroll from one paper towel roll onto the other.

10. Store the picture scroll in the classroom library.

Something to think about
Some teachers frame the picture scroll by cutting a television screen from the top of a heavy cardboard box, placing round holes in the top for the towel rolls and letting the children roll the picture scroll across the television screen.

STORY STRETCHER

For Classroom Library: Predictions

What the children will learn
To predict what will happen in the next chapter based on the events read each day

Materials you will need
Chart tablet or posterboard, marker, cassette tape, recorder

What to do
1. Make a chart listing the chapters you will read on each day.

2. Read the first three chapters on the first day. After the reading, write four or five children's names beside the chapters.

3. Ask the children whose names are on the chart to come with you to the library.

4. Ask them to retell what happened in the chapters you read.

5. Then turn on the tape recorder and let each child make a prediction about what will happen in tomorrow's reading.

6. Continue the process with different children each day until the end of the reading.

Something to think about
If time allows, each day before the read-aloud session, play the short tape of the children's predictions, then read the book and confirm whether or not the children were right. A variation on this activity is to have the children recall something in each chapter that surprised them.

ANOTHER STORY STRETCHER

For Classroom Library: Reading Response Log

What the children will learn
To write their responses to the day's reading

Materials you will need
Writing paper, construction paper, pencils, colored pencils

What to do
1. Teach children about reading response logs by modeling them with your read-aloud session of THE MOUSE AND THE MOTORCYCLE.

2. Make a large version of a reading response log by turning a chart tablet into the Big Book Response Log.

3. Each day write a class entry on the large chart tablet.

4. After a few days, have the children begin their own reading response logs by writing a sentence or two about what happened in the story. Later add other ways of responding, such as what surprised them, what they think will happen next, or a particularly vivid scene that the author expressed really well.

Something to think about
For first and second graders, begin with them writing what happened in the story. Some children may prefer to draw a small scene and add a caption.

STORY STRETCHER

For Writing Center: What If?

What the children will learn
To construct other Keith and Ralph stories

Materials you will need
Chalkboard, chalk, writing paper, pencils, art supplies for illustrations

What to do
1. After you have finished reading THE MOUSE AND THE MOTORCYCLE, ask what might happen if Ralph had decided to take Keith up on his offer to come and live with him in San Francisco.

2. Let the children begin to brainstorm story ideas.

3. Write key words from those ideas on the chalkboard.

4. Ask the children to write other adventure stories for Ralph, using the ideas based on their living together in San Francisco, or other possibilities the young authors prefer.

Something to think about
Teams of third graders who are experienced readers can write a variety of Keith and Ralph stories and organize them as "choose your own adventure" books. First and second graders can draw other adventures for Ralph and compose their stories on tape to store at the listening station for others to hear, or write their stories and then record them.

MACHINES AND THINGS

THE NEIGHBORHOOD TRUCKER

By Louise Borden

Illustrated by Sandra Speidel

Elliot Long loves trucks and wants to be a trucker when he grows up. He knows the names of all the eighteen wheelers on the road. His favorite trucks are the cement mixers from Sardinia Concrete, which is near his house. Elliot's favorite is Slim, the driver of truck number 44 for the company. For his birthday party, Elliot takes all the children to Sardinia Concrete where they get caps with a big "S" on the front. Elliot's special surprise is getting to ride in number 44 truck with Slim. Then Slim gives him patches like truckers wear on their jackets. One patch has Sardinia stitched on it and the other has Slim stitched in red. Sandra Speidel's pastel chalk drawings are warm, expressive and realistic; the trucks come roaring off the pages.

Read-Aloud Suggestions

If you have a baseball cap, wear it while reading the book. Have the children look at the front cover of THE NEIGHBORHOOD TRUCKER. Introduce them to Elliot and turn the page to the beginning of the book. On the page showing the different kinds of trucks, let the children tell what they think these trucks might be hauling. Read THE NEIGHBORHOOD TRUCKER and let the children who have truck drivers in their families tell what their parents haul in their trucks. Announce the story s-t-r-e-t-c-h-e-r-s about the big machines and trucks. This book is an excellent one for a unit on machines, transportation or community helpers.

STORY STRETCHER

For Art: Decorating Trucks

What the children will learn
To design a logo

Materials you will need
Large sheets of manilla paper or butcher paper, scissors, scraps of construction paper, colored pencils, markers, glue

What to do
1. Let the children cut the sheets of paper to look like the long rectangular trailers of big truck rigs.

2. Look at the illustrations in the book and notice the signs, letters and pictures used on the sides of trucks to let passersby know the trucking company or what the trucks are hauling.

3. Have the children design their own logos for their own trucking company using scraps of construction paper, cutting shapes, designs or letters, or drawing pictures.

4. On another day, design the tractors or the cabs of the eighteen wheelers.

Something to think about
Make the design project three-dimensional by covering cracker boxes with butcher paper, and having the children make designs all around the trailer of the rig. Or, let children who have toy models of eighteen wheelers bring their toys to school, and cover the trailers with papers with the children's logos on them.

STORY STRETCHER

For Creative Dramatics: Which Machine Do I Use?

Materials you will need
Variety of dress-up clothes for trucker, mechanic, house cleaner, chef, librarian, office worker, fisherman; paper bags

What to do
1. With four or five children a day, discuss what they would like to be when they grow up. Discuss the fact that everyone uses machines. Have the children think about what machines they will use in their jobs when they grow up.

2. Ask the children to collect clothing from home so they can dress up and let the other children guess what they want to be when they grow up.

3. Each day, have the small group of creative dramatics students dress up in their clothes and pantomime themselves doing their grown-up jobs.

4. Let the other children guess what the jobs or careers are. Then have the dressed up children explain the many different machines they will use in these roles.

Something to think about
Younger children can pantomime adults using machines at home.

STORY STRETCHER

For Science And Nature: Mixing Cement For Concrete

What the children will learn
To recall the steps in mixing cement for concrete

Materials you will need
Ready mix variety of cement, sand, water, wheelbarrow, shovel, rake

What to do
1. Invite a person who does his or her own cement work to come to class and demonstrate how it is done.

2. Involve the children in measuring, mixing, pouring and smoothing the cement mixture.

3. Look around the school at all the places where concrete is used for building and for paving.

4. Have the children observe the drying process, test it periodically as it is setting up and record their observations as the mixture turns from a liquid to a solid.

Something to think about
Make the project a useful one. Pour a small slab of cement somewhere around the school where it is needed.

STORY STRETCHER

For Special Event: A Trucker Comes to Our School

What the children will learn
To know the parts of a truck and the important contribution truckers make to our community

Materials you will need
Eighteen wheeler, driver

What to do
1. If you have a parent who is a trucker, invite him or her to bring an eighteen wheeler to school. Talk with the driver about your study of community helpers, the transportation system and how machines work.

2. Plan for children throughout the school to have time to see the truck, but begin with your class.

3. Have the parent visit the class and talk about what he or she does. Let that parent's child add information.

4. Visit the truck in the school parking lot while it is parked and let the children look inside the cab, try shifting gears, look at the sleeper compartment, stoop and walk under the trailer and explore all around.

5. Have the driver start the motor and idle the truck for the children to hear the different sounds at varying rpm rates.

Something to think about
While the big tractor trailer rigs are most exciting, ask parents who drive delivery trucks, cement trucks, tankers, flat beds and even pickup trucks to drive their trucks to school. Help children make the connections between the work that their parents do and the ways it helps the community.

STORY STRETCHER

For Writing Center: What I Want To Be When I Grow Up

What the children will learn
To see themselves in jobs they could do as adults and think of machines they would use

Materials you will need
Writing paper, pencils, art supplies for choice of illustration media

What to do
1. Read THE NEIGHBOR-HOOD TRUCKER again. After the section about what the other children in the neighborhood were pretending to be, ask your students what they think they might like to do when they grow up.

2. Ask the children to write about what they want to be when they grow up, and to tell why they think they are especially suited for the job.

3. Have the children add illustrations of themselves using the machines that would be a part of their grown-up lives.

4. Discuss the many different careers and professions you thought about as a child and why you enjoy being a teacher.

Something to think about
Consider collecting all the children's writing and having the children edit their work and binding it into a class book. Place it in the classroom library for the children to read.

THE CABOOSE WHO GOT LOOSE

By Bill Peet

Katy is a caboose, a machine confined to the tracks, but she wants to be free. She doesn't like being the last car pulled by the big engine up front. It is too noisy, and she is often afraid of getting backed into other trains or smashed by falling rocks, and she doesn't like the dark tunnels either. Then one day, the coupling breaks, and when Katy goes around a mountain curve, she is flung free. She lands between two evergreen trees and becomes a happy home for squirrels and birds. In typical Bill Peet fashion, the pictures and the rhyming text are both delightfully funny, and Katy the caboose gains the reader's sympathy.

Read-Aloud Suggestions

Talk about trains as machines. Have the children make the sounds trains make: clickety-clacking down the track and screeching to a halt. If children have traveled on trains, encourage them to talk about their trips. Mention the difference between passenger trains and freight trains. Read THE CABOOSE WHO GOT LOOSE, but do not show the children the cover of the book or the title page. Begin with the illustration of the long train stretched around the mountain, over the river bridge and puffing smoke in the far distance. Point out the little red caboose at the end of the train and introduce the caboose as Katy. Near the end of the book, when Katy breaks away from the rest of the train and is thrown into the air while going around a mountain curve, let the children predict what will happen to Katy. Involve as many children as possible in the predictions before reading the end of the story.

STORY STRETCHER

For Art: Katy's View

What the children will learn
To draw or paint landscapes they imagine

Materials you will need
Easel, tempera paint, newsprint or manilla paper

What to do
1. Look at the illustrations in THE CABOOSE WHO GOT LOOSE.

2. At the end of the story when Katy is stuck in the spruce trees, she looks out and sees a beautiful view. Ask the children to paint Katy's view from her new home high in the evergreen trees.

Something to think about
Let the children help you decorate a bulletin board as a big red caboose. Display the children's paintings on the bulletin board shaped like Katy the caboose.

STORY STRETCHER

For Classroom Library: Verbal Cloze Reading

What the children will learn
To complete the rhyming couplet

Materials you will need
Cassette tape and recorder

What to do
1. With a small group of children, read THE CABOOSE WHO GOT LOOSE again.

2. As you read, pause at the second rhyming word of the couplet and let the children fill in the pause. This is a process called verbal cloze.

3. After practicing at least once, tape-record while you read and the children say the rhyming words.

4. Record an introduction to the book, telling the listeners where to turn to begin reading, taping a page-turning signal and encouraging the listeners to join the children on the tape in completing the rhymes.

Something to think about
Since Bill Peet is a favorite author of many primary age children, let a child recommend other books by the author at the end of the tape.

STORY STRETCHER

For Music And Movement: She'll Be Comin' Round The Mountain

What the children will learn
To change the lyrics to a song to match the story

Materials you will need

Chart tablet or posterboard, marker

What to do

1. Sing the old folk song, "She'll Be Comin' Round the Mountain When She Comes."

2. Rewrite the lyrics to fit the story of THE CABOOSE WHO GOT LOOSE. For example, sing,

"She'll be the last car on the freight train when she comes,
Ca-boose.
She'll be the last car on the freight train when she comes,
Ca-boose.
The last car on the freight train,
the last car on the freight train,
the last car on the freight train when she comes,
Ca-boose."

3. Let the children write other verses and print them on chart tablet paper for the class to sing throughout the week.

Something to think about

Make a *Big Book of Music* for the songs the children have rewritten. Use the pages of a chart tablet as the pages of the song book and decorate the cover with musical notes.

STORY STRETCHER

For Special Project: Trains On Display

What the children will learn

To assemble a train set

Materials you will need

Table or large area, trains, shoe boxes, scissors, popsicle sticks, construction paper, glue, playdough

What to do

1. Ask a parent or volunteer who is a train enthusiast to come to class and assist the children in assembling a train set. Have the adult bring a set that the children can play with, and not one that is too delicate or used for exhibits only.

2. When the volunteer is directing the assembling of the set, ask him or her to use railroad terms and labels for the cars of the train, the tracks and the coupling mechanisms.

3. Assign small groups of children each day to assemble the set.

4. Let the set designers add props by making tunnels from shoe boxes, construction paper trees from popsicle sticks stuck upright in playdough, and cutouts of people attached to popsicle sticks.

Something to think about

If you have several children who have train sets, ask them to bring them on different days. Take instant print pictures of the train set-ups.

STORY STRETCHER

For Writing Center: Katy's New Friends

What the children will learn

To extend the story

Materials you will need

Chalkboard, chalk, writing paper, pencils, art supplies for illustrations

What to do

1. Read the end of the story again where Katy is stuck in the spruce trees and the squirrels and birds are around her.

2. Brainstorm with the children about what they think will happen next. Write key words from the children's ideas on the chalkboard.

3. With writing partners, let the children write stories about Katy and her new friends.

Something to think about

If there are children who are already involved in writing other pieces, do not assign this one. Make it a choice for those children who have finished. Writing with partners helps children to write more; however, partnerships take time to develop. Consider letting partners write several pieces together so they learn to collaborate.

Tricia Tusa
Stay Away from the Junkyard!

STAY AWAY FROM THE JUNKYARD!

By Tricia Tusa

Set in Jasper, Texas, STAY AWAY FROM THE JUNKYARD! is a most inventive tale of a little girl named Theo who finds a way to get the townspeople to like Old Man Crampton, the junkyard man, and his pig named Clarissa. A creative, touching, humorous tale, a terrific story which children will savor. The illustrations are as enchanting as the unusual story, with jaunty angles, caricatures of relatives and store owners—with just the right exaggeration of adults from a child's eye view.

Read-Aloud Suggestions

Ask the children if they have ever been to a junkyard and why they went there. Find out if they think their parents would want them to go there alone and why. Show the cover of the book and point out that the housekeeper is shouting, "Stay away from the junkyard!" to Theodora—Theo—as she leaves the house. Ask the children if they think Theo will heed her advice. After reading the book, have the children recall the two people in town who believed Mr. Crampton would be an interesting person. Announce the story s-t-r-e-t-c-h-e-r-s for the book and discuss the marvelous machines which could come from a junkyard.

STORY STRETCHER

For Art: Beautiful Junk Sculpture

What the children will learn
To recycle household items

Materials you will need
Egg cartons, cardboard boxes, gift wrap paper, wire, coat hangers, wire pliers, large styrofoam packing, scissors, knives, tape, glue, ribbons, twine, yarn, scraps of wood and fabric, etc.

What to do
1. Look at Mr. Crampton's beautiful junk sculpture at the end of the book.

2. Assemble all the beautiful junk you and the children have collected.

3. Ask them to make a sculpture they like.

4. Let the children work on the sculptures for several days and then display them around the room.

Something to think about
Children become better at art with practice, just as they do with many other things they learn. Let them enjoy the experience without a great deal of emphasis on the product.

STORY STRETCHER

For Creative Dramatics: Readers' Theatre

What the children will learn
To read with expression

Materials you will need
Chalkboard, chalk, scraps of paper, writing paper, pencils

What to do
1. With a group of seven children, read the book again.

2. Make a list of all the characters in the book.

3. Write the children's names on scraps of paper, place the names in a hat and draw them out to assign who will be each character. Print their names on the chalkboard beside the characters' names.

4. Have the children who are playing Mrs. Percy, Mr. Doogan, Miss Betty Anne and Aunt Mazel copy their dialogue from the book. Theo, Mr. Crampton and the narrator can look at the book together for their lines.

5. Read the story as a readers' theatre production. Have the children practice reading their lines with expression and on cue.

6. Do the entire readers' theatre production of the book for the rest of the class.

Something to think about
The readers' theatre production can be done on other days with other children. Choose books for readers' theatre plays which have a lot of dialogue between two characters at a time, rather than interaction between many all at once.

For Mathematics: Flea Market Equations

What the children will learn
To barter and trade

Materials you will need
Tables, objects to trade, index cards or Post-it notes, pencils

What to do
1. Discuss the fun of going to flea markets and let children who have helped with garage sales tell about their experiences.

2. Announce that the class will have their own flea market and each child should bring some things to class that he or she wants to trade. Explain that they should be sure they want to trade the objects. Talk about the difference between a flea market where items are sold, and a market where people barter and trade.

3. Set up the flea market so that half the children display their wares and half the children take their items around to tables and try to trade.

4. After the flea market, have the children write their equations for the trades they made. For example, one matchbox car equals three baseball cards or three picture puzzles equals one game.

5. Post all the trade equations.

Something to think about
For older children, have a flea market with a one-dollar limit, and let the children see how many items they can purchase for a dollar. For younger children, have a pretend flea market. Store the items for them to use over and over, and practice making change as they sell the objects.

For Special Projects: An Invention Convention

What the children will learn
To use common objects to solve a problem

Materials you will need
Egg cartons, cardboard boxes, gift wrap paper, wire, coat hangers, wire pliers, large styrofoam packing, scissors, knives, tape, glue, ribbons, twine, yarn, scraps of wood and fabric, and other materials which fit the problems

What to do
1. Show the children an invention you have made to solve a problem: for example, connecting two long handles to a dust mop to make it long enough to sweep cobwebs from the ceiling. A hem comes undone on a piece of clothing you are wearing, and you don't have needle and thread, so you tape the hem in place.

2. Help children to see that inventions come from having a problem and needing a solution.

3. Let the children recall inventions they have made.

4. Throughout the day as you encounter problems, pause and say, "I wish someone would invent something that would . . . ."

5. With the children decide on a special day to have an Invention Convention. Plan it at least a week in advance so the children have time to think of something to invent.

6. On the day of the Invention Convention, let the children decide on categories for the inventions, such as household, school, just for fun, etc.

7. Display the inventions and have the children take turns demonstrating them.

Something to think about
For older children, have them write about their inventions, telling about the problems which inspired the inventions, the directions for construction and how to operate the inventions. (Idea adapted from one discussed by Wende Gannon in a graduate course at George Mason University.)

For Writing Center: Clarissa's Adventures

What the children will learn
To write from a different perspective

Materials you will need
Butcher paper, markers, chart tablet, marker, writing paper, pencils, optional—art supplies for illustrations

What to do
1. Let several volunteers make a giant Clarissa Pig for the writing center.

2. Ask the writers to think about what Clarissa might say if she were telling the story of Theo visiting Otis Crampton.

3. As each child begins brainstorming, draw a story web of what he or she is saying. For example, print "Clarissa" in a large circle in the center of the chart tablet paper. Draw lines radiating out from the circle for each different character with whom Clarissa speaks.

4. Let children work in pairs and, as one child tells the story, the other can draw the story web.

5. After the webs are made, encourage the children to write their Clarissa stories for other children to read.

Something to think about

Story webs are excellent pre-writing devices because they help children plan their stories. With older children, use more story elements in the web, such as setting, problem, episodes, solution. Model more complex webs by making webs of books from this unit. Story webs can be designed in many ways, from the very simple to quite elaborate webs with interlinking lines showing details and main ideas. They are also called story maps or cognitive maps. All are graphic representations of the story.

References

Borden, Louise. (1990). Illustrated by Sandra Speidel. **THE NEIGHBORHOOD TRUCKER**. New York: Scholastic Inc.

Cleary, Beverly. (1965). Illustrated by Louis Darling. **THE MOUSE AND THE MOTORCYCLE**. New York: Avon Camelot.

Cole, Joanna. (1986). Illustrated by Bruce Degen. **THE MAGIC SCHOOL BUS AT THE WATERWORKS**. New York: Scholastic Inc.

Peet, Bill. (1971). **THE CABOOSE WHO GOT LOOSE**. Boston: Houghton Mifflin Company.

Tusa, Tricia. (1988). **STAY AWAY FROM THE JUNKYARD!** New York: Macmillan.

Additional References For Machines And Things

Burton, Virginia Lee. (1943). **KATY AND THE BIG SNOW**. Boston: Houghton Mifflin Company. *Katy was a tractor who belonged to the highway department. One winter there was such a big snow that Katy was the only machine strong enough to plow out the city.*

Cleary, Beverly. (1984). **LUCKY CHUCK**. Illustrated by J. Winslow Higgenbottom. New York: William Morrow and Company. *Chuck loves his motorcycle, but he learns the hard way that driving it safely is a must. We learn a lot about the workings of a motorcycle in the process.*

Flack, Marjorie. (1946). **THE BOATS ON THE RIVER**. Illustrated by Jay Hyde Barnum. New York: Viking Press. *Rhythmic text about all the different kinds of boats to be seen on the Hudson River. This is a classic Caldecott Honor Book.*

Scarry, Huck. (1979). **STEAM TRAIN JOURNEY**. New York and Cleveland: Collins Publishers. *Climb aboard and join the engine driver and his dog as they take the steam train on an imaginary journey to see the old trains of many lands. The many detailed illustrations invite children to browse and learn.*

Thomas, Patricia. (1990). **THE ONE AND ONLY SUPER-DUPER GOLLY-WHOPPER JIM-DANDY REALLY-HANDY CLOCK-TOCK-STOPPER**. Illustrated by John O'Brien. New York: Lothrop, Lee and Shepard Books. *A grouchy porcupine who wants to stop the ticking of his clock, and a rabbit who is more than willing to help, produce a hilarious mechanical marvel.*

ANIMAL LIFE

The Puffins Are Back
The Salamander Room
Frogs, Toads, Lizards, and Salamanders
Charlotte's Web
Nate's Treasure

THE PUFFINS ARE BACK

By Gail Gibbons

Only a few years ago, the puffins which lived on the rocky coast of Maine were few in number. But now "the puffins are back," thanks to the National Audubon Society and a unique, successful program of repopulating the puffin colony with birds born in Newfoundland. Children will enjoy the facts of the life cycle of the puffins, told in a straightforward manner but with a touch of wonder, as the scientists wait to see if their venture will work. The mixed media illustrations in watercolor, colored pencil and pen and ink tell the story of the scientific project.

Read-Aloud Suggestions

Show the cover of the book and let the children think of some nicknames for the birds. They are called puffins, but many of the locals also call them "clowns of the sea" and "sea parrots." Read the story of the National Audubon Society's project and the puffins' return to Maine. When you have finished reading, turn back through the illustrations and let the children talk about what interested and surprised them, or let them retell the story in their own words.

STORY STRETCHER

For Art: Audubon's Sketches Of Birds

What the children will learn
To recognize the famous bird sketches made by John James Audubon

Materials you will need
Copies of Audubon bird books, hand-held magnifying glasses, bookmarks

What to do
1.   Show the children the Audubon bird books. Talk about what a treasure they are and that they are very costly, but that the library has agreed to let them look at the books.

2.   Leave the books in a special display at the art center for the entire week.

3.   Encourage the children to place bookmarks at their favorite bird pictures.

4.   At a session of the whole group, let different members of the class tell about the birds they selected and why they like the pictures.

Something to think about
Have the children make their own bookmarks by sketching birds on strips of posterboard or unlined index cards. Laminate them, punch a hole in the bottom and tie a bright piece of yarn through it. The children can use their bookmarks to mark their favorite birds in the Audubon books.

STORY STRETCHER

For Classroom Library: Read More About Birds

What the children will learn
To find out more about birds

Materials you will need
Children's reference and resource books about birds, chart tablet, marker

What to do
1.   Contact the school librarian and city library for good reference books.

2.   Help children understand how to use a resource book.

3.   Begin with birds that are common to your area and read about them.

4.   Make a chart of birds from your area and mark on the chart whether or not they are an endangered species.

5.   After a few days, review the chart.

Something to think about
Young children will enjoy looking at the pictures in adult reference books on birds. Even if some children are not able to read all the text, they still benefit from looking at it.

STORY STRETCHER

For Mathematics: A Diet Of Two Thousand Fish

What the children will learn
To visualize how many two thousand is

Materials you will need

Chalkboard and colored chalk or chart tablet and different colored markers

What to do

1. Discuss the fact that the puffin chicks ate two thousand fish in six weeks. Wonder aloud how many fish two thousand are.

2. Draw off a grid on a chalkboard or chart tablet. Make each square of the grid large enough for ten hash marks across and ten marks down.

3. Let the children take turns filling each square with 100 hash marks in rows of 10 across and 10 down.

4. Change colors of chalk or markers and let another child start the next 100.

5. Continue until you have 20 squares completed.

6. Talk about each hash mark representing one fish.

Something to think about

Older children can calculate how many fish were eaten each week. Others can decide how many trips it took the parent puffin if he brought back 10 fish at a time or 8 fish at a time or another number. First and second graders will enjoy simply counting the hash marks.

STORY STRETCHER

For Science And Nature: Observing From A Bird Blind

What the children will learn

To observe birds through binoculars

Materials you will need

Binoculars, curtains, bird feeder, plastic netting, fat, bird seeds, note pad, pencil

What to do

1. If you do not have a bird feeder which can be seen with binoculars from the classroom window, construct one. Fill a plastic orange net with fat cut from meat. Make a ball of fat about the size of a grapefruit. Roll the ball in bird seeds and place in the orange net. Hang the net in a nearby tree.

2. Close the curtains at the window or hang two pieces of fabric across a rod to make a blind.

3. Explain to the children that the reason it is called a blind is that the birds cannot see you, but you can see them. Recall how the scientists in THE PUFFINS ARE BACK hid in a blind to watch the puffins and their chicks.

4. Demonstrate how to adjust the binoculars for the children to see.

5. Let the children take turns watching the bird feeder.

6. Have them record on the note pad the time they watched the feeder and how many birds they saw.

7. After a week of bird watching, check the note pad and try to determine the best times for watching from the blind.

8. Schedule the following week of bird watching according to the best times.

9. Compare the number of birds seen in the first week and with the second week.

Something to think about

With older children, record the weather conditions as well, which may affect the number of birds.

STORY STRETCHER

For Writing Center: Write To The National Audubon Society

What the children will learn

To compose a group letter requesting materials

Materials you will need

Chalkboard, chalk, overhead projector, transparencies, markers, typewriter or computer, paper, pen

What to do

1. Talk about the puffin project as Gail Gibbons described it in THE PUFFINS ARE BACK.

2. Tell the students that in addition to wildlife preservation projects, like the one for the puffins, the National Audubon Society has other projects.

3. Suggest that, as a class, you compose a letter to the Society to find out more about their wildlife preservation projects and other activities.

4. Let the children brainstorm about what to include in the letter, such as telling the Society that the class read THE PUFFINS ARE BACK.

5. Write the children's questions on the chalkboard.

6. With the questions in mind, begin composing a letter and write your first draft on a transparency.

7. Reread the letter, crossing out and adding any words or phrases as well as adding information about the class, so that the National Audubon Society can respond to their requests.

8. Type or let a child print the letter.

9. Mail the letter to the Education Director, National Audubon Society, 613 Riversville Road, Greenwich, CT 06830.

Something to think about

Contact the wildlife authority for your state and ask for materials written for the primary grades. Also find the location of the nearest bird sanctuary and plan a field trip there.

THE SALAMANDER ROOM

By Anne Mazer

Illustrated by Steve Johnson

Brian finds an orange salamander in the forest and takes him home. When his mother asks him where the salamander will sleep, the question raises an avalanche of changes that would be necessary for Brian to take care of the animal. The answer to each question is for Brian to bring more and more of the forest into his room. Finally, it is clear that it is best for the salamander to live in the forest. The book is charmingly written without any adult lecturing, yet speaks to the feelings many children have about wanting to own animals. Beautifully illustrated with rich colors, unusual perspectives, and a warm glow which captures the mood and adds to the child's wonder at the natural world.

Read-Aloud Suggestions

Ask the children about their pets. Then ask if any children have tried to make pets of wild animals. Read THE SALAMANDER ROOM in a quiet, relaxed tone. Read the mother's questions in a curious tone, rather than an accusing one. The immediate response to this book when we read it to children was, "Read it again." Read the book a second time and pause for the children to suggest other things the child could do to try to make the salamander like his new home. End the session by talking about the importance of leaving animals in their natural habitats. Explain that when they study animals and insects in school, teachers always return them to the place where they were found or donate them to a zoological park.

STORY STRETCHER

For Art: Indoors/Outdoors Pictures

What the children will learn
To compose a picture with unexpected elements

Materials you will need
Manilla or drawing paper, choice of media—colored pencils, crayons, markers, tempera paints, brushes

What to do
1. With small groups of children at a time, look again at the illustrations in THE SALAMANDER ROOM. Call attention to how Brian's room looked more and more like a forest.

2. Ask the children to draw their own rooms and think of an animal they would like to live with them. What kind of changes would be needed in their room for the animal to be comfortable?

3. Have the children add elements of a stream, woods, forest or desert—whatever the natural habitat would be for the animal.

4. Display the indoors/outdoors pictures in the library corner with the book cover of THE SALAMANDER ROOM.

Something to think about
Because the illustrations in the book have such rich green foliage, let the children experiment with mixing green paints to achieve the various shades of green shown. Experiment with painting on a soft yellow color of construction paper to achieve the glowing tone.

ANOTHER STORY STRETCHER

For Art: Camouflage

What the children will learn
To conceal an animal by using a camouflage technique

Materials you will need
Drawing paper, crayons, colored pencils, markers

What to do
1. Look through the illustrations of THE SALAMANDER ROOM and talk about how the little salamander was hidden under the leaves.

2. Discuss how animals use camouflage as protection from their predators.

3. Suggest that the children draw a forest scene and hide a little animal in their picture by using similar colors to camouflage the animals location.

Something to think about
Look at the bird pictures from the Audubon books in the art story s-t-r-e-t-c-h-e-r for THE PUFFINS ARE BACK and see the way the female bird is often camouflaged.

For Classroom Library: True Or False, Comparing Facts

What the children will learn
To compare facts from an informational book and a fiction book

Materials you will need
Reference materials on salamanders (see FROGS, TOADS, LIZARDS, AND SALAMANDERS in this unit), chart tablet or posterboard, marker

What to do
1. Talk with the children about THE SALAMANDER ROOM, which is a fictional book, yet there are many facts they can learn from the book.

2. Read the book again and pause for the children to dictate a list of facts they can infer from the book. For example, on the first page of the story, we can assume salamanders are found in the woods because that is where Brian found his.

3. Read a reference book on salamanders and compare the facts to those listed from THE SALAMANDER ROOM.

4. Check each fact on the list and write true or false beside the item.

Something to think about
Read about salamanders in FROGS, TOADS, LIZARDS, AND SALAMANDERS, another one of the story s-t-r-e-t-c-h-e-r books for this unit. Third graders might try comparing more than one reference book.

For Creative Dramatics: Can I Keep Him?

What the children will learn
To improvise a scene

Materials you will need
None needed

What to do
1. Divide a small group of children into pairs. Have each pair of children pretend to be a parent and a child.

2. Ask the pairs to think of an animal they might find in the woods that they would like to ask their parents if they could keep.

3. Let the pairs plan together what they will say to each other, based on what the animal is and what the animal would need to live anywhere other than the forest.

4. Have the small group act as the audience for the pairs to act out their scenes. Begin each scene with "Can I keep him?"

5. After the pairs have played their scenes for the small group and made any changes they wish to improve the scenes, let them role play before the entire class.

Something to think about
Encourage the children to bring dress-up clothes and other props from home if they need them to improvise.

For Writing Center: Letters To A Zoologist

What the children will learn
To express their concern for the animal

Materials you will need
Writing paper, pencils

What to do
1. After the activities where children express their feelings for small animals, let them think of questions they would like to ask zoos about the care of the animals that are moved from their natural habitats.

2. Let the children write a list of their questions.

3. Working with small groups of children, write to the zoo and ask about particular animals which interest them.

Something to think about
Invite a zoologist to come to the school and talk about what zoos are doing to build better habitats for animals, and about their projects to repopulate endangered species in their natural environments.

FROGS, TOADS, LIZARDS, AND SALAMANDERS

By Nancy Winslow Parker

and Joan Richards Wright

Illustrated by

Nancy Winslow Parker

An informational book about small amphibians and reptiles with a funny rhyme on the left page and scientific information on the right. The book contains simple illustrations, scientific and common names, measurements, male and female symbols, a glossary, life cycle charts and range maps. Especially interesting to the budding scientist whose curiosity extends beyond the "what is it" question, this book includes four species of salamanders, four frogs and four of toads, as well as four kinds of lizards. Colored pencil drawings are featured on the funny rhyme pages and scientifically correct illustrations on the informational pages.

Read-Aloud Suggestions

Ask the children to name kinds of frogs. Write the frog names on the board. Often someone will mention a toad. Ask if there are any differences between toads and frogs. Without answering the children's questions just yet, show them the cover of the book and mention that this is really two books in one. First read the book through from beginning to end, only reading the left side, the rhyming pages, letting the children see the drawings of the animals. Read the book a second time, only reading particularly interesting facts from the scientific pages. End the discussion with the children explaining differences between frogs and toads.

STORY STRETCHER

For Art: Discovering An Amphibian Or A Reptile

What the children will learn
To draw an appropriate habitat for a salamander, toad, frog or lizard

Materials you will need
Drawing paper, colored pencils

What to do
1. Show the children the first illustration of Nick finding a hellbender, a type of salamander, in a brook where he was fishing.

2. Let the children choose an animal they would like to find.

3. Read about the animal and have the children draw a picture which shows them discovering this animal in a place where it would typically be found.

Something to think about
Display the children's drawing in the science and nature center.

STORY STRETCHER

For Classroom Library: Amphibians And Reptiles On Tape

What the children will learn
To say their lines on cue

Materials you will need
Cassette recorder, tape, glass, fork

What to do
1. Ask a few children to come to the classroom library. Tell them that FROGS, TOADS, LIZARDS, AND SALAMANDERS is a must for the class taped book collection because the scientific information is hard for even some adults to read.

2. Let the children practice reading the rhyming couplets for each page.

3. Record them reading the rhyming couplets in unison like a choral reading, then you read the scientific information.

4. Be sure to include an introduction so the listener knows where to begin in the book, and record a page-turning signal by tapping a glass with a fork.

Something to think about
Bring a terrarium to class, or ask a parent volunteer to make the tape recording with the children.

ANOTHER STORY STRETCHER

For Classroom Library: Read More About It

What the children will learn
To compare facts

Materials you will need
Reference books—see the list at the end of FROGS, TOADS, LIZARDS, AND SALAMANDERS; chart tablet or posterboard; marker; index cards or large Post-it notes; tape

What to do

1. Collect as many of the reference books as possible and others the school or city librarian recommends for the age children you teach.

2. Display the books in the classroom library or the science and nature center.

3. Ask the children which of the animals they want to know more about.

4. Read about one of the animals in FROGS, TOADS, LIZARDS, AND SALAMANDERS. Then read about the animal in the reference book and compare the facts.

5. Make a chart for each of the animals in the Parker and Wright book by asking a child to draw a sketch of the animal at the top of the chart, and printing the common name.

6. Draw a line down the center of the chart and on the left write at least five pertinent facts the children select as important from the Parker and Wright book.

7. After the children read more from the reference books, they can write any new facts they want to remember in the right column. Write the information on an index card or a Post-it note, then tape the fact to the chart.

Something to think about

For first and second graders, make a KL chart. Write what the children already "knew" about the animals on the left-hand side, and what they "learned" from reading FROGS, TOADS, LIZARDS, AND SALAMANDERS on the right-hand side of the chart.

For Science And Nature: Frogs And Toads

What the children will learn
To list the habitat and food needs of frogs and toads found in their area

Materials you will need
Terrarium, frog or toad, magnifying glass, food

What to do

1. Consult with a high school science teacher who may have a live toad or frog that one of her or his students could bring to your class. Let the secondary student act as the consultant by telling the children about the animals. Leave the terrarium in the class for a few days. As an alternative source, call a teacher supply store and ask about suppliers of animals for classroom observation.

2. Place the terrarium in the science center.

3. After the children have spent time enjoying having an animal in the classroom, encourage them to describe what they see: the appearance, needs and behaviors of the frog or toad.

4. Compare the frog or toad in the terrarium to one illustrated in FROGS, TOADS, LIZARDS, AND SALAMANDERS.

Something to think about
If you live in an area where you can catch frogs or toads, then find the animals and tell the story of your discovery. After a week or two, return the animal to its natural habitat. If possible, bring a salamander or lizard to class in the terrarium and observe the animal closely.

For Writing Center: Science Learning Log

What the children will learn
To write or draw their observations

Materials you will need
Writing paper, pencils

What to do

1. With any species on exhibit in the science and nature center, encourage the children to observe closely, describe verbally and then write down new information they have learned.

2. As a way to help children appreciate their prior knowledge, have them divide their papers into two columns. On the left side, they can list what they already knew about frogs, and on the right side, what they learned from the book and from observing the animal in the terrarium.

3. Encourage students to sketch what they see to help their words come to life when they reread the entries.

4. Have a sharing time where students read their new discoveries and hear the descriptive language of other students.

Something to think about
Some children may prefer to write about their own experiences discovering frogs, toads, lizards or salamanders in the wild.

ANIMAL LIFE

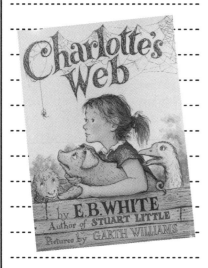

CHARLOTTE'S WEB

By E.B. White

Illustrated by Garth Williams

This classic story has become a child-hood favorite. E.B. White's CHARLOTTE'S WEB is an excellent chapter book to read aloud because there are natural breaks in the story. Wilbur the pig, lovingly raised by Fern, is a barnyard animal whose plight captures the heart of the young listener. In danger of being butchered, Wilbur is saved from his fate by the inventive thinking of Charlotte, the spider, who has helped him endure the scorn and teasing of the other barnyard animals. With tears and giggles, young children, particularly third graders, find Fern, Wilbur, Charlotte, Templeton the rat, and the other barnyard animals as appealing today as they were when the story was written in 1952. Garth William's scant pen and ink sketches highlight one or two of the main scenes in each chapter.

Read-Aloud Suggestions

Many of the children may have already heard CHARLOTTE'S WEB read to them by their parents or in a child care setting, or they may have seen the animated movie version. Ask them not to tell what is going to happen in the story, but to enjoy it again because all good stories can be enjoyed more than once. Decide ahead of time how many chapters to read each day. The twenty-two chapters are short, so plan to read four or five chapters a day so the book can be read in one week. Each day, before reading the next chapters, have the children recall what happened the day before. At the end of the book, be sure to provide time for the children to talk about their feelings so that the mood of the story can be shared. Tell the children how you feel so that they know it is all right for them to be open with their emotions.

STORY STRETCHER

For Art: Spider Web Prints

What the children will learn
To make an abstract representation

Materials you will need
Pictures of spider webs, scrap paper, pencils, black construction paper or posterboard, white tempera paint, white glue, measuring cups and spoons, margarine tubs, cotton swabs

What to do
1. Look at the picture of the spider web at the beginning of chapter thirteen in CHAR-LOTTE'S WEB. Find photographs of real spider webs. Notice the way the web begins with a tightly spun core, then long lines radiating out to the edges, then connecting lines around the perimeter.

2. Let the children describe the patterns they see.

3. Give them scraps of paper to practice drawing lines which look like a spider web.

4. Mix about a half-cup of tempera paint and about a teaspoon of white glue in a margarine tub.

5. Demonstrate how to dip a cotton swab in the paint mixture and use it like a pencil to draw white spider webs onto black paper.

6. Allow the spider webs to dry overnight, then display them around the room.

Something to think about
If you have shrubbery near your school, in the early morning go out and look for spider webs extending across the tops of the shrubs. The morning dew helps them to be seen more readily. The children's webs will be more interesting after observing real spider webs.

ANOTHER STORY STRETCHER

For Art: Charlotte's Portrait Gallery

What the children will learn
To draw or paint from their imaginations

Materials you will need
Choice of art media—tempera paints, pastels, crayons, markers; collage materials, glue, construction paper or heavy texture paper, scissors, old picture frames, hammer, picture-hanging wire and nails

What to do
1. Ask for volunteers to make portraits of the main characters in CHARLOTTE'S WEB. Tell them to use their imaginations without regard for Garth Williams' versions of the characters.

2. Let the children volunteer to draw an animal or human of their choice.

3. Help each artist decide which medium and frame best fits the portrait of their character.

4. Cut the paper or posterboard to fit the frame.

5. After the portraits have been drawn or painted, let the children frame and hang them in the library.

Something to think about
If framing is not possible, mat the pictures with heavy construction paper or posterboard.

STORY STRETCHER

For Classroom Library: Voices For CHARLOTTE'S WEB

What the children will learn
To modulate their voices

Materials you will need
Cassette tapes, recorder, stapler

What to do
1. Have the children recall the main events of the chapters read that day. Look at Garth Williams' illustrations and ask the children to recall your voice, as you were reading that part. Describe your voice as excited, somber, hurried, slow, soft-spoken.

2. Make a list of what happened in the chapters, and let the children take turns telling about the events in a voice which reflects the mood.

3. Let the children practice retelling the chaptesr, then tape-record them. Be sure to record an introduction telling the chapter titles.

4. Ask a parent or friend to read the chapters on the opposite side of the tape.

5. Place the tapes in the library collection for the listening station.

Something to think about
Use different children each day until all the students have been involved in the story retelling on tape. Let younger children mimic the voice of a character without having to retell whole scenes with multiple characters.

STORY STRETCHER

For Writing Center: Reading Response Log

What the children will learn
To summarize what happens and predict events

Materials you will need
Notebooks or loose sheets of writing paper, pencils

What to do
1. Have the children make a date column down the left side of the page.

2. After the read-aloud time each day, ask the children to note the date in the left column and write in their own words what happened in the story in the right column.

3. Have them write at least one prediction for what will happen the next day.

Something to think about
Let older children predict what each of the main characters, Fern, Wilbur and Charlotte, will do in the following chapters.

ANOTHER STORY STRETCHER

For Writing Center: Attention-Getters, Good Beginnings

What the children will learn
To write opening lines for their stories which will make readers want to read more

What to do
1. After you have read the entire book, read the opening sentences from several chapters.

2. Discuss with the children how E. B. White helps the reader see the sights, smell the smells and feel the suspense of the story from the very first opening lines. Read again the first three or four sentences from chapter three which help the reader sense the barnyard through sight, smell and mood.

3. From some of the children's previous writing, select a few which have good attention-getters as beginnings. Emphasize that the opening lines make the reader or the listener want more.

4. Ask the children to select one or two pieces of their writing and rewrite the opening lines to be vivid attention-getters.

Something to think about
As an alternative, have the children write catchy captions for drawings from CHARLOTTE'S WEB.

NATE'S TREASURE

By David Spohn

Nate's dog Bruno and a skunk have a fight. Bruno is sprayed by the skunk and has to spend time away from the house until the smell goes away. The next morning, Nate finds the skunk has died. He notices how beautiful the animal is and carries it away to the far edge of the hillside. The seasons come and go, and in the spring, Nate finds the small white skeleton of the skunk. He places each little piece in a special leather bag and keeps his treasure in a special place. Told with sensitivity, NATE'S TREASURE is an excellent book with a simple story respectful of animals and a young boy's curiosity. The half-page illustrations use pointillism in a simple style which complements the text.

Read-Aloud Suggestions

Ask the children if they have any special objects they keep in special places. When someone mentions something from nature, such as a beautiful rock or stone or bird feather, talk about unexpected treasures we find in the animal world. Show the cover of the book and let the children guess what Nate might have in the little bag. Tell them they will be surprised. Pause after Bruno's banishment to the yard and let children who have had experiences with skunks tell about them. Go on to read the remainder of the story without pausing for discussion. At the end, let the children talk about the story and ask them to bring to class any "natural treasures" they have which they would like to share. Set up a display table near the classroom library.

S T O R Y   S T R E T C H E R

For Art: Pointillism For A Part Of A Picture

What the children will learn
To create the effect of pointillism

Materials you will need
Tempera paints, margarine tubs, small brushes, chalks, different textures of paper, sponges, scissors

What to do
1. Look at the illustrations in NATE'S TREASURE and let the children think of how the artist might have created the tiny points of color.

2. Have them experiment with rolling small brushes in paint and barely touching the surface of the paper.

3. Let them experiment with painting with sponges, lightly dipped in paint and pressed gently on the paper.

4. Have them experiment with a roughly textured paper by lightly rubbing chalk over the paper.

5. Ask them to paint a picture and make at least part of their picture using one of the techniques with which they experimented.

Something to think about
Leave the art supplies out for several days for the children to experiment with various combinations.

S T O R Y   S T R E T C H E R

For Classroom Library: A Display Of Our Natural Treasures

What the children will learn
To listen to other children's descriptions and stories

Materials you will need
Chart tablet, marker, table, solid color tablecloth, tape, index cards, Post-it notes

What to do
1. Talk with the children about the fact that when they go to the library they often see special displays there to encourage children to read a book or series of books on a topic. Explain the display they will create with their "natural treasures."

2. Make a chart of the days of the week and let four or five children at a time sign up to bring one of their "natural treasures" to share each day.

3. On the first day of sharing, have the children tell about their treasures, where they were found, where they keep them at home, how long they have had the treasure, and answer any other questions the children may have.

4. Set up a display table in or near the classroom library. Cover a low table with a solid color tablecloth. Place the book, NATE'S

TREASURE, in the center of the table.

5. Let the children who talked about their treasures place them on the display table. Ask them to write a title for their item using their names and the word "treasure." For example, "Brian's Treasure" or "Melinda's Treasure."

6. Leave the display of natural treasures in the classroom library for at least a week.

Something to think about
Have older children write more about their natural treasures by writing a few sentences on an index card and taping it to their display.

STORY STRETCHER

For Science And Nature: Skeletons

What the children will learn
To see how bones fit together

Materials you will need
Guest speaker, note pad, pencil, skeleton, dark cloth, magnifying glass, index cards, tape

What to do
1. Ask a high school science teacher or a veterinarian to come to class and bring a skeleton of a small animal for the children to see.

2. Involve a small group of the children in helping to set up the speaker's equipment.

3. During the speaker's presentation, write down the questions the children ask and the speaker's answers.

4. Leave the skeleton on display and let the children take time to observe it, handle the bones and ask questions.

5. Label the main bones of the skeleton by printing little tags and

attaching or placing them on a cloth near the skeleton.

6. Print the children's questions on one side of the index cards and write the speaker's responses on the other side. Place the cards on the display at the science table.

Something to think about
Also write down other questions which you think of and ask them after the presentation, so that you have the answers to questions the children may ask after the speaker has gone.

ANOTHER STORY STRETCHER

For Science And Nature: The Seasons

What the children will learn
To classify weather and activities into seasons

Materials you will need
Drawing paper, choice of crayons, markers, colored pencils, paper, magazines, scissors, glue

What to do
1. Have the children look again at David Spohn's illustrations in NATE'S TREASURE. Notice how he shows the weather for the different seasons.

2. Talk about seasons as a time of change in the life cycles of plants, animals and people.

3. Have the children fold a large sheet of paper twice, creating four rectangles. With crayons or markers, draw the lines created by the folds.

4. Ask the students to draw a small sketch of each of the four seasons.

5. Have the children fold a second large sheet of paper twice, creating four rectangles. Again, draw the lines created by the folds with crayons or markers.

6. Let the students look through magazines and find pictures of activities people do during the four seasons. Cut out the pictures and glue them onto the appropriate rectangles.

7. Display the collages and drawings around the room.

Something to think about
Remind the children that this story takes place in Minnesota. Compare the seasons in the area of the country where you live to the ones in Minnesota.

STORY STRETCHER

For Writing Center: Science Learning Logs

What the children will learn
To record their observations in writing

Materials you will need
Note pads or writing paper, pencils

What to do
1. No doubt the skeleton and displays of "natural treasures" in the library area will prompt a lot of talk.

2. Casually write down some of the children's comments as they are looking at the skeleton and the display table.

3. In the writing center, read the comments to the children and talk about how good their observations are.

4. Help the children distinguish between an observation—something one can actually see—and an event they recall.

5. Encourage the children to take their science logs to the science and nature display of the skeletons and to the "natural treasures" display and to write in as descriptive terms as possible, what they see. For example, one child might write, "I see a blue jay's feather. It

is as long as my hand is wide. It is blue and black with two streaks of white. Some white is on the tip of the feather and some is between the black and the blue."

Something to think about

At another writing session, talk with the children about how scientists make discoveries: they "wonder" about something and then try to find answers. Have the children "wonder aloud." Write down some of the things they wonder about and then proceed as a class or small group of investigators to try and find the answers.

References

Gibbons, Gail. (1991). **THE PUFFINS ARE BACK**. New York: Harper Collins Publishers.

Mazer, Anne. (1991). Illustrated by Steve Johnson. **THE SALAMANDER ROOM**. New York: Alfred A. Knopf.

Parker, Nancy Winslow, & Wright, Joan Richards. (1990). Illustrated by Nancy Winslow Parker. **FROGS, TOADS, LIZARDS, AND SALAMANDERS**. New York: Greenwillow Books.

Spohn, David. (1991). **NATE'S TREASURE**. New York: Lothrop, Lee & Shepard Books.

White, E. B. (1952). Illustrated by Garth Williams. **CHARLOTTE'S WEB**. New York: Harper and Row.

Additional References for Animal Life

Dorros, Arthur. (1991). **ANIMAL TRACKS**. New York: Scholastic, Inc. *Guessing games enliven the simple, informative text and help the reader identify animal tracks which can be found in the city as well as in the woods.*

Parnall, Peter. (1990). **WOODPILE**. New York: Macmillan Publishing Company. *What lives in the cracks and crannies of the woodpile? And where did the wood come from? A woodpile is full of stories.*

Ryder, Joanne. (1990). Illustrated by Dennis Nolan. **UNDER YOUR FEET**. New York: Four Winds Press. *This book explores the animal world which exists under the earth in a series of poetic questions addressed to an observant child.*

Tejima. (1985). **FOX'S DREAM**. New York: Philomel Books. *Wandering through the snowy forest, a lonely fox has an enchanting vision and then finds the companionship for which he has longed.*

van der Meer, Ron & Atie. (1990). **AMAZING ANIMAL SENSES**. Boston: Little, Brown and Company. *The many movable parts in this ingeniously designed book show how animals use their senses to survive.*

LIFE IN THE SEA, REAL AND IMAGINED

When the Tide Is Low

Swimmy

Antarctica

The Fish Who Could Wish

Ibis: A True Whale Story

WHEN THE TIDE IS LOW

By Sheila Cole

Illustrated by Virginia

Wright-Frierson

A beautifully illustrated text to accompany a wonderful interaction between a little girl and her mother about going to the beach. Eager to go to the beach to see what the tide has washed up, the child asks over and over again when they can go. The mother's reply is that the beach is not there now because the tide is high: the sea is covering the sand and the rocks. The mother explains the rising and falling of the tide by swinging the little girl in the swing. They recall the many sea animals they have seen at low tide. Finally, the tide is low, and they rush off to the beach to see what sea life has washed ashore. The watercolors washed over pencil sketches are fresh, almost translucent, like a sunny beach day.

Read-Aloud Suggestions

Look at the beautiful cover of WHEN THE TIDE IS LOW and let the children talk about their experiences exploring the beaches. Show the children some shells you have collected and talk about discovering them at low tide. If you have clam shells, pass them around for the children to hold as you read. Announce that the shells will be at the science and nature display throughout the week. Read WHEN THE TIDE IS LOW and pause for the children to predict what the little girl will do to occupy her time until they can go to the beach, until the tide is low. After the reading, make a list of all the sea animals mentioned in the story. Turn to the back of the book and read the paragraphs about the animals in the glossary. Place the book in the science and nature center for the children to explore on their own.

STORY STRETCHER

For Art: Sea Shells Washed Ashore

What the children will learn
To use a color-resistant technique

Materials you will need
Pencils, white or light blue construction paper, watercolors, brushes, margarine tubs filled with water, sponges or paper towels, clear glue, masking tape

What to do
1. Have the children draw some sea shells on white or light blue construction paper.

2. Demonstrate how to paint over the shells with the glue. Explain that when the glue dries you can paint over the shells with watercolors, and the paint will not be absorbed into the sea shell areas.

3. Let the glue dry overnight.

4. Show the children the end papers of WHEN THE TIDE IS LOW and point out how they look like water.

5. Tape the paper to the table by placing a line of masking tape half on the paper and half on the table all around the edges. This holds the paper taut and lets it dry without crinkling up.

6. Have the children paint over their entire sheets of paper with the watercolors.

7. Leave the watercolor paintings taped to the tables and let them dry overnight.

8. Take the watercolor paintings off the table either by removing the tape from the edges or trimming it to look like a frame.

Something to think about
Try the paint resisting technique with pictures of other sea life and hang the paintings on a bulletin board.

ANOTHER STORY STRETCHER

For Art: Our Beach Adventures

What the children will learn
To paint or draw a time at the beach and what made it an exciting place

Materials you will need
Choice of media—paints, watercolors, crayons, pastels, colored pencils, markers

What to do
1. Tell the children that Virginia Wright-Frierson's illustrations of WHEN THE TIDE IS LOW are so beautiful that you are reminded of a time when you visited the beach.

2. Ask the children to draw a time when they went on a beach vacation, or have them imagine what they would do if they could

go to the beach when the tide is low.

3. Tell them of your plan to bind their pictures into a book.

4. Give the children plenty of time throughout the week to work on their beach adventure pictures.

Something to think about
Pictures are compositions, just as writing is a composition. Let the children tell about their beach compositions in the library area or take them to the writing center to write about the experience they had or a trip they would like to take to the beach.

STORY STRETCHER

For Classroom Library: Book Of Beach Adventures

What the children will learn
To compose a beach story

Materials you will need
Pictures from the art story s-t-r-e-t-c-h-e-r above, cardboard, contact paper, scissors, stapler, paper

What to do
1. Select paper the same size as the children's art pictures of their beach adventures.

2. Stack the pictures by placing clean sheets of paper between each of the drawings.

3. Place two sheets of clean paper on top of the stack of drawings and paper.

4. Staple the paper and the pictures together along the left margin, using three to five staples.

5. Have the children decide on a title for their collection of beach pictures. Leave the first page blank, then print the title on the second sheet of clean paper.

6. Then let each child title his or her drawing and write the title on

the clean sheet of paper you placed in front of his or her picture.

7. Continue the binding process by following the directions as shown in the Appendix.

8. Place the beach pictures in the classroom library.

Something to think about
Make three or four class books of beach adventure pictures. Group them according to themes in the pictures, such as sea life, sand castles, family fun and beach towns.

STORY STRETCHER

For Music And Movement: A Sea Song

What the children will learn
To write their own lyrics to a familiar tune

Materials you will need
Chart tablet, marker

What to do
1. Print the words to the familiar round, "Row, Row, Row, Your Boat."

2. Teach the children the song in rounds.

3. Rewrite the lyrics using a sea variation. For example,

"Flow, flow, flow the tide,
Gently from the sea.
Merrily, merrily, merrily,
See the little crabs flee.

Roar, roar, roar the tide
Blowing from the sea.
Crashing, splashing, dropping,
Shells upon the beach.

Away, away, away the tide,
Gently go to sea.
Merrily, merrily, merrily,
Playing time for me."
(Raines, 1991)

Something to think about
Let older children take each of the animals mentioned in the story and described in the glossary and write more lyrics about them. Place this

song and others the children learn in a class *Big Book of Music*, which you have constructed from a large chart tablet.

STORY STRETCHER

For Science And Nature: Sea Shells As Animal Homes

What the children will learn
To classify the shells by which animal once inhabited them

Materials you will need
Sea shells, baskets, posterboard, marker, reference book on shells

What to do
1. Let the children sort the shells by type.

2. The next day, print on posterboard the question: "What animals once lived in these shells?"

3. Provide some picture reference books on shells and let the children read them to find out the answers to the question.

4. If you teach first graders, this story s-t-r-e-t-c-h-e-r is an excellent one to involve older students, by having third graders investigate the question with the first graders. Second graders could have partner investigators from their own class.

5. Let the children each select a type of shell and write the answer in their own words.

Something to think about
If possible, give each child a collection of sea shells, particularly if you live in a community where few children have visited the beach. (Idea adapted from one by Leah Curry-Rood.)

SWIMMY

By Leo Lionni

Almost a classic and certainly a favorite, this Caldecott Honor book is the story of a fish and how he teaches a lesson in cooperation and survival in the sea. In wonderful Lionni style, the sea is alive with motion, color and adventure. Swimmy marvels at the other inhabitants of his world, yet finds his own life scary because he is afraid of being eaten by a big fish. Ingeniously, he teaches the little red fish to swim in formation like a big fish and scare the big fish away. In masterful watercolors and collage, Lionni invents a beautiful underwater experience, visually and verbally.

Read-Aloud Suggestions

Have the children recall that WHEN THE TIDE IS LOW was a story with real people and that could really happen. SWIMMY, on the other hand, is fiction. It is imagined, but it includes some of the same sea animals mentioned in WHEN THE TIDE IS LOW. Recall some of the animals from WHEN THE TIDE IS LOW. Read SWIMMY from beginning to end without pausing for discussion. Almost instantly, the children will ask you to read it again. Read it a second time, and each time an animal is mentioned, have the children decide whether or not it was in WHEN THE TIDE IS LOW or not. End with a brief discussion of cooperation, and let the children talk about some of the ways they cooperate throughout the day.

STORY STRETCHER

For Art: Swimmy's World Prints

What the children will learn
To use a variety of materials to paint

Materials you will need
Large sheets of newsprint or butcher paper, tempera paints, brushes, sponges, scissors, scrap paper, paper towels, doilies

What to do
1. Look at Lionni's illustrations of SWIMMY. Have the children notice how he swirls the paint, leaves some space blank and has some textures in his paint.

2. Let the children experiment with making textures by using different materials for brushes and different strokes. Dip sponges in the paint and press onto the paper. Crush paper towels into a ball, dip in paint and press onto the paper. Cut doilies into pieces and paint

over them, then gently lift off the paper, leaving an imprint of the form.

3. After they have experimented, ask the children to make an underwater scene and use at least one of the printing techniques they tried.

4. Display the SWIMMY'S world prints in the art area and classroom library.

Something to think about
Art materials need to be available for the children every day. When teaching new techniques, leave the supplies out for several days for the children to refine their experimentation.

ANOTHER STORY STRETCHER

For Art: Tissue PaperCollages

What the children will learn
To use dye as watercolor

Materials you will need
Construction paper or manilla paper, tissue paper, glue, water in margarine tubs, paper towels or brushes

What to do
1. With the children, look through Leo Lionni's illustrations of SWIMMY. Pay particular attention to the medusa.

2. Demonstrate for the children how to glue their tissue paper onto construction paper or manilla paper. Then dip a brush or a ball of paper towel into the water. Blot the water onto the tissue paper and watch how the dye in the tissue paper runs to create a watery effect.

3. Let the children practice the technique. Then ask them to make an underwater scene with one of the sea animals from SWIMMY, using a wet tissue paper collage.

Something to think about

Let the children experiment with layering different colors of tissue paper, wetting them and seeing what colors result.

(Idea adapted from one by Heather Emler, student teacher from George Mason University.)

For Classroom Library: Swimmy And Friends, Flannel Board Story

What the children will learn

To retell the story in their own words

Materials you will need

Cardboard or flannel board, chalkboard, chalk, construction paper, scissors, colored pencils, watercolors, pastel chalks, glue, old emery board

What to do

1. Make flannel board characters to retell the story of SWIMMY. Cover cardboard or a flannel board form with blue fabric to represent the ocean.

2. Let the children look through the book and list the sea life, plants, coral and rock forms found in the book. Write the list on the chalkboard.

3. Have the children volunteer to make one of the items from the list by using the art materials listed above which best meet the design for the items.

4. When the children finish making their flannel board pieces, glue a piece of old emery board to the back of the construction paper so it will adhere to the flannel board easily.

5. Retell the story of SWIMMY with the flannel board pieces the children have created.

6. Place the flannel board, pieces and a copy of the book in the classroom library for the children to retell on their own.

Something to think about

One child called flannel board stories, story puzzles, an appropriate choice of words that explains why flannel boards are popular with young children.

For Science And Nature: Aquarium

What the children will learn

To care for an aquarium and the fish and plant life

Materials you will need

Aquarium and supplies, posterboard, marker

What to do

1. Ask a parent who has an aquarium to set it up in the classroom for a few weeks or invite a tropical fish store owner to place one in the classroom for display.

2. Have the parent or store owner involve the children in setting up the aquarium.

3. Write specific directions on a poster for each day's care of the fish and plants.

4. Let the children take turns taking care of the aquarium.

Something to think about

If possible, keep an aquarium in the classroom for the entire year. However, before purchasing an aquarium, check with parents to see if someone wants to donate one to the class.

For Writing Center: Swimmy's Speech To The Little Red Fish

What the children will learn

To write from a main character's perspective

Materials you will need

Flannel board Swimmy, writing paper, pencils, art supplies for illustrations

What to do

1. Read again the part of the book where Swimmy discovers a school of red fish hiding among the rocks and convinces them to swim in formation to look like a bigger fish.

2. Let the children hold the Swimmy from the flannel board story in their hands and improvise a speech he might say to the red fish.

3. After their improvisations, let the children pair up. One child is Swimmy while the other pretends to be the "spokesfish" for the school of red fish.

4. Have the children write the dialogue between Swimmy and the fish.

5. After they have finished, let the children add illustrations to their compositions.

Something to think about

Young children may draw illustrations of the scene and write captions. They can also dictate longer dialogue, but may become fatigued if required to invent spellings for long scenes. Encourage their inventive spellings and writing, but do not overwhelm them with the task.

10

LIFE IN THE SEA, REAL AND IMAGINED

ANTARCTICA

By Helen Cowcher

Emperor penguins, Weddell seals, and Adélie penguins are the featured Antarctic animals in Helen Cowcher's award winning book, ANTACTICA. The life cycle of the emperor seal is told at the beginning of the book, and a little information is provided about the Weddell seals and the Adelie penguins. At the end, the reader is introduced to a frightening scene, the arrival of ice-crushing ships, helicopters and men setting up a base camp there. The bold illustrations of white ice and snow and the black penguins and seals create a powerful visual image for group sharing of the book. The blues, grays, browns and the muted colors of underwater seas and glowing sunsets make the book a dramatic one to be enjoyed again and again.

Read-Aloud Suggestions

Show the children where Antarctica is on a map and a globe. Tell them that the climate is very cold at the South Pole, so cold that no people are native to that area, but it is inhabited. Look at the cover of the book, and have the children tell you what animal is pictured there. Point out the end papers of the book with the water drops, blues and grays. Enjoy the title page with its vast sense of open space, filled with long washes of pink, mauve, yellow, blue and purple as four tiny penguins walk into the sunset. Read ANTARCTICA without stopping for the children to discuss the story. After reading, go back and either read the story again or turn the pages slowly for the children to enjoy the illustrations. Have a child who has not shown much interest in reading place the book in the library area and join him or her there in a few minutes to have a closer look at the book together.

STORY STRETCHER

For Art: A Study In Contrasts

What the children will learn
To use bold contrasting colors in their pictures

Materials you will need
Black and white construction paper, glue, scraps of other colors of construction paper

What to do
1. Look through the illustrations of ANTARCTICA again with a small group of children who choose to come to the art center during choice time.

2. Read the back book jacket of ANTARCTICA which explains that Helen Cowcher is an award-winning author/illustrator. Ask the children what they like about the illustrations.

3. Point out the way the author/ illustrator, Helen Cowcher, uses contrast to show the icebergs in stark white and the colors of the black and white penguins.

4. Suggest to the children that they make collages using contrasting colors. They can take a part of ANTARCTICA they would like to interpret, or make another contrast scene of their choosing.

Something to think about
Artists inspire other artists. Talk about how great painters and illustrators learn from each other. Have the children look at each other's contrasting pictures and talk about what they would like to try that they have seen their friends doing in their paintings and illustrations.

STORY STRETCHER

For Classroom Library: More About Antarctica

What the children will learn
To share new facts and pool knowledge

Materials you will need
Reference books on Antarctica and cold seawater animals, chart tablet, markers, index cards and tape or Post-it notes

What to do
1. Make a KWL chart about Antarctica and sea animals. Use chart tablet paper or posterboard and draw a chart with three columns. Print a large K at the top of the first column, a large W at the top of the second column and a large L at the top of the third column.

2. Begin by having the children tell what they already know about Antarctica from reading Helen Cowcher's book, and what they already knew before you read it to

140

them. Print their comments in the "K" column.

3. Have the children think of some questions they still have. Print these in the column marked with a "W" for "what we want to know."

4. Let the children read and look at the reference materials on Antarctica and sea life. As they find answers to their questions, they can print them on index cards or Post-it notes and tape them in the column marked "L" for "what we have learned."

Something to think about
For older children, begin a larger data retrieval system. Classify their questions by content. For example, some questions will be about weather, animals, human survival, icebergs and land masses. Organize separate KWL charts for each category.

ANOTHER STORY STRETCHER

For Classroom Library: D.E.A.R. And Partner Books

What the children will learn
To read to each other

Materials you will need
The book

What to do
1. Talk with the children about how much you enjoy reading aloud to them. Suggest that they might like to read to each other.

2. Form reading partners for a week based on a random drawing of names.

3. Establish a "D.E.A.R." time each day for the children to "drop everything and read." At the end of D.E.A.R. time, let the children meet with their reading partners and read aloud to each other.

Something to think about
ANTARCTICA and picture books with powerful storylines are excellent ones for partner reading because there is a good match between the text and the illustrations.

STORY STRETCHER

For Music And Movement: Penguins Walk And Seals Swim

What the children will learn
To mimic the animal movements

Materials you will need
Optional—recording of instrumental music with a short, choppy, perky beat

What to do
1. Coordinate with the music and physical education teachers and use the story s-t-r-e-t-c-h-e-r at three different instructional times.

2. Let the children improvise movements in their classroom.

3. Have the physical education teacher use the movements the children improvised, and design others.

4. When the music teacher comes to the classroom or the children go to the music room, add instrumental music to the movements.

Something to think about
Not all schools have the luxury of so many different specialists. Even with the specialists, it remains the teacher's responsibility to integrate art, music and movement into the curriculum.

STORY STRETCHER

For Science And Nature: Trip To A Sea Life Aquarium

What the children will learn
To identify the animals from ANTARCTICA

Materials you will need
Parental permission forms, transportation, identification badges, parent volunteers

What to do
1. Visit the nearest sea life aquarium and talk with the education director. Decide on a time limit and exhibits that best fit your students' needs.

2. Bring back materials about the aquarium for the children to see.

3. Make the arrangements your school system requires for field trips.

4. Prepare the children and the volunteers for the visit by having the children come up with a list of safety rules for field trips, including which children will go with which adults.

5. After the field trip, extend the activity through art, additional reading and writing.

Something to think about
Compose individual or group letters thanking the education director for the visit to the aquarium. Have the children tell about the animals they enjoyed seeing.

THE FISH WHO COULD WISH

By John Bush and Korky Paul

Told in rhyme, this is the story of a magic fish who gets anything he wishes, a castle, a car, snow under the sea, and a number of other funny and unexpected wishes for a fish. But one day, he makes a mistake: he wishes he could be like all the other fish, and that is his last wish. The bright watercolor illustrations are as humorous and quirky as the fish's wishes.

Read-Aloud Suggestions

Collect all the books you have read to the children from the unit on Life in the Sea, Real and Imagined and discuss which titles are factual or based on truth, and which ones are fiction. Look at the cover of THE FISH WHO COULD WISH and decide whether the book is reality or fantasy. Immediately, the children will know it is fantasy. Read the book through once without discussion. Read it again for the children to enjoy the humor in the illustrations, and pause for them to complete the rhymes as they "read along" with you. Ask the children which of the fish's wishes they think are the most outrageous and the most predictable.

STORY STRETCHER

For Art: Unexpected Things In Unexpected Places

What the children will learn
To add a touch of humor to their drawings or paintings

Materials you will need
Choice of art media—crayons, colored pencils, chalk, tempera paints; brushes; paper; construction paper; stapler

What to do
1.   Talk with the children who come to the art center during choice time about what makes THE FISH WHO COULD WISH so funny. The illustrator has painted "unexpected things in unexpected places." For example, there is a snowstorm under the sea, a fish who travels through space and a fish wearing designer suits.

2.   Let the children brainstorm a picture that they could draw which would have unexpected things in unexpected places. Some possibilities are a little bird who sees fish swimming in the sky, or a squirrel who discovers sea shells in his nest, or a child who suddenly finds a giraffe in her room.

3.   After the brainstorming session, let the children draw and paint their "unexpected things in unexpected places" pictures.

4.   Staple a cover sheet over the top of the drawing or painting, and let the child print on the cover a title for his or her artwork, like "The Little Bird Who Could Wish" or "Jennifer Wishes for a Giraffe."

5.   Let the children share their funny pictures with each other and display them around the room, especially in the library and the writing center.

Something to think about
Let the children who enjoy this funny art continue with the project for a few days and design even more "unexpected things in unexpected places."

STORY STRETCHER

For Classroom Library: Reading Confidence Builder

What the children will learn
To read along with the tape recording

Materials you will need
Cassette tape, recorder, glass, fork

What to do
1.   Record yourself reading THE FISH WHO COULD WISH on one side of the tape. Be sure to record an introduction, telling the listener where to begin reading by describing the title page, then tell what the page-turning signal will be, such as tapping a glass with a fork.

2.   With a small group of children, read the book using a verbal cloze process on the other side of

the tape. Read the first lines of a couplet and let the children fill in the blanks. Be sure to keep the rhythm of the language flowing.

3. After a practice session, record the children "reading along" with you, filling in the ends of the rhyming lines.

4. Place the tape and book at the listening station in the classroom library.

Something to think about
Encourage the children who are reluctant readers to listen to the "read along" tape. Children are particularly drawn to books with humor because reading them is enjoyable. Add books to the classroom collection that have rhymes, because they help the reader predict what will come next and build the confidence of readers.

STORY STRETCHER

For Creative Dramatics: What Doesn't Belong?

What the children will learn
To determine the item which doesn't belong

Materials you will need
Dress-up clothes, full-length mirror

What to do
1. Let the children dress up in clothes to look like adults going to work, or in costumes, or in clothing their favorite storybook characters would wear.

2. Have them add at least one item which doesn't belong, such as a tie on a skeleton costume, a hair bow on a father going to work, a screwdriver for the mother dressed for the office, etc.

3. Plan a parade of funny costumes and let the audience enjoy sighting the "unexpected things in unexpected places."

Something to think about
Ask parents to contribute uniforms and old clothes which evoke a lot of imaginative responses.

STORY STRETCHER

For Music And Movement: If I Could Wish Like A Funny Fish

What the children will learn
To write and sing new lyrics to a familiar tune

Materials you will need
Chart tablet, posterboard, marker

What to do
1. Teach the children the familiar song, "I've Been Working on the Railroad."

2. Let them use the tune and rewrite the song to fit the story of THE FISH WHO COULD WISH. For example,

> *"I've been swimming in the o-cean,*
> *All the live-long day.*
> *I've been swimming in the ocean,*
> *Just to pass the time a-way.*
> *Don't you see the fishes swim-ming*
> *Swimming so early in the morn.*
> *Don't you see the fishes swim-ming*
> *Fish, wishing some more.*
> *Fish, won't you wish,*
> *Fish, won't you wish,*
> *Fish, won't you wish some mo-or-ore,*
> *Wish some more,*
> *Wish some more,*
> *Fish, won't you wish some more!"*
> *(Raines, 1991)*

Something to think about
Let the children who show enthusiasm for composing find other songs that could have lyrics rewritten, and let them teach their new lyrics to the rest of the class.

STORY STRETCHER

For Writing Center: Fish Who Could Wish Stories

What the children will learn
To compose funny rhymes

Materials you will need
Pictures from the art story s-t-r-e-t-c-h-e-r, writing paper, pencils, index cards, stapler

What to do
1. Have the children look at their illustrations of "unexpected things in unexpected places."

2. Read some of the rhymes from the funny pictures in THE FISH WHO COULD WISH.

3. Let the children compose some funny rhymes for their own illustrations. For example,

> *"In the clear blue sky,*
> *In the clear of the sky,*
> *Flew a little bird with a*
> *Mind so absurd.*
> *He wished and*
> *His funny wishes came true.*
> *How absurd for a bird!"*
> *(Raines, 1991)*

4. Have them print their funny rhymes on an index card and staple them to the bottom of their "unexpected things in unexpected places" pictures.

Something to think about
For the children who are inspired to continue writing and who find this style particularly enjoyable, let them think of more funny rhymes and outrageous picture combinations.

10
LIFE IN THE SEA, REAL AND IMAGINED

IBIS: A TRUE WHALE STORY
by John Himmelman

Ibis is a story based on some real events which happened to a humpback whale calf who lived near a fishing village. Ibis and Blizzard, two whales, like looking at the little fish, particularly the starfish. Friendly whale-watching boats cause the whales to lose their fear of all boats and ships. Unfortunately, one boat brings a fishing net and Ibis is entangled. With the net wrapped around her mouth, she cannot eat and does not respond to her friend Blizzard's approaches. Blizzard, knowing something is wrong, pushes Ibis's body to the surface where whale watchers find a way to rescue her. Ibis responds to the humans wiggling their fingers in the water because it reminds her of starfish. John Himmelman's watercolor and ink drawings accurately capture the mood of the book.

Read-Aloud Suggestions

Show the cover of IBIS: A TRUE WHALE STORY and read the book. Also read the afterword, where John Himmelman tells about the origin of the story. Based on Himmelman's account in the afterword, discuss what is fact and what is fiction in the story. It is fact that Ibis, the whale, was entangled in the nets and that the whale watchers rescued her. We do not know if she really thought about starfish or wished for Blizzard to play with her. The story is based in truth but has some parts we cannot prove. This is one of the books that the children will want you to read again because it evokes such sympathetic feelings and a sense of triumph when Ibis is rescued.

STORY STRETCHER
For Art: Underwater/Overwater Scenes

What the children will learn
To show different views

Materials you will need
Pencils, paper, choice of watercolors, margarine tubs with water, brushes or colored pencils

What to do
1. Look again at John Himmelman's illustrations of IBIS: A TRUE WHALE STORY. Have the children notice the way they can see part of IBIS above the water and part below the water.

2. Encourage them to experiment with drawing the whales and the hulls of boats partly out of the water.

3. When the children have finished their underwater/overwater scenes, display them in the library area with the book jacket from IBIS: A TRUE WHALE STORY.

Something to think about
For younger children, let them fold their papers horizontally, and on one side draw above the water, then make a line on the fold to indicate the water line, and then turn the paper over and draw the rest of the whale's body and the water.

STORY STRETCHER
For Classroom Library: Story Retelling

What the children will learn
To retell the story in their own words

Materials you will need
Paper bag, scraps of paper, pencil, optional—cassette tapes and recorder

What to do
1. With a small group of five children, look through the illustrations of IBIS: A TRUE WHALE STORY and let the children recall what was happening in each scene.

2. Ask the children to retell the story.

3. Print the numbers 1, 2, 3, 4, 5 on scraps of paper. Place them in a paper bag and have the children draw out a number. That is the order in which they will take turns telling the story.

4. Let them sit in that order around you and pass the book from person to person, or select one child to hold the book.

5. If the children are interested, let them retell the story and tape-record it.

Something to think about
Books with powerful themes and a sense of suspense are excellent choices for story retelling.

For Music And Movement: Writing A Song For Ibis

What the children will learn

To write a song which tells a story

Materials you will need

Chart tablet, marker, optional—recording of whale sounds

What to do

1. If you can get a record of whale songs, play it for the children. Discuss how different sounds communicate different needs.

2. Ask the children to write a song telling the story of IBIS. Choose a familiar tune as the base for the song. For example, use the tune of "Row, Row, Row Your Boat." Sing,

> *"Row, row, row your boat*
> *Out to see the whales.*
> *Merrily, merrily, merrily,*
> *There a big whale blows.*
>
> *Row, row, row your boat*
> *Out to see the whales.*
> *What's that, what's that, what's that,*
> *I-bis is caught.*
>
> *Row, row, row your boat*
> *Out to see the whales.*
> *Help her, help her, help her*
> *What are we to do?*
>
> *Row, row, row your boat*
> *Out to see our whale.*
> *Attach a float, attach a float,*
> *Pull her on home.*
>
> *Cut, cut, cut the net*
> *Off our dear Ibis.*
> *Feed her well, feed her well*
> *Feed her well again.*
>
> *Swim, swim, swim I-bis*
> *Swim out to sea,*
> *Wave good-bye, wave good-bye,*
> *So long.*
> *Wave good-bye, wave good-bye, wa-ve,*
> *   wa-ve, wa-ve*
> *Good-bye! "*
> *   (Raines, 1991)*

3. Print the words on chart tablet paper for the *Big Book of Music*.

4. Record the song on the flip side of the book recording of IBIS: THE TRUE WHALE STORY.

Something to think about

If your school has a music teacher, ask the teacher to play the tune on the piano, write in the appropriate musical notes and teach the song to other classes.

For Science And Nature: Like Ibis, Different From Ibis

What the children will learn

To compare other whales to Ibis, the humpback

Materials you will need

Reference books on whales, charts or pictures of whales if possible, chart tablet or posterboard, marker

What to do

1. The story of Ibis will undoubtedly cause more interest in whales. Send a small group of children, "reference checkers," to the school library and have them tell the librarian about the Ibis book and the class' interest in whales.

2. Let the librarian collect an array of reference books, charts and pictures and have the "reference checkers" decide which books would be most helpful to the class.

3. Place the books on display along with IBIS: THE TRUE WHALE STORY in the science and nature center.

4. After the children have had a few days to browse through the books and find out more about whales, let them talk about what they have learned.

5. In the discussion, mention similarities and differences, and help the children see how scientists studying a species begin to classify them.

6. Let a child draw a sketch of Ibis or paste a picture of a small humpback whale at the top of a chart.

7. Ask the children to compare other whales to Ibis, according to what they have read and seen in the reference books on whales.

8. Draw a line down the center of the chart. On one side print, "Like Ibis," on the other side write, "Different from Ibis."

Something to think about

Let the children continue their studies by looking at dolphins and sharks. Younger children can compare dolphins, sharks and whales, rather than trying to discern similarities and differences among whales.

For Writing Center: Inquiring About Rescues

What the children will learn

To compose group letters asking questions

Materials you will need

Chalkboard and chalk or chart tablet and marker

What to do

1. Read the afterword again from IBIS: THE TRUE WHALE STORY in which the author tells about the work of the Center for Coastal Studies in Provincetown, Massachusetts.

2. Have the children think of some questions they would like to ask the people who work there: for example, Have they ever rescued any other whales? Does Ibis come back to that area?

3. After they have thought of questions, form small groups and

work with each group composing a letter to the director of the center.

4. If interested, request any additional materials about the work of their center.

5. Mail the letters to Center for Coastal Studies, PO Box 1036, Provincetown, MA 02657.

Something to think about

If you live near a coastal area, find out about any sea life rescue efforts in your area and contact them instead of the Provincetown Center.

References

Bush, John, & Paul, Korky. (1991). **THE FISH WHO COULD WISH.** Brooklyn, NY: Kane/Miller Book Publishers.

Cole, Sheila. (1985). Illustrated by Virginia Wright-Frierson. **WHEN THE TIDE IS LOW.** New York: Lothrop, Lee & Shepard Books.

Cowcher, Helen. (1990). **ANTARCTICA.** New York: Farrar, Straus and Giroux.

Himmelman, John. (1990). **IBIS: A TRUE WHALE STORY.** New York: Scholastic Inc.

Lionni, Leo. (1968). **SWIMMY.** New York: Pantheon.

Additional References for Life in the Sea, Real and Imagined

Gerstein, Mordecai. (1986). **THE SEAL MOTHER.** New York: Dial Books for Young Readers. *Based on a Scottish folktale, this book tells the story of a seal who becomes a human woman on Midsummer Eve. She marries and bears a son, and after seven years, she brings him to meet her seal family beneath the sea. He grows up as part of both worlds, and brings his own children to dance with the seals at Midsummer.*

Jonas, Ann. (1987). **REFLECTIONS.** New York: Greenwillow Books. *A magically illustrated book which chronicles a child's busy day by the seaside. The pictures transform themselves when you turn the book upside-down.*

McDonald, Megan. (1990). **IS THIS A HOUSE FOR HERMIT CRAB?** Illustrated by S. D. Schindler. New York: Orchard Books. *When the hermit crab outgrows his old house, he must go on a search along the shore for a new one. He finds many different kinds of things, but most of them just won't work as a house. This is a very informative adventure for the young reader.*

Ryder, Joanne. (1991). Illustrated by Michael Rothman. **WINTER WHALE.** New York: Morrow Junior Books. *After running through a warm rain, a young boy imagines himself as a humpback whale in the tropical sea where the humpbacks winter. This humpback meets many other sea creatures, and the reader swims through the experience of sea life with them all.*

Stock, Catherine. (1990). **ARMIEN'S FISHING TRIP.** New York: William Morrow and Company. *While visiting his aunt and uncle in the South African village of Kalk Bay, Armien stows away on his uncle's fishing boat and learns a great deal about the unexpected ferocity of the ocean.*

PETS, DOGS AND CATS

Hot Fudge

Rosalie

Minou

Will You Please Feed Our Cat?

Riptide

PETS, DOGS AND CATS

HOT FUDGE

By James Howe

Illustrated by Leslie Morrill

The story is told by Harold, the dog, and includes other family pets—Chester, the cat; Howie, the dachshund; and Bunnicula, the rabbit. The pets' adventure in the Monroe household revolves around Harold's attempts to guard the hot fudge, his favorite food. The pets soon find themselves dozing off, and the fudge disappears out from under their noses. The suspenseful tale ends with a visit to a bake sale and a special plate of fudge purchased just for the animals. The dialogue among the animals and the secure family life of bustling activities make the book an excellent one for primary children. Morrill's illustrations are humorous and realistic. The actions and expressions are a perfect match to the story.

Read-Aloud Suggestions

If you are a chocolate lover, tell the children about a time when you smelled fudge candy and your mouth began to water. Show the cover of HOT FUDGE and have the children predict what might happen. Have them notice how the illustrator indicated the wonderful aroma of freshly baked fudge. Tell the children that one of the pets is not shown on the cover, and have them look for the missing one. Read HOT FUDGE and pause during the reading for the children to confirm or reject the predictions they made based on the cover. There are several places where "predicting" can add to the drama of the story: when the entire family leaves, when the animals are trying to guess what happened to the fudge, and when they see the thief. Do not pause for predictions when you feel it may detract from the mounting intrigue. At the end, have the children recall the pet who was not shown on the cover. Read the note at the end of the book about not giving your pets chocolate because it makes them sick. Plan to read other Harold and Chester adventures that include more about Bunnicula.

STORY STRETCHER

For Art: I Wonder What Happens When I'm Not Home

What the children will learn
To contrast two scenes

Materials you will need
Variety of art supplies, paper, crayons, colored pencils, markers

What to do
1. Have the children talk about what their pets do when they are home.

2. Recall how Harold, Chester, Howie and Bunnicula acted differently when Toby and his family were away. Then lead the children to wonder what their pets do when they are not home.

3. Let the children fold a sheet of construction paper in half like a greeting card. On the outside, ask them to draw their pets and themselves together at home.

4. On the inside, they can illustrate what they imagine their pets do while they are away.

5. Display the contrasting pictures near the classroom library.

Something to think about
If children do not have their own pets, they can draw about playing with their friends' pets and imagine an adventure the animals have when no family and friends are around.

STORY STRETCHER

For Cooking: Mr. Monroe's Famous Fudge

What the children will learn
To follow a recipe

Materials you will need
Saucepan, oven mitts, hot plate, deep saucepan, wooden spoon, measuring cups and spoons, pie plate, knife, ingredients listed in the book, milk, glasses, napkins

What to do
1. Making fudge requires adult supervision; however, children can be involved in the measuring and take turns beating the fudge if precautions are taken, such as wearing an oven mitt to protect from hot fudge spattering.

2. Ask a parent or grandparent to come to class and demonstrate how to make fudge.

3. Select three or four children as candy makers. Let them take turns

assisting the volunteer in measuring, stirring and beating the fudge.

4. Have one child test to see if the fudge is ready by dropping a small amount into a cup of cold water, then seeing if it can be formed into a soft ball.

5. After the fudge cools, slice with a warm moist knife and serve with cold milk.

Something to think about
Microwave some fudge brownies as an alternative. Plan a "chocolate lovers sharing," and let the children bring one of their families' favorite chocolate recipes.

For Mathematics: How Much Does Fudge Cost?

What the children will learn
To read prices

Materials you will need
Ingredients from the fudge recipe, tray, Post-it notes, pen

What to do
1. Arrange the boxes and packages of ingredients on a tray.

2. Write the price for each item on a Post-it note and stick it to the box or package.

3. Let the children read the price tags and sequence the ingredients from the least expensive to the most expensive.

Something to think about
Second and third graders can count out play or real money to equal the amount for each ingredient. Older children can total the cost of the fudge.

For Science And Nature: What Pets Need To Stay Home Alone

What the children will learn
To decide solutions for common pet problems

Materials you will need
Chart tablet or posterboard, marker, pet toys, reference books

What to do
1. Discuss what the children already know about pets' needs for attention, food, water, places to sleep.

2. Talk about what animals do when their owners are away at school. Let some children tell how their animals have been destructive by chewing shoes or clawing furniture.

3. Draw a line down the center of a sheet of chart tablet paper or posterboard.

4. On the left side, write a list of problems pet owners have experienced.

5. On the right side, list solutions pet owners found for keeping their animals occupied and entertained while they were away.

6. With the children's help, create a display of toys and activities that keep animals entertained while their owners are away.

7. Add reference books on pets to the display.

Something to think about
Younger children can print a replica of the poster to take home to their family members to help with pet problems. Older children can plan a brochure on "Keeping Your Pet Happy While You Are at School." The information for the brochure can come from the veterinarian, the children's own experiences and reference materials.

For Writing Center: Pet Tales

What the children will learn
To tell a story from a perspective other than their own

Materials you will need
Photographs of their pets, writing paper, pencils, optional—art supplies for illustrations

What to do
1. Discuss that HOT FUDGE is told by Harold, the dog.

2. Let the children show the photographs of their pets to each other and begin brainstorming what their pets might say if they could talk.

3. Encourage the children to write a rough draft of their pet tales.

4. Take several days and let the children work in editing groups. (See the Introduction for more about the writing process and editing groups).

5. Display the children's stories in the class library with the other pet books for the unit.

Something to think about
Consider binding the children's stories into published books for the unit on pets. (See the binding directions in the Appendix.) Keep copies of the children's books, and use them in future years to expand the collection of pet books. This also helps young children see that you value the students' writing enough to keep copies to read to others.

ROSALIE

By Joan Hewett

Illustrated by Donald Carrick

Cindy lovingly tells about her old family pet, Rosalie. She remembers how Rosalie looked and played when she was young. Now that she is an old dog, Rosalie still likes to be near the children when they are playing, but she only watches. The affection between Cindy and Rosalie as well as the family and friends' feelings toward the pet make it a touching story. Carrick's full-page, colorful watercolors are realistic views of modern family life with just the right light and shadow for emphasis.

Read-Aloud Suggestions

Show the children the cover of the book and ask them to tell you the age of the dog. Discuss how they can tell that she is an older animal. Find out if any of the children have older dogs as pets. Ask if their animals are as old or older than they are. Read ROSALIE without pausing to discuss the story. Then let the children who have older dogs relate some cautions their parents tell them when taking care of their pets. Describe some of the story s-t-r-e-t-c-h-e-r-s planned for the study of older pets, and end the session by looking back through the pictures and letting the children recall what is happening as well as the beauty of the illustrations.

STORY STRETCHER

For Art: Then And Now Pictures

What the children will learn
To represent changes in their pets' lives

Materials you will need
Choice of art materials—paper, crayons, markers, watercolors, brushes

What to do
1. Look again at Carrick's watercolor illustrations in ROSALIE. Discuss the difference in the dog's appearance when she was young and now that she is older. Carrick shows gray around her eyes, a slightly curved spine and a bit of droopy skin.

2. Have the children talk about how their pets' appearances have changed. Even if they have puppies or kittens, they can describe more subtle changes.

3. Ask the children to make two illustrations, one showing their pets when they first got them and one how they look now.

Something to think about
Display the "then and now" pictures in a variety of ways: glue them back-to-back and hang them like mobiles; add masking tape across the tops of the pictures, punch holes in the tape, add a long string and hang them on bulletin boards so they can be turned from front to back to see the difference in appearance; or fold papers like greeting cards with "then" pictures on the outside and "now" drawings on the inside.

STORY STRETCHER

For Classroom Library: Books On Tape

What the children will learn
To read dialogue

Materials you will need
Cassette tape, recorder, chalkboard, chalk, stapler

What to do
1. Read the story of ROSALIE again, and each time you read dialogue, write the speaker's name on the chalkboard.

2. Let the children volunteer to read the dialogue each character speaks. Write the volunteers' names beside the characters' names on the chalkboard.

3. Have the children practice reading their lines.

4. Select a child to be Cindy who is a fluent reader.

5. Determine a page-turning signal, such as the click of the stapler, and assign a child assigned to record the signal on cue.

6. Record the story more than once if the children are not satisfied with their reading.

Something to think about
Practice with a child who is not a fluent reader, and let that child become Cindy after the extra practice. It is easier to read the dialogue in this story because the speech is very natural.

For Mathematics: Sixteen Is Almost 100?

What the children will learn
To think about what ratios mean

Materials you will need
Counting blocks or unit blocks, baskets or small paper bags

What to do
1. Read again the first page of ROSALIE where Cindy says that Rosalie is 16 years old and the vet says that is almost 100 in human terms.

2. Let the children discuss the meaning of "16 being almost 100."

3. Divide 100 by 16. Place 100 blocks on a table.

4. Have the children count out sets of 16 blocks and fill the baskets or bags. They will find out how many sets they can make.

5. After they have made six sets of 16 blocks and have four left over, discuss what these 100 blocks represent in human years, and the six sets of sixteen represent in dog years.

Something to think about
Younger children can practice counting to 100 and making sets of 16. Third graders who are learning division can use the mathematical symbols. Older children can research other ratios of length of pet lifes to human life and think of ways to represent these symbolically.

For Science And Nature: Caring For An Older Dog

What the children will learn
To consider an older dog's needs

Materials you will need
Chart tablet, markers

What to do
1. Recall the veterinarian or animal control officer's visit (a RIPTIDE story s-t-r-e-t-c-h-e-r in this chapter) and some of the pointers he or she mentioned about taking care of an older pet.

2. Draw a line down the center of a sheet of chart tablet paper and, on the left side, write a list of problems Rosalie had because she was getting older, such as loss of hearing, sleeping in places where children were playing, keeping out of traffic, illness.

3. On the right side of the paper, make a list of the things Rosalie and her family did to take care of Rosalie's problems.

4. In a different colored marker, write any problems the children have in taking care of their older pets on the left side of the paper.

5. On the right side of the paper, print in a different colored marker how the children and their families take care of their older pets' problems.

Something to think about
Talk about the problems of older cats and the changes cat owners must consider to take care of their pets' needs.

For Writing Center: Young Pet, Old Pet Stories

What the children will learn
To write descriptive stories contrasting young and old

Materials you will need
Paper, pencils, selection of art supplies for illustrations.

What to do
1. Read ROSALIE again and listen to Cindy's descriptions of how Rosalie looked, moved, played and interacted with the family when the dog was younger . Then listen for the descriptive words the author used as Cindy tells about Rosalie now.

2. Ask the children to take a sheet of paper, draw a line down the center and print their pet's name at the top of the paper.

3. On one side write words that describe how the pet was when she or he was younger, and on the other side, list words that describe the pet now.

4. Encourage the children to compose a story about their pet and use the descriptive words in their writing.

Something to think about
Younger children often prefer drawing before writing. The drawing can substitute for the contrasting word list. Drawing seems to focus their attention and lets them work out the action in the story before beginning to write. Again, please keep the writing topics open. If a child is engaged in another piece of writing, do not assign this one.

MINOU

By Mindy Bingham

Illustrated by Itoko Maeno

Minou is very happy living with Madame Violette, a painter, in Paris. Then Minou's owner becomes very sick and is taken away in an ambulance, and the cat must fend for herself. Fortunately, she meets Celeste, another cat, who helps her learn to be independent. Eventually, she finds a home at the rectory near Notre Dame Cathedral. Itoko Maeno's exquisite watercolors are wonderful works of art with street scenes of Paris and familiar landmarks. At the end of the book, there is a legend telling about each of the famous landmarks Minou saw. The end papers are maps of Paris. Proceeds from the book benefit the Girls Clubs of America, and the book emphasizes their theme of independence.

Read-Aloud Suggestions

Show the children the cover of MINOU and look at the street scene. Ask if the cat lives in the city or in the country. Look at the back cover of the book and tell the children that this famous landmark, the Eiffel Tower, gives them a clue to the city in France where the story takes place. Talk with the children about what being "independent" means. Discuss how they make choices throughout the day and take care of themselves so that they can be "independent." After reading a few pages, have the children decide whether or not Minou is an independent cat or a dependent cat. Continue the story without interruption, but at the end, return to the discussion of how Minou learned to take care of herself, to become independent.

STORY STRETCHER

For Art: Postcards From Paris

What the children will learn
To match photographs to watercolors

Materials you will need
Postcards or pictures of Paris

What to do
1. Look through the illustrations in MINOU, and tell the children the names of the landmarks seen in the illustrations.

2. Show the children the back of the cover of MINOU, which is a watercolor of the Eiffel Tower. Match it to a postcard or picture of Paris.

3. Look at other postcards and photographs and see if the children notice any that match the illustrations in the story.

4. Let them leisurely look at the postcards, photographs and illustrations and match as many of them as possible.

Something to think about
Emphasize enjoying the beauty of the postcards and the watercolors in the book.

ANOTHER STORY STRETCHER

For Art: Minou's Stained Glass Windows

What the children will learn
To arrange colors for stained glass effects

Materials you will need
Black construction paper, scissors, colored tissue paper, waxed paper, iron, glue stick, clear tape

What to do
1. Show the children the watercolor illustrations of the stained glass windows in Notre Dame Cathedral in MINOU.

2. On black construction paper, let the children draw an outline of a shape for a window. The outline frame should be about one-fourth to one-half inch in width.

3. Cut out the window frame.

4. Cut a sheet of waxed paper large enough to fit in the window frame.

5. Cut or tear pieces of colored tissue paper to represent broken pieces of colored glass.

6. Arrange the colored pieces of tissue paper onto the sheet of waxed paper. Lay the window frame on top to check the positions of the colored tissue paper.

7. When the tissue paper is arranged the way the children want it, cut a second sheet of waxed paper and place it over the top.

8. Iron the pieces together with a warm iron set on low heat.

9. Position the black construction paper frame over the waxed paper and glue into place.

10. When the glue has dried, trim off excess waxed paper from around the frame.

11. Tape the paper stained glass windows to the classroom windows for light to shine through them.

Something to think about
Older children can make duplicate frames for the front and back of their windows. To hang stained glass windows like mobiles, place a small piece of black electrician's tape at the top, punch a hole through the tape and construction paper, string nylon fishing wire or thread through the hole and hang from the ceiling or in windows.

STORY STRETCHER

For Cooking: Sidewalk Cafe

What the children will learn
To bake croissants

Materials you will need
Refrigerator pastry croissants, baking sheet, toaster oven, basket, napkins, knives, butter or margarine, jelly, milk

What to do
1. With a group of children who volunteer to be bakers, read the directions on the package.

2. Bake enough croissants for the entire class.

3. Wrap hot croissants in a napkin and place in a basket.

4. Serve hot croissants with butter or margarine, jelly and cold milk.

5. Remind the children of the part of Minou's adventure when she visited a sidewalk cafe and saw the people having croissants, eclairs and other French pastries.

Something to think about
Warm prepared croissants and serve with an array of French pastries. Teach the children the names of the pastries. Set up a dramatic play area as a sidewalk cafe and let the children pretend to be waiters, chefs, customers.

STORY STRETCHER

For Science And Nature: Classifying By Breed

What the children will learn
To recognize the features of cat breeds

Materials you will need
Cat pictures from old calendars and magazines, scissors, tape, large index cards, glue, reference books on cats

What to do
1. Let the children search through magazines and cut out pictures of cats and glue them onto index cards.

2. Cut out pictures from the cat calendar and reinforce the edges if needed.

3. Have the children find a cat like Minou, a Siamese.

4. Let them name other breeds they recognize.

5. Provide the reference books, and let the children go through them, matching their pictures with those in the book or books.

6. Have the children print the name of the breed at the bottom of the cat pictures they found in magazines or calendars.

7. Display the pictures in the science area along with a copy of MINOU and the reference books.

Something to think about
Invite a cat owner who has an unusual breed to bring his or her pet to class. Instruct the children ahead of time about how to observe the cat.

STORY STRETCHER

For Writing Center: What If Minou, The Cat, Were Lost In Our Town?

What the children will learn
To describe landmarks of their communities

Materials you will need
Chalkboard, chalk, drawing paper, colored pens, writing paper, pencils, optional—brochures about the area

What to do
1. Discuss how we knew Minou was lost in Paris. List the famous landmarks and scenes.

2. Ask the children what Minou would see if she came to our town. List the well-known places and any famous landmarks.

3. Let the children begin sketching a favorite spot in their town.

4. Suggest that spot be the place Minou begins her journey to independence.

5. Have the children write their Minou stories and edit them.

6. Display the stories in the writing area near the science exhibit of the pictures of different cat breeds.

Something to think about
Younger children, who have less of a sense of the larger community, can write about Minou's visit to our school or to the street where they live. Older children could also write Minou stories for other famous cities and bind these into books for the class library.

11

PETS, DOGS AND CATS

WILL YOU PLEASE FEED OUR CAT?

By James Stevenson

When Mary Ann and Louie are left in charge of the neighbor's pet, it reminds Grandpa of the time he and his brother Wainey were asked to feed their neighbor's cat. Grandpa and Wainey rig up all kinds of elaborate contraptions to feed the cat and other animals. This zany, preposterous tale entertains and fits children's growing sense of the responsibility of pets. In comic book style, Stevenson draws dialogue balloons, yet adds text along the top and bottom of the page. Some illustrations are full-page and others are a series of smaller prints, like comic books panels.

Read-Aloud Suggestions

Have the children tell what they do at home to take care of their pets. Ask if any children have ever taken on the responsibility of helping to care for the neighbors' pets when they were out of town. Tell about any experiences you may have had taking care of someone else's pet. Read WILL YOU PLEASE FEED OUR CAT? Because this is such a funny book, the children will immediately request that you read it again. Emphasize the way the author used a cartooning technique of placing the characters' speech in balloons. Show the children a comic book or a comic strip from the newspaper and have them notice the balloons for the dialogue. Select cartoons and comic books that have pets or animals as characters.

STORY STRETCHER

For Art: Cartoons About Pets

What the children will learn
To draw speech balloons

Materials you will need
Comic books, comic strips, drawing paper, crayons, markers, colored pencils

What to do
1.   With the children who come to the art center, look again at the comic books, comic strips, and at James Stevenson's illustrations in WILL YOU PLEASE FEED OUR CAT?

2.   Ask them to draw a picture that involves themselves taking care of a pet.

3.   Add speech balloons to the picture.

Something to think about
Draw dialogue or speech balloons onto Post-it notes. Keep the top of the balloon at the top of the Post-it note, so that the adhesive is still present even after the balloon is cut out. Let children write comments for each other's pictures and change the balloons. This lets children see how actions can be interpreted in many different ways.

STORY STRETCHER

For Cooking: Pet Stories And Grandpa's Lemonade

What the children will learn
To make homemade lemonade

Materials you will need
Dozen lemons, knives, juicer, strainer, pitcher, water, sugar, ice, glasses

What to do
1.   Show the children how to cut a lemon in half, place it over the curved top of the juicer and twist.

2.   Demonstrate how to pour the juice through the strainer.

3.   Add water to the juice in the pitcher.

4.   Add sugar to sweeten.

5.   Serve over ice.

6.   Let everyone sip lemonade while you read again the story from WILL YOU PLEASE FEED OUR CAT? that Grandpa told to the children while they were sipping lemonade on his front porch. Read other Grandpa and Wainey stories by James Stevenson.

Something to think about
Try homemade limeade and pink lemonade. Also compare the tastes of homemade lemonade, frozen lemonade and drink mix lemonade. Make a comparison study of drink preferences among the class members.

For Science And Nature: Taking Care Of The Class Pet

What the children will learn

To list, describe, divide and share responsibilities for taking care of the class pet

Materials you will need

Posterboard, marker, calendar

What to do

1. Discuss what the class pet needs: attention, food, water, place to live.

2. List all the jobs associated with taking care of the class pet.

3. Discuss each job and decide how often it needs to be done—daily, weekly, monthly—to be responsible pet owners.

4. Decide on the supplies needed to do each job. List them and the quantities needed. Use specific mathematical terms as much as possible: for example, place one-fourth cup of gerbil food in the cage; keep water bottle filled to at least one-half cup for the weekend; place four sheets of newspaper in the bottom of the cage.

5. Mark each job on the calendar and assign each child in the class some responsibility on a rotating basis.

Something to think about

Consider what is to be done with the class pet over long weekends and holidays. In the parent newsletter, describe the class pet and ask for volunteers to keep the pet during school breaks. If your school does not allow pets, seek permission to have children's pets, ones that are easy to care for to come for a week.

For Science And Nature: Strings And Things Inventions

What the children will learn

To design inventive ways to use strings

Materials you will need

Twine; yarn; strings; scissors; tape; staplers; cardboard; other recyclables—styrofoam egg cartons, plastic straws, plastic cups, paper towel rolls

What to do

1. Let the children look at the inventions Grandpa and Wainey made to feed the neighbor's cats and other pets.

2. Ask the children to describe some of the inventions they have made at home.

3. Place the materials listed above on an "inventions table." Let the children brainstorm some ways the materials could be used. Do not insist on an invention, but provide the materials as motivation. Allow a week for the children to tinker with the materials.

4. Have a display of "strings and things invention" associated with pets and pet care.

5. Use as many of the other inventions as possible throughout the classroom.

Something to think about

Children are wonderful tinkers. Talk about how great inventors often had many inventions that failed. Encourage them to experiment, because even when an invention fails in some respect, it may work in others.

For Writing Center: My Cat Is My Responsibility

What the children will learn

To write specifically and descriptively about their cats and what their cats' needs are

Materials you will need

Writing paper, pencils, chalkboard, chalk

What to do

1. Let the children who have cats as family pets discuss what their pets' needs are.

2. After a few children have talked, ask other students who do not have cats as pets to summarize what they are hearing.

3. On the chalkboard, write a summary the group composes.

4. From the summary, ask the pet owners to write specifically about their cats. For example, instead of saying, "cat," use the pet's name. Write exactly where in the house the cat naps in the sun. Describe specifically the household objects the cat plays with, etc.

Something to think about

As a writing extension, have the cat owners tell who takes care of their cat when they are away for vacation and what specific written instructions they leave for the "cat-sitter."

RIPTIDE

By Frances Wade Weller

Illustrated by Robert J. Blake

RIPTIDE is the true adventure of a dog who became the nineteenth lifeguard at a beach because of his heroism in saving a little girl from drowning. Rip belonged to Zach's family, who ran a fruit and vegetable stand near Nauset Beach, but he spent most of his time romping and playing on the beach and diving and swimming in the ocean. The problem was that no dogs were allowed on the beach. The lifeguards ran him off the beach all summer until one hot, sultry day when there was a tremendous storm with huge riptides. A little girl was pulled out to sea and was drowning. Rip swam out to her, and she caught his tail while he pulled her over to the lifeguard. Blake's oil paintings are truly works of art with deep blue, turquoise and azure seas, white-capped waves, sandy beaches with lapping surf and beautifully sunny days with billowing clouds as well as stormy skies.

Read-Aloud Suggestions

If you live near a beach and many of your children have visited the seashore, ask them about the rules at the beach. Find out if dogs were allowed on the beach. Discuss why animals might be prohibited. If many of your students do not know about beaches, tell them about your own experiences and about the rules. Show the children the cover of the book and tell them that this story is based on a real dog. Read RIPTIDE without pausing to ask questions or discussing the story. At the end of the book, read the author's note about the newspaper clipping and interview information used to write the story. The book is such a popular one with children that they will want you to read it again. Do not hesitate to read it a second time, or show the beautiful paintings that illustrate the book, pausing for the children to recall what happened in each scene.

STORY STRETCHER

For Classroom Library: Pictures And Pet Stories

What the children will learn
To tell information about their pets in a way that will interest listeners

Materials you will need
Photographs of pets, cassette tapes and recorder

What to do
1. Ask the children to bring pictures of their pets or of pets they would like to have.

2. In small groups, have the children show their pet pictures and tell a bit about their animals and what they would like to say on the tape. Tape-record the discussion.

3. Listen to the tapes and let each small group brainstorm some ideas for stories based on what the children said. For example, one child might tell about the day she went to the animal shelter to select her dog. Another child might tell why he wants a certain pet that he does not have. Someone else might talk about a time when her pet was heroic, or was lost and found his way back, or about all the steps when moving a pet to a new home.

4. Ask each child to make an individual tape about a pet.

5. Place the tapes and the photographs of the pets in the classroom library.

Something to think about
Have older children work with partners and interview each other like television reporters. First graders can make their tapes in a "show-and-tell" manner, by placing their pet pictures on the bulletin board in the classroom library, then telling about their pet on tape.

ANOTHER STORY STRETCHER

For Classroom Library: Collection Of Animal Adventure Books

What the children will learn
To find other animal adventure stories

Materials you will need
Librarian's reference books

What to do
1. Talk with the librarian ahead of time and tell her or him that some of your children will be coming to the library to find more true animal adventure stories.

2. Ask the librarian to conduct the research steps that she or he would use to locate the books with the children.

3. With a small group of children who are particularly interested in RIPTIDE and other adventure stories, go through the steps of finding the books. Let the children browse through them and decide whether or not to check them out for the classroom collection.

Something to think about
Teachers have learned that when children are allowed to select books on topics which interest them, they read more difficult stories. Even if the children cannot read all the words, they can get information from the pictures, scan the text and learn to seek answers from more than one source.

For Mathematics: How Many Children In Our Class Have Pets?

What the children will learn
To prepare a graph and compare total numbers by categories

Materials you will need
Note pads, pencils, chart tablet or posterboard, black marker and three other different colors of markers

What to do
1. Illustrate how to make a simple bar graph by asking questions and answering questions.

2. With a black marker, draw a baseline across the bottom of the posterboard or a sheet of chart tablet paper.

3. The first question is, "How many children do we have in class?" Answer the question by letting each child mark a horizontal straight line an inch or two long. Start the lines at the baseline or the bottom of the chart tablet or posterboard.

4. The second question is, "How many students have one pet at home?" Using another marker, let each child who has one pet draw a line in a second column up from the baseline.

5. The third question is, "How many students have more than one pet at home?" Use a third color and let each child who has more than one pet make a mark.

6. Look at the answers to the questions and call the information "data." Have the children decide what the answers to their questions are.

7. Discuss how to make the bar graph more readable. One idea is to label each bar, telling what it means by writing the questions or a shorter version, such as "number of children," "one pet," "more than one pet." Consider drawing a straight black line across the column when ten children have made their marks. This allows the children to count more easily.

8. Let the children think of some other questions they would like answered. For example, "How many different kinds of pets do the people in this class own?" Help them formulate questions.

Something to think about
For older children, survey all the classes in one grade level and make comparison graphs with different colored lines showing numbers and kinds of pets. Another in-class project could include graphing numbers of different kinds of pets and favorite pet names.

For Special Event: Visit From Veterinarian Or Animal Control Officer

What the children will learn
To learn the safety laws and recommendations for their communities

Materials you will need
Posterboard or chart tablet, marker

What to do
1. Invite a veterinarian or an animal control officer from your community to visit the classroom and discuss how to practice good safety for an animal in your community.

2. Talk with the guest ahead of time and discuss some of the important points you want to emphasize.

3. Prepare a "KWL" chart. Under the "K" column, let the children list all the safety precautions for pets they already "know." Under the "W" column, list their general questions, or what the children "want to know."

4. After the guest shares information with the class, complete the chart in the "L" column by answering the questions and listing other information the students "learned."

Something to think about
Invite someone in your community who has a seeing eye dog or other dog trained to work with a handicapped person to come to your classroom and talk about the special care and training the pet received and how the dog works for them.

STORY STRETCHER

For Writing Center: My Pet

What the children will learn

To use drawing as a pre-writing device and to determine at least three main events

Materials you will need

Manilla paper, colored pencils, markers, crayons

What to do

1. Talk with the children about the three main events in RIPTIDE: the dog's enjoyment of the beach, the lifeguards chasing him away, and the time he saved the little girl's life.

2. Fold a sheet of manilla paper into thirds. Tell the children that if you were illustrating this story, you would place each of the main events on a third of the paper.

3. Ask the children to fold their papers, then think of three main events that tell their pet's story.

4. Have the children draw their main events.

5. Then ask the students to write about each main event in the story.

Something to think about

The children who made the listening tapes may be interested in writing a story for the other side of their tapes. They can write the story, then read it into the microphone to record it on the second side of their cassette tapes about pets. The children's stories can then be stored with the tapes, and other students can read the written story while the child reads it on the tape.

References

Bingham, Mindy. (1987). Illustrated by Itoko Maeno. **MINOU**. Santa Barbara: Advocacy Press.

Hewett, Joan. (1987). Illustrated by Donald Carrick. **ROSALIE**. New York: Lothrop, Lee & Shepard Books.

Howe, James. (1990). Illustrated by Leslie Morrill. **HOT FUDGE**. New York: William Morrow.

Stevenson, James. (1987). **WILL YOU PLEASE FEED OUR CAT?** New York: Greenwillow.

Weller, Frances Ward. (1990). Illustrated by Robert J. Blake. **RIPTIDE**. New York: Philomel Books.

Additional References For Pets, Dogs And Cats

Baker, Leslie. (1987). **THE THIRD-STORY CAT**. Boston: Little, Brown and Company. *Alice is a cat who lives in a third-floor apartment. In this very believable story, she has a scary but exhilarating outdoor adventure.*

Bayley, Nicola, & Mayne, William. (1981). **THE PATCHWORK CAT**. New York: Alfred A. Knopf, Dragonfly Books. *Tabby has a well-loved and well-worn patchwork quilt to sleep on, but one adventurous day she has to rescue it fron the trash.*

Cleary, Beverly. (1961). Illustrated by DyAnne DiSalvo-Ryan. **TWO DOG BISCUITS**. New York: William Morrow and Company. *One day, Janet and Jimmy had two dog biscuits to give away. None of the dogs they met seemed quite nice enough to get a present, but it turns out that **cats** eat dog biscuits too!*

Cole, Joanna. (1973). Photographs by Margaret Miller. **MY PUPPY IS BORN**. New York: Morrow Junior Books. *The photographs record Dolly's birth, and the young narrator's joy at welcoming the new puppy and watching her grow.*

Pizer, Abigail. (1988). **CHARLIE THE PUPPY**. Minneapolis: Carolrhoda Books, Inc. *Charlie the puppy looks all over the farm for someone to play with, and he gets into very puppy-like trouble everywhere he goes.*

ANOTHER TIME AND PLACE

Song and Dance Man
Miss Rumphius
Flossie and the Fox
When I Was Young in the Mountains
Roxaboxen

12

ANOTHER TIME AND PLACE

SONG AND DANCE MAN

By Karen Ackerman

Illustrated by Stephen Gammell

A Caldecott Medal book, SONG AND DANCE MAN is the story of three children who learn to appreciate the past by seeing it through their grandfather's eyes. They look at posters and pictures, dig through the attic trunk and pretend to be on stage. But Grandpa is the one who makes the past come to life when he puts on his tap shoes, his striped vest and bowler hat and becomes the vaudeville SONG AND DANCE MAN. Told affectionately, the story makes a hero of Grandpa, but the pages vibrate with Stephen Gammell's bright colors, the acrobatic moves of the tap dancer and the delightful expressions of the cheering audience of three.

Read-Aloud Suggestions

If possible, bring an old trunk or suitcase from home and fill it with dress-up clothes. Place the trunk by your side. Do not open it until after you have read SONG AND DANCE MAN. Then pretend to sprinkle some powder on the floor and dance a few soft shoe dance steps. By this time, the children will be clamoring to find out what is in the trunk. Unpack a few dress-up clothes, and as you bring out each item, let a child claim it to wear for creative dramatics. End by announcing all the story s-t-r-e-t-c-h-e-r-s for SONG AND DANCE MAN.

STORY STRETCHER

For Art: Vaudeville Poster For Our Class

What the children will learn
To paint a poster announcing a special event

Materials you will need
Posterboard or large sheets of paper, tempera paint, brushes, easels

What to do
1. Look at Stephen Gammell's Caldecott Medal winning illustrations. Have the children tell why they think he won the medal for the pictures in SONG AND DANCE MAN.

2. Examine the picture which has Grandpa's posters tacked to the attic wall.

3. Ask the children to make posters announcing their own performances for the "Attic Stage."

4. Attach the posterboard or paper to the easel. Fill paint jars with primary colors.

5. Display the posters on easels for the children's pretend performances in the creative dramatics story s-t-r-e-t-c-h-e-r.

Something to think about

As an alternative activity, younger children might enjoy painting pictures of themselves pretending to perform as singers, dancers, comedians or musicians.

STORY STRETCHER

For Classroom Library: New Invention For An Old song

What the children will learn
To use a videotape camera

Materials you will need
Chalkboard, chalk, videotapes, camera, tripod, videotape player

What to do
1. Discuss with the children that Grandpa told his story by taking the grandchildren to the attic and performing for them. Talk about the fact that Grandpa said he was a vaudeville performer before there was television. Obviously, he was a performer before videotape cameras and VCR players as well.

2. Read SONG AND DANCE MAN again and let the children think of how they could dramatize that part of the story and videotape their dramatization.

3. Write their ideas for the different scenes on the chalkboard.

4. Divide up the class members into technicians, performers and directors. The technicians will videotape the scenes. The performers will get their costumes ready and act out the scenes, while the directors will cue the actors.

5. Have the children improvise dialogue that goes with each scene.

6. Videotape the children dramatizing the entire book.

7. Also videotape yourself reading THE SONG AND DANCE MAN.

Something to think about

If needed, you pretend to be Grandpa and dress up for the part. You can keep the momentum of the story going.

For Creative Dramatics: Attic Stage

What the children will learn

To pretend to be a performer

Materials you will need

Trunk, dress-up clothes, canes, hats, full-length mirror, optional—tap shoes

What to do

1. Include the entire class in the production and let every child participate as a performer. Help them to understand that the attic stage is a magic stage where everyone can pretend.

2. Leave the trunk in the read-aloud area.

3. Let the children unpack the clothes and watch the improvising and drama which takes place naturally as they try on the clothes.

4. Encourage the pretending by joining the group and dancing or singing with a child.

5. Let the children who are interested make up songs, dances, jokes and magic acts and perform them for the attic stage audience—who are the other children in the classroom.

Something to think about

Avoid turning this pretend activity into a real stage production for parents and a larger school audience. When asked to put on a production or participate in a school-wide entertainment event, have the children sing some songs and read poetry which are a normal part of your classroom. Parents will be just as entertained, and the chil-

dren will not develop that awful fear of public speaking that many adults trace back to those early "forced" performances in the primary grades.

For Music And Movement: A Little Soft Shoe

What the children will learn

To do a few simple dance steps

Materials you will need

Recording of music for tap dancers, record or tape player

What to do

1. Ask a grandparent who is a dancer, a dance teacher, a parent volunteer, or an older student who takes dance lessons to come to class and teach the children a few dance steps.

2. After the dancer has gotten the children to dance, let them perform for their appreciative audience.

3. Continue the dancing throughout the week so the children can enjoy the steps and recall them easily.

Something to think about

Enjoy learning the steps with the children. The first step in creating a warm, emotionally safe and expressive environment for young children begins with the teacher's enjoyment of the activity. Drama, music and movement with young primary children is most effective with a teacher who feels uninhibited.

For Writing Center: Another Time and Place Stories With Illustrations

What the children will learn

To find out and write about their grandparents' or parents' past

Materials you will need

Drawing paper, crayons, chalk, markers, colored pencils, writing paper, pencils

What to do

1. Have the children begin by drawing a picture of what they see their grandparents, or parents doing now, and then find out what they used to do when they were younger.

2. They can fold a sheet of drawing paper down the middle and on the one side draw their grand-parents and parents as they know them now.

3. Look at old photo albums or ask their parents and grandparents about what they liked to do when they were younger.

4. After the children's investigations, they can complete the other side of the drawings.

5. Then they can write about their "Now" and "Another Time and Place" drawings of their parents or grandparents.

Something to think about

Display the stories and illustrations on a bulletin board in the writing center. Attach an old photograph of the child's grandparents or parents to the story.

MISS RUMPHIUS

By Barbara Cooney

Winner of the American Book Award, MISS RUMPHIUS is a beautiful story about the life of Alice and how she became known as the Lupine Lady. As a child she made three promises to her grandfather, to live by the sea, to travel to faraway places and to make the world more beautiful. When she grew up she became Miss Rumphius, the librarian. She traveled to faraway places and she lived by the sea, but she did not know what to do to make the world more beautiful. Finally, she thinks of spreading lupine seeds over the countryside and becomes known as the Lupine Lady. She has made the world more beautiful by sowing blue, purple and rose-colored flowers. Barbara Cooney's distinctive style of fragile lines yet strong messages is painted in acrylics with pencil. She captures the stages of Alice's life—childhood, adult Miss Rumphius and the aging Lupine Lady—with an exquisite, delicate touch.

Read-Aloud Suggestions

Show the cover of MISS RUMPHIUS and tell the children that the flowers on the front are lupines. Read the story of the Lupine Lady without pausing for discussion. Let the children recall Alice's three promises to her grandfather. Leaf through the pages and have the children tell what they like about the story or about Barbara Cooney's illustrations. Read the story again and end by letting the children tell what they could do to make the world a more beautiful place.

S T O R Y   S T R E T C H E R

For Art: Blue, Purple And Rose-Colored Flowers

What the children will learn
To mix painting techniques

Materials you will need
Paper; brushes; blue; purple and rose tempera paints; scissors; sponges; margarine tubs

What to do
1. Demonstrate for the children how to mix brush and sponge painting. For example, with a brush, paint a straight stem for a flower, and then print textures onto the paper to make the blossoms by dipping small pieces of sponge into paint and pressing them onto the paper. Avoid painting a model for the children to replicate.

2. Let the children experiment by making flowers of their own design.

3. Display the flower paintings on a bulletin board under the title "Miss Rumphius Likes Lupines."

Something to think about
Some children may enjoy the art work Alice did as a child when she helped her grandfather paint scenes from the sea.

S T O R Y   S T R E T C H E R

For Classroom Library: Three Voices Of Miss Rumphius

What the children will learn
To associate the voices with stages of life

Materials you will need
Cassette tapes, recorder, stapler

What to do
1. Ask a child, the school librarian and an older friend to help you record the story of MISS RUMPHIUS.

2. Divide the story into three parts and have the child read the sections which describe Miss Rumphius as Alice. Ask the school librarian to read the section of the book where she is known as Miss Rumphius, and the older friend read the section where she becomes the Lupine Lady.

3. Record an introduction to the tape and click a stapler near the microphone of the cassette recorder as the signal for the listener to turn the page.

4. Place the tape of the "Three Voices of Miss Rumphius" at the listening station in the classroom library. Let the children discover it on their own.

Something to think about
Since the story is written as if Miss Rumphius' niece is telling it, have a child read the entire story on the other side of the tape.

S T O R Y   S T R E T C H E R

For Science And Nature: Growing Lupines

What the children will learn
To grow plants from seeds

Materials you will need

Seed catalog, lupine seeds, poster-board, marker, potting soil, pots, plastic cups, small spades, watering can, trays

What to do

1.   Order some lupine seeds from a catalog. Show the children how you filled out the order blank.

2.   Post a picture of the flowers in the science and nature center.

3.   When the seeds arrive, reprint the planting directions on poster-board.

4.   Let each child plant some lupine seeds. Plant some extra ones in small potting trays.

5.   Let the children replant the tiny seedlings into larger containers according to potting directions.

6.   Follow the package instructions for the amount of sun and water.

7.   When the flowers are hardier, plant them outside the classroom and let the children watch the cycle of plant life.

Something to think about

Write for materials from the National Wildflower Society and find out about Lady Bird Johnson's project to sow wildflowers along American highways.

STORY STRETCHER

For Writing Center: A Written Portrait

What the children will learn

To write vivid descriptions of interesting people they know

Materials you will need

Writing paper, pencils, optional—materials for illustrations

What to do

1.   Read MISS RUMPHIUS again and discuss how the author painted a written portrait of the stages of Alice's life.

2.   Ask the children to write a very descriptive piece about someone they know. Brainstorm the main ideas: for example, how does the person look, what does he or she do that is so special, what do they talk about.

3.   Let each writer draw a web of their character portrait by drawing a circle in the middle of the page. Write the person's name in the middle, and with little lines radiating out from the circle, write appearance, actions, talk or stories.

4.   From their webs, the children can write portraits of interesting friends.

Something to think about

Younger children can write portraits of their friends in the classroom. Older children might like to try written portraits of teachers and helpers at their school.

ANOTHER STORY STRETCHER

For Writing Center: Making My World More Beautiful

What the children will learn

To express their feelings in writing

Materials you will need

Writing paper, pencils, optional—art materials

What to do

1.   Remind the writers of some of the things children said at read-aloud time, when they talked about how they would like to make the world more beautiful.

2.   Let the children think of things which they feel to be beautiful.

3.   Ask the children to write about the beautiful things they enjoy, what they would do if they were Miss Rumphius, or what they personally would like to do to make their world more beautiful.

Something to think about

For younger children, let them write about how to make the school more beautiful or their home more beautiful.

163

12
ANOTHER TIME AND PLACE

FLOSSIE & THE FOX

By Patricia C. McKissack

Illustrated by Rachel Isadora

Set in another era, this folktale is the story of how a little girl outsmarts a sly fox by refusing to believe he is the fox. Sent by her grandmother to take eggs to a neighbor, little Flossie encounters the fox along a path in the woods. Calling him a rabbit, a rat, a cat and a squirrel, Flossie has the fox trying to convince her he is really a fox, but she outwits him again and again. Told in black dialect from another time, Flossie's cunning, quick-thinking retorts have children cheering for the heroine. In the author's note, Patricia McKissack attributes this tale to her grandfather. Isadora's illustrations are rich with warm earth tones, auburns and woodsy greens with streaks of sunlight along the paths.

Read-Aloud Suggestions

Show the cover of FLOSSIE & THE FOX and let the children suggest why Flossie is smiling and why the fox is smiling. Ask if they think this story is set in the past or in the present. Read the "author's note" at the beginning of the book in which McKissack remembers being a little girl and hearing her grandfather tell stories. Read FLOSSIE & THE FOX without pausing for discussion. At the end of the story, have the children tell what they felt when Flossie first met the fox, then what they felt at the end when she scared him away by tricking him. If any children ask about the dialect, discuss that this is the way Flossie's family talked a long time ago. This is one of the stories children like to hear read over and over again because they enjoy the suspense and they like the little girl being so clever.

S T O R Y   S T R E T C H E R
For Art: Woodsy Scenes

What the children will learn
To use colors to indicate light

Materials you will need
Easel, paper, brushes, tempera paints including yellow and white

What to do
1. Look through Rachel Isadora's illustrations of FLOSSIE & THE FOX. Call attention to the way she showed the sunlight streaming through the trees and the interesting play of light and shadow along the path.

2. Ask the children to think how they might show the light in their paintings.

3. Leave the children to paint on their own any subject of their choosing. But as they finish their art work, if they have attempted to show light and shadow, discuss how they made it.

Something to think about
Allow as much choice as possible for children in terms of subjects for their art work and media.

S T O R Y   S T R E T C H E R
For Classroom Library: Reading Response Log

What the children will learn
To express their opinions, likes and dislikes

Materials you will need
Writing paper, pencils, stapler, construction paper

What to do
1. Have the children make a reading response log by stapling sheets of paper together and making a cover.

2. Devise two charts which have at least the following three items—date, title of the book and "What I think about this story." One chart is for the children's own reading of books they select from the classroom collection as well as from the school library. The second chart is for their reactions to the books you read aloud in class.

3. Ask the children to write in their reading response logs each day.

Something to think about
Show FLOSSIE & THE FOX to the black families who have children in the classroom. Also share with them the many books you read aloud that have black characters, so they understand that you purposefully select literature of racial and ethnic diversity.

For Cooking: Flossie's Boiled Eggs

What the children will learn
To boil eggs

Clear glass or plastic measuring cup, cookbook, eggs, crayon or permanent marker, egg timer, saucepan, water, hot plate, salt and pepper, napkins, saltines

What to do

1. Demonstrate for the children how to tell if an egg is fresh. Drop it into a clear measuring cup filled with water, and if it sinks to the bottom, it is fresh. If it rises to the top, it is spoiled.

2. Let the children test their eggs for freshness.

3. Show the children how to find a recipe in a cookbook. Read recipes for simple dishes and then read how to boil eggs.

4. Let the children decide how they want their eggs cooked: soft-boiled, medium, or hard-boiled.

5. Gently mark each egg with the child's initials using a wax crayon or permanent marker pen.

6. Group the children who want their eggs cooked the same way and have them gently place their eggs into cold water.

7. Set the timer once the water has begins to boil.

8. Show the children how to cool their eggs by running water over them and how to peel their eggs.

9. Serve the eggs with saltines.

Something to think about
Invite a parent or grandparent to help the children prepare stuffed eggs.

For Music And Movement: The Big Red Fox

What the children will learn
To compose new lyrics for a familiar tune

Materials you will need
Chart tablet, markers, optional—cassette tape and recorder

What to do

1. Print the words to "Pop Goes the Weasel" on the chart tablet and sing it with the children.

2. Let them compose new lyrics which fit the story of FLOSSIE & THE FOX. For example:

> *"All a-long the forest path,*
> *The fox talked to Flos-sie;*
> *The fox thought 'twas all in fun,*
> *Pop! Look at fox run.*
>
> *I've no time to tarry here,*
> *No time to linger in this lane;*
> *Here come Mc-Cutchin's hounds,*
> *Pop! Look at fox run.*
> *Pop! Look at fox run."*
> *(Raines, 1991)*

3. Sing both versions and tape-record them for the classroom library listening station as the "flip-side" of the recording of the book.

Something to think about
Continue adding to the *Big Book of Music* by printing the old tunes and the new ones. Sing and read the songs like big books.

For Writing Center: Flossie's Story

What the children will learn
To write a retold version of the story

Materials you will need
Writing paper, pencils

What to do

1. Discuss what the children think that Flossie will say to her grandmother when she returns from taking the eggs to the neighbors' house. She will probably tell what happened to her.

2. Let the children work with writing partners and compose Flossie's retelling of the story. One child can pretend to be Flossie and the other, the grandmother. They can write down the dialogue the two of them shared.

3. After the stories have been drafted, let the writing partners decide if they want to rewrite and edit their story to final publishing stage (See the Introduction for editing suggestions and the Appendix for binding suggestions).

Something to think about
Young children may prefer to tape-record their retellings or draw pictures which illustrate the story.

12
ANOTHER TIME
AND PLACE

WHEN I WAS YOUNG
IN THE MOUNTAINS

By Cynthia Rylant

Illustrated by Diane Goode

This Caldecott Honor book is a collection of scenes from a little girl's childhood in the mountains where she lived with her grandfather and grandmother. Rylant evokes a special warmth as she recalls how Grandfather looked when he came from working in the mines, Grandmother's wonderful cooking, the johnny-house, the swimming hole, the Crawfords who ran the general store, pumping water from a well, church and baptisms, posing for a traveling photographer, shelling beans on the front porch and listening to the sounds of the birds. Diane Goode's colored pencil drawings with delicate misty colors help children think of the story's occurring in another time and place.

Read-Aloud Suggestions

Ask the children who have lived in other areas of the country to tell where they have lived. Have some children tell where their parents grew up. Ask the students where their grandparents live now, and if they know where they grew up. Show the cover of WHEN I WAS YOUNG IN THE MOUNTAINS and share any special feelings you have about the mountains. If your students come from a mountain area, have them talk about what they enjoy about living in the mountains. Read the book and linger on each page for the children to savor the illustrations.

S T O R Y   S T R E T C H E R

For Art: What It Might Have Been Like Long Ago

What the children will learn
To illustrate with colored pencils

Materials you will need
Drawing paper, colored pencils, scraps of paper, pencil sharpener

What to do
1. Look closely at the illustrations in WHEN I WAS YOUNG IN THE MOUNTAINS. Call attention to how the artist created a sense of another time, with misty views, old clothes, different hair styles.

2. Examine the illustrations for how the artist used colored pencils to fill in lines and show perspective.

3. Let the children experiment with using colored pencils on scraps of paper. Show them how to sharpen the pencils and use the side of the waxed lead rather than the end of the pencil.

4. Ask the children to draw a picture of the mountains, or to illustrate something from when they were young, or their parents were young or when grandparents were young.

Something to think about
Many young children are developing a sense of their own growth and cannot easily think of their parents and grandparents being young. Ask them to look at family photographs and bring in pictures that show themselves or their parents or grandparents living in a different place than they do now.

S T O R Y   S T R E T C H E R

For Classroom Library: Interviews With Parents

What the children will learn
To compose and use an interview guide

Materials you will need
Chalkboard, chalk, cassette tape, recorder

What to do
1. Look back through the pages of WHEN I WAS YOUNG IN THE MOUNTAINS and have the children list all the subjects the author mentioned in the book: for example, Grandfather coming home from work, Grandmother's cooking, going to the general store, the children playing.

2. Have the children think of questions they would like to ask their parents or grandparents to find out what it was like when they were young. For example, Mother, where did Grandfather and Grandmother work when you were growing up? What games did you play when you were young? Where did you swim? What were your favorite foods? Did you have a bathroom in the house? What was your favorite book when you were growing up?

3. The children can use the questions to interview their parents and write or record their responses.

4. Have the children meet in the classroom library after their interviews with parents and decide how they can share what they found out. They may want to show old photographs and tell about them. They could place tape recordings of their interviews at the listening station, or go to the writing center and write stories with their parents or grandparents as the main characters.

Something to think about
If the children's grandparents live far away, they can mail them the questions and have the grandparents return a cassette tape recording of their responses.

For Cooking: Hot Corn Bread

What the children will learn
To bake corn bread

Materials you will need
Corn bread mix, eggs, water, muffin tins, skillet or corn stick- shaped baking pan, mixing bowl, measuring cup, wooden spoon, oven, oven mit, chart tablet, marker, optional—margarine, milk

What to do
1. Choose the type of baking pan or skillet which is often used in your area of the country for baking corn bread.

2. On a sheet of chart tablet paper, print the recipe for scratch corn bread or the mixing and baking directions from a package of corn bread mix.

3. In small groups, have the children prepare batches of corn bread by following the steps of the recipe. Let one child be in charge of collecting all the ingredients and utensils. Have another child be responsible for measuring, someone

else for mixing and pouring. Another child can set the timer for cooking, tell you when to remove the corn bread from the oven and help serve it.

4. Serve the corn bread with melted butter or margarine and a glass of cold milk.

Something to think about
Vary the recipe to fit the area of the country where you live. For example, in the Southwest, corn bread often includes green and red peppers. In the South, a sprinkling of sugar on the top makes the corn bread brown evenly.

For Creative Dramatics: Old-Fashioned Dress-Up

What the children will learn
To pretend to live in another time and place

Materials you will need
Old trunk, dress-up clothes including long dresses, overalls, coveralls, hard hat, full-length mirror

What to do
1. Look at the pictures in WHEN I WAS YOUNG IN THE MOUNTAINS and have the children decide all the ways the illustrator let them know that this story is about another time and place.

2. Collect some old clothes from parents and place them in a trunk.

3. Let the children decide who they would like to dress-up as in the story, and search through the clothes to create a costume.

Something to think about
If you have children whose parents or grandparents came from another country, have them dress like their relatives did when they were young in the other country.

For Writing Center: When My Parents Were Young

What the children will learn
To write about another time and place

Materials you will need
Writing paper, pencils, optional—art supplies for illustrations

What to do
1. Use the information the children gained from the interviews, or from what they already know about their parents or grandparents, to brainstorm about possible stories. Some children can look back at the pictures in WHEN I WAS YOUNG IN THE MOUNTAINS for "pre-writing" ideas, and to decide what the contents of their compositions might be.

2. Let the children write about themselves, their parents or grandparents during another time and place.

3. Encourage the students to refine and edit their stories.

4. Have the children illustrate their edited stories and bind them into a published book which they can share with their parents or grandparents.

5. Glue a family photograph of the subject of the composition into the front of the book.

6. Leave the books in the classroom collection for a few weeks for the children to enjoy.

Something to think about
First graders can write about themselves when they were young. Second and third graders can write about their parents and grandparents at another time and place.

12
ANOTHER TIME
AND PLACE

ROXABOXEN

By Alice McLerran

Illustrated by Barbara Cooney

A pretend place in another time, but with real children as the players, ROXABOXEN connects one generation of children and the games they played to the next generation. Roxaboxen is the story of a town created by children on a desert hill strewn with rocks which became the outlines of streets and yards. The children from the neighborhood are led by Marian, who has a vivid imagination. In Roxaboxen there are houses, shops, schools, a town hall, and even their own currency, black pebbles. Barbara Cooney's illustrations are as magical as the place, with desert colors, children dressed from another era and pictures painted across the pages and across time.

Read-Aloud Suggestions

Ask the children if they ever pretend to build a city or a town with other children from their neighborhood. Have them describe the places where they play and their favorite parts of playing together. Show the children the cover of ROXABOXEN and tell them that these children lived in their grandparents' time and created their own town, Roxaboxen. Have the students list some games and "pretending" activities they think the children will play in Roxaboxen. Read the story from beginning to end without confirming or rejecting what the children listed. Immediately after you finish the story, the children will ask you to read it again. Read the book a second time, and whenever a game or an activity occurs which the children wrote on their list, comment about it. End by noting that children of every generation are very much alike in what they like to play.

STORY STRETCHER

For Art: A Miniature Roxaboxen

What the children will learn
To design a pretend town cooperatively

Materials you will need
Chalkboard, chalk, sand table or child's plastic swimming pool, pebbles, rocks, small pieces of wood and colored glass, markers, paper for signs, instant print camera

What to do
1.   Let the children help make a list of all the materials they would like to have to make a miniature Roxaboxen. Write their list on the board and have them sign up to bring items from home.

2.   Borrow a sand table from a kindergarten classroom or use a child's plastic swimming pool filled with sand for the building site.

3.   Have the children draw names to decide who the first week of Roxaboxen players are.

4.   Take instant print pictures of each group's Roxaboxen and display them in the classroom library with a copy of the book.

Something to think about
Let the students make dioramas of the different places in Roxaboxen, such as Frances' house with desert glass, the bakery, the ice cream parlor, the forts.

STORY STRETCHER

For Cooking: Old-Fashioned Roxaboxen Ice Cream

What the children will learn
To make ice cream

Materials you will need
Ice cream freezer, ice, milk, eggs, flavoring, bowl, long-handled wooden spoon, measuring cups and spoons, ice cream salt, ice cream scoop, small bowls, spoons

What to do
1.   Read the directions for operating the ice cream freezer and the recommended recipes for that freezer.

2.   Measure and mix the ingredients. Pour into the freezer.

3.   Pack the freezer in ice and add salt on top of the ice as recommended by the manufacturer.

4.   Let the children take turns cranking the freezer and adding the salt to the ice.

5.   Check on the freezing process and let the children see how to check the consistency of the mixture.

6. Serve the ice cream for a snack, and while the children are enjoying it, read the story of ROXABOXEN again.

Something to think about
Make ice cream with an old-fashioned hand-cranked freezer with a new motorized one which doesn't use salt, and compare the taste. The children's favorite can be officially named Roxaboxen Ice Cream.

S T O R Y   S T R E T C H E R

For Creative Dramatics: Roxaboxen In Our Room

What the children will learn
To dramatize scenes

Materials you will need
Chart tablet, markers, posterboard, easel, optional—old-fashioned dress-up clothes, hats, other props

What to do
1. Have a brainstorming session with a few of the children and let them determine how they could dramatize a scene from ROXABOXEN.

2. Assign main characters: Marian, Frances, Anna May, little Jean, Eleanor, Jamie, Paul and extras.

3. Let the children decide how to stage each scene. On the chart tablet, write staging notes about the scene so that each character knows what to do.

4. Print posters announcing the title of each scene, such as River Rhode, buried treasure, Main Street, Marian the mayor, Frances' house, Roxaboxen ice cream, cars in Roxaboxen, horses in Roxaboxen, forts and pirate ships, poor lizard, Roxaboxen is always there. Place the posters on the easel.

5. Have an announcer change the posters for each scene.

6. Wait for the children to arrange themselves according to stage directions and pose absolutely still until you or a narrator starts reading that scene from the book.

7. Repeat the process for each scene.

Something to think about
Have a different director for each scene. That person can come out on stage with each scene to change and position the players. For younger children, choose main characters and let them improvise as you read, rather than follow elaborate stage directions.

S T O R Y   S T R E T C H E R

For Mathematics: How Many Black Pebbles Does It Cost?

What the children will learn
To price items and establish equivalencies

Materials you will need
Pebbles, small boxes, index cards, tape, flea market items

What to do
1. Read again the third scene in ROXABOXEN where the children find the round black pebbles which become the currency for their imaginary town.

2. Collect an assortment of items from around the house that children might like, such as a jigsaw puzzle, heart-shaped valentine candy box, costume jewelry, sports caps.

3. Bring in pebbles in boxes and let the children decide how they can establish a currency system. They can assign each item a certain number of pebbles—as one valentine candy box equals five pebbles, for example. Older chil-

dren might have a currency system with denominations or values set by the size of a pebble: for example, two small pebbles equal one large pebble.

4. Write prices on the index cards, tape them to the items and open the ROXABOXEN FLEA MARKET with the pebble currency.

Something to think about
Let the children bring in items from home that they are interested in trading or giving away.

S T O R Y   S T R E T C H E R

For Writing Center: A Roxaboxen Adventure

What the children will learn
To substitute main characters

Materials you will need
Writing paper, pencils, optional—book-binding and illustration materials

What to do
1. Discuss how often we hear a story and imagine how we would act if we were the main character in the story.

2. Ask several children what they would do in Roxaboxen if they were Marian. Have them talk about how the story would be different and how it would stay the same.

3. After this pre-writing stage, let the children begin writing or drawing to organize their thoughts.

4. With small editing or listening groups, help the children revise their works for possible publication.

5. Share the children's Roxaboxen stories by having them read their composition aloud. Let the authors sit in the special author's chair for reading their finished compositions.

References

Ackerman, Karen. (1988). Illustrated by Stephen Gammell. **SONG AND DANCE MAN**. New York: Alfred A. Knopf.

Cooney, Barbara. (1982). **MISS RUMPHIUS**. New York: Penguin Books.

McKissack, Patricia C. (1986). Illustrated by Rachel Isadora. **FLOSSIE AND THE FOX**. New York: Dial Book for Young Readers.

McLerran, Alice. (1991). Illustrated by Barbara Cooney. **ROXABOXEN**. New York: Lothrop, Lee & Shepard.

Rylant, Cynthia. (1982). Illustrated by Diane Goode. **WHEN I WAS YOUNG IN THE MOUNTAINS**. New York: E. P. Dutton.

Additional References for Another Time and Place

Allen, Thomas B. (1989). **ON GRANDADDY'S FARM**. New York: Alfred A. Knopf, Inc. *The author describes childhood in the 1930s, when he and his cousins spent the summers on their grandparents' farm in the hills of Tennessee.*

Cooney, Barbara. (1990). **HATTIE AND THE WILD WAVES**. New York: Viking Penguin. *From the emerging neighborhoods of Brooklyn to the seascapes of Long Island, Barbara Cooney creates the world of newly arrived Americans: the first generation born in this land of possibilities, yet still secure in the strength of their family traditions.*

Hall, Donald. (1979). **OX-CART MAN**. Illustrated by Barbara Cooney. New York: Penguin USA. *A simple evocation of the self-sufficient life of an early nineteenth century New England family, seen through the changing of the seasons.*

Schroeder, Alan. (1989). **RAGTIME TUMPIE**. Illustrated by Bernie Fuchs. Boston: Little, Brown and Company. *Turn-of-the-century St. Louis is vividly brought to life in this beautifully illustrated account of the childhood of Josephine Baker, the famous dancer.*

Winter, Jonah. (1991). Illustrated by Jeanette Winter. **DIEGO**. New York: Alfred A. Knopf. *In words and pictures we learn the story of the early life of the Mexican muralist Diego Rivera, and we see the determination and the passion for justice which made him an artist. The text is written in both English and Spanish.*

NATIVE AMERICAN LEGENDS AND FOLKTALES FROM OTHER COUNTRIES

Rainbow Crow
The Legend of the Indian Paintbrush
Bringing the Rain to Kapiti Plain
One Fine Day
Eyes of the Dragon

13

NATIVE AMERICAN LEGENDS AND FOLKTALES FROM OTHER COUNTRIES

RAINBOW CROW

Retold by Nancy Van Laan

Illustrated by Beatriz Vidal

Different tribes depict the crow as the creature who brings fire to the earth. RAINBOW CROW is an adaptation of the Lenape tribe's legend of the fire bearer, as told by Elder Bill "Whippoorwill" Thompson and retold by Nancy Van Laan. Crow was once a beautiful bird with rainbow-colored feathers who rescued the forest animals from a snowstorm by bringing fire to earth to melt the snow. In the process of bringing the fire from the Great Spirit, Rainbow Crow's feathers were burned and blackened. Beatriz Vidal's bright, colorful, full-page illustrations of the magnificent Rainbow Crow and the fire make this book excellent for reading to an entire class.

Read-Aloud Suggestions

Ask the children what color feathers crows have. Show the cover of RAINBOW CROW and have the children imagine how the crow's feathers turned from these beautiful colors to black. After a few children have offered possible explanations, read the story. Pause at the scene in which the snow is getting higher and higher, and let the children predict what they think will happen to the animals. Read on, and have one or two children tell what might happen when Rainbow Crow approaches Great Spirit in the Sky. Continue reading until the end of the book. Then go back and read the author's note about when she first heard the legend of Rainbow Crow. Read the book again and let the children join you in the chants and songs that the animals and Rainbow Crow sang.

STORY STRETCHER

For Art: Feather Painting

What the children will learn
To use feathery strokes for painting

Materials you will need
Paper, feathers or construction paper, scissors, meat trays, tempera paints, brushes

What to do
1. If you do not have feathers available in a craft store, fold scraps of construction paper to make several thicknesses. Cut along one side in a curved line, and snip into the edge of the curve to make feathery wisps.

2. Pour bright colors of tempera paint into separate meat trays.

3. Gently float the real feathers on top of the tempera paint or dip the construction paper feathers into paint.

4. Lay the paint-covered feather onto the paper and gently pull it along the paper to paint.

5. Continue painting with the feathers, or switch to brushes after the feathers become saturated with paint.

Something to think about
Leave the feather in the painting, and as it dries, it will adhere to the picture. (Idea adapted from one by Milissa Earl.)

STORY STRETCHER

For Classroom Library: Storytellers—Keeping The Oral Tradition Alive

What the children will learn
To listen appreciatively

Materials you will need
None needed

What to do
1. Invite a Native American storyteller or a skilled storyteller from another cultural tradition to come to class and share a particularly exciting tale.

2. Select an animal story from an anthology for storytellers.

3. After a few practice sessions at home, tell the story to the class.

4. Invite children who are interested to learn a story to tell.

Something to think about
In addition to the importance of keeping the oral tradition alive for its own sake, much research has shown that improving children's listening skills improves their reading. Good storytellers are certain to have a profound effect on young children's desire to listen.

For Classroom Library: Geographic Native American Folktales And Legends

What the children will learn
The names of the Native American tribes or Indians who once lived in your geographic region

Materials you will need
Reference books, map

What to do
1. Research the names and some interesting facts about the Indians who lived in your geographic region.

2. If possible, find a legend or an often-told tale which is credited to the native people of your area.

3. Invite a Native American to tell the story to the class.

4. With permission, record the story and write it up for the children to read.

Something to think about
Indians lived in all areas of the United States before the Europeans came. Be sure to introduce the Native Americans from your area in terms of their ancient tales and customs and where they live now and their modern lives and homes. It is difficult for young children in the first and second grades to have an historical perspective, so treat the storytelling as just that—a story to be enjoyed, but identify it as an Indian story told by a certain people.

For Music And Movement: Rainbow Crow's Chant

What the children will learn
To chant and keep the rhythm in a spoken piece

Materials you will need
Chart tablet, marker, drum

What to do
1. Reprint Rainbow Crow's song to Great Sky Spirit and the animals appreciation song on chart tablet paper.

2. Let the children practice reading the songs a few times.

3. Have them hear the rhythm of the words and gently pat their knees or clap their hands together to keep the beat.

4. Chant the songs keeping the rhythm, and then add a drum to keep the rhythm the children are making.

Something to think about
Ask the school music teacher to teach the children other authentic Native American rhythms, chants and songs.

For Writing Center: An Animal Tale Of A Great Feat

What the children will learn
To create their own folktale

Materials you will need
Chalkboard, chalk, scrap paper, writing paper, pencils, optional— art supplies for illustrations

What to do
1. Have the children recall that Native American folktales and legends are often about an element, such as fire or water, or about creation or animals with supernatural powers.

2. Discuss how Rainbow Crow performed an heroic deed and burned his beautiful feathers to save his animal friends.

3. Let the children brainstorm an idea they have for a story where an animal performs an heroic deed. When the group has generated enough ideas, ask the writers to draw what might happen at the beginning, middle and end of their story on a scrap of paper and discuss it with a writing partner.

4. After the "pre-writing" activity of drawing, let each child write his or her own piece for a classroom collection of animal tales.

Something to think about
Younger children can draw three illustrations: the first drawing showing the beginning of the story where the animal or animals are introduced; the second picture showing the problem which has to be solved; and the third drawing showing how one animal saves the others. Let the children write simple captions for their compositions and tell about their stories, rather than write long pieces.

13

NATIVE AMERICAN LEGENDS AND FOLKTALES FROM OTHER COUNTRIES

THE LEGEND OF THE INDIAN PAINTBRUSH

Retold and illustrated

by Tomie dePaola

Little Gopher is a young Plains Indian who paints pictures of the hills and meadows of what is now Texas and Wyoming. While Little Gopher has a great talent as a painter, he is small and wishes he could be like the other children and learn to hunt and be brave. After going into the hills to think about becoming a man, he has a vision that he will keep the stories of his people alive through his pictures. He strives to paint better and better pictures. As a reward for staying true to his talent, Little Gopher's paintbrushes become the Indian Paintbrush flowers which emblazen the countryside every spring, and his people rename him He-Who-Brought-the-Sunset-to-the-Earth. Illustrated in classic dePaola style, the ancient legend comes to life with simple lines, earthy tones, brilliant sunsets and dramatic splashes of color, a beautiful complement to the book.

Read-Aloud Suggestions

If possible, find a photograph of real Indian Paintbrush flowers. Show the children the pictures and let them admire them and read about where they grow and when they blossom. Read THE LEGEND OF THE INDIAN PAINTBRUSH without pausing for discussion. At the end, look back through the illustrations and let the children tell which pictures they like best and why. Talk about dePaola's use of line and color. Ask the children what they think it means when the author says that Little Gopher stayed true to his gift or true to his talent. Do not belabor the point, but discuss talents as something we really enjoy doing and do well. Those things are our gifts, our talents.

STORY STRETCHER

For Art: Painting On Paper Buckskin

What the children will learn
To paint pictures of scenes from nature

Materials you will need
Brown paper bags, scissors, tempera paints and brushes or crayons and markers

What to do
1. Look at dePaola's illustrations of Little Gopher painting on buckskin or leather.

2. Help the children make paper buckskin by cutting open a paper bag and cutting out an irregular shape which looks like a piece of leather.

3. Roll the paper up into a ball, crushing it. Repeat this process several times until the paper feels more pliable.

4. Spread the paper out flat and let the children paint or draw some scenes from nature which Little Gopher might have seen, such as landscapes, animals and plants or natural things they enjoy.

5. Have the children write captions for their "Buckskin Paintings" and label them as painted by "Brian Little Gopher" or "Tina Little Gopher."

Something to think about
Make the paper even more pliable by wetting it and crushing it into a ball, then spreading it out to dry overnight. (Adapted from an idea by Kim Gerber, student teacher at George Mason University.)

STORY STRETCHER

For Classroom Library: Flannel Board Story Of Little Gopher

What the children will learn
To retell the story using flannel board characters

Materials you will need
Chalkboard, chalk, felt, scissors, markers, flannel board, pieces of old emery boards, glue, large plastic sandwich bag, masking tape, marker

What to do
1. Look at the LEGEND OF THE INDIAN PAINTBRUSH and let the children decide which characters and landscapes are needed to retell the story. Print their list on the board and have them practice retelling the story by recalling each person or scene.

2. Have them draw the characters and landscapes on pieces of felt, cut them out and glue a piece of old emery board onto the back of the felt to make the piece adhere to the flannel board easily.

3. Let the children who helped with the construction of the flannel

board pieces use them first for re-telling the story.

4. Children can form partners with one child reading or retelling the story while the other places the appropriate pieces on the flannel board.

5. Store the flannel board pieces in a large plastic sandwich bag with a zip-lock top, and place it in the library area with a copy of the book. Write the title of the story on masking tape and place it on the outside of the storage bag.

Something to think about
Let the children make the flannel board pieces from construction paper by drawing and cutting out the characters. Then laminate them, cut them out again and glue the old emery board or a piece of sand-paper to the back.

S T O R Y   S T R E T C H E R

For Science And Nature: Indian Paintbrush Flowers

What the children will learn
To recognize Indian Paintbrush and where it grows

Materials you will need
Photographs, reference books, map

What to do
1. Look at pictures of the Indian Paintbrush flowers in reference books.

2. Read about where they grow, how they grow, when they blos-som, the conditions under which they grow best and whether or not the plant is endangered, as many wildflowers now are.

3. Locate on a map the areas of Texas and Wyoming where the In-dian Paintbrush is indigenous.

4. Place the reference books in the science and nature center for children to look at the photographs on their own.

Something to think about
Write to the tourism departments in Texas and Wyoming and re-quest brochures with pictures of the Indian Paintbrush.

A N O T H E R   S T O R Y
S T R E T C H E R

For Science And Nature: Planting Wildflowers

What the children will learn
To read and follow planting direc-tions

Materials you will need
Writing paper and pencils, chart tablet, marker, wildflower seeds, potting trays, potting soil, pots, hand spade, large plastic dishpans, science learning logs

What to do
1. Order wildflower seeds from a seed catalog or secure them from a wildflower association in your state.

2. Read aloud the directions for planting the seeds and have the children list all the equipment and provisions which the class will need.

3. Have two children work to-gether to write the planting direc-tions in their own words and draw simple rebus illustrations of each step. Let them make a chart of their directions and post it in the science and nature center for the other children to follow as they plant their seeds.

4. Plant the seeds and let the chil-dren record the growth of their plants by observing them each day: noting when they watered the plant, how it is growing, etc.

Something to think about
Invite a horticulturist from a local nursery, community college or uni-versity to bring to class samples of wildflowers grown from seeds not taken from the wild.

S T O R Y   S T R E T C H E R

For Writing Center: Two Stories From One Painting

What the children will learn
To interpret paintings in more than one way

Materials you will need
Writing paper, pencils

What to do
1. Look at Tomie dePaola's illus-trations of Little Gopher's Dream-Vision and the paintings he makes throughout the story. Discuss how Little Gopher's paintings told the story of his people.

2. Have the children look at the buckskin paintings they did for the art story s-t-r-e-t-c-h-e-r and write the stories their paintings tell.

3. Without reading their stories to each other, randomly pass out the children's buckskin paintings o each other and let each child write a story for someone else's painting.

4. At a group sharing time, have the two children read or tell their stories while the group looks at the painting.

Something to think about
Young children can dictate long stories to a parent who can type them on a computer. The children can see their spoken words becom-ing print.

NATIVE AMERICAN LEGENDS AND FOLKTALES FROM OTHER COUNTRIES

BRINGING THE RAIN TO KAPITI PLAIN

By Verna Aardema

Illustrated by Beatriz Vidal

A Nandi tale from Kenya, this book's bright full-color illustrations and the rhyming pattern with repeated phrases make it irresistible to young listeners and young readers. Ki-pat is a herdsman who watches his cows go hungry and thirsty because there is no rain to make the grass grow. When a huge cloud shadows the ground, but it still does not rain, Ki-pat makes an arrow from an eagle feather and shoots it into the cloud. It rains. The grass grows, his cows are fed and Ki-pat goes back to watching his herd. Vidal's illustrations are rich with color, bold in design and captivating with or without the tale.

Read-Aloud Suggestions

Show the children the cover of BRINGING THE RAIN TO KAPITI PLAIN. Introduce the herdsman on the cover as Ki-pat and ask the children why these animals would like living on Kapiti Plain. Read the tale through from start to finish. The children will begin saying the recurring phrases with you. Encourage them to "read" with you. Read the tale again and pause for the children to say the repeated phrases with only minor prompting. Read the last page of the book for comments "about the author," "about the artist" and "about the tale." At another group time, read "The House that Jack Built," and see if it reminds the children of BRINGING THE RAIN TO KAPITI PLAIN. This Nandi tale reminded Sir Claud Hollis, an anthropologist who first wrote down the tale, of the nursery rhyme.

S T O R Y   S T R E T C H E R

For Art: Collage Of Animals On A Plain

What the children will learn
To combine media

Materials you will need
Manilla paper, construction paper, scissors, glue, pencils, tempera paints, brushes

What to do
1. Have the children look at the way the artist, Beatriz Vidal, showed the grasses of the Kapiti Plain.

2. Let the children cut green or brown construction paper or paint with green or brown paints to construct a representation of Kapiti Plain. If they made the plain of construction paper, have them glue it onto manilla paper.

3. Make animals by drawing them on scraps of construction paper, then cut them out and glue them onto the grassy plain to create a collage.

4. Display the collages on a bulletin board with the title, "Ki-pat's Kapiti Plain."

Something to think about
Mixing media like paint and collage gives children many more possibilities for creative expression.

S T O R Y   S T R E T C H E R

For Classroom Library: Reading With The Tape

What the children will learn
To read along with the tape

Materials you will need
Cassette tape, recorder, stapler, listening station, headphones

What to do
1. With a small group of children or the entire class, read BRINGING THE RAIN TO KAPITI PLAIN. Pause for the children to say the recurring phrases with you.

2. For the tape recording, have one child read the title of the book and the names of the author and illustrator.

3. Click the stapler near the microphone of the cassette recorder and tell the children to turn the page when they hear this sound. Assign one child to click the stapler each time you turn the page.

4. Record the reading of the story with the children saying the repeated phrases with you.

5. Place the tape and the book in the classroom library at the listening station.

Something to think about
BRINGING THE RAIN TO KAPITI PLAIN is an excellent book for beginning readers. Letting them read along with the tape is a confidence builder for reading aloud.

STORY STRETCHER

For Music And Movement: Pat-A-Syllable

What the children will learn
To hear the rhythm of the language

Materials you will need
None needed

What to do
1. Have the children sit in a semicircle with their legs crossed and their hands on their elbows.

2. Begin reading BRINGING THE RAIN TO KAPITI PLAIN and pat your knees to the sound of each syllable so that there is a sing-song chanting. Pause at the end of each line and skip a beat. Stop at the end of each page for three or four beats.

3. Continue reading to the end of the tale, keeping the beat and pausing for dramatic emphasis and at the end of each scene.

4. Let the children take turns reading different pages of the tale while the others chant and pat the rhythm.

Something to think about
For young children, have them pat their knees for each syllable of the phrase, "on Ka-pi-ti Plain."

STORY STRETCHER

For Science And Nature: Animals On Kapiti Plain

What the children will learn
To recognize the animals in the illustrations and compare them to photographs of real animals

Materials you will need
Chalkboard, chalk, reference books on African animals, index cards, pencils

What to do
1. Look through Vidal's illustrations of BRINGING THE RAIN TO KAPITI PLAIN and identify as many animals as possible and list them on the chalkboard.

2. Show the children how to use the reference books to find pictures and information about the African plains animals.

3. Let them compare the illustrations to the photographs.

4. Have each child identify one African plains animal from BRINGING THE RAIN TO KAPITI PLAIN and find out more about that animal. Ask each child to write on an index card something interesting she or he learned about the animal.

5. Leave the cards the children wrote, the animal pictures and reference books in the science and nature center for the children to explore on their own.

Something to think about
Find out more about the acacia trees which also live on Kapiti Plain.

STORY STRETCHER

For Writing Center: Writing A Cumulative Tale

What the children will learn
To use a familiar pattern to write a different story

Materials you will need
Chalkboard, chalk, chart tablet, marker

What to do
1. Read BRINGING THE RAIN TO KAPITI PLAIN and help the children recognize the pattern.

2. Begin a different tale and let the children work with you in small groups to make up a story.

For example,

> *"This is the great Kansas Plain,*
> *All moist and green from the Midwestern rains"*

or

> *"This is the great busy highway*
> *All crowded with trucks, cars and buses*
> *all day"*
> *(Raines, 1991)*

3. Continue composing the cumulative tale. Edit it and let volunteers reprint it onto chart tablet paper for the class to read together.

Something to think about
Have the children add illustrations in the margins of the chart tablet and use it like a Big Book for a shared reading experience.

ONE FINE DAY

By Nonny Hogrogian

This Caldecott Medal book published in 1971 is an Armenian folktale. An old woman sets down a pail of milk and gathers firewood. A fox comes along and drinks the milk, which makes the woman so angry she chops off his tail. The fox begs for his tail back but the old woman will not put it back until the fox replaces the milk. So begins his journey to find the cow who will give the milk. But the cow will not give the fox the milk until he brings some grass, and so the tale continues. In the end, the old woman carefully sews the fox's tail back on so that none of his friends will laugh at him. With its vivid colors and stylized drawings of the bright orange fox, this book has become a favorite among young children and beginning readers.

Read-Aloud Suggestions

Draw a large circle on the chalkboard. Write the title of the book in the middle of the circle and make a slash mark on the circle for each scene of the story. At the top of the circle make a slash mark for the beginning where the old woman chops off the fox's tail. Make the next slash mark when you read about the cow, another for the fox talking to the grass, then the stream, and so on. Read the story through to the end where it returns to the top of the circle, and the old woman sews on the fox's tail. After completing the story, go back and write a key word beside each slash mark, such as tail, cow, grass, stream, jug, bead, peddler, egg, hen, grain and tail again. The story ends where it began, with the fox's tail. Tell the children this is a circle story.

S T O R Y   S T R E T C H E R

For Art: Picture Circle Stories

What the children will learn
To use graphic representations for scenes

Materials you will need
Pizza cardboard forms, pencils, scissors, construction paper or posterboard, brad, crayons or markers

What to do
1. Draw large circles on construction paper or posterboard by tracing around the pizza cardboard forms.

2. Cut out the large circle.

3. Have the children mark off ten equal "pie pieces" around the circle and use these as the frames for small pictures or graphic representations that tell the story. For example, in the first frame the children can draw the fox's bushy tail; the second, the cow; the third, the grass; and so on.

4. Cut out another large circle from construction paper or posterboard and cut an opening in it the size of one of the story frames.

5. Place the second circle over the circle story illustrations and hold it loosely in place with a brad.

6. The children can turn the picture frame cut in the cover circle to the different illustrations and retell the story.

Something to think about
For first graders, who may have difficulty drawing small pictures, eliminate the cover circle.

S T O R Y   S T R E T C H E R

For Classroom Library: Circle Stories

What the children will learn
To retell a story with graphic reminders

Materials you will need
Circle stories from the art story s-t-r-e-t-c-h-e-r above, other folktales and similar stories, chart tablet, marker

What to do
1. Have the children exchange circle stories and retell each other's story by looking at the story frames.

2. Let the children find other folktales and see if they fit the story circle format, for example: MILLIONS OF CATS by Wanda Gag and IT COULD ALWAYS BE WORSE by Margot Zemach.

3. Make a collection of circle stories by drawing them onto chart tablet paper and leaving the tablet on display in the library area along with the books.

Something to think about

Try a variety of graphic representations of stories, for example a fan with a symbol for each scene drawn on its folds or a sheet of paper folded to make three columns where the children can illustrate three wishes tales.

STORY STRETCHER

For Creative Dramatics: Readers' Theatre

What the children will learn

To read lines in unison and with expression

Materials you will need

None needed

What to do

1. Read ONE FINE DAY as a readers' theatre piece by dividing the children into seven character groups, one for each of the following: the cow, the grass, the stream, the maiden, the peddler, the hen, the miller.

2. Ask another child to read the part of the fox, and you read the part of the old woman.

3. Have the character groups read their lines together. Rehearse for expression.

Something to think about

Make paper bag masks to represent each character. Divide the class into character readers and mask wearers. As each character's lines are said, the mask wearers can walk across the group time area or stand in place. In the end, the mask wearers can take off their masks and say in unison, "And that is the story of how the red fox lost and found his tail on One Fine Day."

STORY STRETCHER

For Music And Movement: Where, Oh Where Can My Fox Tail Be?

What the children will learn

To sing the story by rewriting a familiar song with new lyrics

Materials you will need

Chart tablet, marker

What to do

1. Teach the children the old song, "Where, Oh Where Has My Little Dog Gone?" Print the words on a chart tablet.

2. After the children have learned the tune, let them brainstorm how they might change the song to tell the story of ONE FINE DAY. For example, for the first verse sing,

> "Oh where, oh where can I get some milk?
> Oh where, oh where can it be?
> With-out the milk my tail is gone,
> Oh where, oh where can it be?"

Second verse

> "Oh where, oh where can I get some grass?
> Oh where, oh where can it be?
> With-out the grass, no milk have I,
> Oh where, oh where can it be?"

Third verse

> "Oh where, oh where can I get some water?
> Oh where, oh where can it be?
> With-out the water, no grass have I,
> Oh where, oh where can it be?"

Continue substituting for each item the fox must bring back, a jug for the water, a bead for the maiden, an egg for the peddler and some grain for the hen.

Something to think about

One need not be an accomplished vocalist to sing with children. Choose simple songs with familiar tunes. Also, if you have a music specialist in your school, accompany the children to their music lessons and learn along with them.

STORY STRETCHER

For Writing Center: Writing Circle Stories

What the children will learn

To create a story which begins and ends in the same place

Materials you will need

Writing paper, pencils

What to do

1. Discuss the circle stories the children made in art and the additional ones they found and illustrated in the classroom library. Suggest that the children write their own circle stories, with only one stipulation, that the story begin and end in the same place.

2. Let the children brainstorm in small groups or with a writing partner and then begin to write individual circle stories.

3. When the writers have finished, let them draw their own circle illustrations of their story.

Something to think about

Have the children read their stories in the author's chair while their writing partners show the story circle. Place the children's circle stories in the classroom library, and the children can retell each other's stories by looking at the circles.

EYES OF THE DRAGON

By Margaret Leaf

Illustrated by Ed Young

Bold reds and greens on the cover and beautiful full-page pastel chalk drawings lure the reader and listener into this folktale set in China. Little Li's grandfather was the magistrate of the town and it was his responsibility to protect the people, so he built a wall around the village. To decorate the wall he hired Ch'en Jung, a great dragon painter. Ch'en Jung agreed to paint a fierce and beautiful dragon, except that he would not paint eyes on the dragon. The dragon was painted on the wall. When the magistrate insisted he finish the painting, Ch'en Jung was forced to paint the eyes, and magically, the dragon came to life. Magnificently illustrated in a burst of color, the tale ends with no harm to anyone, but also with no dragon and no wall.

Read-Aloud Suggestions

Show the cover of the book and talk about what the creature on the front might be. Tell the children that you will read the book through from beginning to end without stopping, but when you finish, you will show them the pictures again because they are so beautiful. Read EYES OF THE DRAGON and, near the end, heighten the suspense in your voice without frightening the children. Ask the children what they think the moral of the story is. The magistrate did not keep his bargain and did not heed the warning of someone with experience. If possible, collect Chinese paintings and kites with dragons. If you have Chinese families among your class members, invite them to tell about the meaning of the dragon in Chinese folklore as well as the huge paper dragons in Chinese New Year's celebrations.

STORY STRETCHER

For Classroom Library: Dramatic Reading Of EYES OF THE DRAGON

What the children will learn
To read with expression

Materials you will need
Cassette tape recorder, tape, glass, fork, optional—brass gong

What to do
1. Select a narrator, the magistrate, Li, three village elders, and Ch'en Jung, the painter.

2. Read the book through and let the children rehearse reading their lines with expression.

3. Have the narrator introduce the book on tape by reading the title, the names of the author and illustrator, and telling the listener what the page-turning signal will be. Gently tap a glass with a fork or strike a small brass gong as the signal.

4. Record the tape with the children reading, and on the other side, ask a reader who speaks Chinese to read the book in English but to say a few appropriate phrases in Chinese.

Something to think about
Choose a child who is not a particularly good reader and rehearse with him or her ahead of time so that the child feels comfortable and enjoys making the tape.

STORY STRETCHER

For Cooking: Chopsticks And Veggies

What the children will learn
To manipulate chopsticks and to taste Chinese vegetables

Materials you will need
Chopsticks, forks, rice, small bowls, portable wok, water, cooking oil, cutting board, knives, variety of fresh or frozen Chinese vegetables, forks

What to do
1. If you have a family of Chinese heritage among your students, invite the parent to show the children how to cook using a wok, or invite someone who enjoys Chinese cooking to prepare the snack.

2. Take the usual precautions when cooking in the classroom, such as placing the cooking area away from heavy traffic paths, having an adult present at all times, making sure the electrical outlets can handle the extra wattage needed as well as keeping cords off the floor.

3. Let the children help chop the vegetables.

4. When the wok is hot, cook the vegetables briefly and serve them over rice prepared ahead of time.

5. Show the children how to use the chopsticks, and let them try to use them to eat their vegetables and rice.

6. After they have practiced for a while with their chopsticks, provide forks for them to finish their snack.

Something to think about
Wash the chopsticks and let the children take them home to use.

For Creative Dramatics: Chinese Clothes And Robes

What the children will learn
To dress in clothing and play together using their imaginations

Materials you will need
Chinese clothes and robes, full-length mirrors

What to do
1. Look at the illustrations of the adults and children in EYES OF THE DRAGON. Have the students notice the long shirts with high collars the children wear and the loose-fitting robes which close in the front that the elders wear.

2. Ask a family of Chinese heritage to bring the clothing to school for the children to see and try on. If this is not possible, have the children bring clothes and robes from home which remind them of those in the story.

3. Let the children put the Chinese clothes and robes on over their clothing and pretend to be Little Li, the magistrate, the elders and Ch'en Jung, the painter.

4. Do not direct their play, but instead let them improvise their own playing together in the clothes and robes.

Something to think about
All primary age children need to play together. Play provides opportunities for creative expression, mutual problem solving and negotiation among players, language development and vocabulary expansion. As the children play, they use words associated with whatever their theme is.

For Mathematics: Eighty-One In A Row

What the children will learn
To use 9's in counting, multiplying and dividing

Materials you will need
Eighty-one items to count which are of the same size and shape, such as Unifix cubes, centimeter blocks or poker chips; rulers; tape; crayons; chart tablet paper or graph paper; optional—Chinese abacus

What to do
1. Read the part of the book where the magistrate and Li count the number of fiery red dragon scales. There are eighty-one because nine is a lucky number and nine times nine is eighty-one.

2. With small groups of children, have them count out eighty-one poker chips or other items.

3. After they have a sense of how many eighty-one is, have them group the objects in stacks of nine. Count the number of stacks or groups they have. Tell them they have just "divided" eighty-one by nine. $81 \div 9 = 9$.

4. Ask the children to make rows of nine items across and nine items down to show eighty-one. With younger children, tape a ruler horizontally across a table and let them place nine items across the ruler.

Skip some space and repeat the process to create an array of 9 x 9. Let the children count their arrays and prove that 9 x 9 = 81. Tell them they have now multiplied by nine.

5. With at least one array left on the table, let the children find the answers to 9 x 1 = ___, 9 x 2 =___, 9 x 3 =___, and so on.

6. Use chart tablet paper or graph paper and mark off rows. Let the children place nine check marks on each row, to make a representation of their array.

7. Let the children color a row of eighty-one fiery red dragon scales which look like fish scales.

Something to think about
Simplify or complicate this exercise to fit the needs of the age you teach. However, always start with items they can hold in their hands and count. Avoid setting up materials and demonstrating yourself; with them, instead be sure the manipulatives get into the hands of the children.

For Special Project: Paper Dragon

What the children will learn
To work cooperatively on an art project

Materials you will need
Butcher paper, scissors, tempera paints, brushes, tape, coat hangers, stapler, construction paper or fabric scraps, egg-shaped hosiery container, flourescent paint, fishing wire or yarn, crepe paper

What to do
1. Spread a very long length of butcher paper from one end of the room to the other. Taper it at the end like the end of a tail.

2. Let the children use bright tempera paints to color the scales of the dragon.

3. Tape the body of the dragon along one wall of the classroom.

4. Assemble a head for the dragon by straightening two coat hangers and bending them into a round shape.

5. Cover the circle with butcher paper and staple the paper on the back.

6. Read the description of the dragon's head from EYES OF THE DRAGON. Have the children paint his head in bright colors—without eyes, of course—and use construction paper, fabric scraps or whatever they think would be appropriate to make the head as the author described it.

7. Make the rainbow pearl which goes under the dragon's chin by painting a plastic egg-shaped women's hosiery container with florescent paints. String it on some fishing wire or yarn to hold it in place.

8. Cut crepe paper streamers and staple them around the edge of the head.

9. Hang the head from fishing wire so that it floats at the end of the wall with the dragon's body.

Something to think about
The children can make small individual versions of the dragon and decorate theirs however they like. For older children, make dragon kites.

References

Aardema, Verna. (1981). Illustrated by Beatriz Vidal. **BRINGING THE RAIN TO KAPITI PLAIN**. New York: Dial Books for Young Readers.

dePaola, Tomie. (1988). **THE LEGEND OF THE INDIAN PAINT-BRUSH**. New York: G. P. Putnam's Sons.

Hogrogian, Nonny. (1971). **ONE FINE DAY**. New York: Macmillan.

Leaf, Margaret. (1987). Illustrated by Ed Young. **EYES OF THE DRAGON**. New York: Lothrop, Lee & Shepard Books.

Van Laan, Nancy. (1989). Illustrated by Beatriz Vidal. **RAINBOW CROW**. New York: Alfred A. Knopf.

Additional References for Native American Legends and Folktales from Other Countries

Aardema, Verna. (1991). Illustrated by Will Hillenbrand. **TRAVELING TO TONDO**. New York: Alfred A. Knopf. *A wonderfully illustrated animal fable from the Nkundo people of Zaire: a fable with a message about using your common sense!*

dePaola, Tomie. (1983). **THE LEGEND OF THE BLUEBONNET**. New York: G. P. Putnam's Sons. *A Comanche legend which tells the story of a young girl who saved her people from drought and famine through her courage and sacrifice. The Texas state flower symbolizes her love for her people.*

Grifalconi, Ann. (1986). **THE VILLAGE OF ROUND AND SQUARE HOUSES**. Boston: Little, Brown and Company. *This village really exists in West Africa, and the story explains how it came to pass that the women live in the round houses and the men in the square ones.*

Lee, Jeanne M. (1985). **TOAD IS THE UNCLE OF HEAVEN**. New York: Henry Holt and Company. *A Vietnamese folk tale which tells how Toad convinced the King of Heaven to send rain to Earth.*

Steptoe, John. (1984). **THE STORY OF JUMPING MOUSE**. New York: Lothrop, Lee & Shepard Books. *Jumping Mouse, with his hopeful and unselfish spirit, undergoes a profound transformation on his journey to the "far-off land." This is a retelling of a Native American story.*

Other References Mentioned in the Chapter

Ga'g, Wanda. (1928). **MILLIONS OF CATS**. New York: Coward-McCann.

Zemach, Margo. (1977). **IT COULD ALWAYS BE WORSE**. New York: Farrar, Straus and Giroux.

MYSTERIES, SECRETS AND ADVENTURES

Nate the Great

Flat Stanley

Two Bad Ants

Rembrandt's Beret

Anatole

NATE THE GREAT

By Marjorie Weinman Sharmat

Illustrated by Marc Simont

One of a series of NATE THE GREAT mysteries, The book features Nate, a young investigator who helps people find lost things. When Annie calls requesting his help to find a lost picture, Nate is sure this will be a simple case. He collects all the facts, searches for evidence and leads the reader through the mystery until he solves the case. This confident young Sherlock Holmes will capture the imagination of primary students and have them begging for more mysteries. Simont's illustrations are simple, comical and fit the story "sleuthfully."

Read-Aloud Suggestions

Introduce Nate by having the children look at the cover of the book and describe what they see. Ask if the way Nate is dressed gives them a hint as to what the story is about. Read the story without showing all the pictures, but as Annie's brother and his painting are introduced, show the pictures. Pause after the illustration of Nate looking at the pictures in Harry's room, and let the children try to solve the mystery of Annie's missing picture. Finish reading the story and confirm that the children are indeed good mystery solvers and good detectives. Read the titles of other NATE THE GREAT mysteries and ask the children to list, on a poster in the classroom library, the titles of the Nate books they have read.

STORY STRETCHER
For Art: Mystery Colors

What the children will learn
To mix primary colors to make secondary colors

Materials you will need
Primary colors of tempera paint, brushes, paper, meat trays

What to do
1. Let the children paint pictures using the red, yellow and blue colors. While the paint is still wet, paint over the top of the color with another primary color paint. For example, paint over the blue with yellow, and see green appear. Paint over the blue with red, and see purple appear. Try many different combinations of layers.

2. On another sheet of paper, have the children paint a picture with colors they have mixed on their meat tray palette, rather than layering the colors.

3. Ask the children to paint a picture of their room at home as if it were painted in their favorite colors, like Annie's yellow room in the story.

Something to think about
Another day, show the children how to mix black and white with primary and secondary colors to create shades.

STORY STRETCHER
For Classroom Library: Collecting Leads

What the children will learn
To listen for the clues

Materials you will need
Cassette tape, recorder, stapler, note pad, pencil

What to do
1. Record yourself reading NATE THE GREAT. Tape an introduction and tell the children to listen for the clicking sound of the stapler as the page-turning signal.

2. Pause after each of Nate's clues and tell the children to press the "stop" button on the tape player and jot down on the note pad the clue or lead which Nate should investigate. When they have finished writing the clue or lead tell them to press "play" and continue listening to the story.

3. Direct the children to turn off the tape player after each of the following scenes: Annie eating pancakes, Annie asking who has seen her picture of her dog, Fang burying the bone, Rosamond waving goodbye with her cat in her arms, Harry's face covered with paint, Nate looking at Harry's room, Nate looking at the picture of the orange monster.

4. At the end of the tape, tell the child to write the name of the de-

tective. For example, "Michelle the Great."

Something to think about
Announce the titles of some other NATE THE GREAT mysteries and tell the children some clues or leads as to where they are hidden around the classroom.

For Cooking: Nate's Pancakes

What the children will learn
To follow the directions in a pancake recipe

Materials you will need
Posterboard or chart tablet paper, marker, pancake mix, mixing bowl, measuring spoons, eggs, electric skillet, butter or margarine, syrup, paper towels, milk, napkins, forks, plates

What to do
1. Have two children read the recipe for making pancakes from the side of the box.

2. Ask them to print the directions and draw any pictures which will help the pancake makers to understand what to do. For example, draw pictures of an egg, wooden spoon, any ingredients or utensils the children need to follow the steps in the recipe.

3. Supervise small groups of children mixing the batter and cooking the pancakes in the electric skillet.

4. Wrap the pancakes in paper towels to keep them warm until everyone has helped with the mixing and cooking.

5. Serve the pancakes with butter or margarine, a little syrup and cartons of cold milk.

Something to think about
Instead of using sugary syrup, cut up fruit and spoon over pancakes, along with a tablespoon of yogurt.

For Games: Following Cold Trails Or Hot Leads

What the children will learn
To give clues

Materials you will need
Picture, small items to hide

What to do
1. Tell the children that NATE THE GREAT reminds you of a game of "hide-and-seek," but instead of hiding themselves, the children will hide things around the room and others will have to try to find them by listening to clues the hiders give.

2. Before the game starts, take one of the children's pictures from a bulletin board, roll it up and hide it.

3. Exclaim in distress, "Oh no, Damien's picture is missing!"

4. Have two children leave the room and pretend to be Nate the Great. While they are out, show the other students where Damien's picture is hidden.

5. Brainstorm with the children some clues they could give to the Nate the Great's looking for Damien's picture. For example, it is near a place where people sing. It is like a newspaper. It is beside something red.

6. Select two children to alternate giving the clues until the picture is found.

7. While the detectives are looking and following the clues, have the children who are watching chant, "cold trail," if the detectives are not close to the hiding place. If they are near the hiding place, chant, "hot lead."

8. Repeat the process several times by hiding objects around the room and using different children as Nate the Great detectives and clue givers.

Something to think about
With younger children, omit the clue giving and have them look for the item by moving around the room while the audience simply says, "cold trail" or "hot lead."

For Writing Center: Lost And Found

What the children will learn
To write announcements for lost and found items

Materials you will need
Random items and pieces of clothing from around the classroom, construction paper, markers, crayons or colored pencils

What to do
1. Read the description of Annie's picture in NATE THE GREAT.

2. Have the children think of what they would need to say on a lost or found poster to describe Annie's picture.

3. Let children who have lost or found pets tell of their experiences in writing lost and found announcements.

4. Tell the children you have lost something—a glove, a coffee mug, a set of keys. Ask them to help you compose a "lost announcement."

5. Speak to a child ahead of time and take a glove, scarf, belt or hair ribbon and tell the class you found this object. Have them help you write a "found announcement."

Something to think about
As an alternative, have children write notes to their parents explaining how they are helping a friend solve a mystery, just as Nate wrote a note to his parents.

FLAT STANLEY

By Jeff Brown

Illustrated by Tomi Ungerer

A terrifically silly adventure which lures the young listener and reader into imaginary possibilities, FLAT STANLEY is an excellent read-aloud selection for class or for primary readers. A huge bulletin board falls on Stanley while he is asleep and when he awakes, he is flat. His parents, though distressed, find Stanley's unusual size most convenient. He helps his mother find a ring which has dropped into a street grate, and Stanley himself enjoys entering rooms by sliding under the door. His most daring feat is helping capture art thieves at the museum. Complete with sibling rivalry, the story ends on a happy note when Stanley's brother helps him return to normal shape by pumping him up with a bicycle tire pump. The comic illustrations are just the right touch for Stanley's peculiar predicament.

Read-Aloud Suggestions

Have the children look at the cover of FLAT STANLEY and notice that he is tall and wide, but he is not very thick. Let them imagine how Stanley might have gotten so thin. Read the book and at the end, let several children tell what they thought the most exciting parts of the story were. Ask when they felt sorry for Stanley. Discuss not making fun of other people's appearances when they look different from us.

STORY STRETCHER

For Art: Flat And All That, Paper Dolls

What the children will learn
To follow directions for cutting

Materials you will need
Typing paper, scissors, crayons or colored pencils, optional—lightweight cardboard

What to do
1. Remind the children that Flat Stanley looked like a paper doll.

2. Demonstrate how to fold the paper and cut paper dolls. If the children have difficulty visualizing your directions, cut one example and then show them how you did it.

3. Place the paper horizontally and fold it in half, then fold again.

4. Hold the paper together and draw the outline of one half of a doll, leaving the base and the arms extending all the way to the edge.

5. Cut according to your outline.

6. Let the children practice the folding, drawing and cutting and when they get shapes they like, have them decorate their Flat Stanleys with crayons or colored pencils.

7. When the children become skilled at cutting paper dolls, let them cut a lightweight cardboard backing for their favorite paper doll. Glue it onto the cardboard, leaving a margin at the bottom. Cut in from the sides of the base and then fold back along the cut. This will provide a base for the paper doll to stand upon.

Something to think about
Put the children's paper dolls in envelopes and mail them to their homes. List the return address as Flat Stanley, the school street address, city, state and zip code.

STORY STRETCHER

For Science And Nature: Bicycle Pump

What the children will learn
To observe the effects of air under pressure

Materials you will need
Bicycle pump, balloons, inflatable rafts, beach balls and other inflatable toys

What to do
1. Show the children how a bicycle pump works. If any children still have bicycle tires with inner tubes, bring one to school and pump up the tube.

2. Demonstrate how to blow up balloons, inflatable toys, beach balls and rafts by attaching the end of the pump hose over the valves.

3. Have the children continue pumping so they can feel the resistance as they depress the pump handle.

4. Take some items off the hose and feel the air coming out.

Something to think about
Do not let children put balloons in their mouths. Do not release balloons into the environment because they can harm wildlife.

For Science And Nature: Stanley Kites

What the children will learn

To construct and fly a kite

Materials you will need

Strips of balsa wood, butcher paper, tempera paint, paintbrushes, crayons or markers, stapler, masking tape, string, fabric or crepe paper streamers

What to do

1.   Make a cross of balsa wood about 2' x 3' and staple it together in the middle or bind tape around it to hold the arms in place.

2.   Cut butcher paper about two inches longer and wider than the kite shape.

3.   Let the children decorate their kites by painting or coloring them.

4.   Fold the edges several times to strengthen them and make the butcher paper fit the balsa wood kite frame.

5.   Attach the paper to the end of the balsa wood by stapling it in place. Tape over the staples so they do not come loose.

6.   Make a tail for the kite with strips of lightweight fabric or crepe paper streamers.

7.   Attach the tail to the bottom of the balsa wood.

8.   Staple one end of the string to the middle of the kite where the wood crosses. Place masking tape over the staple and continue wrapping the masking tape around the center of the crossed wood to attach it firmly.

9.   Fly the kites on a windy day. Teach the children the safety rules about kite flying, such as staying away from power lines, traffic and trees. If possible, have parent volunteers help with the kite flying.

Something to think about

Let the children make self-portrait kites of themselves as Flat Stanleys.

STORY STRETCHER

For Writing Center: Another Stanley Adventure

What the children will learn

To write a story appropriate for the main character

Materials you will need

Chalkboard, chalk, writing paper, pencils, large brown envelopes, optional—art supplies for illustrations

What to do

1.   Read again the part of the story where Flat Stanley is put into an envelope and mailed to California.

2.   Let the children discuss some places they would like to be mailed if they were Flat Stanley. List these on the board as the children tell the beginning of an adventure which might occur when they arrive at their destination. Tell them to keep the rest of their idea a secret.

3.   Have the children write very secretively and seal their stories in large brown envelopes. They can add illustrations if they like.

4.   Each day, open several of the large brown envelopes and let the writers sit in the author's chair in the classroom library or group time area to read their FLAT STANLEY adventures to the class.

Something to think about

Mail some of the children's FLAT STANLEY adventures to another classroom and let the children take turns reading their stories to the other class. Be sure the other teacher has already read FLAT STANLEY to her or his class before the children share their adventures.

ANOTHER STORY STRETCHER

For Writing Center: Newspaper Account Of Stanley's Heroics

What the children will learn

To review their writing for who, what, where, when, why and how information

Materials you will need

Newspapers, chalkboard, chalk, writing paper, pencils, optional—art supplies

What to do

1.   Select a few brief newspaper articles of interest to the children and read them aloud.

2.   After reading each article, print a list of the following questions on the chalkboard, "who, what, where, when, why and how." Let the children recall the answers to all these questions from the article.

3.   Read again the account of Flat Stanley's heroic deed in helping to stop the art thieves.

4.   Ask the children to write an account of Stanley's adventure in the museum.

5.   Suggest they critique their writing to determine if it is a thorough account by reading their articles and checking that they have written answers to the questions, "who, what, where, when, why and how."

Something to think about

Let the children read their newspaper accounts to each other and have the listeners check off the answers to the good reporting questions.

TWO BAD ANTS

By Chris Van Allsburg

An adventure told from two ants' perspective, this exciting tale takes the listener and reader through the tunnels of the ant colony where the queen lives. When a scout ant finds a sweet-tasting crystal and delivers it to the queen, she proclaims it to be the best thing she has ever tasted and sends all the ants out to find more. When the treasure is located, two small ants decide to stay behind and taste the crystals for themselves. But danger lurks in their new home. In the end, they are glad to return to the ant colony. The artist's perspective, telling the story visually from an ant's eye view, is ingenious, with gray, taupe and brown colors and lines and textures that heighten the sense of adventure, of something unusual happening.

Read-Aloud Suggestions

If you have read other Chris Van Allsburg books to the children, collect them and let several children tell why they like his books. Invariably, someone will comment about the illustrations. Tell the children that Van Allsburg creates a certain mood with his choice of colors, but this story has an added dimension, they will see the world from an ant's perspective. Have them imagine how a tiny ant feels walking through the grass. Read TWO BAD ANTS without pausing for the children to make predictions. Create a heightened tension in the story by almost whispering when the ants decide to stay behind. After the reading, let the children tell what they thought the most suspenseful parts were.

STORY STRETCHER

For Art: Imagining An Ant's Eye View

What the children will learn
To represent a scene from a perspective other than their own

Materials you will need
Charcoals; gray, brown and black chalks; black construction paper; pencils; other choices of art media

What to do
1. Look again at Chris Van Allsburg's illustrations in TWO BAD ANTS. Let the children talk about what they see and how unusual the visual perspective is, as the ants see the human mouth approaching the lip of the coffee cup, for example.

2. Cut tiny pieces of black construction paper about the size of ants and place one in the palm of each child's hand.

3. Let the children imagine how the ants see their hands. Place one of the tiny pieces of paper beside a pencil and say that the ant would probably see it like a huge fallen tree. Have the children put their ants in different places and think how the ants might see their surroundings.

4. Have the children glue their ant onto some paper and draw a scene around the ant.

5. Encourage the children to write captions for their pictures.

Something to think about
Perspective is difficult for young children, and their drawings may be rather flat, with enlarged items around a tiny speck of an insect; however, this is an excellent beginning.

STORY STRETCHER

For Creative Dramatics: Adding Dialogue

What the children will learn
To improvise dialogue to fit the two bad ants' adventure

Materials you will need
None needed

What to do
1. With a small group of children, the actors, read TWO BAD ANTS again. Pause for every scene after the one where the ants are marching through the woods, and imagine what different ants in the column are saying. Improvise some dialogue.

2. Let two children volunteer to be the two bad ants and improvise dialogue for each of the scenes where the ants stay behind.

3. After a rehearsal of the improvised dialogue, plan how to present the dramatization to the class. Take the children's suggestions for staging. Emphasize that it is not important to say the dialogue exactly as it was practiced.

4. Read TWO BAD ANTS and pause for the actors to improvise their dialogue for each scene.

5. On subsequent days, choose other actors.

Something to think about
Tape-record the children's version of the story with the added dialogue.

For Music And Movement: The March Of The Ants

What the children will learn
To march in silence while keeping a beat

Materials you will need
Recording of march music

What to do

1. Have the children seated in a circle.

2. Play a recording of march music and let the children clap the rhythm with their hands.

3. March around the room and tap a few children to join you, without skipping a beat.

4. Before the record is over, have all the children up and marching.

5. Play the record again and form a long line of single file marchers. Call them "ants on parade."

6. Have the children sit again. Then start humming the march music and begin clapping your hands softly to the beat. Encourage the children to join you.

7. When everyone seems to be keeping the rhythm of the march, begin marching around the room and have the children join you as they hum and clap.

8. Repeat the process another time without the humming and clapping and march as silently as ants.

Something to think about
For older children, try two-column marches and have children march side-by-side as well as in a line.

For Science And Nature: Magnifying Crystals

What the children will learn
To see refined sugar and sugar suspended in a liquid

Materials you will need
Crystal sugar, brown sugar, spoons, magnifying glasses, glasses, water, black construction paper, white construction paper, optional—microscopes

What to do

1. Spoon a small amount of white refined sugar onto a piece of black construction paper. Show the children how to separate out a few granules.

2. Let the children examine the sugar through the magnifying glasses and see if they can see the sugar as a crystal shape.

3. Repeat the process with brown sugar on white paper.

4. Let the children place a teaspoon of white sugar in a glass of water. Place black construction paper behind the glass so that the children can see better. Have them watch how the sugar floats to the bottom of the glass of water. Explain that the sugar is heavier than the water.

5. Have the children stir the water briefly and watch the water as it becomes cloudy because, when the granules of sugar are broken into smaller pieces, they are suspended in the liquid.

6. Compare a clear glass of water to the sugar water.

7. Let the children repeat the process with brown sugar.

Something to think about
Mix packaged drink mixes and observe the suspension of the granules in the water, then serve the drinks for a snack.

For Science And Nature: Ant Colony

What the children will learn
To observe the behavior of the ants

Materials you will need
Ant farm, magnifying glass, reference books which contain pictures of ants

What to do

1. Order an ant farm from a school supply store, or if you are teaching this unit in the spring, search the school grounds for ant colonies.

2. Have the children observe the ants tunneling, searching for food and their excited movements when disturbed.

3. Encourage the children to watch the ants for at least five minutes at a time so they can make accurate descriptive statements about what ants do.

4. Place tiny bits of food or granules of sugar in the ant colony and watch what happens.

5. Place reference books about ants in the science and nature area as well as in the classroom library.

Something to think about
The ants in the ant farm will eventually die, so after a week of observation, let the children take them to a wooded area, open the ant farm and let them go.

REMBRANDT'S BERET

By Johnny Alcorn

Illustrated by Stephen Alcorn

While a little girl's grandfather is painting her portrait, she stares at a Rembrandt painting of a child in a beret with a feather. She thinks the boy has the same eyes as her grandfather. While she poses, Grandfather tells her a story about when he was a little boy. One day at siesta time, he was accidentally left in the museum. While the rest of the city slept, he sneaked into the Hall of the Old Masters where the famous paintings were kept. The people in the paintings came to life and talked to him. The rest of the afternoon he met other painters, and before the afternoon was over, Rembrandt had painted his portrait. And that was the painting at which the little girl is staring while her grandfather paints her portrait. Cleverly written and masterfully painted, the story's mystery, secret and adventure let children imaginatively enter the world of art.

Read-Aloud Suggestions

Have the children recall Anatole and his beret. Read the title of the book, REMBRANDT'S BERET, and the subtitle, OR THE PAINTER'S CROWN. If possible, wear your beret and find a feather to adorn it. Read REMBRANDT'S BERET without stopping. Then look back through the illustrations for the children to enjoy the colors and the drama of the story. Place your beret with the feather on a child's head and announce, "Melissa with Painter's Crown." Suggest to the children that they paint self-portraits and add a painter's crown if they like.

STORY STRETCHER

For Art: Prints Of Rembrandt's Paintings

What the children will learn
To enjoy Rembrandt's paintings, especially, "Portrait of the Artist as a Young Man"

Materials you will need
Prints or a book of prints of Rembrandt and other Old Masters, tape, magnifying glasses

What to do
1.　Look at the illustrations in REMBRANDT'S BERET and read the portrait title of the mentioned in the book: "Portrait of the Artist as a Very, Very Young Man."

2.　Show the children the print of the Rembrandt painting.

3.　Hang the prints at the children's eye level for them to enjoy.

4.　Leave the reference book and book of prints in the art area for the children to enjoy. Place a magnifying glass there so they can look for brush strokes and layers of color.

Something to think about
Show the children prints of paintings by other Old Masters, Caravaggio and Rubens, for example.

ANOTHER STORY STRETCHER

For Art: Self-Portraits With Painters' Crowns

What the children will learn
To paint self-portraits

Materials you will need
Easels, mirrors, manilla or heavy paper, brushes, tempera paints, berets, posterboard

What to do
1.　Have the children try on their berets and look at themselves in the mirrors.

2.　Talk about how many famous artists painted their self-portraits at different times in their lives. If possible, show the children prints of self-portraits.

3.　Have the children paint their self-portraits, let them dry, then mat or frame them with posterboard.

Something to think about
Invite a painter who uses oils to come to class and show the children the paints, palette, canvases and some of her or his paintings.

STORY STRETCHER

For Classroom Library: Rembrandt Speaks

What the children will learn
To read dialogue with expression

Materials you will need
Cassette tapes, recorder, writing paper, pencils, stapler, listening station, headphones

What to do
1.　Ask children to volunteer for the parts of the little girl, the guard, Sir Curator, Caravaggio, Rubens, Rembrandt. You read the

part of Grandfather because he is the narrator.

2. Have the children copy their dialogue from the book and practice reading it with expression.

3. Select another child to be responsible for taping the page-turning signals. Clicking a stapler near the microphone or tapping a glass with a fork works nicely.

4. Ask another child to write an introduction and read it into the tape recorder. Have the "introducer" tell the title of the book, the names of the author and illustrator, the names of the children reading the dialogue, the page for the listener to turn to begin with, and the page-turning signal.

5. Rehearse the tape recording of the book with the children reading the characters' dialogue.

6. Record the story and place the tape at the listening station in the classroom library. If possible, place a print of the "Portrait of the Artist as a Young Man" on a bulletin board near the listening station.

Something to think about
Many public libraries loan fine art prints. Find out what your local library has available, and let the class help decide which prints to request for the classroom.

For Special Event: Visit To An Art Museum Or Gallery

What the children will learn
To appreciate a collection of art as well as to express their preferences

Materials you will need
Procedures required for field trips, permission forms, name tags

What to do
1. Visit a museum or art gallery in your city or a neighboring one. Talk with the curator about the length of a tour and choices of galleries and paintings which would interest your students. Bring back brochures or pamphlets for the children and volunteers to see.

2. Find out the procedures for scheduling field trips and make the appropriate arrangements.

3. Conduct a brief session for volunteers to help them understand what will happen on the field trip, what you would like the children to learn and any special safety precautions required.

4. Prepare the children for the trip by reviewing what will happen, special paintings the children will see and the required safety precautions.

5. Let the children make name tags for themselves in the shape of a "plumed Rembrandt's beret."

6. If possible, arrange for the children to receive brochures, some postcard prints or small prints of paintings, and if parents approve, place their families on the mailing list for the museum or the gallery.

7. After the field trip, let the children tell which paintings they enjoyed and share their small copies of the prints.

Something to think about
Invite art majors from a local college or university to accompany the children as volunteers for the field trip.

For Writing Center: Story Parallels, Mysteries In Museums

What the children will learn
To write a story parallel

Materials you will need
Chalkboard, chalk, writing paper, pencils, optional—art supplies for illustrations

What to do
1. Look back through the story of REMBRANDT'S BERET at each of the illustrations and list on the chalkboard a few words or a phrase which describes each scene. For example: grandfather painting, the boy Tiberius caught in the storm and ducking into the museum, Old Curator and the boy, walking into the Old Masters Hall, etc.

2. After the special event field trip to the museum or art gallery, ask the children to imagine that they are Tiberius visiting the local museum.

3. Using the list of scenes from REMBRANDT'S BERET, ask them to write their own story which parallels the book, but change the setting to your town's museum or gallery. They also can change the name of the story to their own names and title them "Melissa's Beret," for example.

4. Have those writers who are interested, write, edit, publish and illustrate their stories. (See the Introduction for more information on the writing process).

Something to think about
Find out the names of famous artists from your state and display prints of their works in your classroom. Let the children use their names as characters in their stories.

14
MYSTERIES, SECRETS, AND ADVENTURES

ANATOLE

By Eve Titus

Illustrated by Paul Galdone

A Caldecott Honor book, ANATOLE is the story of a little mouse who secretly earns his keep by becoming the taster in a cheese factory. One night while searching for food, Anatole hears the humans talking disgustedly about the mice stealing their food. Determined to give the humans something in return, he sneaks into the Duval Cheese Factory, tastes the cheese and leaves notes for the cheese makers as to what each batch of cheese needs to taste better. He signs each note, "Anatole," but no one knows who Anatole is. The Duval cheeses become the rage of all of France and Anatole deserves the credit. The president of the company leaves a letter in the cheese-tasting room thanking Anatole and asking him to identify himself, but Anatole keeps his identity a secret forever. Galdone's charming illustrations are in charcoal with blue and red splashes of color on alternating pages.

Read-Aloud Suggestions

Practice reading the story with a French accent to fit the setting of a small village outside of Paris. If possible, wear a beret on the day you read ANATOLE and tie a scarf around your neck. Show the cover of the book and ask the children whether this is a story that could really happen or an imaginary one. They will comment that it is imaginary because mice do not ride bicycles or wear berets and scarves. Tell them the mouse on the cover is Anatole and he has a secret. Read through the scene where Anatole hears what the humans say about mice and pause for two or three children to predict what Anatole will do. Stop again at the scene where the president of the company begs Anatole to come forward and identify himself. Let the children decide whether they think Anatole will come forward or keep his secret. At the end of the read-aloud session, show the children the other ANATOLE books from the classroom library which you have collected for them to read.

STORY STRETCHER
For Classroom Library: More Anatole Adventure Books

What the children will learn
To record their preferences

Materials you will need
Chart tablet, posterboard, markers, paper and pencils

What to do
1. Make a large chart of a "Reading Response Log." Have a column for dates, names, book titles, brief recommendations.

2. Supply smaller copies of the "Reading Response Log" for the children to keep.

3. Whenever the children finish an Anatole book, have them record the date, their name, the title of the book and a statement or two about why they like the book.

4. When most of the children have read at least one of the Anatole stories, have a group sharing time and let the class compare the books to the first adventure of Anatole in the cheese factory. Have the children wear their Anatole berets and scarves when discussing his adventures.

5. Extend the activity by looking at the story elements and comparing them across the stories.

Something to think about
Make tapes of the children reading the different ANATOLE adventures and share them with the kindergartners in the school. Be sure to select some children to help with the tapes who are not good readers and help them build their confidence by practicing and rehearsing before making the tapes.

STORY STRETCHER
For Cooking: Cheese Connoisseurs

What the children will learn
To identify cheeses by name and select the ones they prefer

Materials you will need
Variety of cheeses, knives, trays or large plates, toothpicks, plates, water, seedless grapes and other fresh fruits, crackers, chalkboard, chalk, optional—cheese boards, cheese cutters

What to do
1. Prepare an appealing arrangement of cheeses on one tray. On another tray arrange the fruit nicely.

2. Let the children help cut off slices or small chunks of the different cheeses, place toothpicks in

them and arrange them on plates. Place the slices or chunks of one type of cheese on one plate. Prepare as many plates as you have varieties of cheese.

3. Ask each child to take at least one piece of fruit and begin tasting the different varieties of cheese.

4. Prepare a chart on the chalkboard naming all the types of cheese with columns marked "like a lot," "like a little," "don't like." After the children have tasted each type of cheese, let them vote by placing a check mark in the different columns to indicate their likes and dislikes.

5. Have the children take bites of their fruit or crackers or sips of water in between tasting the different cheeses.

Something to think about
Do not force or even strongly encourage children to eat or taste foods they do not like. Instead model your enthusiasm for the tasting and honestly tell the varieties you enjoy and the ones you do not.

S T O R Y   S T R E T C H E R

For Creative Dramatics: Berets And Accents

What the children will learn
How to wear a beret

Materials you will need
Clothing catalogs, scissors, glue, construction paper, berets, mirrors, scarves

What to do
1. Have a few children look through fall and winter clothing catalogs and advertisements to find pictures of men, women and children wearing berets. Ask the children to cut out the pictures and glue them onto construction paper. Place the pictures on display in the classroom near the mirrors so the

children can see how to put on berets and tie scarves.

2. Ask parents to send in any berets and scarves they have at home.

3. Let the children dress up in the berets and scarves and practice saying a few words in French.

4. As the children are trying on their berets and scarves they can pretend to be French. Encourage their pretending by speaking to them in a French accent and using a few French phrases.

Something to think about
If you have friends or families from the classroom who speak French, invite them to teach the class some familiar phrases.

S T O R Y   S T R E T C H E R

For Music And Movement: Anatole's Song

What the children will learn
To sing songs in rounds and to compose new lyrics to fit the story

Materials you will need
Chart tablet or posterboard, marker, optional—cassette tape recorder and tapes

What to do
1. On chart tablet paper or posterboard, print the words to the traditional round "Are you sleeping, Are you sleeping, Brother John? Brother John?"

2. Teach the children the round and sing it with the whole class in unison.

3. Sing the song in rounds by dividing the class into three groups. The second group begins when the first group has finishing the first phrase, "Are you sleeping?" The third group begins when the first group has finished singing, "Brother John."

4. After the children know the tune and words to the English

round, teach them the French version, which is "Frère Jacques."

5. Tell the students that it is most appropriate that they learn the French version because Anatole is French.

6. Have the children compose a round which would fit the ANATOLE mystery. For example,

> *"Are you working, tasting cheese*
> *An-a-tole? An-a-tole?*
> *Factory doors are opening.*
> *Cheese makers arriving.*
> *Run, Anatole, run,*
> *Run, Anatole, run."*
> *(Raines, 1991)*

7. Print all three versions in the class *Big Book of Music* and let the children enjoy singing all the variations.

Something to think about
If you do not know these traditional rounds, ask a music teacher for a copy of a song book and a recording. Also ask the music teacher to sing these rounds with the children, and then have them practice in class.

S T O R Y   S T R E T C H E R

For Writing Center: Anatole And Gaston Adventures

What the children will learn
To retell a story from Anatole's perspective

Materials you will need
Anatole stories, writing paper, pencils, optional—art supplies for illustrations

What to do
1. After the children have read several of the ANATOLE adventures in the classroom library, they will have a keen sense of the character and will be able to imagine him in other situations.

2. Read the end of ANATOLE again, where Anatole invites Gaston to work with him in the cheese factory.

3. Have the children imagine what Anatole will tell Gaston about his mysterious disappearances every night and how he has kept his work a secret.

4. Encourage the children to write the story Anatole will tell Gaston.

5. Extend the writing possibilities by having the children imagine a secret thing Anatole could do at night in their classroom to help the class, or what he could do at their homes.

6. For the children who are interested, continue working with them until their stories are written, revised, edited and published. (See the discussion of the writing process in the Introduction.)

Something to think about
Series books like the ANATOLE ones are excellent for inspiring primary age children to write. Adopting Anatole as a main character for their stories helps them move beyond writing stories where they are the only main characters.

References

Alcorn, Johnny. (1991). Illustrations by Stephen Alcorn. **REMBRANDT'S BERET OR THE PAINTER'S CROWN**. New York: Tambourine Books.

Brown, Jeff. (1964). Illustrated by Tomi Ungerer. **FLAT STANLEY**. New York: Harper & Row.

Sharmat, Marjorie Weinman. (1972). Illustrated by Marc Simont. **NATE THE GREAT**. New York: Coward-McCann, Inc.

Titus, Eve. (1956). Illustrated by Paul Galdone. **ANATOLE**. New York: Bantam.

Van Allsburg, Chris. (1988). **TWO BAD ANTS**. Boston: Houghton Mifflin.

Additional References for Mysteries, Secrets and Adventures

Allard, Harry, & Marshall, James. (1977). **MISS NELSON IS MISSING!** Boston: Houghton Mifflin Company. *The kids in Room 207 don't appreciate Miss Nelson until one day she is replaced by the substitute, Miss Swamp. Will they ever see Miss Nelson again?*

Smith, Carla Lockhart. (1990). **TWENTY-SIX RABBITS RUN RIOT**. Boston: Little, Brown and Company. *The twenty-six rambunctious rabbit children must join forces to hunt every time the baby turns up missing! Charming, detailed illustrations.*

Steig, William. (1969). **SYLVESTER AND THE MAGIC PEBBLE**. New York: Simon and Schuster Inc. *In a moment of fright, Sylvester asks his magic pebble to turn him into a rock, which it does. Now the question is, how can he ever wish himself back into his own shape again? This well-loved Caldecott Medal winner has a happy and affectionate ending.*

Titus, Eve. (1957). Illustrated by Paul Galdone. **ANATOLE AND THE CAT**. New York: McGraw-Hill Book Company. *Anatole, the mouse of action, sets about to rid the cheese factory of the cat who is disturbing his work as cheese taster extraordinaire. Being Anatole, he succeeds, much to our delight.*

Tusa, Tricia. (1987). **MAEBELLE'S SUITCASE**. New York: Macmillan Publishing Company. *In this gentle fantasy, Maebelle, an independent, inventive, 108 year old woman, figures out a sweet way to help a young bird make his first flight south.*

BEARS IN TALL TALES, FUNNY TALES, STORIES AND POEMS

The Narrow Escapes of Davy Crockett

Big Bad Bruce

Berlioz the Bear

Bear in Mind: A Book of Bear Poems

Little Polar Bear

15

BEARS IN TALL TALES, FUNNY TALES, STORIES AND POEMS

THE NARROW ESCAPES OF DAVY CROCKETT

By Ariane Dewey

This collection of tall tales about the legendary Davy Crockett from Tennessee begins with Davy's favorite yarn about how he met a bear. Readers meet Davy when he is eight years old and weighs two hundred pounds. In addition to the huge, fierce bear, Davy encounters a boa constrictor, a hoop snake, an elk, an owl, several eagles, a few rattlesnakes and wildcats, gets caught in a tornado, rescues a steamer and rides up Niagara Falls. The story of how he met his bride, Sally Ann Thunder Ann Whirlwind, and how he was elected to Congress are also included. This action-packed, rollicking, colorful, picture-filled edition is a perfect introduction to the tall tale genre for the primary grades.

Read-Aloud Suggestions

Ask the children what they know about Davy Crockett. Listen to all comments without correcting them. Some will think Davy Crockett was a real person, while others will think he is a character in a movie or a book. Explain that while Davy Crockett actually lived, there were many exaggerated stories about his life on the frontier in which he is also a tall tale character. Tell the children that Davy Crockett's favorite story was about his narrow escape from a huge hugging bear. Read the beginning of the book about Davy as a child and his encounter with the the bear. At other story times, read the remaining tall tales in the collection.

STORY STRETCHER

For Art: Tall Davy

What the children will learn
To imagine and paint a tall tale character

Materials you will need
Butcher paper, scissors, masking tape, pencils, tempera paint, brushes

What to do
1.   Show the children how to make an outline of their bodies. Stretch out a sheet of butcher paper as long as the child is tall and cut that length of paper.

2.   Tape the paper to the floor.

3.   Have the child lie down on top of the paper and draw around his or her body. Let partners work together to take turns drawing each other's forms.

4.   Then paint the shape to look like a tall tale character.

5.   Cut out the tall character and place masking tape around the

edges on the back of the paper to reinforce the form.

6.   Hang the characters around the room and attach copies of the tall tales the children will write.

Something to think about
Older children may prefer to imagine what their characters should be like and then draw exaggerated bodies. For example, they might have bulky muscles or extremely long hair or huge feet.

STORY STRETCHER

For Classroom Library: Who Was The Real Davy Crockett?

What the children will learn
That Davy Crockett was a real person who was elected to the U.S. Congress as a representative from Tennessee

Materials you will need
Encyclopedia or other reference books, other tall tale books

What to do
1.   Read about the real Davy Crockett and look at his picture in the encyclopedia or other reference books.

2.   Compare the information to the tall tale stories. Explain that tall tales were a form of entertainment for the people who did not have radios or television in those times.

3.   Look at other tall tale books and find tales attributed to Davy Crockett. Also read other tall tale books written by Ariane Dewey.

Something to think about
Call your local chamber of commerce for the address of the Department of Tourism for the State of Tennessee. Write to the office and ask for information about Davy Crockett and the place where he was born in Tennessee.

For Creative Dramatics: Dressing Up Like A Tall Tale Character

What the children will learn
To act boastful and tell exaggerated tales of their feats

Materials you will need
Dress-up clothes, full-length mirror, videotape camera and tape, tape player

What to do
1. Ask parents to donate costumes and old clothes for the children to dress up in and imitate a tall tale character or a backwoodsman who tells tall tales.

2. After the children have read a few tall tales, ask some volunteers to pretend to be a character and make up a tall tale.

3. Have the children sign up and practice their tall tales with a partner. Encourage the partner to be an acting coach and suggest ways to make the telling of the tale more effective.

4. If possible, videotape the tall tale tellers dressed in their costumes and telling their tall tales.

Something to think about
Younger children will enjoy simply dressing up in the clothes. Invite a male who is a good storyteller to come to class and tell a tall tale. Have him introduce himself as one of the great-great-great-great-grandsons of Davy Crockett.

For Writing Center: Rebus Writing

What the children will learn
To use rebus symbols and print to tell a story

Materials you will need
Scrap paper, construction paper, markers, crayons or colored pencils

What to do
1. Look at the cover of THE NARROW ESCAPES OF DAVY CROCKETT and call the children's attention to the way the author combined words and pictures to tell about the book.

2. On scrap paper, have the students write one of their favorite tall tales about Davy Crockett.

3. Turn the construction paper vertically, start at the top of the page and have the children reprint their stories, leaving spaces to draw in pictures which will substitute for the main nouns in each sentence.

4. Display the rebus writing tall tales in the classroom library and the writing center and around the room.

Something to think about
Laminate the stories, punch a hole in the top center, tie a piece of leather or shoelace through the hole and hang the stories on a nail in the classroom library.

For Writing Center: Exaggeration And Fascination Of Tall Tales

What the children will learn
To write a tall tale

Materials you will need
Chalkboard, two colors of chalk, writing paper, pencil

What to do
1. Have a child tell about his or her morning from waking up, getting ready for school, the trip to school and arrival in the classroom this morning.

2. As the child tells about what happened, write exactly what he or she says.

3. Leave space between the sentences.

4. Discuss what exaggeration means. For example, if the child said she woke up late, rewrite it as an exaggeration, "I was three months late for school." If the child says she was hungry, write, "I was as hungry as a bear. I ate thirteen boxes of cereal and drank six quarts of milk before going to the refrigerator to see what else was there."

5. Let the children join you in rewriting the sentences for exaggeration.

6. Have the child who told the original story read the piece again as a tall tale, so exaggerated no one could believe it, but fascinating to read.

7. Suggest that the other children write about something which happened in reality and then rewrite it as a tall tale—with the one stipulation that somewhere along the way, they must meet a bear.

Something to think about
Definitely have an author's chair for the children's tall tales. Choose a special chair in which each author can sit while reading his or her work to the audience. At the end of the author's reading, applaud and shout, "Author, author."

15

BEARS IN TALL TALES, FUNNY TALES, STORIES AND POEMS

By Bill Peet

BIG BAD BRUCE

BIG BAD BRUCE

By Bill Peet

In imaginative Bill Peet style, BIG BAD BRUCE, the bear bully, is brought down to size, but not before he terrifies the whole forest by tumbling rocks and boulders down the hillside, breaking off trees and scaring the wits out of quail and little rabbits. Bruce, the bear, meets his match in Roxy, the witch, who cooks up a blueberry pie filled with a magic shrinking potion. Bruce falls asleep under the tree and, while he snoozes, he shrinks. When he awakens he is smaller than the quail and little rabbits he once frightened. Roxy's cat rescues Little Bruce from becoming a meal for an owl. Bruce lives with Roxy and the cat in her cottage, but sometimes he sneaks into the garden and scares the little caterpillars and bugs by flipping pebbles at them. Peet's comical illustrations complement the story with just the right amount of color and detail.

Read-Aloud Suggestions

Ask the children what a bully is. Show them the cover of BIG BAD BRUCE and tell them this bear thinks a lot of things are funny that other people do not. He picks on animals smaller than he is, but he is in for a surprise. Read BIG BAD BRUCE, pause after the illustration of Roxy rushing back to her little cottage and ask the children what they think Roxy will do. Read on to the end of the story. Ask if the children have other favorite stories which Bill Peet has written.

S T O R Y   S T R E T C H E R

For Art: Shrinking Pictures, Miniatures

What the children will learn
To contrast characters in size

Materials you will need
Construction paper, crayons or markers, colored pencils, pencil sharpener, scissors, scraps of construction paper, glue

What to do
1.   Ask the children to draw a large picture which almost fills the page.

2.   Have them cut a tiny rectangle of construction paper and draw a miniature of the same scene. Use sharp colored pencils instead of crayons or markers for the miniature scenes.

3.   Glue the miniatures onto the larger pictures.

4.   Hang them on a bulletin board with the title, "Big Bad Bruce's Shrinking Pictures."

Something to think about
Show the children miniatures of fine art pictures. Let the children continue to make big pictures and miniatures. Highlight the miniatures by letting the children draw

them on paper folded like a greeting card so that when the viewer opens the little card there is a surprise inside.

S T O R Y   S T R E T C H E R

For Classroom Library: Story Retelling From Pictures

What the children will learn
To use visual cues and listen for appropriate interpretation

Materials you will need
Copy of BIG BAD BRUCE, optional—cassette tapes, recorder

What to do
1.   Explain to the children that tall tales and funny tales like BIG BAD BRUCE are excellent for story retelling.

2.   Suggest that the children work with partners and take turns telling the story. They will have to listen to what their partners say to be sure that all the appropriate information is provided.

3.   Let the children enjoy the shared story telling experience for its own sake. If the students want to prepare their story retelling as a recording for the listening station, assist them in writing an introduction and making page-turning signals.

Something to think about
The oral language tradition of story telling is one teachers can begin to build by story retelling. As children become more confident, they can learn some classic stories meant to be told. If you live in a part of the country where traditional stories that often told, invite a storyteller to class.

For Cooking: Bruce's Blueberry Pie

What the children will learn
To read and follow recipe directions

Materials you will need
Posterboard, marker, muffin tins, butter or margarine, packaged pie crust, knives, toaster oven, blueberry pie filling, saucepan, tablespoons, teaspoons, milk, plates, napkins, optional—whipped topping or vanilla yogurt

What to do
1. Print the directions for making BRUCE'S BLUEBERRY PIES on posterboard. Let small groups of children help you prepare the pies according to the directions.

2. Turn a muffin tin upside down and grease lightly.

3. Cut circles of packaged pie crust and form them onto the bottoms of the muffin tins to make tiny pie crusts.

4. Bake the tiny pie crusts about half the time indicated on the pie crust package.

5. Take the pie crusts out to cool.

6. Heat the blueberry pie filling in a saucepan just until it is warm.

7. Spoon a tablespoon of the warm pie filling into the tiny pie crust.

8. Serve with cartons of cold milk. Optional—serve with a teaspoon of whipped topping or a bit of vanilla yogurt on top.

Something to think about
Have a volunteer come to class and bake the pies from scratch. The children will especially enjoy mixing and rolling the pie crust. (Idea adapted from one by Lisa Lewis for baby apple pies.)

For Writing Center: Shrinking Bullies

What the children will learn
To write a funny tale about a bully who gets his or her "comeuppance"

Materials you will need
Writing paper, pencils, optional—art materials for illustrations

What to do
1. Read BIG BAD BRUCE again to the children who come to the writing center during choice time.

2. Discuss how Bruce the bear was a bully, and what he thought was funny, the other animals thought was terrible.

3. Let the children imagine some bullies and what would happen to them if they ate Roxy's blueberry pie and shrank.

4. Have the children write their "shrinking bullies" stories and edit them if they are interested enough to want to read them aloud to the class.

Something to think about
If children bring up difficulties at school with older students bullying them, have the school counselor investigate. Sometimes children will write about situations that need to be investigated. Talk with the children privately and find out if this is an imagined or real bully in their lives.

For Writing Center: Little Bad Bruce In the Flower Garden

What the children will learn
To write a continuing saga of Bruce the Bear

Materials you will need
Chalkboard, chalk, writing paper, pencils, optional—art materials for illustrations

What to do
1. Read the end of Bill Peet's BIG BAD BRUCE where the now Little Bad Bruce goes into the flower garden and tosses pebbles at beetles and caterpillars.

2. Have the children imagine a sequel to the saga which continues the story. Perhaps a little honeybee mixes up a magic potion and leaves it in the cup of a honeysuckle which Little Bad Bruce eats.

3. When the children have brainstormed some possibilities, let them write their stories on their own, illustrate them if they desire and share them with the rest of the class.

4. Place the Little Bad Bruce stories in the classroom library and in the writing center on bulletin boards marked, "The Continuing Saga of Bad Bruce Bear."

Something to think about
Read other shrinking character stories such as Tom Thumb.

BERLIOZ THE BEAR

By Jan Brett

The bear orchestra is to play for a ball in the village square, but Berlioz is worried about his bass. A strange buzzing sound comes from his bass each time he plays it. The musicians load themselves and their instruments onto the festively decorated wagon. When the mule refuses to pull their wagon, the musicians fear they will miss the concert. A parade of animals comes along to help the stranded musicians, but no one can budge the stubborn mule until a bee comes buzzing out of Berlioz's bass. The bee stings the mule who charges ahead pulling the wagon into the village square where the musicians are greeted by thunderous applause. Jan Brett illustrates the book beautifully with lavishly decorated borders, intricate details on the clothing and charming expressions on the animals' faces. Young readers will pore over each page.

Read-Aloud Suggestions

Show the children the cover of BERLIOZ THE BEAR and ask if they remember any other books by Jan Brett. Tell the children this is a tale with two problems which are related. Read the story and, after the first page, let a child identify the first problem—a buzzing bass. Continue reading and after the scene where the wagon hits a hole in the road and the mule refuses to go on, identify the second problem—a stubborn mule. Finish the story and have the children recall all the animals who tried to help pull the stubborn mule: a rooster, a tabby cat, a schnauzer, a billy goat, a plow horse and an ox all try to pull the mule. Let the children recall how the two problems were related. Call attention to the lavishly decorated borders and have the children notice how the illustrator adds more to the story by the little scenes on the borders.

STORY STRETCHER

For Art: Embroidery

What the children will learn
To embroider a simple design

Materials you will need
Loosely woven fabric, embroidery hoops, embroidery thread and needles, fabric markers, clothing with embroidered decorations

What to do
1. Look again at the illustrations of the beautiful vests, coats, shirts, blouses and dresses of the characters in BERLIOZ THE BEAR.

2. Show the children articles of clothing you have collected which are intricately embroidered. Tell the history of the clothing if you know it. Identify the places where the clothing was made or bought.

3. Invite someone who is good at embroidery and other stitchery to show the children how to embroider.

4. Using a fabric marker, let the children draw a design of flowers, stems and leaves onto a piece of fabric.

5. Show the children how to place the embroidery hoop over the fabric to hold it taunt.

6. Demonstrate how to thread the needle and make the stitches.

Something to think about
For younger children, choose loosely woven fabric like burlap, larger needles and more strands of thread. Some children will enjoy creating "embroidery like" designs with fabric markers or liquid embroidery.

STORY STRETCHER

For Classroom Library: Flannel Board

What the children will learn
To recall the sequence of characters

Materials you will need
Flannel board, construction paper, markers or colored pencils, scissors, laminating film or clear contact paper, glue sticks, old emery boards, large sandwich bag

What to do
1. Let the children make the flannel board characters from the story by drawing the intricate costumes, coloring them, and cutting them out.

2. Laminate the characters.

3. Cut old emery boards into smaller pieces and glue the pieces onto the backs of the laminated flannel board pieces to make them adhere to the flannel.

4. Retell the story of BERLIOZ THE BEAR using the children's flannel board pieces.

5. Store the flannel board pieces in a large zip-lock sandwich bag and place it in the class library along with a copy of the book.

6. Encourage the children to work with partners. While one child reads or tells the story, the other can place the characters on the flannel board.

Something to think about
Cumulative tales where a new character is added in each scene are excellent choices for flannel board stories.

STORY STRETCHER

For Cooking: Outdoor Concert And Picnic

What the children will learn
To prepare a nutritious picnic

Materials you will need
Picnic basket, tablecloth, napkins, fruits, peanut butter, jelly, bread, cheese spreads, crackers, knives, plastic wrap, milk or juice, cassette recording of the "Flight of the Bumblebee"

What to do
1. Talk about how many families enjoy taking a picnic lunch to a concert where an orchestra or band is playing.

2. Plan an outdoor concert based on BERLIOZ THE BEAR. Tell the children that they will prepare their own snacks, and when they take their picnic out on the lawn, they will have an encore performance of Berlioz's music.

3. Let the children make their own snacks of peanut butter and jelly sandwiches, cheeses and fruits.

4. Go outside, spread a tablecloth on the grass and open the picnic basket for the children to get their sandwiches, cheese and crackers, fruit and milk or juice.

5. After the children have settled down to eat, surprise them by playing the recording of the "Flight of the Bumblebee," which was the encore the bears played for their concert in BERLIOZ THE BEAR.

Something to think about
Invite a musician who plays a string instrument to come to the playground, and have your concert while eating your snack.

STORY STRETCHER

For Music And Movement: Strings Concert

What the children will learn
The names of the different string instruments

Materials you will need
As many string instruments as possible, but at least a violin, cello and bass

What to do
1. Invite musicians from a high school or middle school to come to class and bring their instruments.

2. Let each musician play a brief piece and talk about what they had to do to learn to play and to be a part of an orchestra or band as well as what is needed to care for their instrument.

3. If some of the children's parents or grandparents are musicians, invite them to class also.

Something to think about
Be sure to alert the musicians when you invite them that the children will be curious about the instruments. Arrange for the children to have a chance to pluck the strings and pull the bows across the strings.

ANOTHER STORY STRETCHER

For Music And Movement: Flight Of The Bumblebee

What the children will learn
To recognize a famous piece of music

Materials you will need
Recording of the "Flight of the Bumblebee" by Rimsky-Korsakov, tape or record player

What to do
1. Show the children the last page of BERLIOZ THE BEAR.

2. Have someone read the title of the score of music on Berlioz's stand.

3. Play the recording of the famous "Flight of the Bumblebee."

4. Invite the children to move the way the music makes them feel. Have only one rule—they may not touch each other.

5. Call a dance instructor to invite students who have danced to the music to come to class and perform for the children.

Something to think about
If the music is too long for younger children, play only the part with the impatient buzzing of the bees.

BEARS IN TALL TALES, FUNNY TALES, STORIES AND POEMS

BEAR IN MIND: A BOOK OF BEAR POEMS

Selected by Bobbye S. Goldstein

Illustrated by William

Pène du Bois

A collection of bear poems grouped under the headings of springtime, funny bears and honey bears, bear facts, bears on view at the circus and zoo, polar bears, sleep time and teddy bear time. Many favorite poets are included: Lillian M. Fisher, Odgen Nash, Margaret Wise Brown, Karla Kuskin, John Ciardi, Jack Prelutsky, Lois Lenski, Aileen Fisher, Leland B. Jacobs, Lee Bennett Hopkins and Jane Yolen. The bright blue cover and the du Bois illustrations invite young readers into a favorite poetry subject.

Read-Aloud Suggestions

Read poems throughout the unit on Bears in Tall Tales, Funny Tales, Stories and Poems. Read John Ciardi's "More about Bears" and Lillian M. Fisher's "Big Hairy Fisherman" on the day you read THE NARROW ESCAPES OF DAVY CROCKETT. Select Isabel Joshlin Glaser's "Advice for Hikers" to accompany BIG BAD BRUCE. Choose the entire section of "Bears on View at the Circus and Zoo" on the day you read BERLIOZ THE BEAR. To accompany LITTLE POLAR BEAR, read "Polar Bear" by William Jay Smith, "The Polar Bear" by Jack Prelutsky and "Bear Coat" by Leland B. Jacobs. Do not show the children the illustrations in the book. Instead tell them the book will be in the classroom library for them to see the pictures.

STORY STRETCHER

For Art: In My Mind I Saw

What the children will learn
To interpret poems visually

Materials you will need
Wide selection of art supplies—tempera paints, watercolor paints, crayons, chalks, charcoals, markers, manilla paper, construction paper, butcher paper, scissors, tape, scraps of fabric left over from collages

What to do
1.   Tell the children that the reason you did not show them the pictures in BEAR IN MIND: A BOOK OF BEAR POEMS is that you wanted them to think of how to illustrate the poems.

2.   Read a few of the children's requests for poems which have particularly descriptive language or evoke strong visual and have emotional images, such as the sec-

tion of the book titled "Bears on Review in Circus and Zoo."

3.   As each child hears a poem that he or she particularly likes, let that child leave the group and go and collect the art supplies he or she wants to illustrate the poem.

4.   Continue the reading until each child has a poem in mind to illustrate.

Something to think about
Let the children copy the bear poem which inspired their art work and display it with the illustrations on a bulletin board.

ANOTHER STORY STRETCHER

For Art: Adding Dimensions To Pictures

What the children will learn
To emphasize a focal point

Materials you will need
Construction paper, pastels, markers or crayons

What to do
1.   Ask the children to make a bear picture from one of their favorite bear poems or stories in the unit.

2.   Demonstrate how to make a character or item in their picture stand out from the rest. Have the children cut a strip of construction paper which is one-half inch by one inch. Fold the strip like an accordion. Place glue on the ends of the folds and stick one side to the paper and another side to the item they want to stick out from the picture. For example, they might draw a bear cub on construction paper, cut it out, draw the background, then attach the cub to the paper by gluing one end of the strip of paper to the picture and the other to the cutout of the cub.

3. Display the focal point pictures in the art center, classroom library and writing center.

Something to think about
An alternative is to place a cotton ball under their cutout, swab the underneath edge of the cutout with paste or glue and stick it into place. The padded item then becomes the focal point.

STORY STRETCHER

For Games: Teddy Bear, Teddy Bear Turn Around

What the children will learn
To jump rope and keep the rhythm of the chant

Materials you will need
Posterboard, marker, individual jump ropes, longer jump ropes for group jumps

What to do
1. Print the words to "Teddy Bear, Teddy Bear Turn Around" on posterboard and teach it to the children if they do not already know it.

2. Demonstrate how to jump rope to the rhythm of the chant.

3. Let the children jump rope to the chants.

4. When the children are skilled enough, teach them how to jump double dutch and to run in and out of the turning ropes.

5. Encourage jumping rope by always having the ropes available for outside play.

Something to think about
Have third graders come to the first grade and put on a jump rope demonstration. Write down some of the words to the children's favorite jump rope chants.

STORY STRETCHER

For Mathematics: Graphing Our Favorite Bear Poems

What the children will learn
To represent data in another form

Materials you will need
Post-it notes or index cards and tape, chalkboard, chalk, posterboard, marker

What to do
1. Have each child write down the name of her or his favorite bear poem on a Post-it note or index card.

2. Make a list of the favorite poems on the chalkboard by having each child read the name of her or his favorite poem.

3. When the title of the poem is read by more than one child, make a tally mark beside the title of the poem.

4. Ask the children to think of another way they could convey the data about their favorite bear poems.

5. Show them how to group the data, listing the five top vote-getters and grouping all the remaining titles under the category of "other."

6. Draw a large graph on the board. Title it "Our Favorite Bear Poems." Down the left side list the names of the five top vote-getters and "others."

7. Let the children each come to the board with their Post-it notes or index cards and stick them end to end across from the title of their favorite bear poem.

8. If the "other" category has a large number, help the children recall how the data were grouped.

Something to think about
Repeat the process for their favorite bear stories from the books and other bear books.

STORY STRETCHER

For Writing Center: Bear Poems

What the children will learn
To write a short poem

Materials you will need
Chalkboard, chalk

What to do
1. Read again some of the children's favorite selections from BEAR IN MIND: A BOOK OF BEAR POEMS.

2. With small groups of children, compose bear poems. Have several beginnings in mind to get each group started. For example,

> *"My favorite kind of bear is one who doesn't stare,*
> *and doesn't growl or even howl.*
> *My favorite kind of bear is teddy bear."*
> *(Raines, 1991)*

3. If a group gets stuck, make a list of words which describe bears and then see if they can begin to make rhymes.

4. Print the jump rope chant to "Teddy Bear, Teddy Bear, Turn Around" on the board and have the children substitute other bears besides teddy bears. For example,

> *"Polar bear, polar bear, float on ice*
> *Polar bear, polar bear, that's so nice.*
> *Polar bear, polar bear, wrapped in fur*
> *Polar bear, polar bear, please don't stir.*
> *Polar bear, polar bear, swim out to sea*
> *Polar bear, polar bear, stay away from me."*
> *(Raines, 1991)*

Something to think about
BEAR IN MIND: A BOOK OF BEAR POEMS is a wonderful one to introduce primary children to poetry because there are many short but interesting poems in the collection.

15

BEARS IN TALL TALES, FUNNY TALES, STORIES AND POEMS

LITTLE POLAR BEAR

By Hans de Beer

After his first lessons in hunting, Lars, the little polar bear, sleeps so soundly he doesn't hear the ice cracking, and he floats away to sea where his tiny iceberg melts. In a storm, Lars latches onto a floating barrel and is carried to the tropics where he meets Henry, the hippopotamus. Henry tries to help Lars find his way back home. Along the way, Lars meets some beautifully colored and exotic creatures, including a chameleon who can turn any color. Henry takes Lars to Marcus, the eagle, who summons Samson, the whale, to take the little polar bear home. When Lars is delivered safely to his father, he tells him of all the beautiful sights, but his father cannot understand because he has seen only his white world of snow and ice. Hans de Beer's soft full-page illustrations are charming and witty. He contrasts the two worlds well, capturing Lars' enchantment with the new while longing for the familiarity of home.

Read-Aloud Suggestions

Have the children think of opposites, night and day, none and many, hot and cold, sunny and rainy. Ask them to describe what the weather would be like at the North Pole and what colors they might see, and the weather in the tropics and the colors they might see there. Read LITTLE POLAR BEAR and near the end have a few children guess who Samson might be. At the end of this book, the children often request that it be read again. Either read the story a second time or let the children re-tell the story by looking at the pictures. On a globe or map, show the children where Lars started his journey at the North Pole and where the nearest tropics are.

STORY STRETCHER

For Art: Opposites

What the children will learn
To demonstrate visually what opposites mean

Materials you will need
Scraps of construction paper, scissors, stapler, glue sticks, different shades of white paper, white and pastel chalks, light blues and gray construction paper, bright colors or markers, crayons, colored pencils

What to do
1. Ask the children to make two pictures which are opposites. They can choose to focus on the opposites in the story and the two worlds Lars explored—the North Pole and the tropics—or they can make night and day pictures, rainy and sunny days, school days and vacation days—any opposites of their choosing.

2. From the array of art supplies, let the children collect the ones they need to make their two pictures.

3. Separate the pictures into sets of opposites—opposites in weather, opposites in feeling, opposites in location—and group them together for display purposes. Hang the Lars pictures in the library area.

Something to think about
Let some children make white on white pictures to show the different shades of white Lars experienced in his North Pole world. Look at the many different shadings the artist uses in LITTLE POLAR BEAR.

ANOTHER STORY STRETCHER

For Art: Sculpting Polar Bears

What the children will learn
To make a three-dimensional form

Materials you will need
Playdough or modeling clay, plastic knives, scissors, index cards, markers, tape

What to do
1. Give each child who chooses to come to the art center during choice time a lump of clay or playdough about the size of a small orange.

2. Ask them to model Lars, Henry or another animal Lars met in his adventure.

3. Display the sculptures around the classroom. Cut strips of index cards and let the children print the name of their animal and their names on the strip. Tape these in front of the sculptures.

Something to think about
Let the children help you make playdough (see the recipe in the Appendix).

For Classroom Library: Felt Characters For Lars' Journey

What the children will learn
To make and use representations to tell a story

Materials you will need
Chalkboard, chalk, flannel board, index cards, pencils, scissors, felt in many different colors, glue, emery boards, large sandwich bag

What to do
1. Tell the children that you think LITTLE POLAR BEAR would make an excellent flannel board story.

2. Let the students list all the characters in the story and then volunteer to make one.

3. Explain that only the outline of the characters is needed. They do not have to make detailed figures. Give each child a 3 x 5 inch index card and have them sketch their animal on the card first, cut it out, then draw the shape onto the felt and cut any bits of different colored felt they want to complete the animal.

4. Have each child decide what colors of felt they need.

5. Glue a small strip of old emery board onto the back of the felt figures to make them adhere better to the flannel board.

6. Tell the story and, as each character is mentioned, have the maker place her or his felt piece onto the flannel board.

7. Store the characters in a large sandwich bag with a zip-lock top and place it in the class library along with a copy of the book.

Something to think about
Engage the children in planning and making many of the materials you use in the classroom. Teachers often do too much for children. When they help make the materials for the flannel board or for games, they are more likely to use them and to care for them properly.

For Science And Nature: KWL About Real Polar Bears

What the children will learn
To find out what the life of real polar bears is like

Materials you will need
Chart tablet, marker, polar bear pictures, reference books on animal life in the Arctic, index cards, tape, Post-it notes, pencils

What to do
1. Make a KWL chart by drawing three columns on a large sheet of chart tablet paper. Write "Polar Bears" at the top of the paper. Print a large "K" at the top of the first column to represent what the children already "know" about polar bears. Print a large "W" at the top of the second column for the list of questions about what they "want" to know. Print a large "L" at the head of the third column to represent what the students "learned" from reading more about polar bears.

2. Have the children recall what they know about polar bears after reading the story of LITTLE POLAR BEAR. Write the information in the "K" column. They know polar bears live where it is very cold and frozen, eat fish, sleep against snow banks, live on land and swim in the sea.

3. Continue the discussion, listing items in the "K" column raised by children who have observed polar bears at the zoo or read other information.

4. Let the children generate a list of questions about polar bears and print them in the "W" column for "what we want to know."

5. Tell the children that the "L" column will include the answers to their questions and other information they learn while finding out more about polar bears.

6. Whenever a child finds the answers to one of the questions, have her or him print the answer on an index card or Post-it note and attach it to the chart under the "L" column.

7. After a few days of children reading about polar bears on their own in the library area, review the chart.

Something to think about
For older children, group the answers to the questions and their additional information into a data retrieval chart. For example, place all the cards that tell about what the polar bear eats in one group, form another set of cards about where the polar bear lives and ranges, have another set of information about families and still another on whether or not the polar bear is safe or an endangered species.

For Writing Center: Informational And Imagination Writing

What the children will learn
To record facts and to write a fantasy piece

Materials you will need
KWL chart from the science and nature story s-t-r-e-t-c-h-e-r, learning logs, writing paper, pencils

What to do
1. Review the KWL chart and emphasize all the facts the children collected about polar bears.

2. Have the children write in their science learning logs by

noting the date and some of the most interesting facts, at least three, which they learned about polar bears. Ask them to begin each statement with "Fact:" and what they learned.

3. Recall the facts they learned from the fantasy book, LITTLE POLAR BEAR. Discuss how the author uses facts and then blends them with fantasy to create a story.

4. Have the children begin with some facts about polar bears and then extend them and write a fantasy piece.

5. When the students have written their stories, have them read their fantasy pieces aloud, and the audience can listen for what is fact and what is fantasy.

Something to think about
Young children can divide a sheet of paper by folding it in half and on the left-hand side write "Fact" and on the right-hand side write "Fantasy." Then they can draw a picture which illustrates each.

References

Brett, Jan. (1991). **BERLIOZ THE BEAR**. New York: G. P. Putnam's Sons.

de Beer, Hans. (1987). **LITTLE POLAR BEAR**. New York: North-South Books.

Dewey, Ariane. (1990). **THE NARROW ESCAPES OF DAVY CROCKETT**. New York: Greenwillow Books.

Goldstein, Bobbye S. (1989). Illustrated by William Pène du Bois. **BEAR IN MIND: A BOOK OF BEAR POEMS**. New York: Viking Kestrel.

Peet, Bill. (1977). **BIG BAD BRUCE**. Boston: Houghton Mifflin.

Additional References for Bears in Tall Tales, Funny Tales, Stories and Poems

Bishop, Claire Huchet. (1964). Illustrated by Kurt Wiese. **TWENTY-TWO BEARS**. New York: Viking Press. *"In the Wild Woods of Wyoming I met twenty-two bears. That is a lot of bears!" This charming book goes on to detail each bear by name, and ends with a birthday and bedtime for a very special bear: YOUR bear.*

Gage, Wilson. (1983). Illustrated by James Stevenson. **CULLY CULLY AND THE BEAR**. New York: Greenwillow Books. *Cully Cully the hunter is chasing a bear, or is it the other way around? A tall tale in which the bear outsmarts the human in a satisfyingly silly way.*

Ludwig, Warren. (1990). **GOOD MORNING, GRANNY ROSE**. New York: G. P. Putnam's Sons. *Granny Rose and her old dog Henry get caught in a mountain snowstorm. Henry finds a cave and they take shelter, only to be awakened by the startling discovery that their cave-mate is a hibernating bear!*

Milne, A. A. (1926). Illustrated by Ernest H. Shepard. **WINNIE-THE-POOH**. New York: E. P. Dutton and Company. *Wonderful read-aloud stories of that lovable bear, Winnie-the-Pooh, and his many friends in the Hundred Acre Wood. This is the original version, later adapted by Disney.*

Pryor, Bonnie. (1985). Illustrated by Bruce Degen. **GRANDPA BEAR**. New York: William Morrow and Company. *Once upon a time there was a little bear. She was too little to do the things her brother could do, and too big to do the things the baby bear could do. But when Grandpa Bear came to live with them, he and Samantha could share all kinds of imaginative adventures and understanding.*

FUN WITH WORDS

Teach Us, Amelia Bedelia
Old Turtle's 90 Knock-knocks, Jokes, and Riddles
A Cache of Jewels
Alison's Zinnia
The King Who Rained

TEACH US, AMELIA BEDELIA

By Peggy Parish

Illustrated by Lynn Sweat

A favorite funny character for beginning readers, Amelia Bedelia, usually a housekeeper, is mistaken for a substitute teacher. Following the teacher's lesson plan, Amelia takes everything on the list quite literally. She calls the roll by taking a roll from a boy's lunch box and calling to it, and so the zany, wacky day begins. Endearing, confused Amelia Bedelia becomes the children's favorite substitute teacher, but Amelia thinks she prefers housekeeping, even though she loves children. Lynn Sweat's illustrations of Amelia, quaintly dressed in a uniform, have become synonymous with the series.

Read-Aloud Suggestions

At the mere mention of an Amelia Bedelia book, the children often cheer. They like the outrageous situations, and Amelia's literal nature is close to their own interpretations of the world. Have the children recall their last substitute teacher and tell how they helped him or her understand what to do. Read TEACH US, AMELIA BEDELIA and pause to let the children make predictions about what Amelia Bedelia will do in each situation. Survey the children for other Amelia Bedelia books they like and place them in the library. Let the children make recordings of the books.

STORY STRETCHER

For Art: Mixed-Up Pictures

What the children will learn
To illustrate with a sense of humor

Materials you will need
Chalkboard, chalk, choice of art media, paints, crayons, markers, pastels, painting or drawing paper

What to do
1. Look through the illustrations of TEACH US, AMELIA BEDELIA and have the children decide what makes each scene funny. Amelia interprets everything literally, without thinking about the context of the comments.

2. Make a list of other "literal interpretations" which Amelia Bedelia might make. For example, she might interpret "library book" as a book about libraries, "school book" as a book about schools, and "putting up pictures" as holding them in the air.

3. Fold sheets of paper in half. On the left side, let the children choose one of their favorite Amelia Bedelia mix-ups or some-thing Amelia Bedelia might do, and draw or paint a picture.

4. On the right side of the paper, have the children illustrate how Amelia Bedelia should have interpreted the situation.

5. Display the students art work on a bulletin board and enjoy the humor in the illustrations.

Something to think about
Young children may not be able to think of other Amelia Bedelia misinterpretations because they think of the world in literal terms as well.

STORY STRETCHER

For Cooking: Amelia's Taffy Apples

What the children will learn
To follow recipe directions

Materials you will need
Saucepan, hot plate, caramel candies or taffy sauce, wooden spoon, measuring cup and spoons, water, apples, popsicle sticks, marker, waxed paper, trays

What to do
1. Melt caramel candies or warm taffy sauce from a jar in a saucepan, stirring continually with a wooden spoon so the mixture does not stick. Add teaspoons of water to the mixture to keep it from thickening too quickly.

2. Have the children write their names on a popsicle stick and insert the stick into the stem end of an apple. Caution them to make one stab and not to wiggle the stick, because then it would be too loose to stay in the apple.

3. Assist each child in twirling their apple in the warm taffy sauce.

4. Place the apples on a tray covered with waxed paper.

5. Allow the apples to cool and enjoy them as a snack.

Something to think about

Give each child a small piece of waxed paper because invariably some of the apples come off the sticks while the children are eating them. They can use the waxed paper to hold the apples and keep their hands from getting too sticky.

STORY STRETCHER

For Creative Dramatics: Amelia Bedelia Comes To Our School

What the children will learn

To think of literal interpretations

Materials you will need

Housekeeper's uniform

What to do

1.   Dress up like Amelia Bedelia.

2.   Have an aide or another teacher look in on your class as they arrive and tell the children they will have a substitute teacher today.

3.   Come to class and introduce yourself as Amelia Bedelia, the substitute teacher.

4.   Ask for help throughout the day with what you are supposed to do next.

5.   Interpret everything literally. For example, if a child asks to call his mother, say, "What do you want to call her?" When you say, "Take a seat," have the students pick up their chairs and take them to another place in the classroom.

6.   Enjoy the humorous situations which arrive throughout the day.

Something to think about

Teachers of younger children might have a shorter time for Amelia to be in the classroom. Older students can imagine Amelia Bedelia and write the verbal exchanges which would happen as she reports to the office, finds the classroom, meets each student, goes to the cafeteria.

STORY STRETCHER

For Mathematics: Amelia Bedelia Story Problems

What the children will learn

To interpret mathematics problems literally

Materials you will need

Apples, oranges, play money, index cards, pencils

What to do

1.   Read the mathematics problems the children solved in TEACH US, AMELIA BEDELIA.

2.   Solve the problem using real apples.

3.   Read some mathematics problems from the math book you use in the classroom. Select some story problems which can be easily interpreted with apples, oranges, play money and items found in the classroom.

4.   Divide the class into groups of three or four children.

5.   Write the story problems on index cards and randomly distribute the cards.

6.   Have the groups of children dramatize their story problems. One child can read the problem and the other two or three can act it out.

7.   While the children are dramatizing the story problem, write the mathematical problem on the board. For example if Jim and Brian took one apple each for snack on Monday, how many apples would be left in the fruit bowl if their mother bought two apples for each day of school that week. On the board write $1 + 1 = 2$; $2 \times 5 = 10$; $10 - 2 = 8$. The multiplication could be written as repeated addition for younger students.

8.   After modeling one problem, let the children write their own equations as the stories are dramatized.

Something to think about

Collect as many examples of real-life mathematics as possible so that children use mathematics routinely for solving problems.

STORY STRETCHER

For Music And Movement: Amelia Bedelia's Song

What the children will learn

To compose some zany lyrics which fit the character

Materials you will need

Chart tablet, marker

What to do

1.   Tell the students you have written the beginning of a song for Amelia Bedelia. In the story, the author did not tell us what song Amelia sang to the children.

2.   Write the lyrics based on the traditional song, "Mary Had a Little Lamb." For example,

> *"A-me-lia went to school one day,*
> *School one day, school one day.*
> *A-me-lia went to school one day,*
> *To sub-sti-tute teach.*
>
> *She made the children laugh and play,*
> *Laugh and play, laugh and play.*
> *She made the children laugh and play,*
> *When Amelia went to school."*
> *(Raines, 1991)*

3.   Have the children continue writing lyrics for each of the funny situations in the story.

4.   Print the finished song in the class *Big Book of Songs*.

Something to think about

The title of this unit is "Fun with Words." Discuss how a lyricist, a songwriter, has fun making words, fit the pattern of a tune.

OLD TURTLE'S 90 KNOCK-KNOCKS, JOKES, AND RIDDLES

By Leonard Kessler

These 90 knock-knocks, jokes and riddles include many of the childhood favorites as well as a few surprises. The characters are animals and many scenes include a turtle. Some jokes are told in story form, taking two or three pages. In addition, on some pages, there are cartoon bubbles. The black pen sketches are colored with bright watercolors and markers.

Read-Aloud Suggestions

About a week before reading the book to the children, have them begin collecting knock-knocks and other jokes. Ask the students to print their jokes on index cards and place them on a bulletin board. Each morning begin group time by selecting a child's knock-knock to read. Read OLD TURTLE'S 90 KNOCK-KNOCK, JOKES, AND RIDDLES over several days. Read knock-knocks one day, jokes another and riddles on another day. Announce all the story s-t-r-e-t-c-h-e-r activities for the book and encourage reluctant and beginning readers to participate in reading and telling their jokes by scheduling a few practice sessions.

STORY STRETCHER

For Art: Pictures Make Me Laugh

What the children will learn
To represent jokes and riddles in picture form

Materials you will need
Manilla or drawing paper, markers, crayons, colored pencils

What to do
1. Have each child select a knock-knock, joke or riddle to illustrate.

2. Help each person decide how many scenes will be needed to illustrate the joke.

3. Fold the papers so that each scene is represented on a fold. Make greeting card folds, tri-folds or accordion folds.

4. Let the children illustrate their jokes or riddles and print the words below the pictures or use cartoon balloons for the dialogue.

5. Post the illustrations on bulletin boards at the children's eye level.

Something to think about
Collect some of the children's favorite cartoons from the newspaper and have them notice the different illustrator's styles.

STORY STRETCHER

For Classroom Library: Pause For A Riddle

What the children will learn
To use cues to solve riddles

Materials you will need
Collection of riddles, posterboard or large index cards, scissors, marker, paper, large brown envelope

What to do
1. Collect riddles from riddle books and children's magazines.

2. Print them on strips of posterboard or large index cards.

3. Code each with a numeral, letter, or a drawing of one of the animal characters from OLD TURTLE'S 90 KNOCK-KNOCKS, JOKES, AND RIDDLES.

4. Make an answer sheet with the answers marked with the corresponding code.

5. Seal the answer sheet in a large brown envelope. On the outside of the envelope print, "The answer may surprise you," or some other message.

Something to think about
Children's magazines are excellent sources for riddles and jokes. Keep the jokes and riddles the children bring in and use them next year with a new class. Most of the children's favorites are timeless.

For Classroom Library: Class Comedy Club

What the children will learn
To read jokes and riddles with the proper timing and inflection

Materials you will need
Index cards, thumbtacks

What to do
1. From the collection of knock-knocks, jokes and riddles which the children have brought to class, let partners select ones to read aloud.

2. Have the reading partners rehearse their presentation of the knock-knocks, jokes or riddles.

3. Assemble an audience for the joke tellers.

4. On other days, let the partners try their knock-knocks and riddles with audience participation.

Something to think about
Every form of text has a certain rhythm to the way it should be read. The pauses, stops and anticipation in the voice of the reader are what makes the knock-knock, joke or riddle work. Help the children rehearse their timing and inflection.

STORY STRETCHER

For Mathematics: Funny Survey Results

What the children will learn
To represent combined data graphically

Materials you will need
Chart tablet, marker, scissors, construction paper, tape, Post-it notes

What to do
1. Select three children to poll the class on whether they like knock-knocks, jokes or riddles best.

2. When the pollsters have finished surveying all the students, have them meet again and decide how to present their findings to the rest of the class. They can tally the results and simply post the winner, or rank them in order of preference, or state the results in terms of the boys and the girls.

3. Have the surveyors decide whether to make a horizontal or bar graph showing the results. They can cut strips of construction paper for each child's vote and tape the pieces of paper to the chart tablet.

Something to think about
Older students might try a more complicated process of surveying the class before they have read books of knock-knocks, jokes and riddles, and after reading, collecting and writing them. They can compare whether or not the class preferences changed after they learned more knock-knocks, jokes and riddles. They can also break down the results by boys' and girls' preferences.

STORY STRETCHER

For Writing Center: Knock-Knock Book, Joke Book, Riddle Book

What the children will learn
To select knock-knocks, jokes and riddles they enjoy

Materials you will need
Typing paper, ruler, cardboard, contact paper, masking tape, optional—art supplies for illustrations

What to do
1. Have each child construct three blank books—one for knock-knocks, one for jokes, one for riddles. Vary the length depending on the age of your students. (See the directions in the Appendix for binding books.)

2. As the children hear and read knock-knocks, jokes and riddles they want to remember, have them print them in the appropriate books.

3. When the children have finished their books, have them sign up for a day to share their very favorite knock-knock, joke or riddle. However, make one rule. If your favorite has already been shared, tell the class what your favorite is, and then read your next favorite. This process keeps the children returning to their texts over and over.

4. Keep a tally of what the children's favorites are, and if there are three in each category which are clear winners, print these on posters and display them in the room.

Something to think about
Younger children might make one book with three sections, knock-knocks, jokes and riddles, rather than three separate books. Extend the activity by having children cut out favorite cartoons and make a collection of these.

FUN WITH WORDS

A CACHE OF JEWELS AND OTHER COLLECTIVE NOUNS

By Ruth Heller

In beautiful illustrations and rhythmic language, Ruth Heller's A CACHE OF JEWELS AND OTHER COLLECTIVE NOUNS extends vocabulary, plays with language and fascinates. Some pictures are bold and bright, others serene and muted, but all are large full-page compositions which are perfect for group reading. Throughout the book the descriptive language, "a cache of jewels," "a batch of bread," "a school of fish" and the inventive illustrations make the reader want to see what surprise lies on the next page.

Read-Aloud Suggestions

On a colorful piece of fabric, place a jewelry box filled with costume jewelry. Open it and spill some of the strings of beads and other jewelry out onto the fabric. Ask the children what they would call this, a "jewelry box" or a "box of jewels?" Show the cover of A CACHE OF JEWELS AND OTHER COLLECTIVE NOUNS by Ruth Heller. Tell the children you will read the book twice. Read it through once and keep the rhythm of the language flowing, then read it a second time and linger over the pictures for the children to enjoy the beauty of the illustrations and to recall the collective nouns, such as "gam of whales" or "muster of peacocks."

STORY STRETCHER

For Art: Collective Noun Pictures

What the children will learn
To illustrate groups of things, animals or people

Materials you will need
Choice of art supplies—paints, brushes, easels, paper, crayon, markers, pastels, colored pencils—scissors, index cards, tape

What to do
1.   Look again at Ruth Heller's illustrations and have the children think of other collective nouns, such as "herd of cattle," "team of players," "gang of kids," "flock of geese."

2.   Ask each artist to illustrate a favorite collective noun.

3.   When the illustrations are finished, have the children print titles for their pictures and tape them to the bottom of the paper.

Something to think about
Try a collage approach. Have the children make multiples of their subjects, whether people, animals or things, by drawing one, then cutting it out and drawing around it to make others. Then cut smaller and larger ones. Layer these or place in a form characteristic of the subject. For example, to illustrate a "flock of geese," the child could make one flying goose, cut it out and use it as a pattern to draw others, and then glue the geese on the page as if they were flying in formation.

STORY STRETCHER

For Cooking: Collective Fruit Snacks

What the children will learn
To use collective nouns

Materials you will need
Bunches of bananas, clusters of grapes, fruit bowl, index cards, yellow marker, purple marker, knife, scissors, orange juice, napkins

What to do
1.   Place the fruit bowl spilling over with fruit on the table. With a yellow marker, print "bunch of bananas" on an index card. With a purple marker, print "cluster of grapes."

2.   Let the children snip a few grapes off the cluster and cut the bananas in half with a knife.

3.   Serve with orange juice.

Something to think about
For the next day, have collective noun vegetable snacks, bunches of carrots, stalks of celery, heads of lettuce.

For Creative Dramatics: Miming Collective Nouns

What the children will learn
To interpret meaning through movement

Materials you will need
Chalkboard, chalk

What to do

1. Divide the class into groups of at least five children.

2. Have each group look through A CACHE OF JEWELS and decide which collective noun they would like to pantomime.

3. Let the groups practice their miming where they cannot see each other.

4. Ask each group to pantomime their collective noun and have the audience guess what it might be.

5. When the audience has guessed correctly, write the collective noun on the board.

Something to think about
Continue the exercise for several days and pantomime different collective nouns from the book or others the children recall hearing or reading.

For Mathematics: Scavenger Hunt For Sets

What the children will learn
To use the term "sets" to refer to a collection

Materials you will need
What to do

1. Have the children think of how the word "sets" is used in everyday language, such as "a set of dishes," "a set of silverware," "a train set," "a set of encyclopedias," "a pen and pencil set."

2. Ask them to tell in their own words what the word "set" means—a collection of things which belong together.

3. Have partners go on a scavenger hunt for sets in the classroom, the office, the library and the cafeteria. Of course, alert everyone throughout the building about the scavenger hunt.

4. Collect the sets on a large display table.

5. Have the partners tell about where they found their items, what makes them a set and what else they could place with the collection, if anything, which would still make it a set. For example, a "set of dishes" could be a service for four. Add more dishes and it is a service for more. A "set of encyclopedias" cannot have more volumes if it is a complete set. A "train set" might have more freight cars added and still be a set.

6. Explain that in doing mathematics problems we often read the term "set," which is used to describe a number of things belonging together or usually used together.

Something to think about
Have the students think of other ways the term "set" is used: "movie set," a "television set," a "set" for musicians is how long they play without taking a break."

For Writing Center: Writing Descriptions Of Collections

What the children will learn
To use descriptive language in their writing

Materials you will need
Writing folders, writing samples, chalkboard, different colors of chalk

What to do

1. Have the children read back through the writing samples in their folders and find places where they could use a collective noun to add description to their writing.

2. Ask the children to write on the chalkboard the collective nouns they found to add to their writing. Try to fill the board. Keep adding to it throughout the week.

3. Let the students select a collective noun which fascinates them, such as a "brood of chicks," "kindle of kittens" or "litter of pups," and develop a story around it.

Something to think about
Make a poster of collective nouns the children clip from the newspaper or, as they notice them in their reading of library books, have them print the phrases on an index card and add to the poster.

ALISON'S ZINNIA
By Anita Lobel

The author combines the word play of ABC's, girls' names, verbs and flower names to create an absolutely delightful and beautiful book to look at and read. The alphabet book begins "Alison acquired an Amaryllis for Beryl. Beryl bought a Begonia for Crystal. Crystal cut a Chrysanthemum for Dawn." Each page is a large illustration of the flower at the top of the page, and in a smaller strip below, the pictures show children and what they did with the flowers. What a wonderful message, giving flowers to a friend! Rich in detail, each illustration is a painting, a true work of art.

Read-Aloud Suggestions

Place a beautiful flower arrangement near the chair where you sit to read aloud to the class. When the children are all seated around you, have them describe the flower arrangement and name some of the flowers. Continue the discussion by asking children what their favorite flowers are. Show the cover of ALISON'S ZINNIA and tell the children that this book is so beautiful they will want to spend a lot of extra time just looking at the illustrations which are paintings of flowers. The book will be on display in the classroom library for them to see later. Read the book through twice. The first time simply let the children enjoy the beauty of the pictures and notice the way the artist has illustrated the text in the small strip below each flower picture. Before the second reading, ask the children to describe the pattern of the language they are hearing. It matches the ABC's, and the verbs begin with the same letter as the children's names and the name of the flower. Have the children practice some of the tongue twisters with you.

STORY STRETCHER
For Art: Inspired By Real Flowers

What the children will learn
To enjoy what they see and use colors and forms for symbols of reality

Materials you will need
Flowers, lazy Susan, choice of colors of tempera paints, brushes, paper, easels

What to do
1. Bring in some beautiful flowers, either cut flowers or a blooming potted plant.

2. Place the flowers or plant on a lazy Susan and let the children turn it around to observe it from several different angles.

3. Have the children look at it closely and describe what they see in terms of colors, shading, shapes, directions of growth.

4. Place the flowers where they can be seen easily from the easel.

5. Do not require that the children paint the flowers, but encourage those who are interested to use the colors, forms and lines they noticed and show those in their paintings.

Something to think about
Do not expect realistic representations, rather have children enjoy the colors, the forms and the inspiration of the beautiful flowers. To extend the activity, bring in some fine art prints of flowers.

ANOTHER STORY STRETCHER
For Art: Arranging Bouquets

What the children will learn
To arrange flowers

Materials you will need
Fresh flowers, if possible, or dried or silk flowers; variety of vases and containers; scissors; water; instant print camera

What to do
1. Invite a parent, grandparent or community volunteer to come to class and help the children make flower arrangements. If possible, invite a male florist, gardener or nursery owner so that the children do not think of arranging flowers as something that only girls and women do.

2. Involve the children in each step of the arranging, selecting containers, snipping off the ends of the stems, arranging the flowers

and deciding on where to place them in the room.

3. Make several arrangements so that all the children can be involved. Have the florists or flower arrangers "think aloud" to let the children know why they are doing each step and some of the artistic decisions they make.

4. Take pictures of the flower arrangements with the children who helped to make them.

Something to think about
Call a wholesale florist market in your area and ask when they sell their flowers at a discount. They often sell the less than perfect ones at a reduced cost.

STORY STRETCHER

For Classroom Library: Mail Order Seed Catalogs

What the children will learn
To match pictures and descriptions

Materials you will need
Mail order seed catalogs for flowers

What to do
1. Collect catalogs from parents of the children in the classroom and from friends and acquaintances.

2. Give each child who comes to the classroom library during choice time a copy of a catalog to look through.

3. Read ALISON'S ZINNIA again and have the children try to find pictures of the real flowers and compare them to the paintings which illustrate the book.

4. Have each child select one catalog flower and read the description. See if the written description would fit the illustration of the flower in ALISON'S ZINNIA.

Something to think about
Extend the story s-t-r-e-t-c-h-e-r by having the children each select one picture of a flower from AL-ISON'S ZINNIA and write catalog copy or an advertisement which describes this flower.

STORY STRETCHER

For Science And Nature: Growing Alison's Zinnias

What the children will learn
To grow flowers from seeds

Materials you will need
Seed catalogs, packets of seeds, posterboard, marker, plastic dishpans, spades, potting soil, flower pots, watering can, popsicle sticks, markers

What to do
1. Order zinnia seeds from a seed catalog. Involve the children in completing the order form, addressing the envelope and mailing the order.

2. When the packages of seeds arrive, read the directions and let a few children make a large chart of the directions for the entire class to follow.

3. Pour the potting soil into large plastic dishpans. Assemble the spades, pots and seeds on a table.

4. Let each child fill a pot with potting soil. Demonstrate how to pack the soil loosely in the container and moisten it.

5. Sprinkle a few zinnia seeds onto the top of the soil and spread a thin layer of soil over the top.

6. Have the children write their names on popsicle sticks and stick them into their flower pots so they can identify which plants are theirs.

7. Plant a large pot of zinnias for the classroom.

Something to think about
Recycle milk cartons into pots instead of using plastic pots.

STORY STRETCHER

For Writing Center: Class Alphabet Flower Book

What the children will learn
To write using the author's pattern

Materials you will need
Chalkboard, chalk

What to do
1. Print the alphabet in big bold letters along the left margin of the chalkboard.

2. Have the children list their names in alphabetical order on the chalkboard.

3. Print a second list of the letters of the alphabet.

4. Make a list of all the flowers the children can think of.

5. Match the children's names and the flower names.

6. If needed, look at the flower and seed catalogs and add names of flowers to the list until there is a flower listed beside each child's name.

7. Begin writing the story with a child's name, such as "Ann acquired an Amaryllis for Brian. Brian bought a Begonia for Chris," etc.

8. When there is no child's name which fits the next letter of the alphabet, skip it and go on to the next child's name.

9. Let each child illustrate a page of the book by writing the text for his or her letter and flower.

10. Bind the pages into a "Class Alphabet and Flower Book."

Something to think about
Have the children write a book using all the teacher's names in the school. Let younger children write a book using just the names of their family members.

FUN WITH WORDS

THE KING WHO RAINED

By Fred Gwynne

A little girl imagines what her parents mean when they say a variety of phrases, such as "bear feet" for bare feet. When her father says there are forks in the road, the child imagines huge silverware forks connecting the highways. A collection of nineteen phrases and illustrations, the book is an excellent way to introduce homonyms and idioms. The hilarious full-page illustrations make it a favorite for group or partner reading.

Read-Aloud Suggestions

Discuss how Amelia Bedelia always gets things mixed up. Show the children the cover of THE KING WHO RAINED and tell them the little girl in the story also gets things mixed up, but she has a terrific imagination. She visualizes what her parents tell her in funny ways. Read the book and stop on each page for every child to see the illustrations clearly. Plan on lots of giggles. Wait for the children to say it is time to turn the page. At the end, the children will immediately say, "Read it again!" Go through the book a second time and let the children interpret what the parents really meant.

STORY STRETCHER

For Art: Draw What You Say

What the children will learn
To draw interpretations of sayings and homonyms

Materials you will need
Chalkboard; chalk; drawing paper; choice of crayons, markers or colored pencils; stapler; masking tape

What to do
1. Brainstorm a list of sayings which could be interpreted literally. For example, "It's raining cats and dogs," and the children can draw cats and dogs falling from a cloud in the sky. For "He is growing like a weed" the child could draw himself with leaves coming from his hands and around his head." There are many other possibilities, such as "monkey on his back," "chained to her desk," "going around the world to get home," "danced my feet off," "coughed his head off," "elephant ears," "eyes like a hawk," "elbow grease."

2. Brainstorm a list of homonyms, words which are spelled differently but when they are spoken sound the same when spoken— such as "see and sea," "right and write," "night and knight." Some children can choose these words to illustrate in funny pictures.

3. After the children have completed their pictures, have them print their homonyms or phrases on a cover sheet and staple it over the top of their pictures.

4. Place the pictures in the classroom library or tape them along a chalk railing for the children to read and visualize how the artist might have interpreted the phrase, then they can look underneath at the picture.

Something to think about
Younger children can select one of the homonyms or phrases in the book and draw a picture placing themselves or their families in a situation similar to that found in the book. As an extension idea, describe food and draw some illustrations or cut pictures from magazines which would illustrate these sayings. For example, say, "Your milk is as cold as ice." Sketch or cut magazine pictures of a glass of milk standing frozen on an ice cube tray or a glass of milk skating of a frozen pond. Or say, "This apple is as red as a rose," and have the stem of the apple growing a rose. Say, "This orange is so sweet it tastes like honey," and draw a bee buzzing around the orange.

For Classroom Library: What It Really Means

What the children will learn
To interpret homonyms, idioms and funny phrases

Materials you will need
Chalkboard, chalk, cassette tape, recorder, glass, fork

What to do

1. Read THE KING WHO RAINED to the children who join you in the library area. Have the children tell what the parents really meant instead of what the little girl visualized.

2. Tell the students you would like to make a tape of THE KING WHO RAINED to leave at the listening station, but you are concerned that some children might not understand the real meanings. Ask the children what could be done to be sure that everyone understands the real meaning.

3. Decide to make a tape recording of the book. You read what Fred Gwynne, the author, wrote, and let the children record what the parents meant.

4. Tell the children that the introduction to this tape will be very important and have them decide what needs to be said. On the chalkboard, write what they dictate.

5. Let one student read the introduction on the tape.

6. After each phrase you read, have the children say together, "That's so funny." Then let one child tell what the parents really mean.

7. After the child has interpreted the phrase correctly, tap a glass with a fork as the page-turning signal.

Something to think about
Tape-record the children's book from the writing center story s-t-r-e-t-c-h-e-r.

For Creative Dramatics: Improvised Sayings

What the children will learn
To dramatize and interpret a phrase

Materials you will need
Index cards, pencils, chalkboard, chalk

What to do

1. Let children work with a partner.

2. On index cards, print the homonyms, idioms and funny phrases from the art story s-t-r-e-t-c-h-e-r and from the book.

3. Give each set of partners a card and secretly ask them how they will interpret the phrase for other children to see. Let them plan any props or costumes they need and bring them to school the next day.

4. Have the partners improvise a scene which illustrates their phrase, and let the audience try to guess what it is.

5. Print the phrases on the board after the children have guessed them.

Something to think about
Randomly assign partners or pair children who are already reading or writing partners. Letting children choose their partners means many unpopular children are always left out. Start the practice of assigning partners at the beginning of the year and the children will expect it without complaining.

For Writing Center: Partner Writing

What the children will learn
To write interpretations of homonyms, idioms and funny phrases

Materials you will need
Drawings from the art story s-t-r-e-t-c-h-e-r, writing paper, pencils

What to do

1. Pair children who have painted or drawn illustrations of homonyms and funny phrases at the art center.

2. Let each person take his or her partner's drawing and write about a situation in which this saying might be heard, and what is really meant.

3. Have the partner whose picture was written about add information and help edit the description.

4. Place the partners drawings and descriptions in the classroom library for the rest of the class to read.

Something to think about
Writing partners often help children write better as they share ideas.

For Writing Center: Binding Our Own Class Book

What the children will learn
To write and publish a book of funny phrases

Materials you will need
Typing paper, pencils, ruler, colored pencils, cardboard, contact paper, stapler, masking tape

What to do

1. Give each child two sheets of typing paper. Have them draw a margin of about one-half inch along the right-hand edge of one page and along the left-hand edge of the other page. Show them that when these two sheets are stapled together they will look like facing pages in a book.

2. On the left facing pages, have the children print their funny phases. On the right sheet, have the children draw the illustrations.

3. Assemble all the children's writing into a book. Refer the children to books to decide what extra pages need to go in front and back, such as end paper, publisher's information page, title page in the front and an extra blank page or end paper page in the back. Place the extra pages in their book and let them decide on a title for the book, a name for their publishing company and dedicate the book to Fred Gwynne, the author of THE KING WHO RAINED who inspired their writing.

4. Bind the book by following the directions provided in the Appendix.

5. Place the book in the classroom library and share it with other classes at the grade level you teach.

Something to think about

If binding all the children's writing into one book makes it too thick, make several smaller ones. For schools with computers, have the children use word-processing and computer graphics to print their funny phrases. Some can type their own, while younger children will enjoy seeing their words become print as someone else types them.

References

Heller, Ruth. (1987). **A CACHE OF JEWELS**. New York: Grosset & Dunlap.

Kessler, Leonard. (1991). **OLD TURTLE'S 90 KNOCK-KNOCK JOKES, AND RIDDLES**. New York: Greenwillow.

Lobel, Anita. (1990). **ALISON'S ZINNIA**. New York: Greenwillow.

Parish, Peggy. (1977). Illustrated by Lynn Sweat. **TEACH US, AMELIA BEDELIA**. New York: Greenwillow.

Gwynne, Fred. (1970). **THE KING WHO RAINED**. New York: Simon and Schuster.

Additional References for Fun With Words

Lear, Edward. Completed by Ogden Nash. (1968). Illustrated by Nancy Ekholm Burkert. **THE SCROOBIOUS PIP**. New York: HarperCollins Children's Books. *A joyous and playful poem by the incomparable Edward Lear. All the animals in the world gather around the mysterious Scroobious Pip, for they can't figure out whether he's a "fish or insect, or bird or beast." And by the end they still don't know, but they have to accept him on his own terms.*

Johnston, Tony. (1990). Illustrated by Lillian Hoban. **I'M GONNA TELL MAMA I WANT AN IGUANA**. New York: G. P. Putnam's Sons, Inc. *Twenty-three short poems which play with word sounds and meanings.*

Parish, Peggy. (1976). Illustrated by Lynn Sweat. **GOOD WORK, AMELIA BEDELIA**. New York: Greenwillow Books. Literal-minded *Amelia Bedelia does household chores and prepares dinner; humor arises from her literal interpretations of familiar idioms. Children recognize and love this kind of joke.*

Reid, Alastair. (1991). Illustrated by Ben Shahn. **OUNCE, DICE, TRICE**. New York: Harry N. Abrams. *New words, old words, made-up words, words in totally new contexts: a treasure-trove of words for counting, naming, enjoying, defining and simply rolling off the end of your tongue.*

Stevenson, James. (1977). **"COULD BE WORSE!"** New York: Greenwillow Books. *Things are always the same at Grandpa's, even the things he says, but one day he surprises the children with an amazing story.*

POEMS, CHANTS, RHYTHMS AND RHYMES

Nathaniel Talking

A House Is a House for Me

Hailstones and Halibut Bones

The New Kid on the Block

Blackberry Ink

NATHANIEL TALKING

By Eloise Greenfield

Illustrated by Jan Spivey

Gilchrist

Nathaniel B. Free is a nine-year-old who tells us what he thinks in raps, poems, chants and questions. Eloise Greenfield succeeds again in capturing the spirit of the black child. In letting the reader know Nathaniel, she teaches us the depth of a nine-year-old's feelings and thoughts. Nathaniel's questions, ambivalence about growing up, his city neighborhood, his family, his pain and his joys are explored brilliantly. Jan Spivey Gilchrist's black and white pencil illustrations include stark silhouettes, muted shadings to accompany gentle poems, and throughout the book beautifully sketched faces.

Read-Aloud Suggestions

Poetry is meant to be read aloud. Before reading any of the poems aloud to the class, rehearse them. Try the rhythmic pattern Eloise Greenfield suggests for "My Daddy." Select several poems to read at one sitting. Begin with "Nathaniel's Rap" and read it at least twice. Teach the children the repeated verses and let them join you. Continue by reading "Nine" and "Knowledge." Turn to the illustrations of "Missing Mama" and "Mama," and set the mood for the poems by asking the children what the pictures tell us Nathaniel is feeling. At another read-aloud session, share the poems about Nathaniel's family and neighbors. End the session by reading "Nathaniel's Rap" again and "Nathaniel's Rap (Reprise)."

STORY STRETCHER

For Art: Silhouettes

What the children will learn
To illustrate using a contrasting technique

Materials you will need
White construction paper or manilla paper, pencils, black construction paper, scissors, glue

What to do
1. Look at the silhouettes Jan Spivey Gilchrist used to illustrate several of the poems, "A Mighty Fine Fella," "Who the Best," "Aunt Lavinia" and "Education."

2. Have the children draw a picture and completely shade in the figures of the people. Or as an alternative, shade a building in the background or an object they want to highlight.

3. Make another type of silhouette by having the children draw figures on black construction pa-per, cut them out and glue them onto their pictures.

Something to think about
Let the children make silhouettes of themselves.

STORY STRETCHER

For Classroom Library: Poems By Request

What the children will learn
To read poetry aloud

Materials you will need
Overhead projector, transparencies, screen

What to do
1. Let the children who choose to come to the library area during center time select poems from NATHANIEL TALKING for you to read aloud.

2. Write a few of the children's favorites on transparencies, project them on a screen and ask the students to join you in reading the poems.

3. Have each child select one poem to read aloud. Practice with each student individually, then have them read their selection to the audience gathered in the library area.

Something to think about
Third graders can write the poems on the transparencies. For younger students, record yourself reading the entire book and place the tape and the book at the listening station.

STORY STRETCHER

For Music And Movement: Twelve-Bar Rhythm

What the children will learn
To read the poem in rhythm

Materials you will need
Chart tablet or posterboard, marker

What to do

1. Read the author's note on how to feel the beat in "My Daddy."

2. Make a chart like the one in the author's note. Mark the bars to fit the four beat in the twelve bars of the poem. The first verse is already charted, so continue the pattern.

3. Read the poem aloud to the children with the rhythm that sounds like a blues song, as indicated by Eloise Greenfield's chart.

4. Show the children how to tap their feet or pat their thighs to the beat as you read the poem a second time.

5. Have the students join you in reading "My Daddy" with the rhythm that the poet suggests.

Something to think about
Ask a music specialist to play some blues music and help the children tap or clap the beat.

STORY STRETCHER

For Writing Center: I Remember

What the children will learn
To compose a picture of themselves when they were younger

Materials you will need
Writing paper, pencils, optional—choice of art supplies

What to do

1. Have the children close their eyes while you read the poem "I Remember." When they open their eyes, ask them what they visualized. Did they see the pigeons, the fuzzy yellow hat, the baby's potty?

2. Ask the children to sit quietly for a few minutes and think about themselves when they were younger, walking along beside their mother or father in the park or a special place. Tell the children that when they begin remembering what they did, how it felt, seeing themselves as young, then they should write down their recollections as quickly as possible.

3. After the children have written, have them read their recollections aloud to themselves. From hearing the words and visualizing, ask the children to write down their memories in the form they choose—a poem, a song, a letter to a diary, a list.

4. Let children who wish to share what they have written read their compositions aloud.

Something to think about
First and second graders will need more time to talk about a special memory, then write. Some may prefer to draw the day or the scene and then put their memories into words.

ANOTHER STORY STRETCHER

For Writing Center: I See My Future

What the children will learn
To think of themselves as adults

Materials you will need
Writing paper, pencils, optional—art materials for illustrations

What to do

1. Read "I See My Future."

2. Ask the children how they visualize themselves when they are growing up. Let the children talk for a while, not about the things they want to own when they are grown-up, but the kind of people they want to be.

3. Read "I See My Future" again and ask the children to write about what they want to be like as adults. They can write a poem, compose a song, write a letter, draw a picture and write captions, or write descriptive phrases.

4. Let the children who wish to, read or show others their writing.

Something to think about
Encourage the children to illustrate their writing. Ask the students to place a copy of this writing in their writing folders. At the next parent conference, share the children's compositions with their parents.

A HOUSE IS A HOUSE FOR ME

By Mary Ann Hoberman

Illustrated by Betty Fraser

A favorite among children and their teachers, this long rhyme gallops across scenes of insects, animals, people and things with the theme of houses. The recurring phrase, "a house is a house for me," ends each verse. The illustrations surround the words and delight the reader. Also available in big book format, the patterned language and associations make the book excellent for beginning readers, and its cleverness calls older readers back to the verse just to enjoy the sights and sounds evoked.

Read-Aloud Suggestions

Some of the children will already know this favorite book, A HOUSE IS A HOUSE FOR ME. If so, invite them to read along with you when you reach the recurring phrase which is the same as the title of the book. Read to the end almost breathlessly. Immediately, the children will request that you read it again. Pause and ask which houses surprised them. Read the book again and have all the children join you in the repeated phrases, pausing for them to complete the rhyming patterns.

STORY STRETCHER

For Art: Decorating Letters

What the children will learn
To use illustrations for decorative purposes

Materials you will need
Templates of letters, pencils, scissors, construction paper, glue, colored pencils, crayons or markers

What to do
1. Look at the title page of the book. Have the children notice that each letter is an illustration of a house. For example, the "A" is a tepee.

2. Have each child draw a pattern of all the letters in his or her first name by tracing around the letter templates.

3. Suggest they decorate the letters of their names as drawings of houses or of things in their house.

4. After the letters are decorated, have the children cut them out and glue them onto a sheet of brightly colored construction paper.

Something to think about
Have the children brainstorm some other ways they could decorate the letters of their names, such as patterns of their favorite colors, drawing themselves in the shapes the letters make them think of, etc.

ANOTHER STORY STRETCHER

For Art: Surprise Houses

What the children will learn
To illustrate parts of the verse

Materials you will need
Drawing paper, colored pencils, crayons, markers, pastels, stapler

What to do
1. Read A HOUSE IS A HOUSE FOR ME again. Pause for the children to look more closely at Betty Fraser's illustrations. Let them discuss the ones they think are particularly effective.

2. Ask the students to choose a phrase they liked from the book and draw illustrations, or think of other houses they want to illustrate.

3. Encourage the children to select a variety of art supplies.

4. Have the children illustrate the houses on one sheet of drawing paper and write the appropriate caption, such as, "A heart-shaped box is a house for _____."

5. On a second sheet of drawing paper, have the children illustrate who or what lives in that house and write the words to complete the phrase, like "valentine candy."

6. Staple the first sheet on top of the second one and have the children read each other's houses.

Something to think about
Let children cut their illustrations in the shape of the houses: a valentine shape, a beehive shape, a ball glove shape.

For Classroom Library: Shared Book Experiences

What the children will learn
To read with others

Materials you will need
Big book of A HOUSE IS A HOUSE FOR ME, pointer

What to do
1.   Using the big book format of A HOUSE IS A HOUSE FOR ME, read the book through from beginning to end without pausing or pointing out words.

2.   Let the children discuss the book and then point out repeated phrases, such as "a house is a house for me."

3.   Read the book aloud a second time and during this reading run the pointer under the words, pausing where there are natural breaks in the rhyme. Encourage the children to read the recurring phrases along with you at and pause for the children to finish the phrases. For example, they can complete the phrase, "A coop is a house for a_____." Try to keep the flow of the language as natural as possible, rather than word-by-word emphasis.

4.   If the children's interest continues, read the book a third time, with everyone reading along with you.

5.   Leave the big book version in the library area and let the children read it on their own or with their reading partners.

Something to think about
Using the author's language pattern, adapt the children's compositions from the writing center to make a big book of their lines. Each student whose verse appears on a page can help with the illustrations. Read the children's big book version in the same way that you read the commercial big book of A HOUSE IS A HOUSE FOR ME.

For Science And Nature: Houses And Habitats

What the children will learn
To match animals and houses

Materials you will need
Chalkboard, chalk, large index cards, markers or crayons

What to do
1.   Read the last words of A HOUSE IS A HOUSE FOR ME, in which the author tells the reader that the earth is a house for all creatures.

2.   Have the children go back through all of Betty Fraser's illustrations and list all the animals pictured. Write the list on the chalkboard.

3.   Go down the list and have the children tell where the animals live. Write their houses or habitats beside each animal on the list.

4.   Let pairs of children volunteer to illustrate the animals and their houses or habitats. One child will draw the animal on an index card and the other will draw the house or habitat on another card. Have them print the phrases which are appropriate, such as "An African plain is the home of_____." The other child will print on his or her card, "lions that roam."

5.   Let the children play a game with the cards by shuffling and matching animals to houses and habitats.

Something to think about
Involve the children as often as possible in making their own learning materials. Not only does it save the teacher time, but the children learn more.

For Writing Center: Continuing The Verse

What the children will learn
To follow the poet's pattern of language for their verses

Materials you will need
Chalkboard, chalk, writing paper, pencils

What to do
1.   Show the children the illustrations of the little boy in the hammock thinking of all the houses. Let the children tell what the houses are. For example, "A baseball glove is a house for a ball," "an egg is a house for a chick," "a pincushion is a house for pins," "a pouch is a house for a joey kangaroo."

2.   Ask the students to brainstorm a few other houses. Write their list on the chalkboard.

3.   Fold writing paper twice, making four sections. Ask the children to write about at least three other houses, and then in the fourth section write, "but a house is a house for me."

4.   The children who are interested can add illustrations to their writing.

Something to think about
Younger students might think of only one other house and draw larger illustrations. Older students might try rhyming and rewriting their phrases to compose a poem similar to the author's.

17

POEMS, CHANTS, RHYTHMS, AND RHYMES

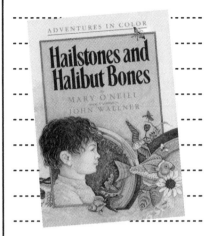

HAILSTONES AND HALIBUT BONES

By Mary O'Neill

Illustrated by John Wallner

Reissued with beautiful new collages of illustrations, this teacher's favorite is now a child's favorite. A celebration of the world of color, each poem is as brilliantly illustrated as it is brilliantly written. Lovingly, longingly, jubilantly, the colors dance on the page in words and shapes, surprised expressions and fanciful associations. Each color's personality becomes a verse. The re-publication of this collection of poems is worth a classroom celebration.

Read-Aloud Suggestions

Wear your favorite color to school on the day you plan to read from HAILSTONES AND HALIBUT BONES. Tell the children why you like that color, what it reminds you of, and how you feel when you are wearing it. Let the children tell their favorite colors. Read HAILSTONES AND HALIBUT BONES, and after you have read about each color, let some of the children who identified a color as their favorite share some of their feelings. As you read on, tell the children that on some days other colors are your favorite. For instance, in the spring, your favorite color is yellow because that is the color of daffodils. In the fall, it is scarlet because that is the color of the sugar maple in your yard. Read as many of the poems as time permits and plan other times during the day and week to read them again.

STORY STRETCHER
For Art: Favorite Colors And Collages

What the children will learn
To shade and tint colors and to design a collage

Materials you will need
Red, yellow, blue, purple, orange, green, black, white and gray tempera paints, manilla paper, tape, various of colors of construction paper, swatches of fabric, magazines, catalogs, calendars, scissors, glue

What to do
1. Have the children paint a piece of paper in their favorite color. If mixing is needed to achieve the color, help the students mix, shade or tint their paints.

2. Tape the solid painted pieces of paper around the room in color families. Place all the yellows together on the bulletin board in the library area, all the greens in the science and nature center, all the blues and purples along the chalkboard rail, etc.

3. Let each child make a collage of their favorite color by finding as many things as possible of that same color to glue onto a heavy sheet of construction paper . They can glue on swatches of fabric, make marks with a crayon, cut the wrapper off that crayon and glue it onto the collage, attach a piece of ribbon, write their names with a marker, cut pictures from magazines, catalogs or calendars, etc.

Something to think about
Display the color collages in the hallway of the school for other students to enjoy. Title the collection, "A Gallery of Color Inspired by Poetry."

ANOTHER STORY STRETCHER
For Art: Color Displays

What the children will learn
To cooperate and to make pleasing designs

Materials you will need
Cotton broadcloth, different sizes of boxes, yarn, scissors, glue, paper

What to do
1. Solicit help from parents and friends in collecting materials for the color displays. Ask parents who sew to donate swatches of fabric.

2. Look at John Wallner's illustrations of the color poems in HAILSTONES AND HALIBUT BONES. Call attention to the fact that each is a collage, or a collection of things, of the same color mentioned in the poem.

3. Invite someone who does window dressing in a department store or a florist who uses color for design purposes to come to class and arrange a variety of things in interesting ways, all within one color family.

4. Inspired by the arrangements they see the professional make, and by the illustrations in HAILSTONES AND HALIBUT BONES, ask the children to make some color displays of their own. Give them a few days to collect materials, and let two or three children who like the same colors work together.

Something to think about
Make arrangements with the office and library to display some of the children's color displays.

STORY STRETCHER

For Classroom Library: Colorful Voices

What the children will learn
To read with inflection and attend to punctuation

Materials you will need
Cassette tape and recorder, tiny bell

What to do
1. Schedule several reading sessions in the classroom library for the children to read and select their favorite color poems.

2. Model effective inflection, and help the children see how the punctuation helps them know how the poet meant the poem to be read.

3. Let each child practice reading her or his favorite color poem.

4. Tape-record the children reading the poems. Tape them in the order that they appear in the book. Tinkle a tiny bell as the page-turning signal. At the beginning of each new poem, have the reader say into the tape recorder, "Poem read by _____."

Something to think about
Let beginning readers who all like the same color read the first two lines of the poem with you and, you read the remainder for the recording.

STORY STRETCHER

For Music And Movement: Dancing With Colors

What the children will learn
To move in response to the music

Materials you will need
Colored scarves and crepe paper streamers, recordings of waltz or blues music, cassette or record player

What to do
1. Remind the children of half-time performances at football games. Have them recall that the performers often carry colorful flags, scarves and streamers, and that they march, dance and move in time to the music.

2. Let the children choose either a colored scarf or a crepe paper streamer.

3. Have the students seated on the floor, and begin with a slow waltz or a blues recording. Begin to gently clap your hands or snap your fingers to the beat.

4. With a few children, stand and begin to sway in response to the music. Then move your scarf or crepe paper streamer back and forth in time to the music while the others continue gently clapping their hands or snapping fingers.

5. Have a few more children join you at a time until everyone is moving and swaying with their colorful scarves and streamers.

Something to think about
If you have children who take dance lessons, ask them to dress in their leotards and help lead the movement sessions.

STORY STRETCHER

For Writing Center: Colors In Thought And Verse

What the children will learn
To write in descriptive ways which help their readers visualize the poem

Materials you will need
Writing paper, pencil, choice of art supplies for illustrations

What to do
1. Have the children who are in the writing center select their favorite color poem from HAILSTONES AND HALIBUT BONES.

2. Read a few selections, and after each is read, let the children pick out some phrases which really made the poem come alive for them.

3. Ask each writer his or her favorite color—and have them talk about that color, what it reminds them of, how they feel about it, some happy or sad associations with the color.

4. Invite the children to write about their favorite colors. Tell them that their writing can be ia poem, or a list of likable things about that color, or a paragraph relating an incident of which this color reminds them, or just a collection of very descriptive phrases.

Something to think about
Have the children who want to share their writing do so, but do not insist, as some may prefer to keep their thoughts private. Other children may like you to read their writing aloud, rather than reading it themselves.

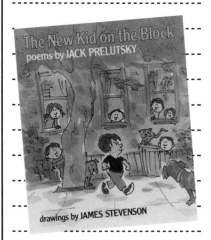

THE NEW KID ON THE BLOCK

by Jack Prelutsky

Illustrated by James Stevenson

Filled with surprises, jokes, riddles and giggles, Prelutsky's one hundred and seven poems range from a rhymed couplet to long narratives and lure primary age children into poetry. The funny animal poems are only surpassed by the funny people poems. The simple, cartoon-like line drawings support the text without overshadowing it. The collection is a good one for read-aloud sessions and for children to read on their own.

Read-Aloud Suggestions

Read the title poem, "The New Kid on the Block." Have the children tell you which line surprised them. Select six or seven other people poems to read at the first of many poetry sessions: "Clara Cleech," "Mabel, Remarkable Mabel," "Euphonica Jarre," "Sneaky Sue," "Dainty Dottie Dee" and "Stringbean Small." At another session, read several animal poems, such as "An Alley Cat with One Life Left," "My Dog, He Is an Ugly Dog," "I Toss Them to My Elephant" and "A Wolf Is at the Laundromat." Plan still another poetry reading session about relationships between children and their parents and brothers and sisters. Read "I Wonder Why Dad Is So Thoroughly Mad," "My Baby Brother," "My Brother's Head Should Be Replaced," "My Sister Is a Sissy" and "My Mother Says I'm Sickening." No celebration of Jack Prelutsky's poetry would be complete without reading the uproariously funny verses about body parts. Read "Be Glad Your Nose Is on Your Face," "Louder than a Clap of Thunder," (a poem about snoring), "I've Got an Itch," "You Need to Have an Iron Rear" and "Baloney Belly Billy." End with "I'm the Single Most Wonderful Person I Know."

STORY STRETCHER
For Art: Illustrate A Giggle

What the children will learn
To portray a funny poem visually

Materials you will need
Drawing paper, colored pencils, charcoals, markers

What to do
1. Have the children look at James Stevenson's illustrations in THE NEW KID ON THE BLOCK and discuss why the simple line drawings are so effective. They allow the reader or the listener to add color or additional scenes to the poem through their own mind's eye rather than the artist's.

2. Ask the children to select one of their favorite poems.

3. Have them read their poems aloud and think of ways to illustrate them by showing what they visualize.

4. Display the poems and illustrations in the classroom library. Arrange the display with the title, "Illustrations of Giggles."

Something to think about
Some children's literature specialists think that all poetry should be read without showing children the illustrations so that the child interprets the meaning for herself or himself.

STORY STRETCHER
For Classroom Library: A Week Of Prelutsky Poetry Readings

What the children will learn
To enjoy reading aloud

Materials you will need
Posterboard, marker

What to do
1. Make posters for poetry readings from THE NEW KID ON THE BLOCK. Make a separate poster for each category. Let the children sign up to read poems about animals, family, people, creatures or events. Ask the children to write the titles of the poems they want to read so that there are no repeats.

2. Schedule Monday as "Animal Poems," Tuesday for "Family Poems," Wednesday for "Funny People Poems," Thursday for

"Creature Poems" and Friday as "It Can Happen Poems."

3. Have the children scheduled to read poetry aloud on other days become the audience for the readers.

Something to think about
Young children can practice the short four line verses or poems with repeated phrases.

ANOTHER STORY STRETCHER

For Classroom Library: Partners Read Prelutsky

What the children will learn
To read in unison

Materials you will need
Cassette tapes and recorder

What to do
1. Let reading partners decide on poems they would like to read aloud.

2. Try various ways to read the poem. For example, one child reads the first verse, the other reads the second verse and they both read the third verse together, or they might alternate lines and read the last lines in unison.

3. Have the children tape-record different ways of reading the poem and use the tape to decide which way they would like to read the poem to the class.

Something to think about
Try choral readings of the poems with several verses and have the entire class read them together.

STORY STRETCHER

For Writing Center: Poems With A Laugh

What the children will learn
To try humorous writing

Materials you will need
Writing paper, pencils, optional— art supplies

What to do
1. Read a number of Prelutsky's funny poems, such as "Be Glad Your Nose Is on Your Face" and "No, I Won't Turn Orange!"

2. Let the children brainstorm some topics which they think are humorous that they could write about. For example, "Be Glad Your Knee is a Part of Your Leg" and "No, I Won't Turn Purple!"

3. Other children may want to write funny poems based on their own experiences. Have them read Prelutsky's "Homework! Oh, Homework!" and "Michael Built a Bicycle" for inspiration.

4. For the students who are interested in writing about feelings, have them read "Ma! Don't Throw That Shirt Out," "Today is Very Boring," "I'm Thankful" and "I'm in a Rotten Mood." They can write about their own feelings or try writing an opposite poem—a poem which expresses the opposite feeling to that about which the poet wrote the original poem.

Something to think about
Encourage lots of experimentation. Avoid giving children the idea that they must always follow the pattern set by another poet. As primary learners, keep them writing, experimenting and enjoying the experience of finding their voices in print.

ANOTHER STORY STRETCHER

For Writing Center: Happy Birthday, Dear Animals

What the children will learn
To use the poet's model to restructure a poem

Materials you will need
Chalkboard, chalk, writing paper, pencils, drawing paper, art supplies for illustrations

What to do
1. Read "Happy Birthday, Dear Dragon."

2. Have the children think of animals to whom they would like to wish a happy birthday.

3. Using the frame of Prelutsky's poem, ask the children to write the poem as if they were saying "Happy Birthday" to the animals. For example, if the children choose a bear, they could begin by describing the bear's den, instead of the dragon's lair.

4. Let the children reprint their poems on drawing paper and add illustrations.

5. Publish the children's verses in a class book of poetry. (See the Appendix for book binding directions.)

Something to think about
For young children, work in small groups and write the poems together. Encourage the children to try their own poetry style without following the poet's model.

POEMS BY EVE MERRIAM

Blackberry Ink

PICTURES BY HANS WILHELM

BLACKBERRY INK

By Eve Merriam

Illustrated by Hans Wilhelm

A collection of twenty-three poems by Eve Merriam, the most anthologized poet in the United States, BLACKBERRY INK entertains, surprises and charmingly ridicules. Eve Merriam knows children and feelings, their need for and lack of social graces, and many poignant and clever ways to observe the world. Many of the children's favorites are here—the title poem, "Blackberry Ink," "Bella had a New Umbrella," "Something's in My Pocket," "How Do You Make a Pizza Grow?" and "I Want My Breakfast." Hans Wilhelm's colorful illustrations decorate the end pages and highlight each page.

Read-Aloud Suggestions

Learn the words to "Blackberry Ink" and make up movements for each couplet. Smile, wiggle your fingers, stick out your tongue and have fun with "Blackberry Ink." Write the words to the poem on the chalkboard and have the children read along with you. Read more poems which you think will become the children's favorites, such as "Bella Had a New Umbrella," "How to Make a Pizza Grow," and "I Want My Breakfast." Use a verbal cloze process for reading "How to Make a Pizza Grow." Read the poem through once, then ask the children to join you in completing the alternating rhyming lines. To end the poetry reading session, read three or four of your favorite poems. Alternate short ones and long ones. Tell the children this book will be in the classroom library on a permanent basis.

STORY STRETCHER

For Art: Illustrations For A Story Poem

What the children will learn
To interpret a poem visually

Materials you will need
Sketch pads or scraps of paper, tractor-feed computer paper, pencils, colored pencils, crayons, markers

What to do
1. Read several of Eve Merriam's character poems, such as "Bertie, Bertie," "Five Little Monsters," and "Xenobia Phobia."

2. Have the children plan different scenes to match scenes or stanzas in the poems. They can sketch out the general idea of each scene on a sketch pad or scraps of paper.

3. Ask the children to draw their stories on computer paper. Make the first sheet of the paper the title page and print the accompanying verse for each illustration on the following pages.

4. Fold the papers back together and place the folded poems in the classroom library.

Something to think about
Let older children use computer graphics to illustrate the story poems.

STORY STRETCHER

For Creative Dramatics: Which Poem Am I?

What the children will learn
To use descriptive language based on the meaning of the poem

Materials you will need
Grocery bags, variety of dress-up clothes

What to do
1. Look through BLACKBERRY INK and select poems which can be easily described and dramatized. Some examples include: "Five Little Monsters," "I Want My Breakfast," "Something's In My Pocket" and "Bertie, Bertie."

2. Privately, ask several children to collect items and dress-up clothes which they could wear to dramatize the poem.

3. Have the actors dress up and one-by-one come to the group reading area and tell the children that they stepped out of the pages of a book of poems by Eve Merriam.

4. Let each actor give some clues and see if the children can guess who they are.

5. If the children have difficulty guessing which poem the actor is, have the actor say the first few lines.

Something to think about
For younger children, print the titles of the poems on the board and let them decide who each actor is with the list as a point of reference.

For Games: Poem Title Word Find

What the children will learn
To recall favorite poem titles

Materials you will need
Chalkboard, chalk, graph paper, pencils

What to do
1. Let the children construct some word finds using the titles of five or six Eve Merriam poems which have been read aloud in class.

2. Show the students examples of word finds: students look horizontally, vertically and diagonally to spot the poem titles among an array of other letters. (See an example of a word find in the Appendix.)

3. Pair the children up and let them design word finds by writing titles horizontally, vertically and diagonally, with one letter in each block on the graph paper, and intersecting where titles share letters.

4. After the children have designed their word finds, copy them and let the students solve each other's word finds.

Something to think about
For younger children, you construct the word find, leave the titles on the chalkboard for reference and use fewer titles and letters.

For Mathematics: Poems Atop The Pop Chart

What the children will learn
To report election results

Materials you will need
Chalkboard, chalk, scraps of paper, pencils, posterboard, marker, wide gift wrap ribbons or fabric ribbons

What to do
1. Let the children nominate their favorite Eve Merriam poems. Write the titles on the chalkboard.

2. From the list on the board, have each child vote for his or her favorite by writing the title on a slip of paper or ballot.

3. Have two children designated as election officials. They can collect the ballots.

4. Have one election official read each title from the slips of paper, and the other child place a tally mark beside the title of the poem.

5. When the results have all been tallied, let the election officials decide how to report them to the class.

6. Extend the activity by reprinting the favorite poems onto posterboard. Let the children make ribbons for the posters which tell the order of the favorites: blue ribbon for the class favorite, red ribbon for the second place poem, yellow ribbon for the third place, green ribbon for the fourth place and white ribbon for the fifth place.

Something to think about
After reading poetry books, let third graders decide which Eve Merriam poetry book they like best.

For Writing Center: Inspired By A Poet

What the children will learn
To write their own variations based on the poet's model

Materials you will need
Large paper bag, chalkboard, chalk, collection of stuffed animals or toys, writing paper, pencils

What to do
1. Place a large paper bag in the writing center and fold the top of it closed.

2. Print the poem "I'm a Prickly Crab" on the chalkboard and read it aloud to the children. After reading it once, go back through the poem and call attention to the pattern the poet used.

3. Have them guess what might be in your bag.

4. List everything they say on the chalkboard.

5. Open the grocery bag and take out a collection of stuffed animals or toys. Using the model of Merriam's poem, have the children write verses for the items in the bag.

Something to think about
Other poems which inspire children to write include: "I'm Sweet," "Night-light" and "Left Foot." Read "Swish Swash" and let the children think of other machines—such as a dishwasher, lawn mower, vacuum cleaner—and write poems using the same pattern but different descriptions.

References

Greenfield, Eloise. (1988). Illustrated by Jan Spivey Gilchrist. **NATHANIEL TALKING**. New York: Black Butterfly Children's Books.

Hoberman, Mary Ann. (1978). Illustrated by Betty Fraser. **A HOUSE IS A HOUSE FOR ME**. New York: Penguin Books.

Merriam, Eve. (1985). Illustrated by Hans Wilhelm. **BLACKBERRY INK**. New York: William Morrow and Company.

O'Neill, Mary. (1961, reissued 1989). Illustrated by John Wallner. **HAILSTONES AND HALIBUT BONES**. New York: Doubleday.

Prelutsky, Jack. (1984). Illustrated by James Stevenson. **THE NEW KID ON THE BLOCK**. New York: Greenwillow.

Additional References for Poems, Chants, Rhythms and Rhymes

Cole, Joanna & Calmenson, Stephanie. (1990). Illustrated by Alan Tiegren. **MISS MARY MACK**. New York: Morrow Junior Books. *A collection of rhymes used in all kinds of street games. Children will recognize some as well as learn new ones.*

Dragonwagon, Crescent. (1986). Illustrated by Jerry Pinkney. **HALF A MOON AND ONE WHOLE STAR**. New York: Aladdin Books. *In this soothing, evocative poem, nighttime slowly deepens around a young girl gradually falling asleep on a summer evening.*

Lessac, Frane. (1987). **CARIBBEAN CANVAS**. New York: J. B. Lippincott. *The vibrant art work of Frane Lessac accompanies and illustrates this collection of poems by various Caribbean poets and traditional proverbs from the islands.*

Lobel, Arnold. (1984). Illustrated by Anita Lobel. **THE ROSE IN MY GARDEN**. New York: Greenwillow Books. *A cumulative poem based on the pattern of "The House That Jack Built." Many garden flowers are introduced and illustrated.*

Merriam, Eve. (1989). Illustrated by Sheila Hamanaka. **A POEM FOR A PICKLE**. New York: Morrow Junior Books. *Simple verses, playful and funny, are a charming introduction to contemporary poetry for children.*

TALL AND FUNNY, FUNNY TALES

Pecos Bill

The Maggie B.

Cross-Country Cat

Possum Magic

Imogene's Antlers

PECOS BILL

By Ariane Dewey

As legend has it, Pecos Bill was a Texan who was raised by coyotes. When he grew up, he met a cowboy named Curly Joe, and that is when his adventures began. He tamed a rattlesnake and made a lasso out of it, rode a mountain lion, captured outlaws, lassoed eagles in flight and roped entire herds of cattle. Other stories in the book include his taming a wild mustang, riding out an Oklahoma tornado with lightning so fierce it traveled all the way to Arizona to make the Grand Canyon, and meeting his bride, Slue Foot Sue, who rode a giant catfish. The illustrations are mostly half-page, colorful and uncluttered, large enough to share in a group reading of the book.

Read-Aloud Suggestions

Have the children recall THE NARROW ESCAPES OF DAVY CROCKETT and discuss how tall tales exaggerate. People do superhuman physical feats, things which could not possibly happen, but which are fun to read about and imagine happening. Show the cover of PECOS BILL and ask how the children know that this, too, is a tall tale. Pecos Bill has a snake coiled around his shoulder and is riding a mountain lion. There are nine tall tales in this book of 56 pages. Decide ahead of time whether to read the book in one session or two. This is one of the books that the children will want you to read again because it is so outrageously funny. After reading the book, point out on a map the states mentioned in the stories: Texas, Oklahoma, Colorado, Montana, New Mexico, California and Arizona.

STORY STRETCHER

For Art: Larger Than Life Tall Tale Characters

What the children will learn
To paint characters as they imagine them

Materials you will need
Butcher paper, pencils, scissors, masking tape, tempera paints, brushes, optional—nylon fishing line

What to do
1. Tear off three long sheets of butcher paper, each one long enough for a child to stretch out on.

2. Have two boys and one girl lie on the sheets of butcher paper.

3. Let other children draw around the outlines of their bodies. These forms will become the out-

lines for Pecos Bill, Curly Joe and Slue Foot Sue.

4. Have the children paint the bodies to look like the three characters.

5. Cut out the tall tale characters.

6. Reinforce the back of the paper characters by placing masking tape all around the outline of the form.

7. Hang the characters from the top of a bulletin board or punch a hole in the top and hang them from the ceiling with nylon fishing line.

Something to think about
As the children write tall tales on their own, let them make their own characters into tall tale figures.

STORY STRETCHER

For Classroom Library: "Reading Rainbow" Book Review Of Tall Tales

What the children will learn
To review a tall tale

Materials you will need
Books of tall tales, videotape, tape player

What to do
1. Have two or three children go to the library and find other tall tale books the students in the class might enjoy or which they would like to hear read aloud.

2. Record at least one program from the PBS television series, "Reading Rainbow."

3. Have the children notice how the children on the series review the books. They do not tell the ending, but enough of the story to interest the listeners in reading the book for themselves.

4. Let the children who found the books read them first and do a "Reading Rainbow" type of book review.

Something to think about

Place all the tall tale books in the class library, and have the children record their responses to the books in their reading response logs.

STORY STRETCHER

For Special Event: Curly Joe Visits The Class

What the children will learn

To listen and participate with a storyteller

Materials you will need

Western clothes, boots, hat, rope

What to do

1. Either dress up like Curly Joe or invite a friend or parent volunteer to come to class and tell Pecos Bill tall tales.

2. Have the children seated, ready to listen to a story you will read when someone knocks on the door.

3. Ask the visitor to take off his hat and have him sheepishly ask permission to tell the children a story.

4. When you say yes, have the visitor change his style to a flamboyant one, saying, "Howdy, I'm Curly Joe."

5. After the stories, have Curly Joe pretend to hear someone calling him—"It's Slue Foot Sue"—and Joe hurries away.

Something to think about

Ask the principal or someone from the school who enjoys drama to play Curly Joe.

STORY STRETCHER

For Writing Center: What If Pecos Bill Came To Our Town?

What the children will learn

To write stories in keeping with the character

Materials you will need

Chalkboard, chalk, writing paper, pencils, art supplies for illustrations

What to do

1. Ask small groups of children in the writing center how they would describe Pecos Bill to someone who had never heard of him. After a few comments, help them understand that they would have to tell some tall tales to characterize Pecos Bill.

2. Pose the problem of "what if Pecos Bill came to our town?" What do they think he would do?

3. As they brainstorm, write key words on the chalkboard. For example, if they say he would lasso big trucks, write "trucks" on the board. If they say he would lasso airplanes instead of eagles, write "planes" on the board.

4. When the students have generated enough ideas to get started writing, ask them to tell their writing partners what they are thinking of writing.

5. Write, edit and publish the tall tales. Place them in the classroom library for the children to read along with the books by famous authors.

Something to think about

Encourage first graders to draw a picture first of what Pecos Bill might do and then begin to write.

ANOTHER STORY STRETCHER

For Writing Center: Slue Foot Sue Tall Tales

What the children will learn

To develop a character

Materials you will need

Chalkboard, chalk, writing paper, pencils, art supplies

What to do

1. Read again the part of PECOS BILL which introduces the reader to Slue Foot Sue.

2. Draw a line down the middle of the chalkboard and on top of the left column write a large "K" for what we "know." At the top of the right column, print "I" for what we can "imagine."

3. Have the children recall all the information they know about Slue Foot Sue from Ariane Dewey's writing. Write their comments on the chalkboard under the "K" column.

4. Ask the children to imagine what Slue Foot Sue might do. Does she keep on riding the giant catfish or learn to ride Bill's wild mustang? Are there some times when Bill goes with her riding down the Rio Grande? What does Slue Foot Sue do on the ranch while Bill and Curly Joe are being cowboys?

5. When the children have imagined Slue Foot Sue and what she might do, ask the students who are interested to write another tall tale for Slue Foot Sue.

Something to think about

With first graders, take dictation from small groups of children and let them compose their Slue Foot Sue stories together.

18
TALL AND FUNNY, FUNNY TALES

THE MAGGIE B.

By Irene Haas

In this ALA Notable Book, Irene Haas tells the tale of a most imaginative little girl, Margaret Barnstable, and the ship of her dreams named after her, THE MAGGIE B. Before going to bed, Margaret wishes on a star for her own little ship, then falls asleep. When she wakes up, she and her brother James are on board the Maggie B. A most unusual ship, it has animals and a little garden with an apple tree and wonderful herbs and spices for cooking. Margaret and James love their life at sea until a storm brews. Safe in their little ship, they ride the storm out. The day on the Maggie B. ends with James asleep and Margaret curled up in her bed. By alternating pages of black and white with lovely soft watercolors splashed with color, the illustrator creates just the right dreamy mood.

Read-Aloud Suggestions

Begin singing "When You Wish Upon a Star" or "Twinkle, Twinkle Little Star." Tell the children some of the things you used to wish for when you were a child. If anyone wants to share what they wish for, let them. Look at the cover of THE MAGGIE B. and tell the children that this is the result of Margaret Barnstable's wishing. Read THE MAGGIE B. At the end of the reading, leaf back through the illustrations and let the children tell what the main event is on each page. Ask the children to recall when in the story they thought something adventuresome was going to happen. Place the book in the classroom library and tell the children about the special cooking story s-t-r-e-t-c-h-e-r planned for the day.

S T O R Y   S T R E T C H E R

For Art: Playdough Maggie B's

What the children will learn
To sculpt three-dimensional forms

Materials you will need
Playdough or modeling clay, plastic knives, index cards, markers

What to do
1. Make or let the children help you make several recipes of playdough. (See the directions in the Appendix.)

2. Ask the children to sculpt a ship or a boat they would like to own.

3. When the models of ships and boats are finished, have the students invent names for their crafts. Print them on index cards and display the sculptures around the classroom.

Something to think about
Ask a craftsperson who makes ships in bottles to come to class and show the children how they are done.

S T O R Y   S T R E T C H E R

For Classroom Library: Read Along With Maggie B.

What the children will learn
To read in unison

Materials you will need
Chalkboard, chalk, cassette tape and recorder, stapler, listening station, headphones

What to do
1. Print the words to Margaret's wish and the sea chantey she sang on the chalkboard.

2. Have the children practice reading the wish and song in unison.

3. Let one child introduce the book, including directions to the listener as to where to begin. Also include information that the page-turning signal will be the sound of the stapler clicking.

4. Record yourself reading the book, and when it is time for Margaret's wish and song to be recorded, have the children read the words in unison.

5. Place the recording at the listening station.

Something to think about
Older children who are fluent readers can form reading groups and record themselves, rotating the reading of the text with reading the song and wishes in unison.

For Cooking: Maggie's Muffins

What the children will learn
To follow the steps of a recipe

Materials you will need
Chart tablet, marker, packaged muffin mix, water, milk, measuring cups and spoons, mixing bowl, wooden spoon, muffin tin, toaster oven

What to do
1. Make a large chart of the package directions for baking muffins.
2. Divide the class into small baking groups so that each child can help with the measuring and mixing.
3. Follow the directions on the chart. Bake several recipes.
4. Serve the muffins hot with cartons of cold milk.

Something to think about
Make the cinnamon peaches also mentioned in the book. Slice peaches in half, sprinkle them with cinnamon and a drop of honey, broil briefly to warm them. Serve with the muffins and cold milk. Also consider making a fish stew like the one Margaret made on the Maggie B.

For Special Event: Boats, Ships

What the children will learn
To use nautical terms

Materials you will need
Parental permission forms, transportation, paper, drawing materials

What to do
1. Find out if any of the families of children in your classroom have boats. It doesn't matter what kind, fishing boats, speedboats, sailboats.
2. Ask the parents if your class can visit the boat. It can be in dry dock or afloat.
3. Secure the proper permission forms to visit the dock or wharf where the boat is kept.
4. Have the captain, the owner, tell about his or her boat and ask them to use nautical terms such as deck, hull, anchor, aft, port, starboard, bow, rudder, the names of sails.
5. If the craft has a cabin, take the children down into the cabin a few at a time and let them see the adaptations needed because the boat is afloat, such as storage for dishes, books, food.
6. Upon returning to the school, let the children draw and write about what they learned.

Something to think about
If you cannot arrange for a field trip to see the boats and ships, ask a parent who has a small boat to bring it to the parking lot of the school and let the children explore it there.

For Writing Center: When You Wish Upon A Star

What the children will learn
To write a wish-comes-true story

Materials you will need
Writing paper, pencils, optional—art supplies for illustrations

What to do
1. Say Margaret's wish from the beginning of the book.
2. Ask the children to tell what they wish for when they wish upon a star, if it is not too private.
3. Talk about how Margaret dreamed about the Maggie B. after she made her wish.
4. Ask the children to write a wish-comes-true story that has happened to them, or that they wish would come true.
5. For the students who are interested in reading their stories aloud, plan a sharing time.

Something to think about
Some children's wishes may be so private that they don't want to share them with the whole class. Respect their wish for privacy.

TALL AND FUNNY, FUNNY TALES

CROSS-COUNTRY CAT

By Mary Calhoun

Illustrated by Erick Ingraham

Henry is a proud Siamese who likes prancing around on his hind legs. Inadvertently left behind at the mountain cabin, Henry finds a way to ski home. With twigs for ski poles and carved shingles for skis, Henry encounters an elk, a snowshoe rabbit, a blue jay and a coyote. The family returns, scouring the road for Henry. The reunion is worth the entire book. In pencil drawings of muted browns and blues with sepia tones, Ingraham's illustrations are fraught with the mystery and intrigue of being lost in a storm in the forest.

Read-Aloud Suggestions

Show the children the cover of CROSS-COUNTRY CAT. Let them decide whether this is a true story or an imaginary one. Look at the first picture in the book and introduce Henry to the children. Ask the children who have cats as pets if their cats are hind-leg walkers. Read the CROSS-COUNTRY CAT. When you finish reading this book, the children will immediately ask you to read it again. Instead of reading it again, turn the pages and let the children take turns telling the story in their own words.

STORY STRETCHER

For Art: Wintry Scenes

What the children will learn
To use charcoals and pencil shading

Materials you will need
Drawing paper, scraps of paper, charcoals, tissues, pencils, white chalks

What to do
1. Have the children look at Erick Ingraham's illustrations of CROSS-COUNTRY CAT. Call attention to the muted shadings.

2. Demonstrate how to shade by placing charcoals and pencils on their sides. Also show how to make the shadings muted by rubbing them with a finger or with a bit of tissue.

3. Ask the children to draw a wintry scene and use some shading in their drawing.

Something to think about
Teachers often think that charcoals are too messy for young children. However, the important point is for the children to experiment with and gain control of a variety of media. Let them explore the possibilities. Learning about the messiness is part of exploring the medium.

STORY STRETCHER

For Classroom Library: Will Henry Make It?

What the children will learn
To say their lines on cue

Materials you will need
Cassette tape and recorder, listening station, headphones

What to do
1. With a small group of children, plan an introduction to the CROSS-COUNTRY CAT.

2. Have a child tell the listeners to the tape that when they hear the children's voices say the phrase, "Oh, Henry" or the question, "Will he make it?" that is their page-turning signal.

3. Plan to change phrases at the scene where Henry first tries to ski.

4. Cue the children each time. Raise one finger when they are to say the first phrase, "Oh, Henry," and two fingers when they are to say the second phrase, "Will he make it?"

5. Record the tape and let the helpers decide whether they are satisfied with the recording or if they want to make another one.

6. Place the tape and the book in the classroom library at the listening station.

Something to think about
Engage a few children in reading the Henry story who need practice with expressive reading. The excitement of the story lends itself to reading with inflection.

For Music And Movement: Cross-Country Skiing

What the children will learn
To move like cross-country skiers

Materials you will need
None needed

What to do
1. Have the children take off their shoes and pretend that they are skiing.

2. Let children who have been skiing tell how to bend the knees slightly and how to hold the poles.

3. Show the children how the cross-country skiers must synchronize their ski poles and their skis. Demonstrate how to hold the poles up, rest arms on knees and pretend to "whoosh" down a slope. Most cross-country skiing is flat and the skiers follow trails.

4. Have the children do the skiing motions and ski around the room. While they are skiing, narrate a trail. "We are just getting started. Slip your feet into your skis, lock them flat into place, stand up, take your poles and push off," and so on."

5. Sing the song that Henry remembered the kids singing, "This Old Man," which helped him to get the rhythm needed to ski smoothly.

Something to think about
Have a real skier bring her or his skis and complete ski outfit to school and talk about skiing.

For Science And Nature: Henry And Real Siamese Cats

What the children will learn
To recognize a Siamese cat

Materials you will need
Cat calendars, magazines, reference books on cats, index cards, pencils

What to do
1. Have the children recall that Henry is a Siamese. Ask them to describe how Henry looked: blue eyes and tan fur with black ears, tail, paws and face.

2. Let the children look through magazines, cat calendars and reference books on cats for pictures of Siamese cats.

3. Make a display of Siamese cat pictures for the science and nature center.

4. Read to or have the children read about Siamese cats, and ask each child to write on an index card at least one new fact he or she learned about Siamese cats and how to care for them.

5. Ask a pet owner who has a Siamese to bring the cat to school. Instruct the children not to handle the cat, except at the pet owner's direction, and then only to stroke the cat's back. Allow the cat to wander around the room at leisure while the children observe it from afar.

Something to think about
Extend the study of cats by learning about cats with a similar body, such as the Burmese.

For Writing Center: Another Henry Adventure

What the children will learn
To think of new stories in keeping with the character

Materials you will need
Chalkboard, chalk, writing paper, pencils

What to do
1. Brainstorm a list of other possibilities for a Henry adventure: Henry at the beach, Henry locked in a cabin, Henry and the skunks, Henry decides to live in the wild, for example.

2. Have the children agree that whatever their Henry adventure is, he must stay true to character. List some of Henry's characteristics on the chalkboard: pride, a hind-leg walker, a dancer, an inventor.

3. Ask the children to write another Henry adventure and when they have finished, reread their stories so that the reader knows Henry has all these characteristics.

4. Let the children decide whether or not to keep working on their drafts, rewriting and editing them through to publishable form. (See the Introduction for more information about the writing process.)

Something to think about
Since the story addresses the fear of being lost or left behind, have young children talk about what they can do if they get separated from their families.

TALL AND FUNNY, FUNNY TALES

POSSUM MAGIC

By Mem Fox

Illustrated by Julie Vivas

Grandma Poss has "possum magic." She can turn the animals different colors and even make them invisible. She makes Hush, the little possum, invisible to protect her from snakes. After a while Hush longs to see what she looks like, but Grandma Poss has forgotten what magical steps are needed to turn Hush back from invisible to visible. Finally, Grandma Poss recalls that for Hush to be visible she must eat people foods, but which foods? And so they begin their trek eating their way across Australia. Every year of Hush's birthday, the animals have a celebration and eat the foods which keep Hush visible. Delightful, endearing illustrations that portray each animal's personality, the watercolor and pen drawings float on a page of white space and little background except for a twig, branch or sandy beach.

Read-Aloud Suggestions

Read the title of the book, POS-SUM MAGIC, and ask the children if this story is fact or fiction, reality or fantasy. Show the cover and introduce the children to the characters on the front, Hush and Grandma Poss. Have the children recall Australian animals they know. Perhaps they will mention kangaroos and koalas. Tell the children they will hear some other Australian animals, some names of Australian cities, and most interestingly, some foods which sound unusual. Read POSSUM MAGIC without stopping for discussion. At the end, list all the animals, cities and foods mentioned in the story. Tell the children they will learn more about these by doing the story s-t-r-e-t-c-h-e-r-s associated with the book.

STORY STRETCHER

For Art: White Space And Watercolor

What the children will learn
To use watercolors sparingly

Materials you will need
White drawing paper, pens, watercolors, brushes, masking tape, paper towels, margarine tubs with water

What to do
1.   Have the children look at Julie Vivas' style of painting. She uses very little background, but instead paints her pictures of the animals almost floating on the page.

2.   Call attention to her use of a pen to draw and watercolors to fill in.

3.   Demonstrate how to use watercolor paints almost dry, like oils, rather than with a lot of water. Place a tiny dab of water onto the

pad of paint, load the brush with color and paint in the outlines.

4.   Ask the children to try drawing a picture and filling it in with watercolor. Call attention to the fact that Julie Vivas, who is a professional artist, lets some of her colors go outside the outline. Talk with the children about the fact that they are learning new watercolor techniques.

5.   Have the children who want to draw and paint a picture do so and ask them to illustrate a favorite scene from POSSUM MAGIC or do a picture of their own choosing.

Something to think about
When the children have finished their paintings, talk with them about their effective use of white space and watercolors.

STORY STRETCHER

For Classroom Library: Tracing Hush's Journey to Visibility

What the children will learn
To find and mark cities on a map

Materials you will need
Map of Australia, push pins, yarn

What to do
1.   Mount a map of Australia in the classroom library.

2.   Read the story of POSSUM MAGIC again and as each city is mentioned, let the children locate it on the map.

3.   Locate Adelaide, Melbourne, Sydney, Brisbane, Darwin and Perth. Have the children notice that Grandma Poss and Hush traveled across the sea to Tasmania, and then find Hobart on the map.

4.   Let the children wrap yarn from one push pin to the other and trace Hush's journey to visibility.

Something to think about
While young children may not understand the vast distances involved in the journey, using the map and marking the locations helps them understand how people use maps.

STORY STRETCHER

For Cooking: Anzac Biscuits

What the children will learn
To make oatmeal cookies

Materials you will need
Refrigerator oatmeal cookie dough, cutting board, knives, cookie sheet, oven, oven mit

What to do
1. Anzac biscuits are like oatmeal cookies. Prepare oatmeal cookies from refrigerated cookie dough or, if possible, make them from scratch.

2. Follow the directions on the refrigerated dough package. Slice dough into one inch rounds. Slice the rounds into quarters.

3. Place on a cookie sheet, allowing space for the cookies to spread when cooking.

4. Bake the cookies in an oven. Watch carefully and do not overcook.

5. Serve the "Anzac biscuits" warm from the oven with cartons of cold milk.

Something to think about
Read the names of the other people foods mentioned in POSSUM MAGIC and let the children prepare those foods on other days: "lamington," a sponge cake dipped in chocolate and rolled in coconut; "pavlova," a meringue shell with fruits and whipped cream; and "minties," peppermint- flavored candy.

STORY STRETCHER

For Science And Nature: Real Australian Animals

What the children will learn
To recognize Australian animals

Materials you will need
Chart tablet, marker, index cards, encyclopedia or reference books on animals

What to do
1. Read through POSSUM MAGIC again, and each time you read the name of an Australian animal, have a child write the name on a sheet of chart tablet paper. Write possum, wombat, kookaburra, dingo, koala, kangaroo, snake.

2. Look through the reference materials on Australian animals and compare the real to the imaginary in POSSUM MAGIC. For example, the tiny emu drawn in the background of the book is really a huge bird.

3. Let the children write facts they want to remember on index cards and attach them to the animal chart.

4. After a few days, read the cards and organize the information by name of animal.

Something to think about
Koalas often interest young children because of their resemblance to teddy bears. Help the children learn that the koala is not a bear.

STORY STRETCHER

For Writing Center: What If I Were Invisible

What the children will learn
To imagine a possibility and to compose a piece others will want to read

Materials you will need
Writing paper, pencils

What to do
1. Collect a small group of writers together and tell them that for a long time Hush enjoyed being invisible. Ask them if they have ever wanted to be invisible. Let them share some experiences.

2. Encourage the writers to write an invisible adventure story with themselves as the main character. Have them imagine what magic would be needed to turn them visible again.

3. When the writers have story ideas, have them write rough drafts and share them with a listening-editing group. Have the listeners ask questions about what else they would like to know. The writers can decide whether or not to add information to their pieces in order to answer the listeners' questions. The author retains control of the story.

4. After several drafts and editing and rewriting sessions, let the children share their finished stories with the class. Call the author's sharing chair, the POSSUM MAGIC chair.

Something to think about
Give children choices. They can continue working on other pieces they are writing or elect to write an invisible adventure story.

IMOGENE'S ANTLERS

By David Small

The outrageously funny tale of Imogene, who wakes up one day to find she has grown antlers. An embarrassment to her family and terribly inconvenient, Imogene's dilemma perplexes the doctor, the school principal, and even her brother Norman, who declares she is turning into an elk. Imogene's mother faints at the sight of her, while the housekeeper puts washing on her antlers to dry and the cook hangs doughnuts on them and sends her out to feed the birds. After trying all types of silly disguises, Imogene wakes up the next day to find her antlers gone. But surprise, when she goes downstairs to breakfast, she has a beautiful fan of peacock feathers. The softly colored illustrations are just as hilarious as the story is preposterously funny. The book is a winner of the Parent's Choice Award.

Read-Aloud Suggestions

If you have students who have already read this book for themselves, ask them not to tell the ending. Show the cover of the book and allow time for the children to laugh at the sight of Imogene leaning out the window with a full head of antlers. Have the children imagine what problems Imogene would have. After several children have commented, read the story. Stop on each page and allow the children to see the illustrations before going on. There will be lots of giggles, so enjoy the laughter, and when it subsides, go on to the next page. This book is another of the "read-it-again" variety, so read the book a second time, and during this reading, point out more of the funny parts of each illustration. Prompt an extension of the story for the writing center by having the children imagine what problems Imogene will now face with her huge fan of peacock feathers.

STORY STRETCHER

For Art: Illustrating "Imogene's Peacock Feathers"

What the children will learn
To draw pictures which complement the stories they compose

Materials you will need
Paper, pencils, choice of art supplies—tempera paints, brushes, crayons, pastels, markers, colored pencils

What to do
1. After the children have written their stories in the writing center, help them decide which scenes of the story need to be illustrated.

2. Have the children take as many sheets of paper as they plan to have illustrations.

3. In pencil, let them jot on the back of each sheet of paper what scene should be drawn on that sheet.

4. Illustrate the scenes and add the pages for the text.

5. Assist the children in selecting an appropriate way to bind the book (see the instructions in the Appendix).

Something to think about
Younger children may choose to illustrate a scene from the beginning of the book, the middle of the book and the end. Introduce the concept of a story board, planning the layout of a book to match text and pictures.

ANOTHER STORY STRETCHER

For Art: Funny Hat Designs

What the children will learn
To invent silly designs

Materials you will need
Straw hats, beach hats, cowboy hats, sombreros, caps, ribbons, lace, scarves, crepe paper, bows, gift wrapping paper, staples, scissors, tape

What to do
1. Wear a big straw hat into the classroom.

2. Read IMOGENE'S ANTLERS again, pausing to look more closely at the illustrations of the milliner and his assistants designing hats to cover Imogene's antlers.

3. Ask the children to bring in some hats and a collection of other materials which could be used to make funny hats.

4. When the supplies have been collected, begin decorating your own hat and make it very silly.

5. Let the children wear their silly hat creations during D.E.A.R. time (see the Introduction for a dis-

cussion of Drop Everything and Read Time).

Something to think about
Have a fashion show of silly hats. Be sure to bring in some silly hats that people wear to football and baseball games to support the team mascots.

For Classroom Library: Giggles, Sillies, Laughter And A Lesson

What the children will learn
To express their reactions

Materials you will need
Cassette tape, recorder, fork, glass, listening station, headphones

What to do

1.   This story is one which prompts lots of giggles and laughter, but one which also has a subtle message of acceptance. Imogene retreated to the kitchen where the housekeeper and cook accepted her no matter how she looked.

2.   With five or six children, plan a recording of the book. Look through the pages and have the children recall how they reacted at each scene. Let them imitate themselves giggling, feeling silly, worrying about whether or not she would have antlers forever, feeling glad the cook and the housekeeper liked her, relieved when the antlers went away, and feeling "here we go again," when the peacock feathers appeared.

3.   Plan an introduction to the book to tell that the listener when they hear your voice, you are reading what is on the page, but when they hear the children's voices, those are reactions. Tell the listeners the page-turning signal—tapping a glass with a fork.

4.   Read the story through and pause to record the children's laughter. Stop at some key points for the children to say what they were thinking when they first heard the story, such as, "I wonder if they will go away?"

5.   On the other side of the tape, record a child reading the story through from beginning to end, with another student making the page-turning signal.

Something to think about
Often the funny children's stories that have a subtle message, such as accepting someone regardless of appearance, get the idea across better than stories that preach a message.

For Cooking: Imogene's Doughnuts

What the children will learn
To make doughnuts

Materials you will need
Doughnut cooker or deep frier, oil, spatulas, paper towels, plates, measuring cups and spoons, mixing bowls, wooden spoons, eggs, flour, baking powder, baking soda, nutmeg, salt, powdered sugar, pastry brush, milk, napkins

What to do

1.   Have a parent or community volunteer assist with frying the doughnuts. Work with only two or three children at a time.

2.   Follow the recipe which comes with the doughnut cooker or deep frier. You can also use uncooked doughnuts, which come packaged like refrigerator rolls and unbaked cookies.

3.   Allow every child to cook at least two doughnuts. Often the doughnuts separate in the hot oil, so plan on extra mix.

4.   Glaze the doughnuts by rolling them in powdered sugar, or mixing a small amount of water with the powdered sugar and brushing on the glaze with a pastry brush. Young children like brushing on the glaze.

5.   Serve for a snack and call the doughnuts, "Imogene's doughnuts." Give the leftovers (if there are any!) and stray bits from the cooking to the birds, just as the cook did in IMOGENE'S ANTLERS.

Something to think about
If it is not possible to have this cooking experience, purchase many kinds of doughnuts and serve them for a snack with cartons of cold milk. Let the children wear their silly Imogene hats while eating the doughnuts.

For Writing Center: "Imogene's Peacock Feathers"

What the children will learn
To imagine preposterous possibilities for another Imogene story

Materials you will need
Paper, crayons, colored pencils, pastels, markers, chalkboard, chalk, writing paper, pencils

What to do

1.   Ask the children to draw Imogene and her peacock feathers, or to imagine themselves with peacock feathers. Suggest that as they draw, they begin to think of all the problems one might face trying to live with a fan of peacock feathers attached to their backs.

2.   Let the children share their pictures with each other and at least one problem they imagine.

3.   As the children talk about their illustrations, write down key

words on the chalkboard that will help recall the ideas.

4. Have the children write their "Imogene's Peacock Feathers" stories. If some of the children are interested in editing them to final form, assist them by calling "listening-editing" groups to prepare for publishing. (See the Introduction for more information about steps in the writing process.)

5. Bind the edited stories into books and place them in the class library.

Something to think about

Bring in an array of David Small books and compare the stories and style of illustrations, and let the children write extensions of some of his other books as well.

References

Calhoun, Mary. (1979). Illustrated by Erick Ingraham. **CROSS-COUNTRY CAT**. New York: William Morrow.

Dewey, Ariane. (1983). **PECOS BILL**. New York: Greenwillow Books.

Fox, Mem. (1983). Illustrated by Julie Vivas. **POSSUM MAGIC**. San Diego: Harcourt, Brace Jovanovich.

Haas, Irene. (1975). **THE MAGGIE B**. New York: Atheneum.

Small, David. (1985). **IMOGENE'S ANTLERS**. New York: Crown Publishers.

Additional References for Tall and Funny, Funny Tales

Brown, Marc. (1986). **ARTHUR'S TEACHER TROUBLE**. Boston: Little, Brown and Company. *With Mr. Ratburn as his teacher, Arthur is sure that third grade spells trouble. He is stunned when he is chosen for the school spellathon, and even more stunned when he wins. The story is full of realistic humor, as are all of the Arthur books.*

Calhoun, Mary. (1991). Illustrated by Erick Ingraham. **HIGH-WIRE HENRY**. New York: Morrow Junior Books. *Henry the cat is disgusted and jealous when a puppy joins the household; so he climbs a tree, stretches his whiskers out for balance, and starts to tightrope-walk along a branch. No one is impressed, until the puppy gets stuck and only a high-wire artist like Henry can rescue him.*

Kellogg, Steven. (1984). **PAUL BUNYAN**. New York: William Morrow and Company. *Here are the traditional American tall tales of Paul Bunyan and Babe, the big blue ox, enhanced by the retelling and illustrations of Steven Kellogg.*

Numeroff, Laura Joffe. (1991). Illustrated by Felicia Bond. **IF YOU GIVE A MOOSE A MUFFIN**. New York: HarperCollins. *"If you give a moose a muffin, he'll want some jam to go with it. . ." , and you will have started something it is VERY hard to stop. The sequel to IF YOU GIVE A MOUSE A COOKIE by the same author and illustrator.*

Willis, Val. (1988). Illustrated by John Shelley. **THE SECRET IN THE MATCHBOX**. New York: Farrar, Strauss and Giroux. *Bobby Bell brings his matchbox to school, but nobody wants to see what is in it. When his teacher confiscates the matchbox and puts it on her desk, Bobby knows there will be trouble, and indeed there is! The secret in the matchbox proves to be a dragon which grows and grows until Bobby gets it back under control.*

BASIC ART DOUGH

the best and easiest uncooked dough

MATERIALS:
4 cups flour
1 cup iodized salt
1¾ cups warm water
bowl

PROCESS:
1. mix all ingredients in bowl
2. knead 10 minutes
3. model as with any clay
4. bake 300° until hard
5. or air dry for a few days

Steps in Binding a Book

 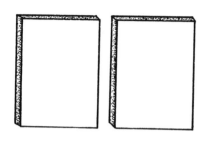 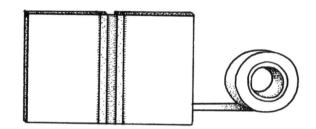

1. Cut two pieces of heavy cardboard slightly larger than the pages of the book.

2. With wide masking tape, tape the two pieces of cardboard together with ½-inch space between.

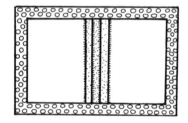 

3. Cut outside cover 1½ inches larger than the cardboard and stick to cardboard (use thinned white glue if cover material is not self-adhesive.)

4. Fold corners over first, then the sides.

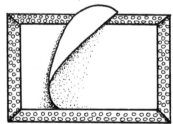

5. Measure and cut inside cover material and apply as shown.

6. Place stapled pages of the book in the center of the cover. Secure with two strips of inside cover material, one at the front of the book and the other at the back.

Sample Rebus Chart
Directions for Making Muffins

1. Preheat

2. Place in

3. Empty  into

4. Add 1  and ½ water

5. Stir

6. Pour into

7. Bake in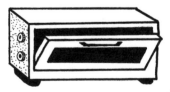

8. Serve and

CONSTRUCTING WORD-FINDS FOR POEM TITLES

Step One: Select titles of poems, preferably short titles.
Write the titles of the poems horizontally, vertically and diagonally.

```
B   O   A   C   O   N   S   T   R   I   C   T   O   R
W       L   F               I
H       I       O               C
O       C           R               K
        E               S   P   A   G   H   E   T   T   I
                        A
                        L
                        E
```

Step Two: Add letters to fill out the puzzle.

```
B   O   A   C   O   N   S   T   R   I   C   T   O   R   T
W   B   L   F   Z   M   K   I   X   A   Z   P   L   C   K
H   P   I   V   O   L   T   W   C   Y   K   S   C   R   J
O   R   C   D   L   R   O   B   R   K   H   Z   O   K   V
M   F   E   C   U   M   S   P   A   G   H   E   T   T   I
P   I   F   R   L   B   K   A   F   F   S   Y   J   U   B
W   T   C   K   V   F   U   I   L   G   B   U   Q   Z   K
A   B   V   Z   I   D   Q   N   D   E   M   A   H   L   T
```

246

INDEX

Titles

This * indicates titles of the books used as the foundation for the STORY S-T-R-E-T-C-H-E-R-S. If only one name is listed, the author is also the illustrator.

Centers or Activities

Art

Classroom Library

Construction Project

Cooking

Creative Dramatics

Games

Terms

A

B

C

D